ATLAS OF AMERICAN MIGRATION

ATLAS OF AMERICAN MIGRATION

Stephen A. Flanders

Facts On File, Inc.

To Carol M. Flanders

Atlas of American Migration

Copyright © 1998 by Facts On File, Inc.

All rights reserved. No part of this book may be reproduced or utilized in any form or by any means, electronic or mechanical, including photocopying, recording, or by any information storage or retrieval systems, without permission in writing from the publisher. For information contact:

Facts On File, Inc.
11 Penn Plaza
New York NY 10001

Library of Congress Cataloging-in-Publication Data
Flanders, Stephen A.
    Atlas of American migration / Stephen A. Flanders
        p.   cm.
    Includes bibliographical references and index.
    ISBN 0-8160-3158-4 (alk. paper)
    1. United States—Emigration and immigration—History—Maps.
  2. Immigrants—United States—History—Maps.   I. Title. II. Title:
American Migration.
    G1201.E27 F5   1998   <G&M>
    304.8'0973'022—DC21   98-13452

Facts On File books are available at special discounts when purchased in bulk quantities for businesses, associations, institutions or sales promotions. Please call our Special Sales Department in New York at (212) 967-8800 or (800) 322-8755.

You can find Facts On File on the World Wide Web at http://www.factsonfile.com

Cover design by Nora Wertz
Text design by Paul Agresti
Layout by Robert Yaffe
Maps by Thomas Nast & Mapping Specialists, Ltd.

Printed in Hong Kong

CREATIVE FOF 10 9 8 7 6 5 4 3 2 1

This book is printed on acid-free paper.

CONTENTS

PREFACE

There are several reasons for a book on American migration. First, and foremost, is that migration is a major national issue and promises to remain so in coming years. Migration is at the heart of the current debate over the nation's multicultural identity. Immigration, in particular, has been a pressing national concern. Has its annual level climbed too high in the 1990s? Should it be curtailed or even halted? Or, as its supporters suggest, is immigration essential to America's continued vitality?

The questions are not new. As recounted in this atlas, immigration has often been a matter of intense concern and debate in the past. It is hoped that this book helps place in perspective the long history of American migration and how it has shaped the pressing issues of today, such as illegal immigration.

Beyond its current relevance, the story of American migration is a compelling, often fascinating subject in its own right. It touches on everything from colonial exploration and the settlement of the West to the building of skyscrapers and the emergence of America as a suburban nation. It is a subject of no little interest to most Americans, as we are all either immigrants or the descendants of ancestors who came from elsewhere.

Why an atlas? Migration, by its very nature, is often best depicted in forms, such as maps and timelines, that convey its movement across space and time. The maps and other visual elements in this atlas are designed to portray and illuminate the many different and often simultaneous migrations described in its text, quotes, and special features.

The overlapping, multifaceted nature of American migration presents special challenges in tracing both its progression and separate movements. The basic organization of the atlas is chronological. Much of American migration does not fit neatly into distinct time periods, though, and the dates in chapter headings should be understood more as historical markers than as fixed start or end points. When a given migration, such as the movement from farms to cities, extends across several time periods, it is addressed in depth in the most germane period. Many of the historical maps depict migration across time. Current state boundaries have often been given in the background as a point of reference.

The first chapter provides an overview of the broad themes of American migration. Chapters 2 to 5 and 8 to 10 follow the many threads of this migration from prehistory to the present. It is mostly a positive tale of willing migrants bettering their lives. Chapters 6 and 7 are dedicated to the two overpowering instances of involuntary American migration, the enslavement of African Americans and the removal of Native Americans.

The story of American migration is very much the story of the different racial and ethnic groups that have peopled America. As much as they continue to influence American society and life, however, there are no set definitions of race and ethnicity. Such definitions, it is increasingly understood, are based on social perceptions rather than empirical science. Racial and ethnic distinctions in this atlas reflect the common identity given to different groups at different times. Thus, for example, Irish Americans were seen as a much more distinct group in the 1840s than in recent decades. Conversely, African Americans continue to suffer a discriminatory racism. Among the many facets to the debate over multiculturalism today is that America, through migration, internal immigration, and intermarriage, is becoming so diverse that racial and ethnic categories are becoming largely problematic.

ACKNOWLEDGMENTS

This atlas is a collaborative effort in the truest sense of the term. It was first conceived by my editor at Facts On File, Eleanora von Dehsen. Its final completion several years later, after a more than normal sequence of glitches and delays, is a testament to her perseverance, patience, and expertise. It was a very much appreciated privilege to have an editor who is also an accomplished historian.

The maps were prepared by Thomas Nast, a very skilled independent illustrative cartographer, and Mapping Specialists, Ltd. The graphics are the work of Thomas Nast and Dale Williams at Facts On File, who also coordinated the overall design of the elements that make this an atlas. The joint effort extends to several other staff members at Facts On File, with particular note due: Jackie Massa and Jeremy Eagle. Also deserving special mention are the copy editor, Paul Scaramazza, and the photo researcher, Lisa Kirchner.

The entire manuscript was edited by Carl Flanders, who somehow always found a way to tighten the writing and make it clearer. For assistance with research and otherwise I am indebted to Joseph Goddu, John Moore, John Orr, and Bruce Tyler. As always, I was greatly aided by the staff of the Sprague Library at Montclair State University.

This book is dedicated to my mother, who, until her death in 1996, was my editorial assistant. She brought a special enthusiasm to the book's early conception and design. It is not surprising that its subject matter fascinated her, as her own life was very much a celebration of America's diversity. I was fortunate to be able to again draw on my personal life for another, informal editorial assistant. Hedy Limb brought much the same interest and dedication to the project, even as she typed seemingly endless drafts. Her help was invaluable in myriad ways.

A SHIFTING MOSAIC
America and Migration

igration is everywhere in the American experience. It is entwined throughout American history and has become part of the very fabric of the nation's identity. It is commemorated in such national landmarks as the Statue of Liberty and the Gateway Arch. Migration, as much as any factor, has built America and made it what it is today.

America is an immigrant nation. Since colonial times, successive waves of immigration from around the world have poured across its shores, creating the most diverse society on Earth. America has been called a mosaic of different peoples and groups, representing a dazzling array of races, ethnicities, religious beliefs, and cultures. It is immigration that provided the pieces.

Immigration, though, is only half the story. The other half is the internal migration that has assembled and reassembled the American people in a shifting mosaic of cities, farms, and suburbs across the continent. Internal migration drove the settlement of the frontier, the industrialization of the Midwest, and the development of Southern California's suburban landscape. It has put the descendants of southern black slaves in northern cities, planted Mexican-American communities in Florida, and relocated Asian-American workers from Seattle to new jobs in Texas.

Its sheer size alone has made American migration unique. Equally remarkable, though, have been its diversity, complexity, and constancy.

Both the scale and scope of American migration are staggering. More than 62 million immigrants have crossed the nation's portals since 1820, when official records were first kept. This immigration is extraordinary not only for its magnitude but also for its variety, having come from literally every part of the globe. Until the 1880s, America was peopled almost entirely by immigrants from northern Europe. This changed dramatically in the early 1900s as a sudden, vast influx of immigrants from southern and eastern Europe brought a stunning new diversity to those arriving in America. In recent decades, newcomers from Latin America, Africa, and Asia have continued to expand the nation's sources of immigration.

Internal migration has been similarly massive and diverse. The western frontier

Statue of Liberty (By courtesy of the Statue of Liberty National Monument)

Gateway Arch   (Archive Photos)

for more than a century was the destination of millions of pioneers. Their travails and triumphs in pressing across the continent helped make the West a mythic place in the American imagination. As the nation underwent a transition from an agrarian to an industrial economy after 1890, even larger numbers of Americans joined in the movement from countryside to city. Among their ranks were some 6 million African Americans who between 1910 and 1970 left the rural South for new and hopefully better lives in the burgeoning urban centers of the North and Midwest. The very size of this internal black exodus gained it the appellation the Great Migration. Since World War II, tens of millions of Americans of every background have poured into the suburbs now extending out from every major city.

American internal migration has been summarized as a movement first to the country, then to cities, and then to suburbs. Yet, this encapsulation fails to capture either the multiplicity or overlapping

nature of the different movements within America at any given point in the nation's history. In actuality, the carving of the West into family farms, the first rapid growth of cities, and the founding of early bedroom suburbs were all part of the 19th-century American experience. Internal migration has been too multifaceted and complex to be traced simply as a linear progression of distinct movements.

The same holds true for immigration. America has always been a nation on the move, with different migrations taking place simultaneously within and across its borders. More often than not, these various movements have been interconnected. In 1849, for example, the surging tide of German and Irish immigrants provided settlers for the frontier in the Old Northwest and workers for the budding factory and mill towns in the nascent manufacturing belt stretching from Philadelphia to Boston. Some of the newcomers became 49ers, joining in that year's mad rush to the California

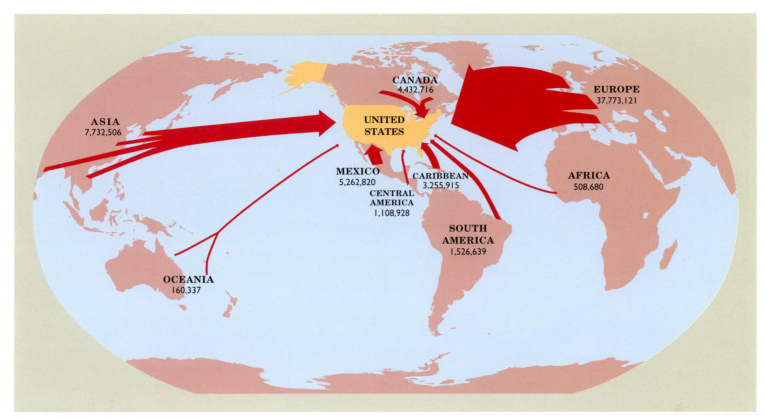

Sources of U.S. Immigration, 1820–1995

Major Internal Migrations, 1790–1890

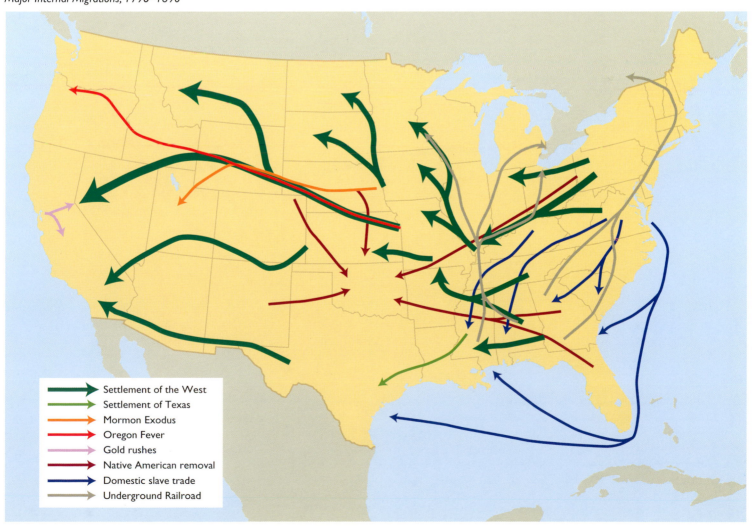

goldfields. Others labored on the railroads that would enable future generations of immigrants to journey westward. In the Far West, Irish railroad hands encountered Chinese contract workers who initially had come to America as part of the California Gold Rush and had then found employment in helping to build the nation's first transcontinental rail lines.

Migration has been the constant of American history since the advent of the colonial era. American migration actually precedes colonial times, reaching back to prehistory. America was first inhabited by Native Americans, themselves the descendants of Stone Age migrants from Asia. Since the arrival of European colonists in the 1500s, migration has been a ceaseless, dynamic presence in the area now comprising the United States. For almost 500 years, there has never been a time at which migration was not reshaping the American landscape and recasting American society. Immigration to America has ebbed and flowed, but it has never fully stopped. Internal migration has been even more

unrelenting. From the first colonial settlements pushing inland to the exurbs forming today on the outer reaches of suburbia, the patterns of American habitation have constantly shifted and changed.

Several broad themes can be found in the long course of American migration. First is the central role migration has played in the development of the American nation. Much higher levels of colonial immigration ensured that the British would prevail in their fight with the French and the Spanish for control of the North American continent. A newly independent United States after 1783 turned its attention to its unsettled western area between the Appalachian Mountains and Mississippi River and then to further territorial expansion. The migration of Americans across the continent became almost a national creed, captured in the phrase Manifest Destiny. Migration eventually carried the American flag as far as Hawaii.

Migration has been equally important to the American economy. The need for workers was a dominant factor in immigration until the 1920s. From colonial times

Major Internal Migrations, 1890—1990

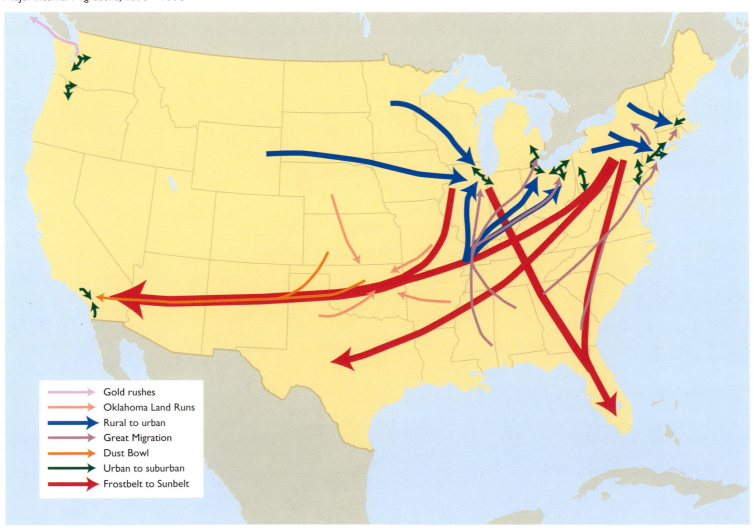

Gold rushes
Oklahoma Land Runs
Rural to urban
Great Migration
Dust Bowl
Urban to suburban
Frostbelt to Sunbelt

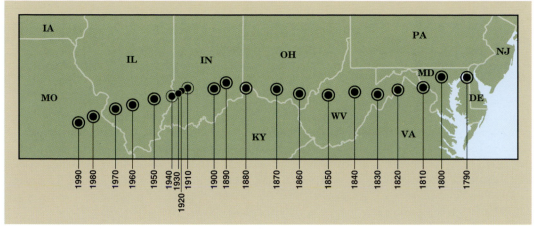

Shifting U.S. Population Center

until the early 1900s, immigrants were recruited to come to America to till its land, build its infrastructure, and work in its factories. Until the mid–1800s, America was largely a nation of small family farms settled by progressive generations of frontier migrants. The notable exception was the South, where a flourishing cotton economy rested on slave labor. Not all those who spurred America's growth were willing migrants, as first the African slave trade and then a very active domestic slave trade supported the extension of cotton cultivation westward to Texas.

In the late 1800s immigrant farmers helped make the Great Plains the major source of crops and livestock for a rapidly industrializing nation. By the early 1900s, due largely to the massive influx of newcomers from southern and eastern Europe, one in every two industrial workers was an immigrant. America's expanding economy also benefited from a very mobile workforce. Settlement of the frontier had accustomed Americans to a tradition of moving for economic opportunity. The new jobs available in the North and Midwest drew millions in the half-century before World War II. In the half-century since the war, the direction of the nation's population flow has shifted to the booming economies of the South and Southwest.

Migration has had a formative impact on American society. From colonial times, a combination of diverse immigration and unfettered internal migration has made Americans a pluralistic people. Migration is also linked indelibly to the nation's sense of its own identity. America has long seen itself as a haven to the oppressed and a land of opportunity for those willing to leave their homelands in the risk of building a better future. The ease with which Americans have migrated internally has been key to the social mobility that has helped tens of millions to actually attain a better life. Migration has contributed to the national character and the noted American traits of restlessness, optimism, and innovative spirit.

THE FORCES SHAPING AMERICAN MIGRATION

Human movement, no matter how personally motivated to those involved, occurs within a broader context. American migration has been constantly shaped and reshaped by external forces. Natural, technological, and social factors have guided and defined the ways in which people have moved to and within America.

NATURE, TECHNOLOGY, AND SOCIETY

Nature until very recently exerted the greatest influence on migration. Modern technology has diminished its role, but the physical realities of the natural world continue to provide the overarching framework to human movement.

Geography is the given of migration. Climate, terrain, and the availability of natural resources have always guided where people live and where they seek to move. Natural routes of transportation, such as rivers, have facilitated migration since earliest times. The Mississippi River and its tributaries in essence provided a vast watery highway system into the American interior. Conversely, both the Appalachian and Rocky mountains posed major barriers to America's westward expansion.

Physiography guided the settlement of the West. The timber, game, and fish riches of the Pacific Northwest sparked an "Oregon fever" among American pioneers, but

MIGRATION TERMS

Those who study migration have developed a number of terms to describe its various aspects and forms. Basically, migration may be defined as the relatively permanent movement of an individual or group over a significant distance. Migration takes place across space and time, but there is no exact rule for the degree of permanence or distance that distinguishes it from other forms of human movement, such as travel or temporary employment. National boundaries are used to differentiate between the two broad categories of migration. *International* migration, called either immigration or emigration depending on the vantage point, involves movement from one country to another. *Internal* migration occurs within a nation's borders.

The study of migration extends across many disciplines, but its basic patterns and statistics are largely the province of demographers. In statistics on international migration, there is a general consensus that a migrant is someone who intends to stay in the receiving country for at least one year. Different nations, however, vary in their definition of internal migration. In the United States, with its long-standing tradition of freedom of movement, there is no formal tracking of internal migration. Records of overall shifts in the population are kept by the Census Bureau, which collects data on residency changes in a 12-month period. The distance that constitutes a migration is linked to county lines. Those who relocate to another county are classified as migrants. Those who remain within the same county are deemed to have stayed in their home area and are listed as movers.

Demographers turn to the human dimension in identifying several basic types of migration. These types, which apply to both internal and international migration, are differentiated primarily by whether the movement is voluntary or involuntary. The exception is *primitive migration*, where distinctions between voluntary and involuntary are often less clear or germane.

Although primitive represents the oldest type of migration, the term itself does not refer to ancient times or preliterate societies. Instead, it connotes the movement of a group in response to such basic, or primitive, factors as climatic changes, shifting natural resources, or famine. Primitive migration is the process by which the area now called the United States was originally peopled by Native Americans.

Voluntary migration, where persons themselves decide to move, can range from a handful of individuals to a massive tide of millions. *Free migration* is used to describe the pioneers, religious dissidents, entrepreneurs, or other inventive or intrepid souls who first set out to build a new life in a different locale. Their numbers are small but they can have a profound effect on subsequent migration. Often they inspire others from their home region to follow. As this process repeats itself, what is known as a *chain migration* develops. This linked movement in turn can lead to a *mass migration*. Although such migrations by their very nature are comparatively large, if not enormous, they are characterized not by their size but by the collective, or mass, behavior involved. For those joining in a larger group movement, the established patterns of migration are often as important as individual motivations.

The waves of transatlantic immigration to America's shores all began as free migrations and then evolved into chain and mass migrations. Much the same pattern was followed in the settlement of the West.

Involuntary migrants include all those induced to move by external force or pressure. This could come from a government, hostile society or community, or other entity or institution capable of imposing its will. If those targeted have no choice about leaving, their movement is termed a *forced migration*. If they do, it is an impelled migration.

The African slave trade, domestic slave trade, and removal of Native Americans were all forced migrations. Many of the refugee movements to America have been impelled migrations.

Demographers call the various incentives that influence migration *push* and *pull* factors. Push factors are those that cause people to consider migrating away from their home areas. Pull factors are those that attract prospective migrants to a new locale. Examples of push factors range from the very personal, such as an addition to the family or the loss of a job, to larger phenomena, such as political upheaval or the exhaustion of natural resources. Pull incentives tend to involve new or better opportunities, whether in employment, housing, or social circumstances.

When push and pull incentives inspire some to move one way, and others the opposite way, this is known as *reciprocal migration*. Reciprocal movements can encompass *return migration*, in which prior migrants journey back to their place of origin. More rarely, a migratory flow is not only halted, but its direction is also turned around in what is known as a *reverse migration*.

Those who move because they hope for something new or better have been termed *innovating* migrants. *Conservative* migrants seek to preserve their way of life by departing an environment that has changed.

Migratory selection is the process by which thousands of individual decisions add up to larger patterns that distinguish migrants from each other and from the society as a whole. In America today, local migrations are generally motivated by housing and other residential concerns. The main incentive for longer migrations, as it is for immigration, is economic opportunity.

the desert Southwest drew few permanent residents until the inauguration of widespread irrigation.

Efforts to subdue nature have not always worked as planned. In the 1930s, a combination of overplanting and natural wind storms forced tens of thousands to flee the Dust Bowl in the southern Plains. In recent years, the spread of suburbs into California's foothills has exposed thousands to dangerous sagebrush fires.

If geography is the destination, technology provides the means. For much of the American past, migration was an arduous and often perilous undertaking. Advances in transportation steadily made it easier, quicker, and safer to move. Development of the steamship enabled millions to immigrate to America. The railroad ushered in mass transportation, while the automobile provided unprecedented individual mobility. These advances also changed the ways in which Americans lived and worked, underscoring how technology's role in migration has transcended transportation.

Starting in the early 1880s, the Industrial Revolution transformed America from a rural to an urban nation. Technology built the modern cities to which generations of farmers, made surplus by the mechanization of agriculture, moved. The suburbanization of the American landscape after World War II, first linked to the automobile, is now increasingly driven by the advent of the Information Age.

Political and economic institutions as well as traditions and customs have shaped American migration. Government has always had a hand in the process. U.S. land policy dictated settlement patterns in the West. U.S. immigration policy has shifted over 200 years, from an open door, to a restricted door, to a closed door, to a reopened door. Foreign governments have also played a major role in immigration, permitting or barring the emigration of their citizens.

The most telling factors affecting American migration have often been economic. Government fiscal and monetary policies have served to promote internal migration. Federal housing programs and tax measures, for example, have aided millions of Americans to attain the dream of a suburban home.

America has been an experiment in fashioning a society of diverse racial, ethnic, and religious groups. The frictions sometimes have been intense. Nativism and prejudice have played a central role in American migration. So has the tension between cultural pluralism and assimilation. For many immigrants, issues of assimilation have posed a difficult dilemma and have often influenced their settlement in ethnic neighborhoods. Race, ethnicity, and socioeconomic status continue to define the choices available to individuals in deciding to migrate.

FREEDOM, FAITH, AND OPPORTUNITY

Migration, most often, is recounted or examined in terms of its broader patterns. Still, it is ultimately individuals who move, not the masses or groups that are recorded in history pages or quantified in statistics. The human face of migration is evident in the choices people make, or have made for them, about where and how to live. In recent decades millions of Americans have relocated from the northern Frostbelt to the southern Sunbelt. Their ranks include retirees lured by Florida's subtropical clime, workers displaced by a decline in manufacturing jobs, and African-American families returning to southern roots. Where exactly a given retiree, worker, or family goes, and why, is very much governed by the myriad personal factors that shape individual lives.

There probably have been as many reasons for coming to America as there have been immigrants who have come. The same could be said for the movement from Frostbelt to Sunbelt. At heart, though, those migrating to and within America have done so largely for political, religious, or economic reasons. The desire for greater freedom, liberty, or human rights has animated the flow of refugees from around the world to America. The promise of religious freedom has prompted the immigration of persecuted groups, from Puritans in the early 1600s to Soviet Jews in our own time. In the 1800s the Mormons moved across the continent to Utah to find a place where they could practice their faith without interference.

Economic opportunity has been the paramount motivation underlying American migration. Most immigrants, from the first colonists to the most recent arrivals, have come to fulfill the American promise of a better life. Many were also driven by the desire to escape the poverty and social rigidity of their native lands. Better economic prospects likewise have always provided the most powerful incentives to the nation's internal migration.

UNWILLING MIGRANTS

American migration is also the story of those made to move against their will. The removal of Native Americans was one of the two main instances of involuntary migration. The other was the forced movement of millions of blacks in the African and domestic slave trades. In a tragic irony, both Native Americans and blacks were brutally relocated for the economic benefit of other migrants.

American history also contains examples of groups compelled to move for other than economic reasons. As far back as the 1750s, French Acadians were forcibly deported from Nova Scotia by British authorities uncertain of their loyalties and dispersed in Britain's American colonies. As recently as World War II, tens of thousands of Japanese Americans, in violation of their rights as citizens, were placed by an espionage-fearing U.S. government in internment camps.

FOOTPRINTS
AND NUMBERS

We know much about the long story of American migration. All its major movements have been chronicled by historians. Census and immigration statistics provide a broad portrait of the many millions who have come to America or moved within its borders. Most of their individual tales, however, were never recorded. Their footprints are largely faded from view, but traces can be found in diaries, personal narratives, newspaper clippings, and other firsthand sources. American migration is an extraordinary, sweeping historical phenomenon that has configured and reconfigured the national mosaic. It is, as well, the experience of the black slave escaping along the Underground Railroad, the frontier woman giving birth on the Oregon Trail, the immigrant processing through Ellis Island, or the World War II veteran purchasing a suburban home.

The story of American migration continues to unfold. Migration remains a central part of American life. As America approaches the 21st century, millions of immigrants still stream across the nation's borders, even as those within continue to move in similar pursuit of a better future.

THE EARLIEST AMERICANS
Pre-Columbian Migration

2

When European explorers first appeared off the coast of North America in the late 15th and early 16th centuries, they found a continent inhabited by unknown, copper-skinned peoples. Christopher Columbus, believing he had reached the East Indies, called these native peoples Indians. This misnomer marked the opening entry in the annals of a centuries-long, often tragic mistreatment and disregard of these original Americans. Only recently have we come to recognize the central place of Native Americans in the American experience.

THE FIRST AMERICANS

The Native Americans were themselves the descendants of immigrants. The human species first emerged in Africa and Eurasia during the Pleistocene epoch, the long period of global cooling better known as the Ice Age. For most of this period, the North American continent was uninhabited by man. But by about 15,000 BCE, small bands of Stone Age peoples first appeared on the North American landmass. These early hunters and gatherers wandered across the Bering Land Bridge from Asia in search of the large mammals of the late Ice Age, such as the mammoth, mastodon, and giant bison.

The Bering Land Bridge had been created during the final glaciation of the Ice Age. This Wisconsin Glaciation at its peak locked up in its vast ice sheets immense amounts of the planet's water supply. It is estimated that as a result sea levels fell by as much as 300 feet. As the Bering Sea retreated during this period, a land bridge linking Asia and North America was exposed. At its maximum the Bering Land Bridge, also referred to as Beringia, ranged up to 1,000 miles wide. While ice at times covered North America as far south as the Missouri and Ohio rivers, the area spanning Siberia, Beringia, and Alaska remained dry, apparently because of lower levels of precipitation.

Exactly when Stone Age hunters from Siberia first meandered across the Bering Land Bridge into North America is uncertain. They did not know, of course, that they were crossing from one continent to another. They were simply following the aimless trails of the various animals they hunted for food. For much of this period, their route farther south from Alaska was blocked by the ice sheets covering Canada. After 15,000 BCE, rising temperatures eventually opened an ice-free corridor down the eastern slopes of the Rocky Mountains to the fertile expanse of the Great Plains. Paleolithic man migrated along this corridor in pursuit of the teeming herds of grass-eating mammals that populated prehistoric America. Another possible route south was along the Pacific coast. Archaeologists agree that small bands of these first Americans had reached the Great Plains by 13,000 BCE. This migration south from Siberia took hundreds, if not thousands, of years.

Migration Across the Bering Land Bridge

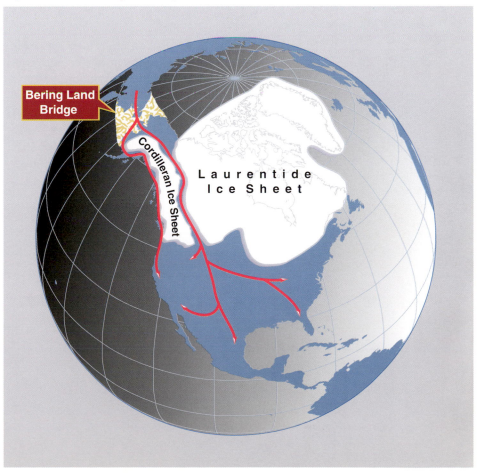

With the end of the Ice Age around 10,000 BCE, rising sea levels again covered the Bering Land Bridge. Native peoples of the region such as the Eskimo would subsequently move back and forth across the Bering Strait, but the gateway to further prehistoric migration from Asia had been closed.

LITHIC PERIOD

From the Great Plains, successive generations of these earliest Americans dispersed throughout both North and South America. This dispersal, which lasted thousands of years, was spurred by a steady population growth resulting from abundant sources of food. By 9000 BCE the ancestors of the Native Americans inhabited all of present-day continental America.

Scholars divide the more than 10,000 years from the initial peopling of America to the arrival of Europeans in 1492 into three broad periods. The first of these is the Lithic Period. The earliest inhabitants of America are known as Paleo-Indians. These first Indians, like their Asian ancestors, were early Stone Age peoples. The Paleo-Indians continued as nomadic big-game hunters. As they tracked the giant herds of the late Ice Age, they took shelter in caves, beneath overhangs, and in brushwood lean-tos. They also gathered wild berries, seeds, and roots.

The Paleo-Indian migratory way of life was essentially uniform across the continent. The key technological innovation of the Lithic Period was the stone spear point. Scholars use the different types of points recovered from archaeological sites to trace the evolution and spread of the Paleo-Indi-

ans. The various Paleo-Indian cultures are named for the sites where their distinctive stone points were first uncovered. Stone points for the most common culture, the Clovis (c. 12,000–8000 BCE), have been found throughout present-day America. The other major Paleo-Indian cultures are the Sandia (before 12,000 BCE) in the Southwest, the Folsom (c. 11,000–9000 BCE) in the Southwest and lower Great Plains, and the Plainview or Plano (c. 9500–4500 BCE) in the Great Plains.

The end of the Ice Age after 10,000 BCE brought dramatic change. As temperatures rose and the ice sheets retreated northward, the climate, topography, and vegetation of North America were gradually transformed. By 5000 BCE the present-day physiography of the continent had taken shape. The changing natural environment caused the extinction of the large Pleistocene mammals. Archaeologists suggest that the Paleo-Indians may have accelerated this extinction through overhunting, in what is called the Pleistocene Overkill. The end of the Pleistocene era marked the beginning of the current geologic period, the Holocene epoch.

ARCHAIC PERIOD

The early Indians adapted to their changing environment. The Paleo-Indians gradually evolved into what have been termed the Foraging Indians, as big-game hunting gave way to a foraging way of life. Scholars generally date the end of the Lithic Period around 7000 BCE. The ensuing Archaic Period lasted until about 1000 BCE. These dates are approximations, as the transitions from one period to the next occurred at varying rates in different areas. Archaic cultures

Timeline of Pre-Columbian Migration

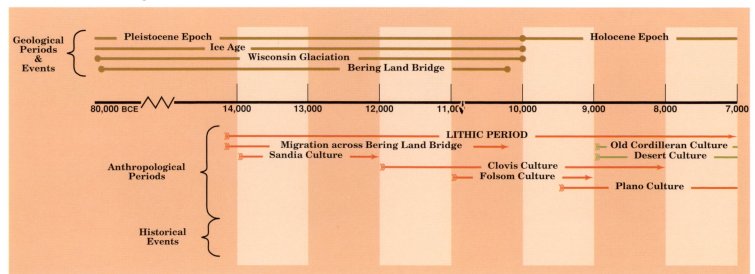

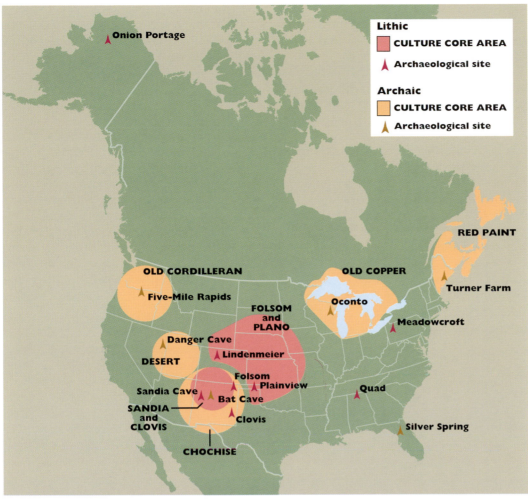

Lithic and Archaic Cultural Core Areas and Sites

had emerged in the Pacific Northwest and along the Mississippi River by 9000 BCE, for example, while Paleo-Indian Plano hunters were active on the Great Plains as late as 4500 BCE.

The Foraging or Archaic Indians hunted and trapped the smaller species of game we know today, developed fishing skills, and gathered diverse edible wild plants. They still led an essentially nomadic existence, but their migratory patterns were more localized as they no longer trailed the Ice Age herds over extended distances. As life became more sedentary, Archaic peoples learned to fashion a wide range of tools and implements out of such materials as

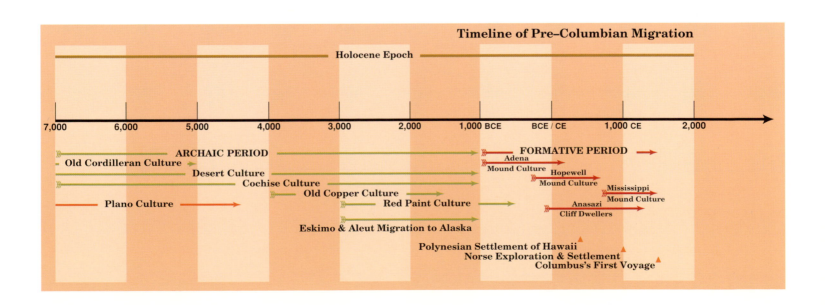

stone, wood, bone, shell, hide, plant fiber, and copper. Archaic advances included the construction of boats and the first woven baskets and clothing.

Scholars distinguish between the Eastern and Western Archaic Traditions, designating the Mississippi River as the rough geographic divider. In the more arid West, Archaic peoples were more dependent on plants, while the game-rich woods of the East gave rise to a denser population. The Archaic Period saw the development of much greater cultural diversity. Major Archaic cultures include the Old Cordilleran (c. 9000–5000 BCE) in the Pacific Northwest, the Desert (c. 9000–1000 BCE) in the Great Basin region, and the Red Paint (c. 3000–500 BCE) in what is now New England. The Old Copper culture (c. 4000–1500 BCE)

was the first to make use of metal in North America, while the Cochise (c. 7000–1000 BCE) led into the famed Cliff Dweller culture of the Southwest.

FORMATIVE PERIOD

The Foraging Indians by about 1000 BCE had begun the transition to the settled village life characteristic of the final pre-Columbian period. This Formative Period spans the roughly 2,500 years from 1000 BCE to contact with Europeans. During this era the Foraging Indians evolved into the Classic Indians that inhabited America at the time of Columbus. In essence, the term Native American as used today corresponds to Classic Indian. Formative refers

Native American Culture Areas

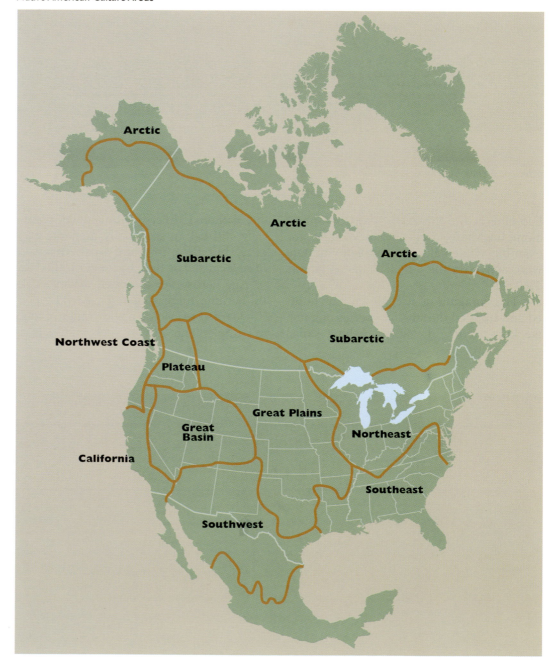

to the emergence and development of the Native American peoples and their traditional cultures. The Formative Period is identified with homes and other dwellings, the spread of agriculture, and the domestication of animals. General cultural advances included pottery, weaving, the bow and arrow, and elaborate religious ceremonies and beliefs. Highly developed civilizations appeared among the Cliff Dwellers in the Southwest and the Mound Builders in the Mississippi Valley.

The combination of technological development and an increasingly settled way of life gradually produced more advanced social organizations. The band, a loose grouping of several families, was the typical social unit of hunting and gathering peoples. During the millennia-long transition from the Archaic to Formative periods, bands joined together into larger social groupings known as tribes. The tribes became the basic Native American social organization. A given tribe, comprised of a number of bands or villages, shared a common descent, territory, history, and culture. The North American pre-Columbian Indians did not have formal political institutions. Authority within a given tribe derived from custom, heredity, or kinship patterns.

northern and western coasts of Alaska. These upper regions were settled by later Stone Age migrants who crossed the Bering Strait in small skin or wooden boats between 3000 and 1000 BCE. Their descendants, the Aleuts in the Aleutian Islands and the Eskimos on the Alaskan mainland, thus were ethnically distinct from other Native Americans. Modern Eskimos prefer the term Inuit, meaning "the people," rather than the imposed name Eskimo, which is Algonquin for "raw meat eater."

The Inuits and Aleuts developed a unique way of life in the harsh Arctic environment. They subsisted primarily by hunting, mainly sea mammals and caribou, which they supplemented by fishing. They also utilized their prey to make clothing, kayaks, sleds, weapons, and tools. The northern Inuits lived in transitory earth-covered abodes and migrated from inland to the coast in warmer weather. (The igloo was found among the Eskimos of north-central Canada.) The more fixed southern Inuits inhabited semi-underground wood and sod dwellings. The Aleuts lived in timber and earth pit houses. The southern Inuits interacted with other Indian peoples to a significant extent. Arctic lifeways went uninterrupted until first contact with Russian explorers in the 18th century.

NATIVE AMERICAN CULTURAL AREAS

The natural environment fundamentally shaped Native American lifeways. Tribes in a given geographic region shared a broad range of cultural traits. Anthropologists consequently divide Native Americans into geographically defined areas. This classification provides a framework for understanding the movements and settlement patterns of the diverse Native American tribes throughout the Formative Period. These cultural areas are not exact, as there were no fixed boundaries between regions. Often there were considerable cultural similarities among different areas, or significant differences between tribes in the same area. Anthropologists have devised various schemes for determining culture areas. The 10 culture areas discussed below represent the most commonly used system.

ARCTIC

The Arctic culture area runs along the top of North America from Greenland to the

SUBARCTIC

The Subarctic culture area also spans North America from the south-central Alaskan coast to Newfoundland. The area encompasses the rest of present-day Alaska other than the sliver of its southwestern coast. The scattered native people of the rugged Alaskan interior pursued a nomadic way of life. They hunted, fished, and foraged in the vast evergreen forests lying below the Arctic tundra. For the northern Koyukon tribe, life revolved around the seasonal migrations of the caribou. Tribes farther south included the Kutchin and Ahtena. Native Americans in western Alaska, like the Eskimos, employed earth-covered dwellings, while those farther east took shelter in double lean-tos. The Kutchin built unique, small, cone-shaped tents out of caribou skin.

NORTHWEST COAST

The Northwest Coast culture area stretches more than 2,000 miles from the Alaska panhandle to the northern boundary of California. At its broadest, this long coastal strip between the Pacific Ocean and the Coast Range mountain chain is only some 150 miles wide. The climate is temperate and moist. The abundant fish and game of the ocean, numerous rivers, and thick forest made possible a relatively dense Native American population, especially to the south. A highly complex culture, built around village life, evolved in the area. The evergreen forests provided lumber for wooden boats and plank houses, as well as for the populace's distinctive giant totem poles. Among the premier Native American woodworkers, the Northwest peoples were also extensive traders. The many tribes included the Tlingit along the Alaskan panhandle, the Makah on Cape Flattery in northwestern Washington, and the Chinook along the lower Columbia River. The river provided an important trade link to the tribes of the Plateau culture area.

PLATEAU

The Plateau Indians lived in the northwestern highlands bounded by the Cascade Mountains to the west, the Rockies to the east, the Fraser River to the north, and the Great Plains to the south. The culture area derives its name from this Columbia Plateau, which is dominated by the long, meandering Columbia River and its numerous tributaries. The Plateau Indians are also referred to as River Indians. Their villages were normally located along riverbanks. They were primarily fishers, particularly of the plentiful salmon in the region. The rivers also served as trade routes. The Plateau peoples did not farm, but gathered berries and other wild plant foods. In colder weather, they inhabited semi-underground earth-covered pit dwellings. As it warmed and they followed the spawning salmon, they occupied temporary wood and bulrush-mat lodges. Plateau tribes included the Spokane, Yakima, Cayuse, Nez Percé, and Flathead.

GREAT BASIN

The Great Basin draws its name from the immense desert basin in western America. Site of Death Valley, the lowest point in the hemisphere at some 280 feet below sea level, this natural, bowl-shaped depression is formed by the Sierra Nevada in the west, the Rockies in the east, the Columbia Plateau to the north, and the Colorado Plateau to the south. The vegetation is sparse in the arid terrain and there is little game. The sparse Native American population existed primarily by gathering. They dug for much of their diet, including roots, seeds, nuts, rodents, snakes, lizards, and insects. Consequently, they are sometimes referred to as Digger Indians. Because there were such limited food sources, these nomadic peoples normally traveled in small bands. They lived in simple, teepeelike structures, with pole frames covered by brush or reeds. Major tribal groupings were the Shoshone, Paiute, and Ute.

CALIFORNIA

The California culture area comprises most of present-day California, for which it is named, and the Baja Peninsula of Mexico. It is bounded by the natural barriers of the Pacific Ocean to the west and the Sierra Nevada and Gulf of California to the east and south. To the north, however, there was no such barrier to interaction with other native peoples, and the northern California and Northwest Coast regions shared many cultural traits. The distinctive feature of the California culture area was its bountiful environment, particularly in the central Great California valley, with plentiful game, many edible wild plants, and fish-stocked rivers.

The California Indians were hunters and gatherers. Even without farming, the California region supported the densest native population on the continent. This population was made up of many different peoples, speaking more than 100 distinct dialects. Most lived in villages of several interrelated families. Dwellings ranged from plank houses in the north and brush, grass, or tule-covered teepees in central California to bark lean-tos and hide or mat wigwams farther south. Social organization above the village was limited. In the absence of real tribal-level structures, the term tribelet is used to describe the various loose groupings of villages. There was little movement of people between the different, relatively isolated tribelets.

SOUTHWEST

The Southwest Indians inhabited a rugged, arid area extending from present-day southern Utah and Colorado through Arizona, New Mexico, and the western corner of Texas into northern Mexico. The terrain in this region varies from mesas and canyons in the north to the Mogollon

Mountains of southern New Mexico and the Painted Desert of Arizona. Despite its harsh environment, the Southwest culture area was the site of the most advanced agricultural civilization in pre-Columbian North America. The scarcity of game and edible wild plants made farming a natural alternative for the Southwest peoples, whose resort to agriculture was strongly influenced by the highly developed Mesoamerican culture in central Mexico. Pre-Columbian Mesoamerica (Middle America), best known for its Mayan and Aztec civilizations, was the cradle of Native American agriculture. Evidence of extensive interaction with Mesoamerica includes early Southwest irrigation systems, textiles, and pottery, as well as the keeping of macaws as house pets.

Under this Mesoamerican influence from the south, three major Southwest civilizations arose out of the Archaic Cochise tradition. The Mogollon Indians were the first Southwest people to farm. Named for the mountain range of their core area, their culture flourished from about 300 BCE to 1300 CE. They used primitive digging sticks to cultivate the basic Southwest crops of corn, beans, squash, cotton, and tobacco, which they continued to supplement by hunting and gathering. The adoption of agriculture enabled the Mogollons to live in fixed villages. They developed semi-subterranean pit houses, with log frames and mud roofs, that were well suited to the region's temperature extremes. Influenced by the later Anasazi culture, they built aboveground pueblos after 1100, with villages containing as many as 30 structures. The Mogollon culture gradually was absorbed by the Anasazi. It is thought the Zuni Indians are descended from the Mogollon.

West of the Mogollon the Hohokam culture thrived from about 100 BCE to 1500 CE in the river valleys of the southern Arizona desert. To cultivate the sandy soil along the rivers, the Hohokam Indians developed remarkable irrigation systems. They dug shallow canals as much as 10 miles long and built diversion dams with woven-mat valves. Their advanced agricultural techniques made possible larger settlements. Snaketown, the principal Hohokam village near present-day Phoenix, covered some 300 acres with more than 100 pit houses. For unknown reasons, possibly prolonged drought or raiding tribes, the Hohokam abandoned their settlements around 1500 and dispersed into smaller groups. These groups, researchers believe, were the ancestors of the Pima and Papago

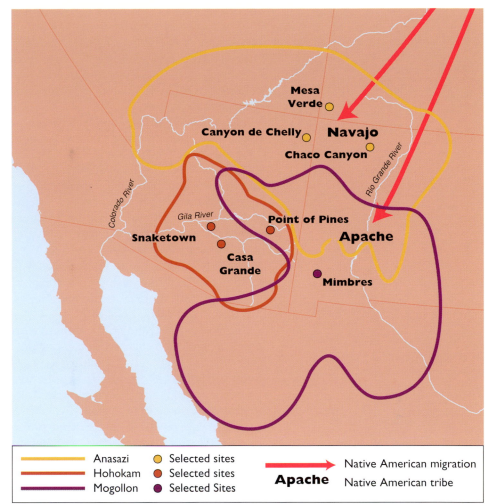

Southwest Pre-Columbian Civilizations

tribes. Hohokam in the Pima language means the "vanished ones."

The Cliff Dwellers

The Four Corners area of present-day Utah, Colorado, Arizona, and New Mexico was the heartland of the third, and most extraordinary, Southwest civilization, the Anasazi. Scholars divide the development of the Anasazi culture in this high plateau region of flat-topped mesas and steep canyons into two distinct periods. The first of these, the Basket Maker period, lasted from about 100 BCE to 750 CE. During this stage the Anasazi Indians mastered the weaving of containers and other objects out of such plant matter as straw and rushes. Hunters and gatherers by origin, they became skilled farmers as well and began to live in villages of Southwest-style pit dwellings.

The Pueblo period, from roughly 750 to 1300, is named for the remarkable new form of architecture devised by the Anasazi. This second period is also called the Golden Age of Anasazi culture. The pueblo is an apartment-like multistoried structure built out of stone and adobe (clay) mortar or adobe brick. The roof of one level served as the floor or front terrace of another. The different stories were connected by ladders. Pueblo, the Spanish word for "village," was first applied to these dwellings, and the Indians that inhabited them, by 16th-century Spanish explorers.

The Anasazi initially built their pueblos atop mesas. The stunning Pueblo Bonito at Chaco Canyon in what is now New Mexico was constructed in a huge semicircle, with five stories and some 800 rooms. These large settlements were supported by the burgeoning yields of an increasingly sophisticated Anasazi agriculture. Advances included canal irrigation and terraced fields. This Golden Age is renowned as well for the superb craftsmanship and artistry of Anasazi pottery, mosaics, turquoise jewelry, and cotton-and-feather clothing.

Between 1000 and 1300 the Anasazi largely abandoned their mesa-top pueblos. They instead built terraced cliff dwellings along the ledges and under the protective overhangs of neighboring canyons, apparently as a defensive measure against raiding Indians. These astonishing pueblos earned the Anasazi the appellation Cliff Dwellers. Famed sites include Mesa Verde in Colorado and Canyon de Chelly in Arizona.

Starting around 1300, the Anasazi mysteriously abandoned their cliff dwellings and migrated elsewhere, primarily to the south. Possible reasons for the relocation include a severe drought around 1275 and the encroachment of warring invaders, particularly the Apache. They built smaller pueblos and passed on many cultural traits to later Pueblo Indians, including the Hopi in Arizona and the Tewa along the upper Rio Grande.

The Apache and Navajo originally inhabited western Canada. Nomadic hunters and gatherers, they eventually migrated to the Southwest. The first Apache bands came around 850 CE and the Navajo arrived some 200 years later. The pre-Columbian Native Americans did not have horses, which were introduced by Spanish colonists in the 17th century. Thus this long trek was made on foot. The Apache and Navajo alike had warrior cultures. They often raided the Pueblo tribes for food, property, women, and slaves. The name Apache comes from the Zuñi word for "enemy." The Navajo, named by the Spanish, called themselves the Dine, meaning "the people."

Over time the Apache and Navajo adopted many of the Southwest lifeways, including farming and basketmaking. The word *Anasazi* is actually Navajo for "ancient ones." The most common dwelling for the Apache was the wickiup, a dome-shaped hut with a wooden pole frame and brush or reed covering. The Navajo lived in cone-shaped log and earth shelters called hogans.

The other major Southwest cultural group was the Yuma, who inhabited the lower Colorado River. These indigenous peoples fished, farmed the riverbanks, and constructed riverside villages of pit houses. Tribes included the Havasupai, Mojave, and Yavapai.

GREAT PLAINS

The Great Plains derives its name from the vast, largely treeless grassland stretching from present-day lower Canada to south Texas and from the Mississippi River to the Rocky Mountains. The seemingly endless plains were the ideal grazing land for the animal so closely identified with the Plains Indians, the American bison, or buffalo. The Great Plains culture area is unique in that its basic way of life did not evolve until well after Native American contact with Europeans. The lifeways built around the nomadic hunting of the buffalo became possible only with the European introduction of the horse, which reached the Great Plains via the Spanish Southwest in the early 1700s.

The descendants of the early Stone Age Plano hunters had largely migrated from the Plains by 1200 CE, most likely because of drought. The earliest Formative inhabitants of the region apparently were agricultural tribes in the river valleys, including the Hidatsa, Arikara, Pawnee, and Wichita. The Mandan, also farmers, migrated westward onto the Plains from the Ohio valley by 1400. The only buffalo-hunting tribes on the Great Plains before 1500 were the Blackfoot and the Comanche.

Known as the Lords of the Southern Plains because of their warrior ways and proud bearing, the Comanche had gained use of the horse by the late 1600s. As these mounted hunters and raiders roamed northward, they helped spread the horse throughout the Great Plains. During the 1600s and 1700s, other tribes entered the Plains, drawn by the new buffalo-hunting lifestyle made possible by the horse. This migration was also driven by conflicts with other tribes and the pressure of an expanding white population.

The Ponca, Kaw, Omaha, Osage, and Quapaw journeyed westward from the Ohio valley to settle on the eastern Plains.

The Iowa, Missouri, and Oto migrated southwestward from the Great Lakes region. These tribes are sometimes referred to as Prairie Indians because they inhabited the tall-grass prairie running west from the Mississippi past the Missouri River. They retained eastern Woodland Indian traits, such as permanent villages and agriculture, while adopting the buffalo-centered, Plains way of life.

The Sioux were also originally Woodland Indians. By the mid-1700s they had begun to migrate westward from their ancestral territory along the upper Mississippi River. A key reason for their exodus was the mounting danger posed by their traditional enemy, the Chippewa, who had been armed with guns by the French. The various branches of the Sioux eventually covered the upper Plains from present-day Minnesota to eastern Montana and Wyoming.

The Cheyenne, Arapaho, and Atsina migrated westward from the Great Lakes region. The Cheyenne probably were pushed westward by the Sioux. The closely allied Arapaho and Atsina separated in southern Minnesota, with the Arapaho heading south and the Atsina (also known as the Gros Ventre) venturing north.

The Crow appeared as a distinct tribe after it split off from the Hidatsa along the upper Missouri in a dispute over buffalo and moved westward to the Yellowstone River. The intriguing migration of the Kiowa captures the dynamic movement on the Plains. About 1700, the Kiowa relocated eastward, from western Montana, across the Rocky Mountains to the Yellowstone River region. From there they moved to the Dakotan Black Hills, where they acquired use of the horse. In the late 1700s they were driven into Nebraska by the Sioux and Cheyenne. The American explorers Lewis and Clark reported their presence along the North Platte River in 1805. Soon after, the Kiowa finally settled to the south in Kansas and Oklahoma.

Migration also occurred from the south. Though of uncertain ancestry, the Tonkawa and other tribes of southern Texas are believed to be related to the Southwest culture tribes of what is now northern Mexico.

The Plains Indians became legendary horsemen, with the horse assuming a central place in their culture. The tribes in the western, drier, shorter-grass Plains adopted a fully nomadic way of life, based on buffalo hunting. The buffalo provided food, shelter, and clothing. The horse enabled these Indians to carry all their possessions. Among these was the teepee, the best-known of Native American shelters, which was quickly and easily assembled out of wooden poles and a buffalo-skin covering.

NORTHEAST

The Northeast culture area encompasses the territory from the Atlantic seaboard west to the Mississippi valley and from the Great Lakes to the Cumberland River in Tennessee, the northern reaches of West Virginia, and the Tidewater region of Virginia and North Carolina. Before modern development, the common feature in this varied terrain of seacoast, mountains, lakes, and river valleys was the heavy forest. The northeastern forests provided a wide variety of game as well as wood for shelters, tools, and fuel. The Northeast Indians are also referred to as Woodland Indians.

The Northeast tribes belonged to two basic groups that were defined by their languages: the Algonquian and the Iroquois. The origins of both remain unclear, though it is thought the Iroquois appeared in the region later and probably migrated from the south. The two groups shared many cultural traits. Both were farmers as well as hunters, fishers, and gatherers. They lived in permanent villages, which were often palisaded for protection. The Algonquins generally made their homes in wigwams, wooden-framed huts overlaid with bark, while the Iroquois became known as the People of the Longhouse. The communal wood and bark longhouse, up to 100 feet in length, housed as many as 20 families. The only other Northeast people, the Sioux-speaking Winnebago west of Lake Michigan, lived in rectangular bark lodges.

The Northern Iroquois around 1000 CE were distributed over western Pennsylvania, New York, and southern Canada from the upper St. Lawrence River to Lake Huron. In the following centuries the scattered Iroquois settlements contracted into 13 tribal areas. This consolidation resulted from both periodic intertribal warfare and the development of agriculture. Trade routes linked the tribal areas and their villages. In a successful effort to halt intertribal conflict, around 1570 five central New York tribes—the Mohawk, Oneida, Onondaga, Cayuga, and Seneca—formed the Iroquois Confederacy.

Adena and Hopewell Mound Cultures
The natural abundance of the Northeast supported the emergence of two advanced cultures, both with sizable populations,

ORIGIN OF THE IROQUOIS

The Native Americans, like other early peoples, explained their origins in myth. Various of these creation legends, part of a vast Native American oral tradition, were later captured in writing. The prominent place commonly given to nature as creative force is illustrated by a brief legend explaining the origin of the northern Iroquois.

Long, long ago, one of the Spirits of the Sky World came down and looked at the earth. As he traveled over it, he found it beautiful, and so he created people to live on it. Before returning to the sky, he gave them names, called the people all together, and spoke his parting words:

"To the Mohawks, I give corn," he said. "To the patient Oneida, I give the nuts and the fruit of many trees. To the industrious Senecas, I give beans. To the friendly Cayugas, I give the roots of plants to be eaten. To the wise and eloquent Onondagas, I give grapes and squashes to eat and tobacco to smoke at the camp fires."

Many other things he told the new people. Then he wrapped himself in a bright cloud and went like a swift arrow to the Sun. There his return caused his Brother Sky Spirits to rejoice.

from Voices of the Winds

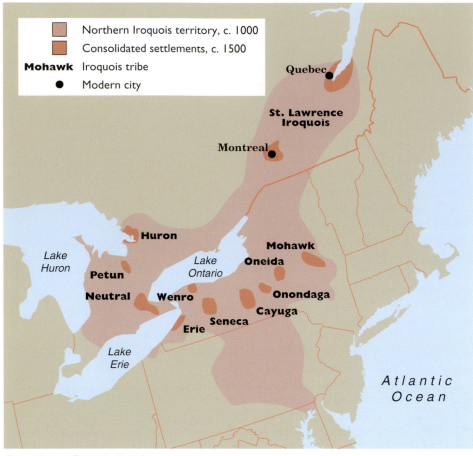

Northern Iroquois territory, c. 1000

Consolidated settlements, c. 1500

Mohawk Iroquois tribe

● Modern city

Quebec

St. Lawrence
Iroquois

Montreal

Huron

Lake
Huron

Petun

Neutral

Wenro

Lake
Ontario

Mohawk

Oneida

Onondaga

Cayuga

Erie

Seneca

Lake
Erie

*Atlantic
Ocean*

Consolidation of the Northern Iroquois

without the development of large-scale agriculture. Because of their remarkable and fascinating earthworks, they are referred to as Mound cultures and their peoples are known as Mound Builders. Scholars are unsure where the Mound Builders came from or what became of them when their cultures faded. Their way of life ranks, with that of the Southwest Cliff Dwellers, as the most complex and organized in pre-Columbian North America. Their larger settlements were virtual small cities.

The Adena Mound Culture lasted from about 1000 BCE to 200 CE. The Adena, named for a 19th-century archaeological site in the heartland of their Ohio River valley area, were primarily hunters and gatherers. They inhabited villages of pole-framed houses with matted walls and thatched roofs. Advanced social organization is seen in their massive earthworks, most of which were burial mounds. Entombed with the dead were beautifully crafted tools and ceremonial objects made from wood, bone, copper, and precious stones. The symbolic Great Serpent Mound near Peebles, Ohio, forms an earth-shaped snake some 15 feet across and 1,330 feet long.

The Adena Indians gradually were displaced by the Hopewell Mound Culture. The Hopewell Indians, also named for a

19th-century archaeological site in Ohio, thrived from approximately 300 BCE to 700 CE. From its core area in the Ohio valley, the Hopewell Mound Culture extended east to Lake Ontario and west along the Illinois and Mississippi river valleys. The Hopewell lived in wigwam-like structures. The cultivation of corn, squash, and other crops helped support a growing population. Hopewell burial mounds were larger than those of the Adena, reaching 30 to 40 feet high. Other earthworks were laid out in geometric shapes. The Hopewell site at Newark, Ohio, covers four square miles. Its construction required a highly organized society. The diverse materials found in Hopewell objects, including obsidian, mica, shells, and alligator teeth, attest to their extensive trading network and wide contacts with other peoples.

The widespread influence of the mysterious Mound Builders is evident in the scattered mound sites found throughout the Northeast. The Hopewell left no clues as to their disappearance. Their culture may have declined because of prolonged drought, crop failures, epidemics, or warfare. It is possible the Hopewell are the ancestors of later Northeast tribes. The Mound tradition did not end with the Hopewell. Within a short span the Temple Mound Culture from the Southeast would occupy much of their previous territory.

SOUTHEAST

The Southeast peoples were also predominantly Woodland Indians. This region stretches from the Atlantic west to the Trinity and Mississippi rivers and south from the Arkansas and Cumberland rivers to the Gulf of Mexico. Much of the Southeast culture area was covered in pine forest. Its diverse terrain also included everglades, marshes, and flood plains.

The majority of Southeast Indians lived in villages along the river valleys. They were farmers, capitalizing on the region's mild climate and long growing season. They also hunted, fished, and gathered. When the soil, which was often sandy, became depleted, they would move their villages. The typical shelter was a rectangular hut of wattle and daub.

There was widespread cultural similarity across the region. Larger tribes included the Catawba, Cherokee, Creek, Chickasaw, and Choctaw. The Seminole, closely identified with Florida, actually did not migrate there until the 1700s, when they broke off from the Creek in Alabama and Georgia.

The original tribes in Florida were the Timucua and Calusa. While the Timucua observed the basic Southeast way of life, the Calusa in southern Florida shared many cultural practices with native peoples across the Gulf of Mexico. These included the use of blowguns, human sacrifice, and cannibalism. Noting their seaworthy dugout canoes, scholars theorize the Calusa may have migrated to Florida from the sea.

Mississippi Temple Mound Culture

The final and most impressive Mound culture emerged along the middle Mississippi River after 700 CE. Known as the Mississip-

pian culture after its core area, this advanced civilization soon produced regional variants farther up and down the river, in the Ohio valley, and along the Red and Savannah rivers. The defining Mississippian earthwork was the temple mound. The often massive mounds typically had sloping sides and a flat top where the wood and thatch temple stood. A log stairway ran up one side.

In addition to obvious Adena and Hopewell antecedents, scholars note the apparent Mesoamerican influence on the Temple Mound Builders. While there is no hard evidence of this influence, the similar use of temple mounds and open village plazas, agricultural techniques, and art

Adena and Hopewell Mound Cultures

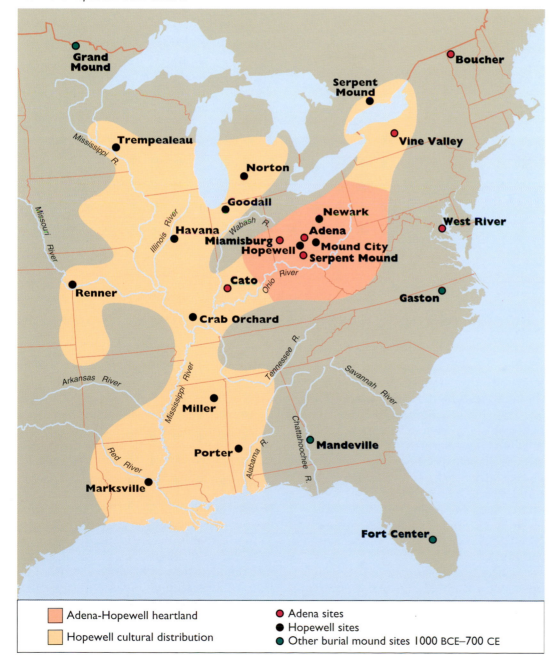

▨ Adena-Hopewell heartland	● Adena sites
▨ Hopewell cultural distribution	● Hopewell sites
	● Other burial mound sites 1000 BCE–700 CE

Mississippi Temple Mound Culture

styles all indicate significant cultural interaction. Contact could have occurred through Mesoamerican migrants or traders.

The Temple Mound Builders established an elaborate and vast trade network. They were master artisans, crafting highly refined tools, pottery, and ceremonial objects. Their society was highly structured. Priests, chieftains, and other officials often lived on the terraced sides of mounds. Ordinary villagers resided in wood and thatch huts or pit houses surrounding the mounds.

Several Mississippian villages developed into small cities. Cahokia, near present-day St. Louis, was the largest pre-Columbian settlement north of Mexico. It covered some 4,000 acres, with 85 temple and burial mounds. The central mound

measured 100 feet high and took up 16 acres. At its peak between 1050 and 1250 Cahokia housed an estimated 40,000 people in its urban center and five suburban areas. The substantial, centralized Mississippian populations were sustained by large-scale farming.

Cahokia was in decline by 1500. In following years the great Mississippian villages were abandoned. Their magnificent earthworks remained, but the Temple Mound Builders vanished into prehistory. Theories as to the cause of their dispersal just decades before the arrival of the first European explorers include overpopulation, war, drought, famine, and disease. Their only verifiable descendants were the Natchez along the lower Mississippi. The Natchez retained many Mississippian cultural traits until their virtual destruction by the French in the 18th century. Many Southeast tribes continued to use the ancient mounds. Scholars suggest that the Creek, among others, may trace back to the Mound Builders.

POLYNESIAN SETTLEMENT OF HAWAII

Sometime around 2000 BCE a second migration started across the Pacific from Asia. This time, there was no land bridge. The migration was accomplished by sea, by some of the most extraordinary mariners in history. Their long journey ended at a small mid-Pacific archipelago, the present-day Hawaiian Islands.

The Polynesian seafarers who first settled Hawaii came originally from Southeast Asia. Between 4000 and 2000 BCE a maritime culture based on seagoing canoes emerged in the islands of Indonesia. These first Melanesian peoples became skilled navigators and traders, plying their canoes throughout the Indonesian archipelago. By 2000 BCE Melanesians from the central Moluccas Islands had colonized the eastern coast of New Guinea. Over the next 1,000 years these Lapita colonists, named after their distinctive red-slipped pottery, continued to spread to the east into the islands of present-day Melanesia. The reasons for this migration are uncertain, but most likely had to do with population expansion. Lapita colonists reached Fiji, the eastern boundary of present-day Melanesia, by 1300 BCE and made their way eastward to the islands of Tonga and Samoa by 1000 BCE.

Mississippi Temple Mound settlement at Cahokia (Courtesy of the Illinois Historical Library)

OTHER EARLY MIGRANTS

In 1947 the Norwegian explorer Thor Heyerdahl, with a crew of five, sailed an exact replica of a traditional South American balsa-wood raft across the South Pacific from Peru to the Tuamo-to Archipelago in western Polynesia. The 97-day voyage aboard the Kon-Tiki was undertaken to test Heyerdahl's theory that Polynesia had been populated by ancient peoples from the northwest coast of South America. In the years since his celebrated feat, anthropologists have largely dismissed Heyerdahl's thesis. The archaeological, racial, linguistic, and ethnological evidence all support the settlement of Polynesia by maritime peoples from Southeast Asia. Similarly, while it is possible there were isolated, random transpacific contacts between the South Pacific and South America, there is no substantive evidence of any migration from Polynesia eastward to the Western Hemisphere.

Heyerdahl was also one in a long line of theorists to conjecture that ancient peoples from Africa or Europe were among the original inhabitants of America. In 1970 he again took to the seas to demonstrate that intrepid mariners from North Africa could have journeyed across the Atlantic Ocean in antiquity. His successful voyage in a traditional North African reed boat is cited by contemporary scholars who suggest variously that ancient Egyptians, Phoenecians, Libyans, or sub-Saharan Africans reached the Western Hemisphere thousands of years before Columbus. Other theorists have raised the possibility of transpacific voyages from Japan or even China.

Anthropologists generally agree that if there were any early contacts between Native Americans and other peoples, they were transitory, circumstantial events (such as a drift voyage) of negligible impact at most. No physical trace of such contacts has been found. Existing archaeological evidence suggests overwhelmingly that the Native Americans, descendants of the prehistoric migrants over the

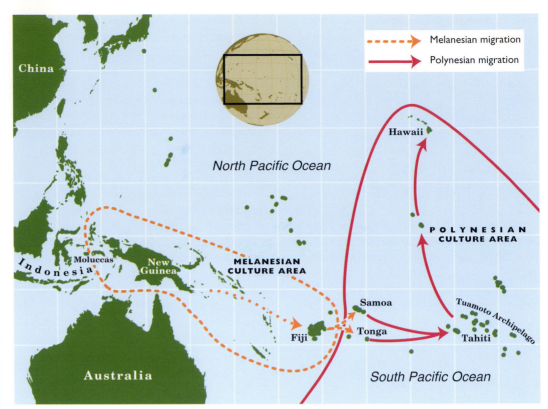

Polynesian Settlement of Hawaii

The Lapita settlements on Tonga and Samoa evolved a new and distinctive Polynesian culture over 1,000 years of geographical isolation. Both the Melanesians and Polynesians were advanced Stone Age peoples. Each made skillful use of stone, bone, and shell tools, cultivated tubers and fruit trees, and kept domesticated pigs, chickens, and dogs. While the Polynesians did not retain the pottery skills of their Lapita ancestors, their double-hulled and outrigger canoes were technological marvels. European voyagers in the 18th century reported seeing double canoes at Tahiti over 90 feet long. Matted leaf sails let the Polynesians sail into the wind by tacking.

Beginning about 150 BCE, Polynesian colonists from Tonga and Samoa launched a remarkable new seaborne migration to the east. Over the next millennium, their descendants spread throughout the vast ocean expanse of present-day Polynesia. Again, the most likely explanation for this dispersal was population growth. The Polynesians first sailed their open double canoes, loaded with livestock and seed plants as well as men, women, and children, to Tahiti and the Society Islands. From there, further generations continued the migration north to Hawaii, east to Easter Island, and south to New Zealand. The Polynesians were arguably the greatest navigators in history. Without aid of navigational tools or devices, they made jour-

neys of up to 2,400 miles across the open ocean from isolated island to isolated island. They relied on observations of star and sun positions, prevailing wind and swell directions, cloud patterns, and homing birds. During their long voyages, they could sustain themselves through the collection of rainwater and fishing.

The first Polynesian settlers reached Hawaii about 400 CE. The Polynesians had no written language and there is no record of this extraordinary migration. Anthropologists believe that Polynesian immigration to the islands may have continued intermittently as late as the 1300s, but that mutual contact between Hawaii and Tahiti had ceased by 1400. The more fertile high volcanic islands of Polynesia permitted the Polynesians to move beyond the subsistence-level social organization characteristic of Melanesia and to develop a richly ceremonial religious, social, and political life. During centuries of isolation, a separate Polynesian culture emerged on Hawaii. The name Hawaii itself derives from the native word for homeland. The Hawaiians were highly skilled fishers and farmers. Taro plants, in particular, were cultivated on irrigated terraces. Their largely wooden villages, with earthen and stone religious sites, were governed by a strict system of laws and taboos administered by local ruling chiefs and priests. When British naval officer Captain James Cook sighted Hawaii in 1778, bringing the archipelago into contact with the outside world, the native population of the islands numbered some 300,000.

NORSE EXPLORATION AND SETTLEMENT

North America remained isolated from the rest of the world until 1492. There was, however, one group that did reach the continent some 500 years before Columbus. Its story is one of enterprise and daring, circumstance, and human drama. While the short-lived settlement of Norse visitors on the North American shore had no lasting impact, their brief foray foreshadowed many of the basic themes of later European migration to the continent.

Between the 9th and 12th centuries, Viking raiders from Scandinavia terrorized much of Europe. These fierce Norsemen rank with the Polynesians as among history's greatest sailors. Setting out across the Baltic in their famed long ships, they explored and plundered their way along the Atlantic coast to the Mediterranean and roamed the major rivers of Russia as far as the Black Sea and Constantinople (now Istanbul). The Vikings were the warriors of the Norse people of present-day Norway, Denmark, and Sweden. Polygamy and concubinage were not uncommon in pre-Christian Scandinavia, and the ranks of the Vikings were filled by illegitimate sons, barred by law from any inheritance, seeking

adventure and opportunity. As population pressures in Scandinavia increased, due largely to a shortage of good farmland, other ordinary Norse put out to sea. Their goal, however, was not plunder but uninhabited lands they could settle.

Norse land-seekers first colonized the Shetland and Faroe islands off the coast of Norway. These Norse ranged westward across the North Atlantic in the versatile knarr, or round ship, a variant of the long ship. Norse shipbuilding was the most advanced in medieval Europe. Like the Viking warship, the shallow-drafted wooden knarr had a huge square woolen sail. Auxiliary power was provided by the distinctive Norse long oar. The knarr, some 60 feet long and 15 feet wide, was designed for cargo. It could carry several head of cattle, sizable provisions, and upwards of 30 crew and passengers. The Norse navigated by what is called "latitude sailing." Using two crude instruments, a notched stick and a sun shadow board, to measure the height of the North Star and the sun, they were able to sail east or west along a given latitude. They had no means to determine longitude and generally followed a coastline when voyaging north or south.

By 870 Norse colonists had reached Iceland, roughly a week's sail west of the Faroes, displacing the hermetic Irish monks already there. Our knowledge of further Norse exploration to the west comes from *The Vinland Sagas*. These Norse oral histories were first written down in Iceland in the 13th century. According to the sagas, Norse colonist Eric the Red, banished tem-

Bering land bridge, were the first and only inhabitants of pre-Columbian America. Anthropologists offer two fundamental observations that support this conclusion. First, all of the native inhabitants of the Americas, from Canada to Peru, share a common genetic inheritance traceable to northeastern Asia. There is no evidence of any other racial presence. Second, all of the Native American languages, while interrelated to various degrees, are completely distinct from any other known languages. If other ancient peoples had somehow migrated to America, there would be some linguistic record of their presence.

Over the centuries speculation about the origins of the Native Americans has produced an array of fascinating and, occasionally, wild theories. Myth, religion, and even science fiction have all figured in efforts to explain the original peopling of America.

Often, these theories stemmed from attempts to explain such impressive accomplishments of pre-Columbian Native American culture as the Mississippi and Ohio valley temple mounds. Possessed of racist, derogatory attitudes about Indians, white settlers found it inconceivable that these massive earthen structures, or the copper and precious stone artifacts they contained, could have been fashioned by Native Americans. The idea took hold that an ancient, and by inference more civilized, white race had to have been in America long before Columbus. At various times Greeks from the legendary island of Atlantis, the mythic 12th-century seafaring Welsh prince Madoc, and even visitors from outer space have been proposed as the source of the more advanced aspects of Native American culture. Among the more fanciful, and more enduring, theories is that St. Brendan and a band of seagoing Irish monks journeyed to America in the 6th century. No early Irish artifact has ever been found in North America, but the legend of St. Brendan continues to exert a powerful allure.

Norse Exploration and Settlement

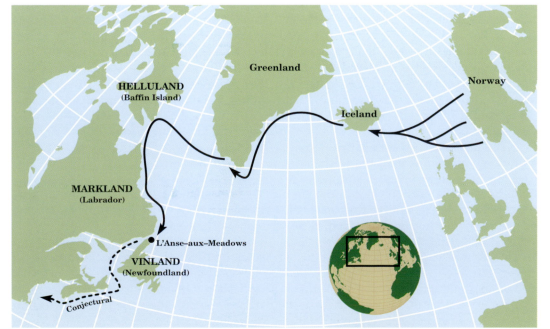

Language Families

Algonquian	Keresan	Muskogean	Sahaptin	Uto-Aztecan
Caddoan	Kiowa-Tanoan	Na-Dene	Salishan	Unknown or no dominant family
Hokan	Lutuamian	Penutian	Siouan	

Apache   Native American tribe

Western Native American Tribes, c. 1492

porarily from Iceland in 982 after a blood feud, sailed to the west and discovered a great peninsula. He named his discovery Greenland, apparently at least in part to attract prospective settlers. Returning to Iceland, he organized an expedition that established a Norse colony on the southwestern Greenland coast in 986.

The same year Icelander Bjarni Herjulfson, blown off course en route to the new settlement, became the first European to sight the North American coast to the west of Greenland. In 1000 Eric the Red's son Leif set out to explore this unknown land. Heading west in Bjarni's knarr, Leif Erickson and his crew first reached the rocky coastline of present-day Baffin Island, which he called Helluland (land of stone slabs). Turning south, they sailed along the southeastern coast of Labrador, which Leif named Mark-

land (land of woods). They finally came to the northern tip of Newfoundland, where they spent the winter. Leif dubbed the area Vinland (land of wine). The following year they returned to Greenland with a cargo of grapes and timber. As far as scholarship has been able to determine, Leif and his crew were the first Europeans to set foot on North America.

Over the next two decades, various members of Leif's family mounted expeditions to Vinland. His brother Thorvald first encountered the Native Americans of the region. The Norse called these Indians *skraelings*, literally "uglies" or savages, and generally treated them with hostility. Thorvald was killed in a skirmish after his crew had slain several Native Americans. Around 1010 the merchant Thorfinn Karlsefni led an expedition of some 65 men and women that established a settlement at the site of Leif's original camp on Vinland. Thorfinn's wife gave birth to a son, Snorri, the first European on record to have been born in North America.

The Norse traded with the Indians for furs, but relations were tense. The settlement was abandoned in 1013 after a pitched battle with Native Americans. The following year Leif's half-sister Freydis returned to Vinland with another expedition. The settlers fought among themselves, however, with the fearsome Freydis herself killing five women with an ax. The Norse presence in North America ended with the survivors sailing back to Greenland.

Voyages from Greenland to North America in search of timber and fur continued over the following three centuries, but no further attempts were made to settle in Vinland. The Norse colony in Greenland eventually died out in the 15th century. The story of the Norse discovery of North America faded into obscurity and was unknown to Columbus and other European explorers of the Age of Discovery. Translation of *The Vinland Sagas* into Latin in the 18th century sparked interest in whether

Eastern Native American Tribes, c. 1492

Language Families		
Algonquian	Iroquoian	Siouan
Caddoan	Muskogean	Unknown or no dominant family
Cherokee Native American tribe		

these seemingly legendary tales recounted actual historical events. A key question was the location of Vinland. Over the years scholars searched without success for Norse artifacts between New England and Virginia, mindful that grapes could not have grown farther north.

In 1960 Norwegian archaeologist Helge Ingstad uncovered the remnants of a Norse stone village at L'Anse-aux-Meadows on the northern coast of Newfoundland, confirming both the underlying truth of *The Vinland Sagas* and the location of Vinland. It is thought the sagas' grapes were actually berries, such as currants, also used by the Norse for making wine. Many have surmised that the Norse continued their exploration past Newfoundland and down the Atlantic coast, perhaps as far as New England, but no other physical evidence of their presence has ever been found.

The hostile Norse response to the *skraelings*, even to this first use of the term "savages," was only too prophetic of future relations between European colonists and Native Americans. The Norse experience paralleled that of later European migrants in other ways, including development of the maritime technology necessary to traverse the Atlantic and the quest for natural resources and land. There is at least an echo of future advertisements for settlers in Eric the Red's naming of Greenland, and possibly even Leif Erickson's use of Vinland.

AMERICA ON THE EVE OF COLUMBUS

In 1492 all of present-day America was inhabited. Native Americans had occupied the North American continent for more than 10,000 years. Hawaii had been home for some 1,000 years to a vibrant Polynesian culture. There were literally hundreds of distinct Native American tribes speaking some 200 to 300 different languages. The Native American population at the time of contact with Europeans is impossible to determine. Estimates for what is now the continental United States range from the commonly cited one to two million to as high as 10 to 12 million. The population density varied widely. The highest concentrations were found along the Virginia, Georgia, and California coasts and on the upper Rio Grande and lower Colorado rivers. The Great Lakes region, New England coast, and Deep South also had higher levels. Population densities were lowest in the Arctic, Subarctic, and Great Basin.

EL DORADO AND THE FUR TRADE
Migration in the Spanish Borderlands, New France, and Russian Alaska

In the late 15th century seaborne European explorers would journey to the Americas, find their way around the horn of South America, and continue across the Pacific Ocean to circumnavigate the globe. Expeditions along the Atlantic and Pacific coasts of the Americas revealed the basic outline of the Western Hemisphere. For the Europeans, these were voyages of astonishing discovery. This sudden burst of exploration and its unveiling of the Americas is known as the Age of Reconnaissance.

The Europeans not only explored America, they also laid claim to it. Five European powers—Spain, France, the Netherlands, England, and Russia—established colonies in the territory of present-day America. Another, Sweden, founded a brief settlement on the Delaware River. These colonies marked the start of the centuries-long migration of peoples from around the world to America that continues to this day. Colonial migration had many causes. The Spanish came to conquer, the French and Russians to trade, and the Dutch and English to settle. The Africans were brought in chains in the holds of slave ships. And the Native Americans became refugees in their own land.

THE AGE OF RECONNAISSANCE

Exploration of the world beyond Europe's shores evolved out of the Renaissance, the period of intellectual and cultural flowering that brought the continent out of the Middle Ages. Also key was the rise of the nation-state. The increasingly unified and centralized European nations had the means and resources to mount expensive seaborne expeditions. Exploration suited their national purposes. The emerging nation-states of Europe looked to trade to spur economic growth. There was a mounting demand for Eastern spices, essential to food preservation, to support expanding European populations. The lack of direct trade routes limited access to the Indies and its trade riches. First Portugal, and then Spain, began the quest for new sea trade routes to the East. This search launched the Age of Reconnaissance.

TECHNOLOGY AND TRANSPORTATION

These maritime expeditions were made possible by late medieval and Renaissance advances in shipbuilding, navigation, and map making. Two distinct shipbuilding traditions developed in Europe during the Middle Ages. The trader ships of the North Sea and Atlantic Coast were heavy-bodied and broad, with a single mast and square sail. The longer, sleeker ships of the Mediterranean had two or more masts and triangular sails.

The Portuguese and Spanish were the first to combine the best elements of the two traditions in the construction of vessels that were truly oceanworthy. These ships, with their multiple masts and sails, were maneuverable and could sail effectively against the wind. Their solid, watertight construction made them highly seaworthy. The ships had two or more decks and were capable of carrying a sizable cargo. The three ships that ferried Columbus and his crew on their maiden trip to America were typical in size. The larger *Santa Maria* was some 85 feet long and carried about 100 tons. The *Niña* and *Pinta*, also tri-masted caravels, were closer to 50 tons and 60 feet in length. These ships and their larger successors soon proved capable of transporting a steady flow of colonists to America.

Mariners braving an oceanic voyage relied on several improvements in navigation. The magnetic compass, adapted for shipboard use, provided direction. Latitude could be determined by using the newly developed astrolabe, an instrument for measuring the height of the sun or stars above the horizon. Advances in chart making and cartography enabled seafaring nations to provide crews with maps for their voyages and to record the results of their exploration for future use.

Europe by the late 1400s had a burgeoning shipbuilding industry. Its ships were manned by a growing pool of experienced and skillful captains and crews.

Among this fraternity was the Genoese seaman Christopher Columbus.

CHRISTOPHER COLUMBUS

Born around 1451, Columbus as a youth decided on a life at sea. He came of age in the multinational Mediterranean seafaring world of the Renaissance, lived in Portugal nine years, and made voyages to Iceland and the west coast of Africa. Since the early 1400s, Portugal had explored southward along the coast of Africa in pursuit of a sea trade route to the lucrative markets of the East. Columbus conceived the idea of sailing west across the Atlantic to the Indies. The ambitious sea captain was fascinated by the 14th-century Venetian merchant Marco Polo's account of his travels to China, which Polo called Cathay.

Contrary to the notion enshrined in popular history, educated opinion in late 15th-century Europe knew that the world was round. What worried explorers in venturing westward was not the prospect of falling off Earth's edge, but the unknown distances involved. Columbus and his fellow mariners were unaware of the Norse exploration of North America some 500 years before. No one in Europe had any

inkling of another hemisphere across the Atlantic. Maps of the time depicted the ocean as an empty expanse between Europe and the Indies. It was generally believed that any crew heading west would perish at sea long before reaching its destination. In one of history's most fateful miscalculations, Columbus estimated the distance between the Canary Islands and Zipangu (the European name at the time for Japan) at 2,400 miles—short by some 8,200 miles. His calculation was actually the approximate distance from the Canaries to America.

When King John II of Portugal declined in 1484 to fund an expedition westward, Columbus moved to Spain. After years of petitioning, he finally prevailed on King Ferdinand and Queen Isabella to back his audacious plan to cross the Atlantic. The Spanish monarchs, hoping for mercantile gain, provided him with three ships, a crew of 90, and a letter of introduction to the Great Khan of Cathay. Columbus's small fleet of the *Niña, Pinta,* and *Santa Maria* sailed from the Canary Islands on September 6, 1492, and into history. On October 12 the voyagers touched land in the central Bahamas.

Columbus believed he had reached a chain of islands off the coast of China. He made a total of four voyages to the Americ-

Early Spanish Exploration of America

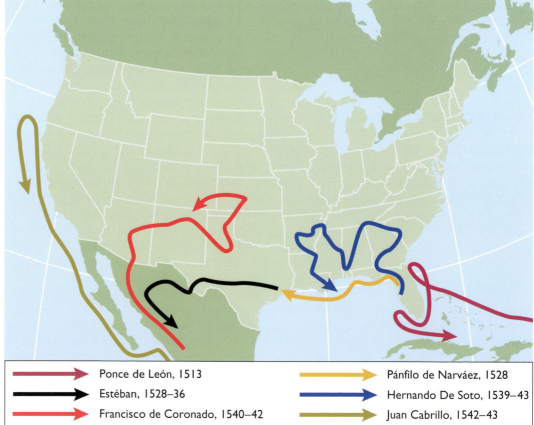

➤ Ponce de León, 1513	➤ Pánfilo de Narváez, 1528
➤ Estéban, 1528–36	➤ Hernando De Soto, 1539–43
➤ Francisco de Coronado, 1540–42	➤ Juan Cabrillo, 1542–43

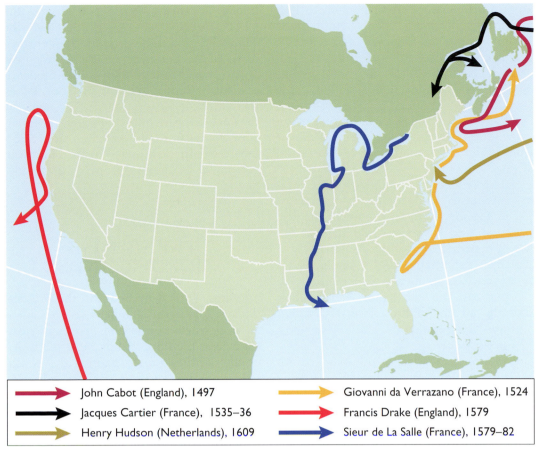

→ John Cabot (England), 1497		→ Giovanni da Verrazano (France), 1524	
→ Jacques Cartier (France), 1535–36		→ Francis Drake (England), 1579	
→ Henry Hudson (Netherlands), 1609		→ Sieur de La Salle (France), 1579–82	

Other Early European Exploration of America

as, searching the Caribbean in vain for a passage to the Asian mainland and its prospective riches. Key among the hoped-for treasures was gold. Returning to Spain to extraordinary acclaim in 1493, Columbus set forth again across the Atlantic later the same year with a fleet of 17 ships carrying more than 1,000 colonists. This second journey set a basic pattern for European contact with the Americas and its native inhabitants. The colonists, most lured by the promise of gold, founded the first permanent European settlement on the island of Hispaniola. The island's natives were soon enslaved and put to work in gold mines. Catholic priests undertook what became a tradition of forcibly converting the Indians to Christianity. For the Spanish Crown, this first colonial expedition served to further exploration of the Indies and to forestall any possible Portuguese competition.

EUROPE ENCOUNTERS A NEW WORLD

For Europeans, the Americas were a New World. Florentine navigator Amerigo Vespucci, who explored the South American coast for both Spain and Portugal, suspected as early as 1502 that the Americas were not part of Asia. This suspicion was confirmed by the Spanish expedition led by Ferdinand Magellan in 1519, which rounded South America and crossed the Pacific to Asia. Magellan was killed in the Philippines, but the expedition's survivors completed the first circumnavigation of the earth, returning to Spain in 1522.

In other correspondence, Vespucci falsely claimed to have been the first European to sight the American mainland in 1497. The feat actually belonged to John Cabot, sailing for England in the same year. Based on Vespucci's unmerited claim, the German geographer Martin Waldseemüller in 1507 dubbed the newly encountered world "America" in honor of the Florentine explorer.

The term New World conveyed the sense of opportunity with which Europeans viewed the Americas. Renaissance Europe was poised to exploit its discovery of a vast new territory across the Atlantic. Its nascent nation states were eager for natural resources to support their domestic industries. The establishment of colonies abetted the procurement of timber, furs, and other sources of wealth and provided new markets for their expanding economies. With Europe's emergence from feudalism, an economic system known as mercantilism came to dominance from the 16th to 18th centuries. Mercantile theory emphasized exports as the key to growth and relied on government regulation of industry and trade. A central tenet of mercantilism was bullionism, the idea that a nation's true wealth was determined by its quantities of gold and silver. The Spanish Empire in the New World rested on the huge quantities of gold plundered from the native Aztecs and Incas.

The Renaissance itself, with its celebration of inquiry and learning, inspired interest in the unknown world across the sea. Religion also played a role in the Old World's penetration of the Americas. Missionaries, especially from Catholic Spain and France, came to convert the Indians to Christianity. The 16th-century Reformation and the advent of Protestantism divided Europe along religious lines. The fierce competition between Catholic and Protestant nations extended to the New World, spurring exploration and the claim of lands for one faith or the other.

When Europeans looked at America, they did not see a millennia-old Native American way of life, but a sparsely inhabited wilderness open to settlement. For successive generations of colonists, America became a haven from the poverty, overcrowding, and religious persecution of their native Europe. America represented hope and a new life.

Colonization followed the pattern of early exploration. In 1494 in the Treaty of Tordesillas, Spain and Portugal divided between them the unknown world they were discovering. Spain claimed all the lands lying west of present-day Brazil. Portugal was allotted Brazil, Africa, and any lands it might find in Asia by sailing east.

Spain took the lead in early exploration of the Americas, but other nations were soon to follow across the Atlantic. At first the search was for the Cathay Passage, the hoped-for route through the lands found by Columbus and onward to the Asian mainland. Later, as it became apparent that another hemisphere lay between Europe and the East, mariners hunted for a water passageway through the Americas to the Indies.

Each nation followed these expeditions with other forays, as explorers progressively mapped out and laid claim to all of the Americas. The Age of Reconnaissance lasted almost three centuries. Scholars generally mark its close with British Captain James Cook's voyages in the Pacific in the 1770s. This long period is also known as the Age of Expansion, when the European colonial powers extended their reach around the globe. The Spanish presence defined the colonial period in the present-day territory of the United States. The colonial settlement of America began with the establishment of a Spanish outpost in Florida in 1565. While the American Revolution in 1776 signaled the demise of the colonial period, the Spanish colonial presence stretched until 1821, when Spain lost its North American colonies as a consequence of Mexican independence.

THE SPANISH BORDERLANDS

The areas settled by Spain in the present-day territory of the United States are known as the Spanish Borderlands. At their greatest extent, the Borderlands included much of the Southeast and spanned the Southwest from Texas to California. These areas represented the remote northern frontier of the Spanish Empire centered in Mexico. As other European powers penetrated North America, the Borderlands defined the boundary between the Spanish Empire and the English, French, and, later, Russian colonies.

EXPLORATION AND SETTLEMENT

Spanish migration in North America was shaped by the sword, the cross, and gold. Spain's conquering approach to the New World was a direct legacy of Spanish history. In the 700s the medieval Christian kingdoms on the Iberian Peninsula were overrun by Muslim invaders from North Africa. Over the next 700 years Christian forces, starting from their mountain strongholds in northern Spain, waged a relentless war to drive the Muslim Moors from the peninsula. The long crusade became known as the *Reconquista,* or Reconquest. The Spanish finally triumphed over the Moors in 1492.

Soon after the Reconquest ended in Spain, its basic aspects reappeared in the Spanish penetration of the Americas. Subjugation of the brilliant Moorish civilization, with its access to the trade riches of the Islamic world, taught the Spanish crown that conquest could bring wealth. Reports of fabulously rich native civilizations in Mexico and in the Andes inspired early Spanish explorers to undertake military expeditions of conquest. Centuries of conflict had given rise in Spain to a warrior class of battle-hardened, ruthless professional soldiers. From its ranks came the conquistadores, who within 40 years of Columbus's first voyage had conquered both the Aztec and Incan empires.

The struggle against the Moors produced a militant Catholicism in Spain. The church developed a doctrine of just war to validate the conquest of lands from infidels, or non-believers. For the Spanish the Native Americans, like the Moors, were infidels. The conquest and conversion of native peoples became a fundamental purpose of the Spanish Empire in the Americas. Two missionary orders in particular, the Franciscans and the Jesuits, believed it their calling to spread the Catholic faith in the New World.

The Spanish conquistadores were spurred by gold. In 1521 Hernán Cortés conquered the Aztec Empire and established the kingdom of New Spain in central Mexico. Aztec gold and jewels filled the coffers of the Spanish treasury. Twelve years later Francisco Pizarro added Incan Peru, with its even greater wealth of gold and silver, to the Spanish New World empire. Tales of even richer native kingdoms inspired further exploration. In South America adventurers searched for the realm of El Dorado, the "golden man." According to legend this kingdom was so awash in precious metals and stones that its ruler was powdered with gold dust to give him a second golden skin. Over time, the name El Dorado became identified with a place, a fabulous realm of untold riches somewhere in the unexplored reaches of the Americas.

Spanish reconnaissance of North America began in 1513, when Juan Ponce de León sailed north from Puerto Rico in search of the mythical Fountain of Youth. Ponce de León found and named the peninsula of Florida, which he thought was an island. Later expeditions to America, lured by stories of golden riches, explored the Gulf coast, the Southwest, and California. None of these expeditions found an American El Dorado, and there was little immediate impetus for further Spanish penetration of the continent. This surge of early exploration, though, sketched the outline of the future Spanish Borderlands.

Spain exercised tight imperial control over its New World empire. In 1524 the Spanish crown founded the Council of the Indies to govern its overseas possessions. A constant profusion of royal laws and edicts regulated colonial life down to the smallest detail. Spanish holdings in the Caribbean and Central America were organized into

CHRONOLOGY OF THE SPANISH BORDERLANDS

1492	Christopher Columbus reaches the Western Hemisphere
1493	First Spanish colony on Hispaniola
1512	Laws of Burgos
1513	Juan Ponce de León explores the Florida peninsula
1521	Hernán Cortés conquers the Aztec Empire
1524	Viceroyalty of New Spain
1528	Pánfilo de Narváez explores America's gulf coast
1539–43	Hernando de Soto crosses the American Southeast
1540–42	Francisco Vásquez de Coronado explores the American Southwest
1542	Indian slavery banned in New Spain
1542–43	Juan Rodríguez Cabrillo sails along the California coast
1565	Founding of St. Augustine
1573	Ordinances of Discovery
1598	Settlement of New Mexico
1680	Pueblo Revolt
1687	Settlement of Primeria Alta
1690–93	Early settlement of Texas
1702–13	Queen Anne's War
1716	Permanent settlement of Texas
1756–63	Seven Years' War
1763	Great Britain gains possession of Florida; Spain acquires French Louisiana
1769	Settlement of California
1783	Florida returns to Spanish control
1800	France reacquires the Louisiana Territory
1819	Spain cedes Florida to the United States
1821	Southwest Borderlands part of newly independent Mexico

the viceroyalty of New Spain. The Ordinances of Discovery in 1573 established strict guidelines for the settlement of Spain's American colonies. All land in Spanish America belonged initially to the king. It was held in trust by the crown until transferred by royal land grant to an individual or group for the formation of a settlement or to the church for the creation of a mission.

Settlement of the Spanish Borderlands began in 1565 as a defensive measure against French encroachment in Florida. The Spanish province of Florida fell under the administration of colonial authorities in the Caribbean. The establishment of Spanish outposts in the Southwest was also largely defensive. The provinces of Texas and California were intended to block French and Russian colonial advances. Settlements in Arizona and New Mexico aided the pacification of Native American tribes that were raiding Spain's lucrative silver mines in northern Mexico. These southwest provinces reported directly to the government of New Spain in Mexico City.

ESTÉBAN

He explored more of the Spanish Borderlands than any conquistador or priest. Yet history scarcely notes his exploits. Estéban was born in North Africa about 1500. A Moor or, more likely, a black African owned initially by the Moors, he became the slave of Spanish conquistador Andrés Dorantes in the 1520s. In 1527 Estéban sailed from Spain with Dorantes as part of Pánfilo de Narváez's ill-fated expedition to Florida.

From April to September 1528 Narváez led some 300 men through the southwest interior of Florida. Under constant attack by native tribes, the Spaniards abandoned their exploration and attempted to sail in small, hastily-built boats along the southeast coast of America to Mexico. Most of the expedition, including Narváez, drowned in a storm off Texas. Among the handful of survivors washed ashore were Estéban, Dorantes, and the conquistadores Cabeza de Vaca and Alonso de Castillo.

The four were captured and enslaved by local Indians. They spent six years among the Native Americans of central Texas, migrating with them in their seasonal search for food. Estéban and his fellow captives finally escaped in 1534 and set out for the safety of Spanish settlements in Mexico. Over the next two years they wandered across present-day Texas, New Mexico, Arizona, and possibly southeastern California. In early 1536 they reached the northern Mexican province of Sonora where they were rescued by a party of Spaniards on a slave-catching foray among the Indians.

Their feat of crossing the American continent, from Florida to the Gulf of California, went unrepeated until American explorers Lewis and Clark did so in 1805. The long trek of the remaining members of the Narváez expedition was not over, however, as they continued overland to Mexico City to meet Spanish authorities. New Spain was enthralled by their reports of golden Indian cities to the north, which soon became known as the Seven Cities of Cíbola. Quite possibly Estéban and his

Spanish authorities relied on three institutions for the colonization and settlement of the Borderlands: missions, presidios, and towns. Catholic priests were in the vanguard of Spanish penetration of new territories, traveling beyond the existing limits of settlement to found missions among the Native Americans. These missions were organized to convert the Indians to both Christianity and Spanish civilization. They were largely autonomous, self-sufficient communities. Labor was provided by Indian converts. Missions were chartered for 10 years. The Spanish crown expected that the Native Americans would gradually adapt to Hispanic acculturation and that the mission communities would become loyal Indian towns. More often than not, however, this assimilation did not occur.

Many Native American tribes resisted conversion, and missions often requested military protection. Colonial authorities responded by establishing presidios, or military garrisons, in close proximity to the missions. Presidios also were strategically placed to protect Spain's territorial claims. An average presidio comprised 50 to 100 soldiers and their families. These remote outposts in the Borderlands relied on supply trains or ships for essential provisions. Civilian settlements often developed near the presidios to provide them such essentials as food, clothing, and manufactured goods.

The Ordinances of Discovery provided detailed directions on how a town should be laid out and its land allocated. These guidelines were adapted from the centralized towns that had emerged in Spain in the Middle Ages. The Spanish did not live on separate farmsteads, but traveled back and forth from their village or town to work their land and tend their flocks and herds. Water rights, arable and grazing lands, and forests were held in common for use by all the town's residents. The communal Spanish town was transplanted first to New Spain and then to the Borderlands.

Each town had a central plaza, surrounded by straight, parallel streets and rectangular blocks and lots. Near the plaza were a church, the municipal buildings, and the residences of officials. Outside the compact town were common grazing lands and small plots for individual cultivation. Settlements were classified as villages, towns, or cities. The largest settlements in the Borderlands, Santa Fe and Albuquerque, never exceeded a population of 7,000 and were designated as towns.

NATIVE AMERICANS

Spanish settlement of the Borderlands proved a centuries-long nightmare of disease, death, and devastation for its native inhabitants. Scholars estimate the Native American population in Florida at the time of Spanish penetration in the early 1500s was around 100,000. By the early 1700s, epidemics, warfare, and enslavement had essentially destroyed the Apalachee, Timucua, and other indigenous tribes. Some 80,000 Indians lived in New Mexico in 1598. Two centuries later fewer than 10,000 remained. Similar decimation occurred in Arizona and Texas. The native populace of coastal California declined precipitously after the Spanish arrival in 1769.

Native Americans were not illness-free before the arrival of Europeans. But, because of their millennia-long isolation from the rest of the world, they had not been exposed to diseases that first appeared in Africa and Eurasia. Consequently, they had no natural immune defenses against many of the germs that Europeans brought to the Americas. Contact with the Spanish triggered devastating epidemics that swept though the native population. Diseases such as smallpox, scarlet fever, typhus, and cholera were particularly deadly. A series of smallpox epidemics, for example, basically wiped out the native population of Florida.

The Spaniards, unlike later European colonists, did not drive the Indians from their lands. Instead, they sought to conquer, convert, and incorporate the native peoples into their New World empire. Columbus and the first Spanish colonists viewed the Indians as unworthy and inferior savages. The Spanish almost from the start made slaves of the Indians under their control. Those that resisted conquest and enslavement were brutally annihilated. Indian slave labor soon became the backbone of the burgeoning economy in Spain's Caribbean possessions.

Under the strong influence of missionary orders, the Spanish crown moved to end Indian slavery. Royal policy sought instead to make the Native Americans into peaceful Christian subjects of the monarchy. The Laws of Burgos, promulgated in 1512, sought to terminate the outright enslavement of Indians. To govern the use of Indian labor, the laws extended to the New World the Spanish feudal institution known as the *encomienda*. The *encomienda* was an official authorization to its holder, or *encomendero*, to collect tribute from the inhabitants of a given area. In New Spain the *encomiendo* represented the right to extract labor from the Native Americans.

The *encomienda* was in effect another form of slavery. Indians subject to its award were compelled to work as many as nine months out of every year. Although the *encomendero* had certain obligations, most notably to provide for the natives' spiritual welfare, these were rarely honored and abuses of Indian workers were rampant. The Spanish crown, aware of its failure as a tool to aid in the conversion of Native Americans, theoretically abolished the *encomienda* system in 1542. The ban was often circumvented by colonial authorities, however, and use of the institution persisted until the early 1700s. In the Borderlands, the award of *encomiendas* was limited to New Mexico, where they were employed as incentives to draw colonists to the remote province. After the Pueblo Revolt of 1680, the *encomienda* system was not reestablished in New Mexico.

To replace the *encomienda*, the Spanish officials authorized use of the *repartimiento*. Also a kind of royal grant, the *repartimiento* gave its holder the right to impose an annual levy of labor on the native populace. While less harsh than the *encomienda*, it still represented what was in essence legal enslavement. The Indians were compelled to submit to the *repartimiento*, but under the law they were entitled to wages and could be pressed into labor only for set periods of time. These legal requirements, however, were almost invariably ignored. The *repartimiento* was widely employed in Florida and New Mexico. While officially eliminated in the early 1600s, forced levees of Indian labor continued to exist in various unsanctioned forms until Mexican independence in 1821.

The 1573 Ordinances of Discovery banned brutal military campaigns of conquest against the Indians and established procedures for their pacification as Spanish subjects. The primary instrument for this subjugation was the mission. In New Mexico and Arizona, the town-like dwellings of the Pueblo Indians facilitated the establishment of mission communities. In Florida, Texas, and California, missionaries gathered the more-scattered native inhabitants into mission settlements to aid in their conversion and acculturation. Disease took a constant toll. The Native Americans often violently resisted Spanish intrusion, but were no match for the Spaniards' superior military technology and tactics. Passive resistance was widespread, though, as they rejected Spanish religion and culture whenever possible.

SLAVERY

European settlement and development of the Americas was linked directly to slave labor. The African slave trade, with its brutal, forced migration of millions, came to dominate colonial economic arrangements.

At the time of European contact with the New World, virtually every religion and society worldwide accepted slavery as a normal part of human activity. Slavery existed in various forms in pre-Columbian America. The Aztec Empire made extensive use of slaves in agriculture. Enslavement of captives apparently was common among the Native American tribes of the Borderlands. Some scholars postulate that a slave trade existed from the Southwest to the more complex Aztec civilization to the south.

The Spanish experience with slavery dated to the Reconquest, when both Christians and Moors enslaved their captives. Fifteenth-century Spain was also familiar with Portugal's exploitation of African slaves to work the sugar plantations on its recently acquired islands off the African coast. Portugal pioneered the African slave trade to the Americas, first bringing slaves to cultivate its sugar fields in Brazil in the early 1500s.

Two distinct slave systems materialized in Spanish America. First was the enslavement of indigenous peoples. From the start, Spanish colonists regarded the Native Americans as conquered infidels who, like captive Moors, were subject to human bondage. As the Spanish colonial presence expanded, slave expeditions were mounted throughout the Caribbean region to maintain a steady supply of Indian labor. Enslaved Africans began arriving in Spain's New World colonies in 1518. At first, they supplemented the enslaved native populace already at work in the mines and plantations on Spain's Caribbean islands. As disease and horrid work conditions reduced Indian populations by as much as 90 percent, the African slave trade became the primary source of labor.

Though Indian slavery was ostensibly banned by the Spanish Crown in 1512, it continued under the guise of the *encomienda* and *repartimiento* systems. Native Americans in the Spanish Borderlands were subjected to what amounted to legalized enslavement into the 18th century. As Indian slavery declined, the number of African slaves imported each year grew steadily. Of the estimated 10 million Africans brought in bondage to the Americas from the early

companions had been fooled by the sun's golden reflection off the adobe walls of distant Pueblo dwellings. An expedition was organized under Franciscan missionary Marcos de Niza to search for the fabled Indian cities. Estéban was purchased by colonial governor Antonio de Mendoza to serve as guide.

The expedition headed north in March 1539. Estéban traveled ahead with a small advance party. In May he reached the Zuñi pueblos in what is now western New Mexico. Treated at first as the incarnation of a god because of his dark skin, Estéban at some point fell out of favor and was killed by Zuñi warriors. On learning of his death, Niza retreated to Mexico. The lure of the golden cities would inspire subsequent exploration of the Borderlands under de Soto and Coronado.

Cabeza de Vaca returned to Spain, where in 1542 he published *Los Naufragios* (The Shipwrecked), an account of the eight-year adventure of the Narváez expedition survivors. In 1935 the Spanish explorer was honored by a 50-cent coin minted in the United States commemorating his pathbreaking journey across the Southwest.

1500s to the abolition of slavery in the mid-1800s, roughly 90 percent went to Spanish and Portuguese colonies.

The journey for almost all of Spain's black slaves ended in the plantations and mines of its Caribbean and Central American colonies. Black slavery was extremely limited in the Borderlands. There was no economic incentive for slaveholding in these sparsely settled areas. The handful of slaves in the Spanish Southwest were domestics or personal servants. There were slightly higher numbers of black slaves in Florida, which was linked to Spain's slave-based colonies in Cuba and Hispaniola.

In their intense colonial rivalry with the English settlements to the north in the Carolinas, Spanish authorities in 1687 made it known that they would free English-owned slaves who escaped to Florida and converted to Catholicism. More than a hundred slaves managed to flee to freedom by the early 18th century, and a settlement, Santa Teresa, was built for them just north of St. Augustine. When England acquired Florida at the close of the Seven Years' War in 1763, 87 freed blacks and some 300 slaves were part of the Spanish evacuation of the colony.

Black slavery was legal in the Spanish Borderlands throughout the colonial period. Florida was absorbed as slave territory by the United States in 1819. Two years later the southwest Borderlands became part of newly independent Mexico, which abolished slavery in 1829.

FLORIDA

Among the mines worked by both Indian and black slaves were the incredibly rich silver deposits found in both the Andes and northern Mexico in the 1540s. Spanish treasure ships soon were sailing from the Caribbean to Spain. French privateers, private warships authorized by the French crown to raid foreign shipping, preyed on the silver-laden merchantmen. The Florida peninsula, lying along the principal Spanish sea route through the Florida Channel, suddenly became strategically important. In 1564 France established a military outpost, Fort Caroline, near present-day Jacksonville on the northeastern coast of Florida.

Spain reacted quickly. In 1565 Pedro Menéndez de Avilés founded a Spanish military garrison at St. Augustine, some 40 miles down the coast. The same year, a military expedition under Menéndez overran Fort Caroline. Spanish authorities were determined not to allow France a foothold on the southeast American coast from which it could base its privateers. The destruction of Fort Caroline ended French inroads in the Southeast. St. Augustine, which survived several bitter colonial wars with England as well as repeated raids by pirates, remains the oldest continuously inhabited European settlement in America.

The Spanish initially considered all of southeastern America part of Florida. Jesuit priests arriving in the province in 1566 established missions from the southern Florida peninsula as far north as the Chesapeake Bay in present-day Virginia. Native American resistance caused the order to abandon the province in 1572. Their missionary charter was assumed by the Franciscans the following year. The English settlement of Jamestown in Virginia in 1607 blocked the reestablishment of Spanish missions north of the Carolinas. The Franciscans concentrated their efforts among the Timucua and Apalachee tribes in north-central Florida and the Guale along the Georgia coast. By 1650 a string of some 40 missions stretched from St. Augustine as far north as Santa Catalina on Saint Catherine's Island in Georgia and across interior Florida to the Apalachicola River in the panhandle.

The missions were administered from St. Augustine, which became the anchor of the Spanish presence in Florida. A small settlement grew up beside the presidio. Throughout the 1600s, the town's Hispanic population hovered around 700, nearly all of whom were soldiers and their families. Florida, like the other Borderlands, was only sparsely settled throughout the Spanish colonial period. The Spanish, unlike the English, never migrated to the New World in great numbers. Over its 300-year history, total Spanish immigration to New Spain was around 300,000. Most of the Spanish colonists in Florida came from Cuba. Almost all had been born in the Americas.

Most of the population growth in New Spain came from natural increase rather than immigration. The shortage of Hispanic women, especially in the Borderlands, led soldiers and settlers to mix freely with Native American women. Their offspring were referred to as *mestizos*. The Spanish developed a complex racial classification system for the new ethnic types emerging in the Americas. The offspring of whites and blacks were called *mulattoes* and those of Indians and blacks *zambos*. As these new groups also intermixed the population of Florida, as well as the other Borderlands, became increasingly diverse.

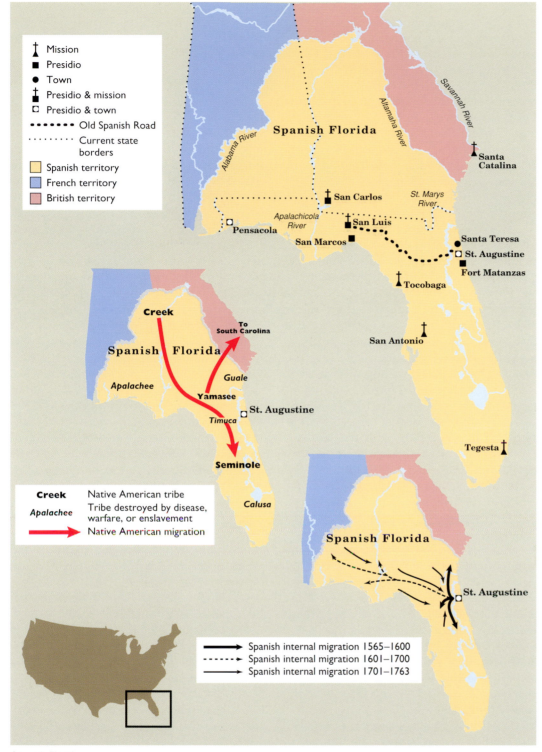

Legend

† Mission
■ Presidio
● Town
⊞ Presidio & mission
□ Presidio & town
••••• Old Spanish Road
····· Current state borders

Spanish territory
French territory
British territory

Creek Native American tribe
Apalachee Tribe destroyed by disease, warfare, or enslavement
→ Native American migration

→ Spanish internal migration 1565–1600
--→ Spanish internal migration 1601–1700
→ Spanish internal migration 1701–1763

Spanish Florida

For more than a century, St. Augustine was the only Spanish town in Florida. The limited settlement of the province followed three separate corridors out of the Spanish outpost. A string of a half-dozen missions and presidios ran along the Georgia coast to the north. The Saint Johns River to the south provided access to the interior for a handful of religious settlements. The principal internal migration extended across northern Florida to the Gulf coast and inland to central Alabama. Missions and presidios were constructed along the colony's main road across the peninsula. Known today as the Old Spanish Trail, it linked St. Augustine with the key settlements at San Luis near present-day Tallahassee and San Marcos on the Gulf of Mexico. Although most of the province's Hispanic inhabitants were soldiers and their families, a few settlers established cattle and wheat ranches in the interior.

French navigation of the Mississippi River and subsequent activity in the Gulf of Mexico in the late 1600s provoked Spanish alarm. In 1698 Spain established a military

THE PUEBLO REVOLT

Native Americans fought desperately against European encroachment on their lands. Despite determined resistance, they were unable to stem the steady advance of better-armed European colonists. The Pueblo uprising against the Spanish stands out as the only Indian rebellion that succeeded in expelling a colonial power from lands it had occupied.

The Pueblo Revolt was led by a charismatic Indian shaman named Pope. Following their settlement of New Mexico in 1598, the Spanish brutally suppressed the native Pueblo culture. A member of the Tewa tribe in the upper Rio Grande valley, Pope grew up under the harsh yoke of Spanish colonial rule. He refused to convert to Christianity and became an influential shaman or religious figure.

In 1675 Spanish provincial authorities moved to stamp out native religious practices. Pope and some 50 other shamans were arrested and taken to Santa Fe, where they were flogged and imprisoned. After a Tewa delegation, threatening violence, won their release, Pope fled to the Pueblo village of Taos. There he secretly plotted a general uprising against the Spanish. Pope was a brilliant strategist and leader. Over the next five years, he united the Pueblo tribes in a coordinated plan to oust the Spanish, becoming the symbol of native resistance. It was said that he had been visited by three fiery spirits from the underworld telling him to drive out the Spanish.

The revolt was timed for just before the arrival of the annual supply train from New Spain. Pope sent runners from Taos with knotted ropes, each knot representing one day, to inform the various tribes of the number of days to the attack. On August 11, 1680, several thousand Pueblo warriors descended on the Spanish settlements and missions. The Spanish were stunned by the fierce onslaught. The survivors held out in the town of Santa Fe for several days before abandoning the colony and retreating hundreds of miles south to present-day El

garrison at Pensacola. This settlement of some 250 people defined the western limit of Spanish Florida, bordering, as it did, the French outpost at Mobile, Alabama, which was founded in 1702. The steady arrival of English settlers in the Carolinas brought pressure on Spanish Florida from the north. Competition over the territory of present-day Georgia soon flared into conflict. A series of English attacks during Queen Anne's War (1702–13) destroyed virtually all the Spanish settlements in northern Florida and drove the Spanish back to St. Augustine.

The colonial warfare also took its toll on the remaining Native Americans. Epidemics in the late 1500s and the 1600s had effectively annihilated the Calusa in southern Florida and devastated the Indians in the northern Spanish missions. By 1763 the Timucua, Apalachee, and Guale, ravaged by a combination of disease and war, had ceased to exist as separate tribes. The remnants of the Apalachee migrated west to Louisiana. In the mid-1700s Creek Indians fleeing the advance of English settlers in Georgia moved south into Florida. Through intermingling with the last survivors of the original Florida tribes, they developed a distinct tribal identity and became known as the Seminoles, the Creek word for runaways.

The Spanish contraction back into St. Augustine, as well as the augmentation of its garrison, increased the town's population to some 2800 in the mid-1700s. When Spain ceded Florida to Great Britain at the close of the Seven Years' War in 1763, the Spanish presence in the province had been reduced to Pensacola, the presidio at San Marcos, and St. Augustine. With the arrival of British rule, roughly 3,100 inhabitants, including virtually all the Spanish residents as well as blacks and Indians, evacuated the colony for Cuba.

During its brief occupation of Florida, the English crown issued land grants to entrepreneurs who in turn recruited agricultural workers. In 1767 British plantation owner Andrew Turnbull brought 1,500 Greek, Italian, and Minorcan settlers to the colony. During the American Revolution, an estimated 19,000 British loyalists fled south to Florida. As part of the Treaty of Paris ending the war in 1783, Great Britain returned Florida to Spain. This second period of Spanish rule saw limited Hispanic migration. St. Augustine was one of the most diverse communities in North America, with Spanish, British, American, German, Swiss, southern European, Creek, Seminole, and African-American residents.

The growing influx of American settlers in northern Florida ultimately induced Spain to cede the province to the United States in 1819.

NEW MEXICO

Spanish advances in the western Borderlands soon followed the initial penetration of Florida. The four provinces eventually established in the Southwest each had a distinct history and pattern of growth. While each of these isolated colonial outposts was closely linked to New Spain in Mexico, there was only limited movement of people or goods between them. Significant migration within the vast region did not occur until the end of the colonial period and the arrival of westward-pushing Americans.

The discovery of massive silver veins in northern Mexico in the 1540s brought rapid Spanish colonization and the waging of a relentless military campaign against the area's nomadic tribes. Spanish settlement of the American Southwest began in 1598 when Juan de Oñate led a party of 129 soldiers and their dependents north from New Spain to the cluster of Pueblo Indian villages along the upper Rio Grande valley. Oñate achieved, often at sword point, the submission of the Pueblos to Spanish authority. When it became apparent that New Mexico was a land of adobe and sand rather than gold and silver, many of the colonists returned to New Spain. Despite the dwindling numbers, Oñate succeeded in securing a lasting Spanish foothold on the upper Rio Grande.

Establishment of the province of New Mexico extended New Spain's frontier hundreds of miles to the north. The province became an outer bulwark of New Spain's defense of its mining towns against Indian attack. The Spanish were never able to subdue either the nomadic Indian raiders of northern Mexico, whom they called *chichimecas* (a derivation of a native term for "sons of dogs"), or the Apache and Comanche of the New Mexican desert.

In the absence of precious metals, settlement of New Mexico was driven by missionary activity. Between 1598 and 1680 the Franciscans established some 50 missions among the Pueblo tribes, stretching from the Rio Grande villages of the Kere, Piro, Tano, and Tewa to the adobe settlements of the Zuñi to the west and Hopi to the northwest. In New Mexico, as in the other western Borderlands, provincial officials generally came from Spain, but almost all the settlers were natives of New Spain. A slow but steady flow of colonists from Mexico gradually settled the upper Rio Grande. The town of Santa Fe was founded in 1610. The famed *Camino Real* or Royal Road, some 1,800 miles long, linked the remote settlement to Mexico City and the outside world. The journey along the rough, dusty trail, normally by ox-drawn wagon, took six months.

Traditional Pueblo culture was suppressed as native inhabitants were forcibly converted to Christianity and compelled to provide labor for the burgeoning colonial farms and sheep and cattle ranches. In 1680 the Pueblos rebelled against the harsh Spanish rule. The Pueblo Revolt drove the more than 2000 Spanish colonists out of the upper Rio Grande valley. The fleeing Spanish regrouped farther down the Rio Grande, where they formed the town of El Paso.

A series of military expeditions beginning in 1693 reestablished Spanish control over Pueblo areas. An armed garrison was maintained at Santa Fe. The town of Albuquerque was founded in 1706, cementing the Spanish hold on the upper Rio Grande. Over the next century Spanish settlement gradually expanded in the El Paso area, along the upper Rio Grande, and to the west of Albuquerque. Further migration was hampered by the Comanche to the east, the Ute to the north, and the Apache to the west. New Mexico became the most populous of the sparsely settled Spanish frontier provinces. When the western Borderlands became part of an independent Mexico in 1821, New Mexico's Hispanic population numbered roughly 35,000.

PRIMERIA ALTA

The province of New Mexico included the northern half of the present-day state of Arizona. Southern Arizona was part of New Spain's northern province of Sonora. This area, from roughly contemporary Phoenix southward, was referred to in the colonial period as the Primeria Alta. Throughout the 1600s, first Franciscan and then Jesuit priests attempted with limited success to establish mission settlements in southern Arizona's Santa Cruz and San Pedro river valleys.

Spanish penetration of the Primeria Alta took hold with the arrival of Father Eusebio Francisco Kino in 1687. Kino galvanized the Jesuit missionary effort and oversaw the conversion of the Pina and Papago tribes to Christianity. The dense villages and fixed, agricultural way of life of the Pina and Papago facilitated their forced incorporation into mission settlements. Disease took a constant toll, such that by 1800 there were only scattered remnants of the two tribes.

Apache raiders from the north discouraged the migration of Spanish settlers into the area. In the mid-1700s colonial authorities constructed presidios at Tucson and Tubac to protect the missionary frontier. Small towns grew around the garrisons. A slow trickle of colonists moved into the adjacent river valleys, where they established cattle ranches. At the time of Mexican independence, the Hispanic population of Tucson and Tubac numbered around 800.

Paso. In little more than a week, more than 400 of the 2,500 Spanish settlers had been killed, including 21 of 33 Franciscan missionaries. The Pueblo death toll was around 250.

The Pueblos had retaken their native lands. Pope and his fellow leaders set about eliminating every trace of the Spanish presence. In his fervor to return to traditional Pueblo ways, Pope himself became increasingly repressive and tyrannical, adopting, ironically, many of the trappings of a colonial official. By the time of his death in 1690, his alliance of Pueblo tribes had all but dissolved.

The Spanish, exploiting the Pueblo disarray, reconquered northern New Mexico in 1693. The Pueblos once again were unwilling subjects of the Spanish Crown. After the Pueblo uprising, though, the Spanish were more tolerant of native culture and ritual. Perhaps the most lasting consequence of the Pueblo Revolt was unrelated to the struggle over land. It was during the rebellion that the Pueblos first acquired their own horses, which had been left by the fleeing Spanish. Use of the horse soon spread to more northern tribes, dramatically changing the native way of life on the Great Plains by the mid-1700s.

The Spanish Southwest

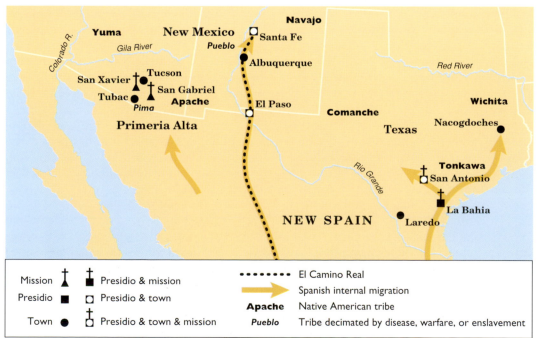

Mission	✝	■ Presidio & mission	········· El Camino Real
Presidio	■	□ Presidio & town	➤ Spanish internal migration
Town	●	✝□ Presidio & town & mission	**Apache** Native American tribe
			Pueblo Tribe decimated by disease, warfare, or enslavement

TEXAS

Spanish colonial authorities in Mexico, like their counterparts in Florida, kept a wary eye on French activity in North America. In 1682 French explorer René-Robert Cavelier, sieur de La Salle, sailing down the Mississippi to the Gulf of Mexico, claimed the river, its delta, and all adjacent lands for France. La Salle's failed attempt in 1685 to found a permanent French garrison at Matagorda Bay on the present-day Texas coast sparked fears in Mexico City over French encroachment on New Spain's northern frontier.

New Spain at the time extended as far north as the Rio Grande. The French threat brought Spanish colonization north of the river. In 1690 a small Spanish outpost was established on the Nueces River in southern Texas. As part of the colonization effort Franciscan friars sought, with little success, to gather the area's nomadic tribes into mission settlements. The territory north of the Rio Grande was organized as the province of Texas in 1691. Two years later, as the potential danger of French colonial competition seemingly receded, the Spanish abandoned their initial settlement of the area.

Spanish interest in Texas was rekindled in 1714 when a small party of French traders from Louisiana appeared along the Rio Grande. Again Spanish officials moved to forestall possible French designs on Texas. In 1716 an expedition of some 80 settlers from New Spain established a presidio and mission at Nacogdoches. This outpost, facing the French trading post at Natchitoches to the east, staked out the northern limit of Spanish Texas. Presidios were also founded at La Bahia (modern-day Goliad) and San Antonio.

Small clusters of settlements formed around the three garrisons. The town of San Antonio was chartered in 1731. Its tiny population was augmented by 16 families from the Canary Islands the same year. The Canary Islanders, sent by the Spanish Crown as colonists for Texas, reached San Antonio after a 13-month trek from Veracruz. Most of the Spanish settlers in Texas were natives of New Spain. The remote northern province never drew large numbers of colonists, and its population grew largely through natural increase.

The vast territory between San Antonio and La Bahia in southeastern Texas and Nacogdoches to the north remained unsettled throughout the 18th century. A rough wagon road linked Nacogdoches with the rest of the colony. The only new settlement during this period, the town of Laredo on the lower Rio Grande, was founded in the mid-1700s. When Texas became part of Mexico in 1821, its Hispanic population totaled only some 2,000.

Renewed efforts after 1716 to incorporate the Native Americans into Spain's Christian realm again proved largely futile. The scattered Franciscan missions made little headway toward inducing the area's nomadic tribes to settle down in fixed religious communities. So few Indians lived in mission settlements that Spanish authorities never obtained an accurate count of Texas's native population. Disease, as always, ravaged those tribes in contact with the colonists. The movement of the French into the Mississippi valley in the early 1700s gradually displaced the Osage, Wichita, and other tribes onto the Great Plains. Their migration in turn pushed the Comanche to the southwest into Apache lands. In a kind of extended ripple effect, the Comanche forced the more eastern Apache tribes farther south and west into New Mexico. Both the Comanche and Apache came closer to the Spanish settlements advancing from the south. Their mobile warriors, on horses acquired from the colonists, kept the Spanish garrisons on the defensive across the Southwest frontier.

CALIFORNIA

For more than two centuries after initial Spanish exploration of its coastline, California held little allure for settlers because it was generally believed to contain neither gold nor other precious metals. Its more habitable coastal areas could be reached overland from New Spain only by crossing harsh desert. Not until the 1760s did Spain, alarmed by the growing Russian presence in the Pacific Northwest, move to establish a colony in California. Also of concern were Spain's traditional colonial foes, the British. French Louisiana had long separated the Spanish Southwest from Great Britain's eastern seaboard colonies. With the departure of the French from the continent at the conclusion of the Seven Years' War in 1763, the Spanish and British colonies were left in direct contact in America.

Because California was intended as the western anchor of New Spain's defensive northern fringe, its settlement was organized and directed by colonial authorities in Mexico City. In 1769 colonial official Gaspar de Portola led a small party north from New Spain to establish a presidio at San Diego. Portola continued north the same year to form a second presidio at Monterey.

Additional garrisons were added at San Francisco in 1776 and Santa Barbara in 1786.

Civilian communities soon developed around these military outposts. Formal towns were founded at San Jose in 1777, Los Angeles in 1781, and Branciforte (now Santa Cruz) in 1800. Los Angeles was expressly created as an agricultural settlement to supply the presidios. The provincial government, eager to build a population sufficient to forestall possible Russian or British advances from the north, actively recruited settlers from New Spain. They came both by ship and by wagon train along the trails connecting California with both northern Mexico and Primeria Alta. Colonists were provided with 120 pesos and provisions, equipment, and livestock for three years. California's coastal terrain proved well suited to the traditional Spanish ranching way of life. Ranches were often awarded to retired soldiers and their families. By 1821 the Spanish population of California had exceeded 3,000.

Portola was accompanied in 1769 by Franciscan Father Junípero Serra. Until his death in 1784, Serra laid the foundation for an extensive mission system in California. Twenty-one Franciscan missions were founded along the coast from San Diego to San Francisco between 1769 and 1823. The diverse native tribes in this area were rounded up by the Spanish and forced to live in the mission settlements. These California Indians soon lost their native cultures as they were converted to Catholicism, taught to speak Spanish, and put to work tending mission fields, livestock, and vineyards. Runaways who were caught were whipped in punishment. With their tribal identities destroyed, the surviving Native Americans became known as Mission Indians. The abrupt, brutal change in their native ways of life reduced their numbers by two-thirds, to little more than 50,000, during the half-century of Spanish colonial rule in California.

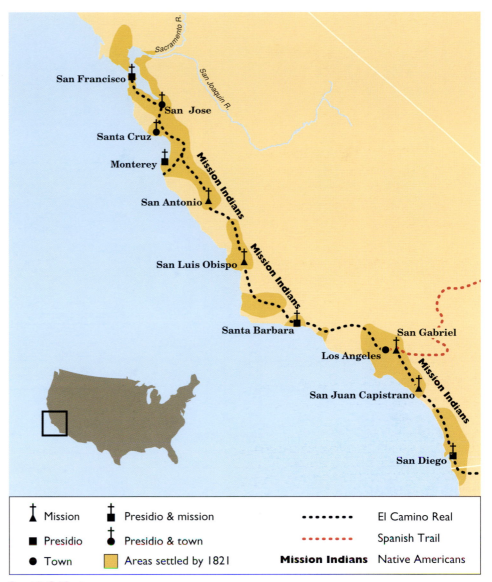

Spanish California

NEW FRANCE

The French colonies in North America were known as New France. At its greatest extent, France's New World empire encompassed much of the present-day continental United States. The French presence stretched from the Appalachian Mountains in the east to the foothills of the Rockies in the west and from the Great Lakes to the Gulf of Mexico.

New France, like the Spanish Borderlands to its south, was only sparsely settled.

A far-flung network of forts, missions, trading posts, and small settlements was established in the Great Lakes region and down the Mississippi River valley to French Louisiana. The limited French migration sealed New France's fate. At the close of the Seven Years' War in 1763, New France east of the Mississippi was absorbed by the much more populous English colonies along the Atlantic coast. French Louisiana west of the Mississippi passed to Spanish control. France's colonial defeat ended French migration in the vast Mississippi valley region, but its legacy endures in the French-speaking Cajun population of present-day Louisiana.

EXPLORATION AND SETTLEMENT

New France was built on European fashion. The French ultimately came to America not

New France

for gold or land but for fur. Most coveted were beaver pelts, which were used in the making of the wide-brimmed, high-crowned felt hats that were in fashion for over two centuries. The pursuit of fur shaped French relations with the Native Americans. New France became a vast fur-trading empire. The French developed an extensive trade network with Native American tribes, exchanging goods, firearms, and liquor for the highly-prized furs.

French penetration of North America began as a search for a northern sea route to Asia. In 1524 Giovanni da Verrazano undertook the first French expedition to the New World in an effort to find a direct passageway to the Far East. While Verrazano failed to locate a northern route, his exploration of the northeastern American coast laid the basis for future French claims to the continent.

A decade later explorer Jacques Cartier resumed the French hunt for the presumed Northwest Passage. Cartier made two voyages to North America between 1534 and 1536, navigating up the St. Lawrence River as far as the future site of Montreal. He called the area Canada, after the Iroquois word for village.

In 1541 Cartier returned to the St. Lawrence, intent on colonizing the area. He abandoned the attempt the following year when further exploration up the St. Lawrence River failed to reveal either a water route through North America or precious metals.

French attention was subsequently drawn from North America by mounting religious strife at home between Protestant Huguenots and Catholics. Two brief attempts were made in the early 1560s to establish a French outpost on the southeastern Atlantic coast. Charlesfort, founded in 1562 at the site of the present-day Marine Corps base at Parris Island, South Carolina, survived less than a year. Fort Caroline, erected near the mouth of northern Florida's St. Johns River in 1564, was destroyed by the Spanish the following year. Over the next 30 years France turned inward as the country was racked by a series of religious civil wars between Huguenots and Catholics. These Wars of Religion ended in 1598 with the Catholic French crown issuing the Edict of Nantes granting religious toleration to the Huguenots.

Throughout the 1500s French fishermen from Brittany and Normandy sailed to the teeming fish banks off Newfoundland and Nova Scotia. The fishermen cultivated an informal trade with the local Indians, bartering iron kettles, axes, and other goods for furs. With the end of the Wars of Religion, France moved to exploit the burgeoning fur trade. The first permanent French foothold in North America was established at Acadia (Nova Scotia) in 1603. Explorer, and later colonial governor, Samuel de Champlain linked New France to the St. Lawrence River when he set up a trading post at Quebec in 1608.

The new French colony drew adventurers, soldiers, and missionaries but few settlers. France, with its still largely feudal social structure, lacked a vigorous middle class, and there was little enthusiasm among the peasantry to emigrate to the New World. Quebec's growing season was a brief 150 days and the St. Lawrence was frozen solid in the winter, cutting off the colony from France six months out of the year. By 1627 the population of New France had barely climbed above 100. In that year Cardinal Richelieu, as chief minister in the French government, oversaw creation of the Company of New France. Patterned on the English East India Company, the quasi-private commercial enterprise was entrusted with the colonization of New France. In return for a monopoly over the fur trade, the company undertook to recruit and bring settlers to the French colony and to support missionary efforts among France's Native American trading partners. The company, not surprisingly, concentrated more on the fur trade than settlement. As a consequence the French Crown, eager to solidify its holdings in North America, made New France a royal colony in 1663.

The recruitment of settlers continued to go poorly. Much of the early peopling of New France was involuntary. The French government swept its prisons and poorhouses to provide settlers for the New World and impressed landless peasants into service as colonial soldiers. This reliance on involuntary labor diminished by the mid-1600s, as New France increasingly turned to contract workers to meet its growing demand for laborers. Known as "36 monthers" after the normal length of their contract, they cleared land, toiled as builders, and worked in the fur trade. At the end of their term they were free to remain or return to France. Many chose to return. Of the roughly 27,000 colonists thought to have entered New France through Quebec, less than one-third put down permanent roots in the colony.

French migration policy hampered efforts to settle New France. The French Crown, intent on preserving New France as a Catholic domain, barred Huguenot immi-

CHRONOLOGY OF NEW FRANCE

1500s	French fishermen visit the coasts off Newfoundland
1524	Giovanni da Verrazano explores the American coast
1534–36	Jacques Cartier sails up the St. Lawrence River
1541–42	Short-lived French outpost on the St. Lawrence
1562–98	Wars of Religion in France
1598	Edict of Nantes
1603	First permanent French settlement at Acadia
1608	Quebec founded by Samuel de Champlain
1615	French missionaries arrive in New France
1627	Company of New France
1642	Montreal founded as a base for fur traders
1663	New France made royal colony
1665	Jesuit mission at Sault Sainte Marie
1682	René-Robert Cavelier, sieur de La Salle, descends the Mississippi River to the Gulf of Mexico
1685	Revocation of the Edict of Nantes
1699	Settlement of Louisiana
1701	Detroit founded in Illinois Country
1702–13	Queen Anne's War
1709	Indian slavery legalized
1717	African slaves arrive in Louisiana
1718	Founding of New Orleans
1724	French *Code Noir*
1755	French Acadians deported by British
1756–1763	Seven Years' War
1763	France cedes New France east of the Mississippi to Great Britain; Spain acquires French Louisiana
1800	France reacquires Louisiana from Spain
1803	Louisiana Territory sold to the United States

DAUGHTERS OF THE KING

French concern over the small population in New France produced one of the most singular migrations to colonial America. Almost all of the early inhabitants of France's North American colony were men—adventurers, traders, soldiers, laborers. Colonial officials struggled with the shortage of women and its impact on New France's growth. A fair number of colonists formed unions, both in and out of marriage, with Native American women. In 1665 the colonial governor encouraged marriage to Indian women by offering to provide each bride with a dowry of 150 livres.

The same year the French crown moved to correct New France's gender imbalance. Over the next decade the government sent at royal expense some 1,000 young women to New France as prospective brides. The women were drawn from orphanages and religious houses of charity. Each was provided a dowry by the crown. They became known as *filles du roi*, or daughters of the king, because they were in essence given away in marriage by the monarch.

Military officer Louis de la Hontan, an eyewitness to the arrival of the first shipload of *filles du roi* at Quebec, recounted how all were married within 15 days. Marriages were concluded "on the spot in the presence of a priest and a public notary, and the next day the Governor General bestowed upon the married couple a bull, a cow, a hog, a sow, a cock, a hen, two barrels of salt meat, and 11 crowns." The hoped-for population increase soon ensued. Immigration to New France remained slight and the descendants of these unions provided many of the French settlers in the Great Lakes region and Louisiana.

The shipment of the daughters of the king graphically illustrated how little 17th-century European women, especially those with few prospects, had to say about their future. Arrival in New France often brought greater autonomy. With their husbands frequently absent on military or trade expeditions, women often assumed responsibility for their families' commercial and other affairs.

gration to the colony. When King Louis XIV revoked the Edict of Nantes in 1685, some 400,000 Huguenots fled religious persecution in France. Many, ironically, immigrated to the colonies of France's bitter North American rival, England.

Few French families migrated to New France and there was a chronic shortage of women. Colonial authorities encouraged, or at least condoned, intermixing with Native Americans. The offspring of the French-Indian unions, known as *métis*, contributed to New France's growing diversity. Beginning in the 1660s the French crown sent several shiploads of single women to the colony. Natural increase soon ensured New France a steady if small population.

The lucrative fur trade filled French coffers. Throughout the 1600s French woodsmen, known as *coureurs de bois* (literally, woods runners), made their way into the American interior to trap and trade for fur. The Spanish, and later the British, penetrated North America by foot, horse, and wagon. The French traveled by water. To do so they adopted an Indian invention, the birchbark canoe. The lightweight, versatile canoe was easily portaged between rivers and could carry 600 beaver pelts, each worth a gold dollar.

New France became a riverine empire as French explorers in canoes traversed the major waterways of the American interior. The French first followed the St. Lawrence River to the Great Lakes region. From Lake Superior, Louis Jolliet and the Jesuit Father Jacques Marquette floated down the Wisconsin River in 1673 to confirm Indian reports of a mighty river to the west, known in Chippewa as the "Father of Waters," the Mississippi. In 1682 René-Robert Cavelier, better known by his title, sieur de La Salle, journeyed all the way down the Mississippi to the Gulf of Mexico, claiming the entire region for France. By 1700 New France extended across the Ohio, Mississippi, and Missouri valleys. The northwestern exploration of Pierre Gaultier de La Vérendrye and his sons in the 1730s and 1740s extended France's fur-trading reach as far as the Yellowstone River in the present-day Dakotas.

The French erected trading posts and forts at strategic points along the interconnected waterways of the Great Lakes region and Mississippi valley. These outposts over time were joined by a handful of small settlements. The French Crown attempted to replicate in New France the feudal farming communities of the French countryside. Land grants were made by the ultimate landholder, the king, in the form of

seigneuries, or lordships. The landholding seigneur in turn provided plots to settlers in return for a small annual rent. New France's riverfront settlements developed the distinctive long lot system. Farms were laid out so that each had access to the river. Each had a frontage on the water of roughly 250 yards and extended a mile or more inland.

The initial settlement of New France in 1603 preceded by only four years the founding of the first British colony in Virginia. Almost from the start, France and Great Britain were locked in a desperate 150-year struggle for supremacy in North America. The long frontier between the two colonial powers was the site of frequent armed conflict. In the Treaty of Utrecht ending Queen Anne's War in 1713, France ceded Newfoundland and Acadia to Great Britain. France was driven from North America in 1763 at the close of the Seven Years' War, also known in America as the French and Indian War. Among the key factors contributing to Great Britain's final victory was its huge advantage in colonial population. New France had some 70,000 French inhabitants in 1763, as opposed to a populace of more than one million in the British colonies.

NATIVE AMERICANS

The French had the most successful and balanced relations with Native Americans of any of the colonial powers. There were several reasons for this. Most importantly, New France's economy was built on the fur trade. This trade rested on friendly relations with the Indians, who not only provided much of the fur but also acted as guides for French trappers and served as intermediaries with more distant tribes. Outnumbered by their English colonial rivals, the French also courted the Indians as military allies. French officials generally sought tribal approval for the use of Indian lands. New France's low colonial population meant there was little competition over land. In French-held territory there were few settlements around the trading and military posts. Thus the wilderness remained largely intact. Other than in the lower Mississippi valley, there was no systematic displacement of Native Americans.

Catholic France felt a strong obligation to spread the Christian faith. Jesuit missionaries proved among the most effective French emissaries to the Indians. The Jesuits did not attempt to relocate Native Americans into separate mission communities. Instead, they lived among the Indians and integrated their missions into native villages. Dubbed the blackrobes by Native Americans for their distinctive garb, the Jesuits adapted Christianity to Native American culture. Jesuit missionaries were at the forefront of French penetration of the American interior. Often they played a key role in New France's network of alliances with Native American tribes.

The efforts of Jesuits and others ultimately did not prevent the disastrous consequences for Native Americans of the French presence. The overhunting of beaver and other fur-bearing mammals disrupted the natural food chain on which Indians depended. Disease took its customary toll, with tribal populations generally suffering a loss of 50% or more after first contact with Europeans. The introduction of alcohol, traded by the French for fur, more often than not had a debilitating impact. Native American population also declined in the face of constant warfare. Northeastern tribes in particular were drawn into the frequent conflict between the French and English. The dislocations brought by the Europeans also unleashed much greater intertribal warfare. The French traded firearms for fur, giving their allies a critical advantage over other tribes.

The French in general exhibited a greater degree of cultural sensitivity to Native American ways of life. In diplomatic and other contacts, the French meticulously observed Native American protocols. While France made harmonious Indian relations a basic policy, French colonial ambitions always took precedence. The French waged ruthless military campaigns, for example, against both the Fox and Natchez.

SLAVERY

The French also made use of Indian slaves. Slavery was a part of New France from the start. French colonists seeking inexpensive, readily available labor were able to capitalize on the Native American practice of enslaving captives from other tribes. Soon the French were purchasing captives from their Indian allies. Many were Pawnees captured farther west, and *panis* became the generic French word for Indian slave. Ownership of Indian slaves was formally legalized in a 1709 colonial ordinance. On the eve of New France's demise in the early 1760s, there were some 3,000 *panis* in the St. Lawrence region. Indian slavery was more limited in the sparsely settled Great Lakes environs. In Louisiana the importation of African slaves by the 1720s had largely supplanted the use of Indian slave labor. Both the English and Spanish officially prohibited Indian slavery on taking possession of their respective parts of New France in 1763.

There was little demand for African slaves in northern New France where the climate did not support large-scale agriculture. Most of the roughly 1,000 black slaves in the St. Lawrence region in the early 1760s were household servants. French Louisiana, with its more conducive climate, saw the widespread introduction of black slavery. Regular shipments of African slaves began arriving in the colony in 1717. A Code Noir (slave code), promulgated in 1724, institutionalized the slave system. About 28,000 African slaves in all were imported into French Louisiana. Most were employed on indigo and tobacco plantations along the Mississippi River. Small numbers of slaves were taken farther north to the scattered French settlements in the upper Mississippi valley. Despite high mortality rates from disease and horrid work conditions, a substantial African-American population emerged, contributing to the evolution of a distinctive Creole culture in the colony.

GREAT LAKES REGION

The first Europeans in much of the American interior were the French. Jesuit missionaries soon followed French *coureurs de bois* into this fur-rich area. They established missions in Wisconsin and Michigan as well as on the upper Mississippi. However, most of the limited French settlement of the northern American interior occurred south of the Great Lakes in an area called Illinois Country after the Native American tribe. Almost all of the region's handful of colonists were from the St. Lawrence region of New France. In the mid-1700s, the French population of the Illinois Country numbered less than 2,000.

The French established friendly relations with most local tribes. The Chippewa, with their relatively large population, became a backbone of the fur trade. Known also as the Ojibwa (especially in Canada), the Chippewa used firearms acquired from the French to expand their lands between Lake Superior and the Missouri River and drive the Sioux and Cree farther west. The French sided with the Chippewa in their warfare with their traditional enemy the Fox. Both the Fox and Sauk in the early 1600s had been forced by Iroquois attacks to migrate into Wisconsin from their historic homelands between lakes Michigan and Huron. In 1734 the remnants of the Fox, driven south by the French and Chippewa,

THE GREAT UPHEAVAL

The most controversial European migration in colonial times involved bitter adversaries Great Britain and France. At the close of Queen Anne's War in 1713, France was forced to cede Acadia to Britain. The British renamed the strategic peninsula, which lies astride both Maine and the Gulf of St. Lawrence, Nova Scotia. The roughly 2,300 French Acadians were given the choice of immigrating to French territory or remaining in Nova Scotia as loyal British subjects. Most remained, but the Catholic Acadians resisted swearing allegiance to the Protestant British Crown. To allay British suspicions of their continued loyalty to New France, the Acadians declared their neutrality in any conflict between Britain and France. British authorities begrudgingly accepted this arrangement and the expression "the neutral French" was often used to describe the Acadians.

Renewed colonial warfare with the French in the 1740s revived British concern over Acadian loyalties. British authorities believed many Acadians had supported France's failed attempts to retake Nova Scotia. As conflict loomed again in the mid-1750s, British colonial officials contemplated removing the Acadians. By 1755 Nova Scotia's Acadian population had grown to about 7,000. When delegates from the Acadian community the same year refused to endorse an unqualified oath of allegiance, the British decided to act.

In the autumn of 1755 some 6,000 Acadians were forcibly rounded up, embarked on transports, and deported from Nova Scotia. Most were dispersed among Britain's American colonies. Others were removed to France and the French West Indies. Many who escaped deportation fled to Île Royale (Cape Breton Island). Acadian lands were given to some 8,000 English settlers from New England. What the Acadians called the Great Upheaval lasted until 1763, as the British continued the deportations after capturing Île Royale in the Seven Years' War.

formed a lasting alliance with the Sauk. Further French attacks pushed the allied tribes to the west. The Huron, located north of Lake Ontario, established especially close ties with the French and often served as middlemen between fur traders and other tribes. In the 1600s and 1700s the Huron were also driven west by the Iroquis. Many eventually migrated into the territory of present-day Michigan, Indiana, and Illinois, where they became known as the Wyandot.

French forts were constructed at key points throughout the Great Lakes region. These outposts guarded the rivers, lakes, and portages that linked together France's fur-trading enterprise. A string of forts in western Pennsylvania was intended to block further English expansion to the west. Fort Duquesne was erected in 1754 on the future site of Pittsburgh. Trading posts were often located at or near the forts. Often linked to the trading posts were small settlements, such as at Detroit and Green Bay.

LOUISIANA

In 1682 La Salle claimed Louisiana for the French crown. Louisiana, which he named after King Louis XIV, was defined by the explorer as the entire Mississippi valley and all its tributaries. Three years later the French attempted to colonize the area but this initial effort was aborted following La Salle's murder by discontented subordinates.

Louis XIV sent a second fleet to Louisiana in 1699. The expedition under Pierre Le Moyne, sieur d'Iberville, established the first permanent French toehold on the Gulf of Mexico at what is now Biloxi, Mississippi. Additional outposts were erected at Fort Toulouse, near present-day Montgomery, Alabama, and at Fort Rosalie, now Natchez, Mississippi. Queen Anne's War (1702–13) diverted royal support for colonization, so much so that by 1717 there were only 27 French families in Louisiana. The same year the French crown turned over responsibility for development of the colony to the mercantilist Compagnie des Indes. Over the next decade the company recruited and shipped more than 7,000 French settlers to Louisiana. About a fifth were forced emigrants. The company also imported thousands of African slaves.

French expansion to both the east and west was limited by the Spanish Borderlands, and the colony developed up the Mississippi River. Disease spread easily in Louisiana's steamy climate and by 1730 the colony's total population of both settlers and slaves amounted to no more than 5,300.

Jurisdictional disputes among Jesuits, Franciscans, and Carmelites limited missionary activity among the Native Americans. French traders and officials, pursuing their colonial interests, courted alliances with the area's diverse tribes. Trade relations were established with the Quapaw and Tunica along the Mississippi and with the Caddo, Osage, and Wichita to the west. Close ties with the Choctaw in southern Louisiana and Mississippi drew the French into tribal warfare with the Chickasaw to the east. The French eventually concluded an uneasy peace with the Chickasaw, who had allied themselves with English traders pushing west from the Carolinas in the 1730s. The Creek in Alabama and Georgia preserved a precarious independence by maintaining relations with the French, English, and Spanish. The contest over farmland around Fort Rosalie led to a French military campaign that destroyed the Natchez in 1729. Most of the roughly 500 Natchez survivors were shipped to the West Indies as slaves. Warfare also broke out between the French and the Chitimacha in the Mississippi delta. In 1718 the remnants of the tribe agreed to settle at a site on the Mississippi near present-day Plaquemine.

In 1731 the French crown resumed direct control of Louisiana. Immigration fell to a trickle and the population grew slowly. In 1760 there were roughly 10,000 inhabitants in the colony. New Orleans, founded in 1718, was the major settlement, with a population of about 8,000.

On taking possession of Louisiana in 1763, Spanish authorities moved to increase immigration. Spain saw colonial development as key to preventing British encroachment from the east. Louisiana's population more than quadrupled between 1760 and 1790. Colonists from the Canary Islands and Spain were settled in the lower Mississippi valley. The Spanish readily accepted French Acadian refugees and British loyalists fleeing the American Revolution. The admixture of French, Spanish, Africans, and Native Americans produced a distinctive Creole culture still associated with Louisiana. By 1790 the colony's diverse population exceeded 40,000.

At the turn of the century American settlers were moving into the region. France reacquired the vast Louisiana territory west of the Mississippi from Spain in 1800. Bowing to the tide of inevitable American expansion, while also satisfying his need for funds to sustain his military campaigns, French emperor Napoleon sold the Louisiana Territory to the United States in 1803.

RUSSIAN ALASKA

As France in 1763 was relinquishing its hold on the Mississippi valley, Russia was extending its reach across the northern Pacific to Alaska. The Russians, like the French, came for fur. For more than one hundred years Russian fur hunters and traders ranged from the Aleutian Islands to northern California. Their primary prey was the sea otter. A single pelt was worth as much as 100 silver rubles. The sea otter's soft, dark, glossy fur was in particular demand in northern China, where it was prized as elegant trim.

The Russian population of Alaska never exceeded 1,000. This Russian presence was sufficient, though, to open the Pacific Northwest to European and American settlement. The Russians' small numbers were of little solace to the region's native peoples, who suffered grievously at their hands.

Russia's exploration and settlement of Alaska was simply an extension of its eastward advance across Siberia in search of "soft gold," the Russian nickname for sable fur. Pursuit of the luxuriant fur, at the time the world's most valuable, brought the development of a class of hardened, often ruthless fur hunters known as *promyshlenniki*. The Russian surge to the east reached the Pacific Ocean in the 1630s. Within another 70 years rapacious *promyshlenniki* had largely depleted northeast Asia of its furs.

Czar Peter the Great, whose royal coffers depended on the fur trade, looked still farther east. In 1725 he dispatched an expedition under Vitus Bering into the North Pacific. Bering sailed as far as the strait that now bears his name. A second royal expedition under Bering in 1741 reached the massive Alaskan peninsula just across the sea from Siberia. Though Bering died of scurvy on the return voyage, his expedition made it back to Russia with some 1,500 sea otter pelts.

The discovery of great numbers of what the Russians called "sea beaver" in the North Pacific sparked a fur rush across the Aleutian Islands to Alaska. Numerous fur-trading companies were chartered. These companies drew on the readily available *promyshlenniki* to mount hunting and trading voyages to the region. The fur rush spurred Russia's development as a maritime power. The Russian ships at first were crudely built out of Siberian timber, with short masts and narrow sails. Some 50 feet in length, they carried a crew of 40 to 50. The ships were called *shitiks* (sewn ones) because their wooden planks were secured by rawhide thongs. Later, as the Russians embarked on longer voyages, they developed larger, more seaworthy vessels known as *gvozdenniks* (nailed ones).

The Russians quickly realized that the Aleuts and Eskimos, with their kayaks and harpoons, were unmatched sea hunters. The *promyshlenniki* employed particularly brutal methods to exploit Native American labor. Typically they would sail to a native village, take the women and children hostage, and compel the men to hunt for furs. Often the women were used as concubines. The disruption of their traditional way of life devastated the native populace, which also was decimated by disease and warfare. An Aleut population that numbered around 10,000 in the 1740s, when the Russians first arrived, dwindled to some 3,500 by the end of the century. A similar decline occurred among Alaska's southern Eskimos.

As overhunting reduced the massive sea otter herds, Russian ships ventured farther east along the Alaskan coast. The need for longer voyages led to the establishment of permanent bases in North America. Fur merchant Grigory Shelikov founded Three Saints, the first Russian settlement, on Kodiak Island off the coast of Alaska in 1784. Shelikov's vigorous promotion of Russian colonization earned him the title of "Russian Columbus." Other outposts in what the Russians called Alakshak (after the Eskimo word for "great land") were established from St. Michael in the Bering Strait to Yakutat on the southeast coast.

In 1799 the crown chartered the Russian American Company and gave it sole responsibility for the development and administration of Russia's North American fur trade. The same year New Archangel was founded on Sitka Island in the Alaskan panhandle. The colonists named the settlement after the northern Russian city on the White Sea in their native region. New Archangel (present-day Sitka) became the capital of Russian America. By 1810 the town had more than 600 Russian and Native American inhabitants, making it the largest settlement on the Pacific Coast north of Mexico. Life in the dank climate was not easy. New Archangel's muddy hodgepodge of wood buildings, however, proved very hospitable to rodents, and residents soon dubbed the settlement Ratville.

The Russians had only limited success in their attempts to trade for furs with the Tlingit and other local tribes. The Tlingits violently resisted Russian encroachment

Few Acadians assimilated into the British colonies. Many migrated to Louisiana, which retained a strong French character after passing under Spanish rule in 1763. Spanish authorities, who favored Catholic settlement, kept Louisiana's door wide open to Acadian refugees. More than 1,000 Acadians from the British colonies and French West Indies had arrived in the province by 1769. With the end of Franco-British war in 1763, many Acadians also found their way back to Nova Scotia. Most of the several thousand Acadian exiles in France chose to immigrate to Louisiana. Some 1,600 came in 1785 when Spain, eager for settlers, chartered six large merchant ships for their transport. The Acadians, or Cajuns, as they soon came to be known, tended to settle in more remote areas, where they prospered as cattle ranchers and farmers. Many of these areas retain a distinctive Cajun quality to this day.

Historians debate British prerogatives in the Acadian removal. On one side, there are those who argue the deportations were unnecessary and set a destructive precedent for later forced emigrations. On the other, there are those who certainly condemn the harsh methods involved, but at the same time concede the legitimacy of Britain's perceived security concerns and place the removal in a wider historical context, noting, for example, the earlier expulsion of Protestants from France after 1685.

CHRONOLOGY OF RUSSIAN ALASKA

1741	Vitus Bering explores the coast of Alaska
1740s	Russian fur hunters and traders frequent the Aleutian Islands
1760s	Russian fur expeditions along Alaskan coast
1761–66	Failed Aleut rebellion against Russian domination
1784	Three Saints established on Kodiak Island
1799	Russian American Company; New Archangel founded on the Alaskan panhandle
1802	Tlingit warriors overrun New Archangel
1804	Russian expedition recaptures New Archangel
1812	Fort Ross established in northern California
1825	First Russian Orthodox mission in the Aleutians
1839	British control of Canada's Pacific coast
1841	Russia settlement in northern California abandoned
1867	Alaska sold to the United States

and there was frequent conflict. The Russians also faced mounting competition from British and American ships drawn by the region's sea otter wealth. Both the British and Americans, with their better goods, such as iron wares, textiles, and firearms, were more successful in establishing trade relations with the Northwest Coast Indians.

The establishment of Fort Ross just north of San Francisco Bay in 1812 extended Russian America as far south as northern California. In part to check Russian expansion, Spain had colonized California as far north as San Francisco in preceding decades. While Russia's primary interest was fur, its California colony also engaged in limited farming, shipbuilding, and brick-

making. Trade relations were developed with Spanish California. The Russian colonists coerced labor from the local Pomo Indians. Over time colonial authorities in Russian America enacted rules to limit the worst abuses of Native Americans, but at best the Indians under Russian control were never more than serfs. The Pomos fought Russian domination, but forced labor and disease decimated their numbers.

The Russian American Company brought schools, churches, and infirmaries to its settlements. However, few Russians immigrated to America. Russian peasants could find better farmland in Russia's new conquests in the Ukraine and Siberia than in faraway Alaska. The roughly 400 permanent inhabitants of Russian America in 1820

Russian Alaska

Tlingit	Native American tribe
Aleut	Tribe decimated by disease, warfare, or forced labor
●	Russian settlement

included only 13 women. Not surprisingly, relations between Russian men and native women, either in concubinage or marriage, were not uncommon. The Russians used the term Creole to describe the offspring of these unions. By the early 1860s there were as many as 1,900 Creoles in Russian America.

In 1839 Russia acquiesced in British control over the Pacific coast of present-day Canada in return for British provision of favorably priced supplies to New Archangel. Two years later the Russian American Company abandoned California, which was by then largely depleted of furs. As the fur trade declined, due both to over-hunting and changing fashion, Russian Alaska became less profitable. By the early 1860s the number of Russian inhabitants had declined to less than 700. Russia sold Alaska to the United States for $7.2 million in 1867. American critics skewered Secretary of State William H. Seward for negotiating acquisition of the remote, seemingly valueless territory, and for many years the Alaskan purchase was derided as "Seward's Folly."

THE PROMISE OF LAND
Migration in New Netherland and the British Colonies

4

Most of the settlers of what was to become British North America came for two very basic and human reasons—economic betterment and religious freedom. Intertwined in both these motives was the promise of land. The vast American wilderness offered the chance to carve out a better life. It also loomed as a haven for groups seeking to practice their faith separate from the religious conflicts of Europe.

The peopling of the British colonies actually involved three distinct migrations: the influx of Europeans, the dispersal of Native American tribes, and the importation of Africans as slaves.

NEW NETHERLAND

In 1609 the Dutch East India Company sent Henry Hudson west to North America in search of the long-hoped-for Northwest Passage to the Indies. Hudson sailed up the river that now bears his name as far as present-day Albany. While he failed to find a more direct route to Asia, Hudson's voyage laid the basis for the Dutch colonial claim to New Netherland. The loosely defined Dutch possession stretched between the Connecticut River in the north and the Delaware River in the south and ran inland as far as the upper reaches of the Hudson. The first Dutch in the area were traders anxious to exploit the region's lucrative fur-trade potential. In 1621 the Netherlands, eager to solidify its hold on the North American expanse, chartered the Dutch West India Company and gave it responsibility for the colonization of New Netherland. Permanent settlers arrived in 1624 when 30 families founded New Amsterdam on the southern tip of Manhattan Island.

Two years later Peter Minuit, governor-general of the colony, purchased Manhattan Island from the Manhattan Indians for 60 guilders ($24) worth of trade goods. Minuit hoped to appease the Algonquian tribes, principally the Delaware and Wappinger, that were wary of the growing Dutch presence. The Dutch were also concerned over encroachment on New Netherland by New

CHRONOLOGY OF NEW NETHERLAND AND NEW SWEDEN

1609	Henry Hudson explores fur-rich Hudson valley
1614	Fort Nassau (Albany) established
1618	Fort Nassau washed away in a spring flood
1621	Dutch West India Company chartered
1624	New Amsterdam and Fort Orange (Albany) founded
1626	First African slaves brought to New Amsterdam
1629	Charter of Freedoms and Exemptions
1631	Patroonships founded at Rennselaerswyck (New York), Pavonia (New Jersey), and Swanendael (Delaware).
1637	New Sweden Company chartered
1638	New Sweden established on the Delaware River; Fort Christina founded
1640–45	Governor Kieft's War
1654	First Jewish settlers in America arrive in New Amsterdam
1655	Dutch seizure of New Sweden and incorporation into New Netherland
1655–57	Peach War
1658–64	Esopus War
1664	New Netherland forcibly absorbed into English colonies

France or the English colonies in New England and Virginia.

Dutch officials at first treated the Indian tribes as sovereign nations, with prior rights to the land. If the Indians were recognized as the original landowners, then the Dutch could assert the legitimacy of their territorial acquisitions to other European powers. The Dutch believed that their claim to New Netherland, based on land purchase, would take precedence over French or English claims based on earlier discovery.

Unfamiliar with European concepts of land ownership, the Native Americans did not realize they were signing away their land rights. They were thus initially amenable to granting what they thought was the use of their territory in return for trade goods. Dutch land purchases at first were limited to small tracts for isolated trading posts and settlements. Later, as their emphasis shifted from trade to the settlement of New Netherland, the Dutch often departed from their original observation of Indian land rights, resorting to cajolery, trickery, and force to obtain new territories. The Dutch, like other European colonists, considered themselves superior to the Indians. But unlike their British, French, or Spanish counterparts, they were willing to accept Indian culture in close proximity to their own and never adopted an official policy of acculturation.

The Dutch were careful to maintain friendly trade relations with the powerful Iroquois Confederacy to the north. Relations with the Algonquian tribes in the lower Hudson valley gradually worsened as the Dutch encroached on their lands. Epidemics in the 1630s and 1640s devastated the Delaware and Wappinger. Their ranks were further depleted by a series of bloody conflicts with the Dutch between 1640 and 1664. The Dutch colonists paid a price for their eventual victory, as, exhausted by prolonged war, they were open to easy conquest by the British the same year. Dutch development of the fur trade sparked conflict between the Iroquois Mohawks and Algonquian Mahicans over the beaver-rich upper Hudson valley. The conflict, part of the so-called Beaver Wars between the Iroquois Confederacy and its neighbors, ended in 1664 when the Mohawks, armed with Dutch-supplied muskets, drove the Mahicans east from their lands around Albany to the Housatonic valley in Massachusetts.

During the Esopus War (1658–64), Governor-General Peter Stuyvesant sold Indian captives into slavery in the Caribbean as part of Dutch efforts to intimidate the native populace. The Dutch did not resort, however, to Indian slavery in New Netherland. While Dutch investors and merchants played a key role in the development of the African slave trade, few slaves ended up in New Netherland, where there was little demand. The first black slaves arrived in New Netherland in the 1620s. Most belonged to the Dutch West India Company and were used in clearing land, agriculture, and construction. Because of the premium placed on physical labor, men outnumbered women among the slaves imported to the colony.

Private ownership of slaves became more common after 1650. Slaves were employed as farmhands, laborers, and domestics. While slavery became entrenched in the colony, it was never codified in law. The Dutch West India Company adopted a policy of freeing slaves who had served the firm well. In 1664 there were approximately 75 free blacks in New Amsterdam, forming the city's first African-American community.

At first the Dutch West India Company's interest in colonization was limited to small agricultural settlements that could provide food and other supplies for its burgeoning fur-trade enterprise. In 1629 Kiliaen Van Rensselaer, an Amsterdam merchant and stockholder in the company, convinced the firm that the future of New Netherland depended on more vigorous settlement. That year the company issued the Charter of Freedoms and Exemptions providing for the creation of patroonships to spur the development of the colony.

Under the charter, any investor who brought at least 50 colonists to New Netherland was entitled to purchase a tract of land from the Indians and receive a deed to it from the Dutch West India Company. This deeded land, known as a patroonship, was essentially a feudal domain. The landholder, or patroon, enjoyed broad manorial powers. Patroons functioned as colonial landlords, collecting rent from the settlers, who in effect were tenant farmers. In return for a normal annual rent of one-third of their crops, settlers were provided farmland, tools, and materials to build their houses and barns. Patroonships were established along the Hudson River as well as on Staten and Long Islands and along the Delaware River.

Several thousand Dutch settlers arrived in New Netherland in the decades after 1630. At first the majority were single men. By the late 1650s the character of this immigration had changed, with the promise of a new start in America drawing more families to the colony. A large proportion of the

New Netherland and New Sweden

colonists came from the province of Utrecht, one of the most depressed regions of the generally prosperous Netherlands. Still, Dutch migration to New Netherland remained limited. Faced with little surplus population to emigrate, the Dutch kept New Netherland open to settlers from other colonies. In addition to the Swedes and Finns absorbed into the colony with the conquest of New Sweden, New Netherland's population included French, Norwegian, Danish, German, and Italian settlers. As many as a third of the roughly 10,000 inhabitants of the colony in 1664 were from countries other than the Netherlands.

New Amsterdam, which became a key port in the transatlantic trade, was especially diverse. In 1654 it became home to the first Jewish community in America, when 23 Dutch Jews from the former Dutch colony in Brazil arrived in the city. From 300 inhabitants in 1630, New Amsterdam grew to a population of some 2,000 in 1664.

At the same time the Dutch were struggling to build New Netherland's population, English colonists were arriving in droves in Connecticut and Massachusetts to the north and Maryland and Virginia to the south. In 1664 the English seized New Netherland, uniting their New England and

Chesapeake colonies. England's King Charles II conferred the captured territory on his brother, the Duke of York. New Netherland was renamed New York in honor of its new owner. While the English conquest ended Dutch colonization in America, New York retained a Dutch flavor for many years. The English reconfirmed all the Dutch patroonships, and Dutch settlers and settlements were left largely undisturbed.

NEW SWEDEN

Sweden's brief foray as a colonial power normally is recorded as little more than an historical footnote. Its one New World venture, the colony of New Sweden on the Delaware River, endured as a separate entity for only 17 years.

Sweden, linked to the Netherlands by extensive maritime ties, closely followed Dutch inroads in North America. In 1637 the Swedish Crown, aided by a syndicate of Dutch investors, chartered the New Sweden Company to pursue its own colonial ambitions. The firm hired Peter Minuit to head its colonizing efforts. In 1638 the former governor-general of New Netherland led a small expedition that established a Swedish toehold along the lower Delaware River. Minuit chose the site because it gave the new colony waterborne access to the fur trade in the interior. He was also aware that there were no specific Dutch claims to the lower west bank of the river. To strengthen Sweden's own claim to the area, Minuit purchased from local Delaware Indians several tracts of land around the present-day site of Wilmington, Delaware, where he founded the settlement of Fort Christina.

The Swedish courted friendly trade relations with the Delaware, and New Sweden soon was sending cargoes of fur back to the mother country. The colony expanded as small farming villages were built along both sides of the river, including a settlement at Salem, New Jersey. Distracted by the Thirty Years' War in Europe, Sweden provided only erratic support to its American colony, whose population hovered around 100. New Sweden remained isolated until 1654, when a Swedish ship bearing 200 new colonists arrived in Delaware Bay.

Startled Dutch authorities were distressed by the Swedish incursion into what they thought was their territory. New Netherland, however, became embroiled in a series of Indian wars that prevented the Dutch from moving against New Sweden until 1655. That year Dutch forces from

New Amsterdam under Peter Stuyvesant quickly overran the Swedish colony. Its conquest, though, did not erase the Swedish presence on the Delaware. Almost all of the colony's 300 inhabitants accepted Stuyvesant's offer to remain in the New World under a largely lenient Dutch rule.

THE BRITISH COLONIES

The seizure of New Netherland was the first in a series of victories that led to British supremacy in North America. On the eve of the American Revolution, Great Britain held sway over the entire present-day eastern United States from the Atlantic Ocean to the Mississippi River. The 13 British colonies that would sign the Declaration of Independence stretched along the Atlantic seaboard from Maine (then part of Massachusetts) to Georgia. Each of the colonies had a distinct origin, history, and character. Over time, larger patterns of immigration and internal migration served to divide the colonies into four broad regions: New England; the Middle Colonies; the Chesapeake Colonies; and the Southern Colonies. Migration shaped a fifth region in British America after 1750 as settlers pushed across the Appalachian Mountains into the western frontier.

EXPLORATION AND SETTLEMENT

England in the early 1500s was an unlikely candidate to gain a vast colonial empire in North America. The small island country was still recovering from a dynastic war, and its agricultural economy provided scant money to finance overseas expeditions. War-weary and weak, England was no match militarily for emerging colonial powers Portugal and Spain.

England's initial goal in the New World was to find a direct northern route to Asia's spice markets. The English organized two expeditions under Venetian sea captain John Cabot to the North American coast in 1497 and 1498. The voyages found no passageway to Asia nor to any of its outlying Spice Islands. English interest in further exploration waned, but the rich fish banks off Newfoundland and New England, first encountered by Cabot, drew English fishermen to these waters. Cabot's exploration of the North American coast also served as the basis for future English claims to the continent.

During the 16th century England was preoccupied by the Reformation at home and by Spain abroad. The island nation also developed as a maritime power. Cut off by Spain from Mediterranean and African markets, England gradually awakened in the 1570s to the commercial possibilities of colonies in North America. Such colonies could provide both new sources of goods and new markets. Interest was also rekindled in western trade routes to Asia. In 1577 the most famous English privateer, Sir Francis Drake, set out in search of a western opening to the presumed Northwest Passage. Drake did not find it, but in exploring the western coast of North America, he laid

COLONIAL MIGRATION AND WAR

Migration was a constant thread in the long colonial struggle over America. The movement of English colonists south from New England into Connecticut and Long Island led to British seizure of New Netherland. English settlers forging inland from New England and New York soon were encroaching on lands also claimed by New France, while English and Spanish colonists eventually came to blows over Georgia and Florida. The major colonial powers—Great Britain, France, and Spain—fought a succession of wars for control of the American continent. The Native Americans, often drawn into the fighting, invariably found themselves worse off as a result.

ANGLO-DUTCH WAR (1665–74) In a surprise attack, a British fleet captured New Amsterdam in August 1664 without firing a shot. The action, which gave Great Britain control of New Netherland, precipitated a series of Anglo-Dutch conflicts. The warfare, fought mainly at sea, ended with the Netherlands ceding its former North American colony to Great Britain.

KING WILLIAM'S WAR (1689–97) The frontier between New France and the northern English colonies erupted in warfare in 1689. The English, allied with the Iroquois Indians, fought the French and their Algonquian allies in a protracted but inconclusive conflict for control of the upper Hudson valley, St. Lawrence valley, and Acadia.

QUEEN ANNE'S WAR (1702–13) The frontier fighting discouraged, but never stopped, the steady press of English colonists inland, and war quickly resumed over the American interior. This reignited conflict pitted France and Spain against Great Britain. Under the Treaty of Utrecht bringing the war to a close, France formally relinquished Acadia, which had been captured by the British in 1710.

WAR OF JENKINS'S EAR (1739–43) Great Britain and Spain went to war in 1739 over attacks on each other's merchant shipping. During the conflict, waged primarily in the Caribbean, British forces in Georgia drove the Spanish back from northern Florida to St. Augustine.

KING GEORGE'S WAR (1744–48) The steady expansion of New England made inevitable renewed hostilities between the French and British over control of the Hudson and St. Lawrence valleys. The relatively brief but bitter war ended with an uneasy restoration of the status quo.

SEVEN YEARS' WAR (1756–63) Fighting broke out between French and British colonists for control of the upper Ohio River valley in 1754. The frontier warfare escalated into global struggle when Great Britain and France formally declared war in 1756. While this larger conflict is known as the Seven Years' War, the extensive fighting that took place in North America is often referred to separately as the French and Indian War (1754–63). Spain's late entry in the war on the side of France failed to prevent Great Britain's ultimate victory in North America. Under the Treaty of Paris ending the conflict, Great Britain gained possession of all of America east of the Mississippi River.

the foundation for later British assertions to possession of the Pacific Northwest.

In 1585 Sir Walter Raleigh mounted an expedition that established the first English settlement in North America on Roanoke Island off what is now the North Carolina coast. Contact with the colony was interrupted in 1587 by a war with Spain. When a supply ship finally reached the island in 1590, the colonists had vanished without a trace. Roanoke, which became known as the "Lost Colony," represented the end of English colonial ventures until the negotiated close of the conflict with Spain in 1604.

The war with Spain marked England's emergence as a major power. A newly confident English crown fixed its colonial sights firmly on America in the early 1600s. The English drive to settle the Atlantic seaboard had several motives, the most basic of which were economic. English merchants wanted markets for their woolens. England also believed colonies could provide it with important products, such as naval stores, wine and oil, which it had to purchase from other nations. Religion played an important role, as the Anglican English crown was unwilling to cede the New World to Catholic Spain and France. England soon also saw its American colonies as an outlet for its burgeoning population.

English colonization of America began modestly with small settlements at Jamestown in 1607 and Plymouth in 1620. By 1650, however, a steady stream of English colonists had carved out the basic shape of both the Chesapeake Colonies and New England. The conquest of New Netherland in 1664 added what became the four Middle Colonies to England's rapidly expanding colonial dominion. The Carolinas were settled by the 1670s, and all of England's American colonies except Georgia (founded in 1732) had been established by 1700.

The formal union in 1707 of Scotland with England and Wales in the single nation of Great Britain aided the flow of Scottish settlers to the American colonies. Until late in the colonial period, British policy encouraged and facilitated the peopling of America. Colonial charters expressly authorized

CHRONOLOGY OF THE BRITISH COLONIES

1497	John Cabot sails along the Atlantic coast from Newfoundland to Maine
1585–90	The "Lost Colony" of Roanoke Island
1607	Founding of Jamestown in Virginia
1619	First Africans in British America arrive at Jamestown
1620	Pilgrim landing at Plymouth in Massachusetts
1622–46	Powhatan War
1629–42	Puritan Great Migration
1633	Maryland settled as a refuge for English Catholics
1635	Puritan settlers establish Hartford in Connecticut
1636	Roger Williams founds Providence in Rhode Island
1653	Settlement of North Carolina
1660s	Black Codes institutionalize slavery in Virginia and Maryland
1664	New Netherland seized from the Dutch and renamed New York; New Jersey established
1670	Charleston founded in South Carolina
1672	Royal African Company given a monopoly over the African slave trade
1680	New Hampshire becomes a separate colony
1682	William Penn oversees settlement of Pennsylvania
1701	Delaware chartered as a separate colony
1707	England, Scotland, and Wales united as Great Britain
1712	African slave trade is opened to private merchants
1733	Georgia established as a haven for debtors and other destitute poor
1755	Formal British policy for Indian affairs
1760s	Settlement of the Ohio valley in western Pennsylvania
1756–1763	Seven Years' War
1763	Great Britain gains New France and Spanish Florida
1770s	Colonial settlers cross the Appalachians into Tennessee and Kentucky
1775–1783	American Revolution
1783	Great Britain accedes to American independence; Florida returned to Spain

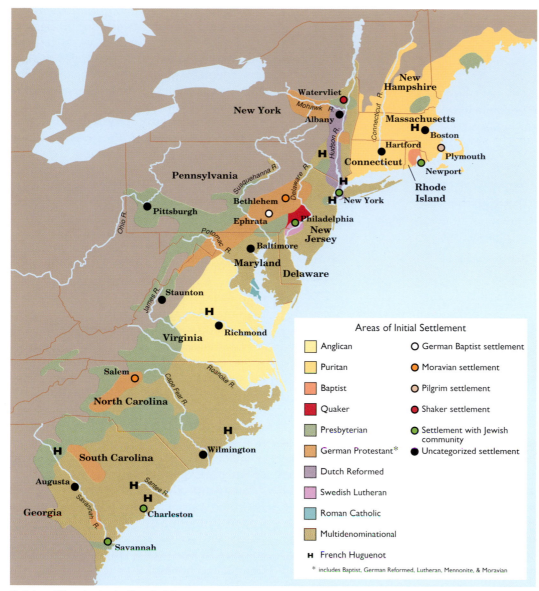

Religious Migration in the British Colonies

THE LOST COLONY

The "Lost Colony" survived only five years, but its fate has captured the popular imagination for centuries. The first English settlement in North America was established on Roanoke Island off the present-day North Carolina coast in 1585. The colonizing expedition of 108 men included the artist John White, whose drawings depicted Native American life at the time of first contact with Europeans. In 1586 the colonists, their supplies depleted, returned to England with Sir Francis Drake, who had stopped at the island in Albemarle Sound on his way home from raiding the Spanish West Indies.

A second expedition of 89 men, 7 women, and 11 children, in three ships, reoccupied Roanoke in 1587. The first English child born in America, Virginia Dare, was delivered shortly after their arrival. The colony subsequently was cut off from England by war with Spain. A relief ship reached Roanoke in 1590, but found only an overgrown, ransacked settlement. The colonists had disappeared without a trace. The only clue to their whereabouts was the word CROATOAN carved into a doorpost.

What happened to the "Lost Colony?" The answer some 400 years later remains unclear. At the time the Croatoan Indians lived on Cape Hatteras, some 60 miles south of Roanoke. Scholars long have surmised the colonists either migrated or were forcibly taken to Cape Hatteras, where they were absorbed into the Croatoan tribe. About 1650 the Croatoans moved to the North Carolina mainland, where they became known as the Lumbees. The Lumbee, who remain in Robeson County to this day, have long pointed to the fair hair and blue eyes of various members as evidence of their Roanoke ancestry. More recently, scholars have speculated the Roanoke colonists relocated to the more fertile mainland of what is now southern Virginia. There, it is suggested, they mingled with the local tribes until 1606, when Powhatan, the powerful chief of the Indians along the Chesapeake Bay, had them killed out of fear of further English intervention. This intervention in fact came the following year with the founding of Jamestown.

the recruitment of settlers. British subjects immigrating to America were assured that they and their descendants would retain all the rights of freeborn citizens and would be governed by British law. To aid the recruitment of colonists from other countries, liberal naturalization laws were passed in the colonies beginning in the 1600s. In 1740 an act of Parliament specifically provided for the naturalization of foreign immigrants, setting a seven-year residency requirement.

Shared Threads

While distinct migratory patterns developed in the four different regions of British colonial America, there were several fundamental shared threads. Religion profoundly influenced migration to the colonies. English Puritans and Quakers, Scotch Presbyterians, and French Huguenots came seeking religious freedom. Maryland was founded as a refuge for English Catholics.

Ethnic as well as religious diversity marked migration to the British colonies. More than 600,000 Europeans journeyed across the Atlantic Ocean to British America. The English were joined by Welsh, Scottish, Irish, Scotch Irish, Swiss, German and French migrants. Also finding refuge in the colonies were several hundred Sephardic Jews of Dutch, Spanish, and Portuguese origin.

The African slave trade constituted the most extreme, but not the only, example of involuntary migration to the colonies. Thousands of British colonists also came to America unwillingly as convict labor.

Many willing migrants journeyed to America as indentured servants. Lacking the money to pay for passage to America, thousands signed a contract, known as an indenture, binding them to work for a specified number of years in return for the cost of transportation to the colonies.

Most indentured servants were under 25, single, and male. Many were recruited

RELIGIOUS MEMBERSHIP IN THE BRITISH COLONIES IN 1775

Denomination	Number
Congregationalist	575,000
Anglican	500,000
Presbyterian	310,000
German Churches*	200,000
Dutch Reformed	75,000
Quaker	40,000
Baptist	25,000
Roman Catholic	25,000
Methodist	5,000
Jewish	2,000

* includes German Reformed, Lutheran, Mennonite, and Moravian

Source: *Encyclopedia of American History*

from England's itinerant population of farmworkers and laborers. England by the 1600s was a mobile society. Population growth, the rise of commercial farming, and industrial development had accustomed the poor in particular to roaming its roads in search of employment, opportunity, and security. The early peopling of the American colonies was largely an extension of domestic migration patterns in England. The Atlantic became in a sense another highway leading to a possible better future.

Land drew the other great mass of voluntary immigrants. These were the English, Scottish, Scotch-Irish, and German settlers who came to the colonies for a homestead of their own. The desire to own a plot of land, with the freedom and self-sufficiency it brought, was a part of American history from the start.

Land Speculation

So was land speculation—the acquisition of land for its future resale or commercial value. Land speculation was at the heart of migration both to and within the British colonies. Contrary to popular myth, land was not just free for the taking in the colonies. British America belonged to the Crown. Ownership of a specific tract of land was transferred to a colony through its charter. The charter's holder, whether proprietor or joint stock company, could allot this land as deemed fit. Settlers obtained

individual plots of land in various ways. Land could be purchased outright, leased, or farmed under a tenancy arrangement. Various colonies had a headright system under which a colonist bringing a specified number of settlers to America was entitled to a land grant.

The steady influx of settlers and natural population increase in the colonies made land an increasingly valuable resource. Political influence was often used, both in London and the colonies, to obtain titles to wilderness tracts. As land speculation grew, so did the demand for settlers. Speculators looked to Protestant northern Europe for the colonists needed to develop their lands. While most early settlers came from England, even the burgeoning English population could not provide all the colonists required. Recruiters in the 1700s turned their attention to Ulster in northern Ireland, the Scottish Highlands, and the Rhineland, where they found many thousands eager to immigrate to America.

In the 1600s the majority of European immigrants to America were indentured servants. In the 1700s the business of migration shifted to settlers. Commercial arrangements were formed among land speculators, shipping merchants, and emigrant agents. Recruiters combed the British Isles and German principalities along the upper Rhine River. Many carried pamphlets and other materials extolling the colonies to prospective emigrants as a land of milk and honey.

These new settlers came as families. The ratio of male to female was roughly equal, as opposed to a ratio of seven to one or more among contract workers. The families came from more provincial areas and generally settled on the frontier in the colonies.

By 1750 most of the prime parcels of land between the Atlantic seaboard and the Appalachian Mountains had been settled. Great Britain's triumph over France in the Seven Years' War added a vast wilderness tract to British America stretching from the Appalachians to the Mississippi River. The British, exhausted by war and eager to avoid hostilities with their Native American inhabitants, designated this area Indian Country and barred settlement there. Colonial governments, however, chose not to enforce this royal policy and settlers hungry for land began working their way west through the natural gaps in the Appalachians.

The end of the French and Indian War in the colonies brought a renewed surge of emigration from Britain. In the 15 years before the American Revolution, approxi-

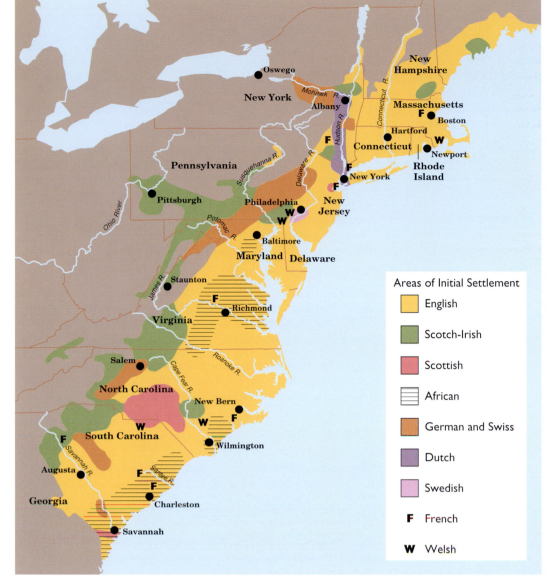

Ethnic Migration in the British Colonies

mately 125,000 emigrants left the British Isles for America. Many were lured by the new frontier lands. Many others were artisans or craftsmen responding to colonial demands for skilled labor. British authorities became concerned this mass exodus would depopulate the realm.

British officials understood the relationship between land speculation and emigration. To discourage the recruitment of settlers, the British crown in 1773 imposed new guidelines governing the distribution of open tracts in the colonies. No longer were colonial officials empowered to make large land grants. Instead, lands were to be sold at public auction in officially surveyed lots at set prices. Though implementation of this new policy was foreclosed by the American Revolution, its basic principles, which favored the individual settler over the land speculator, were incorporated into early U.S. land legislation.

NATIVE AMERICANS

There was an inevitable collision between land-hungry British colonists and the Native Americans who inhabited the Atlantic seaboard. The British drive for land brought death and destruction to the Indians. Those who survived were pushed farther and farther from the Atlantic coast by the relentless advance of colonial settlement.

Like the Dutch, the British treated the Indian tribes as sovereign nations when it suited their purposes, as in concluding treaties with the tribes for the acquisition of their lands. The Indians often were misled about the true nature of the transactions. In their unfamiliarity with European concepts of land ownership, tribes were led to believe they were selling the right to use their land rather than the land itself. A basic pattern emerged in British-Indian relations.

INDIAN WARS AND LAND CESSIONS
1607–1774

POWHATAN WAR (1622–46) In 1622 the Powhatan Indians, alarmed over the seizure of their lands for tobacco cultivation, unleashed a bloody attack on English settlers in Virginia. A newly organized colonial militia waged a relentless campaign that ultimately destroyed the once-powerful Powhatan Confederacy. The surviving Powhatans fled west or were confined to small reservations.

PEQUOT WAR (1636–37) Pequot resistance to English advances into the Connecticut valley was crushed in 1637 by a colonial force that razed the tribe's main village. Pequot captives were sold into slavery in Bermuda or given as slaves to friendly tribes. In 1655 the remnants of the Pequot tribe were settled on the Mystic River.

GOVERNOR KIEFT'S WAR (1640–45) Angered by their resistance to an annual tax payable in corn, furs, or wampum, New Netherland governor-general Willem Kieft in 1640 embarked on a brutal campaign of virtual extermination against the Wappinger and Delaware tribes along the lower Hudson River. By 1645 the Indians, devastated by the war and close to starvation, were compelled to sign a peace treaty relinquishing most of their tribal lands.

PEACH WAR (1655–57) Dutch-Indian hostilities flared again after a Dutch farmer killed a Delaware woman picking peaches in his orchard and her family then slew him. New Netherland's new governor-general, Peter Stuyvesant, deciding against full-scale war, negotiated a gradual halt to the fighting.

ESOPUS WAR (1658–64) Tensions between local Esopus Indians and Dutch settlers around the town of Esopus (now Kingston, New York) erupted in warfare in 1658. A concerted Dutch military campaign finally forced the Esopus to sign a treaty giving up most of their remaining lands and accepting Dutch supremacy.

KING PHILIP'S WAR (1675–76) Worsening English treatment of New England's Indians induced Wampanoag chieftan Metacom, called King Philip by the English after the ancient Macedonian ruler, to organize an alliance with the Narraganset and Nipmuc. In 1675 the Indians attacked English settlements across New England. In a bloody campaign, colonial forces annihilated the three tribes. Metacom was killed and his wife and son were sold into slavery in the Caribbean, as were hundreds of other captured Indians.

ABNAKI WARS (1675–1724) The Abnaki violently resisted the encroachment of English settlers onto their lands in Maine and New Hampshire. Intermittent frontier warfare between the Abnaki and British continued for decades. In 1724 the British overran the main Abnaki stronghold in Maine, breaking the back of further Abnaki resistence. The Abnaki withdrew to French Quebec, where their descendants still live today.

TUSCARORA WAR (1711–13) Friendly relations between the Tuscarora and English colonists in northeastern North Carolina soured as the settlers seized the tribe's lands, cheated it in trade deals, and kidnapped its members for shipment to the Caribbean as slaves. A Tuscarora revolt against the English abuses was crushed by a colonial army in 1713. Many of the surviving Tucaroras migrated to New York, where the tribe became the Sixth Nation of the Iroquois Confederacy.

YAMASEE WAR (1715) In 1687, discontent with Spanish rule, the Yamasee moved from northern Florida to English-claimed South Carolina. In 1715 the Yamasee fought back against mounting colonial infringement on their lands. The South Carolina militia razed the tribe's villages and decimated its war parties. The remnants of the tribe fled back to Florida, where they settled near St. Augustine.

CHEROKEE WAR (1760–61) In 1760, after Virginia frontiersmen attacked a tribal war party on its way home from helping the British capture Fort Duquesne from the French, the Cherokee severed their ties with the British and raided colonial settlements along the Carolina frontier. In the ensuing war the Cherokee were compelled to cede a large swath of their eastern lands, opening the Carolina back country to settlement.

PONTIAC'S REBELLION (1763) Following their seizure of the Great Lakes region from France, the British mishandled relations with the area's tribes. Pontiac, the charismatic chief of the Ottawa, fashioned a broad Indian alliance against British rule. In the spring and summer of 1763, Indian warriors struck British forts and settlements across the northern frontier. The British managed to stem the onslaught and by winter Pontiac's alliance was falling apart. The Ottawa chief reluctantly sued for peace and the fighting subsided. His uprising, however, contributed to the Proclamation of 1763 barring colonial settlement west of the Appalachians.

LORD DUNMORE'S WAR (1774) Virginia's colonial governor, the earl of Dunmore, ignored the Proclamation of 1763. When Dunmore awarded Shawnee territory in the Ohio valley to veterans of the Seven Years' War, the tribe attacked the incoming settlers. In 1774 an army of Virginia militiamen under Dunsmore defeated the Shawnee and forced them to sign a peace treaty surrendering their eastern lands.

The first settlers in an area would peaceably acquire Indian lands, often through trickery or deceit. Continued colonial encroachment on Indian territories eventually would provoke an armed response. In the ensuing hostilities, the British would crush the Native Americans and seize their lands. By the American Revolution, the British had virtually cleared the Atlantic seaboard of its original inhabitants as far as the Appalachian Mountains.

It is estimated that there were as many as one million Native Americans east of the Mississippi River on the eve of British settlement in North America. By the end of the colonial period their numbers had been reduced to about 150,000. European diseases were a more effective killer than any colonial army, as epidemics of smallpox and other contagions ravaged whole tribes. The Indians also were drawn into the century-long colonial conflict between Great Britain and France. Indian ranks were further depleted by intertribal warfare, as the dislocations produced by the European arrival exacerbated ancient tribal rivalries or pitted former allies against each other. Various tribes, most notably the Delaware and Tuscarora, migrated great distances to avoid destruction.

The British demonstrated only minimal respect for Native American ways of life and ancestral land rights. During their wars with the Indians, the British did not seek to conquer but to destroy. Their basic intent was to depopulate the land. Indian villages were razed and the survivors forced to flee west. Native American captives often were sold into slavery in the Caribbean. Over time the British set aside small tracts of land for the remnants of the Indian tribes in the colonies. These lands, which became known as reservations, did not represent an official Indian policy, but rather evolved locally and informally. The first formal Indian reservation was established in Burlington County by the New Jersey colonial assembly in 1758.

The British crown left Indian policy to the colonial governments until 1755, when it assumed overall control of Indian affairs. The British created two Indian departments, each with a superintendent responsible for Indian relations.

The most enlightened approach to Native Americans was in the Middle Colonies. In Pennsylvania the Quakers generally sought to enact fair procedures for the purchase of Indian lands, although evasion of these regulations was not uncommon. In New York British fur traders inherited the close relationship with the Iro-

quois established by the Dutch. The British alliance with the Iroquois Confederacy forestalled white encroachment on Iroquois land until after the American Revolution.

New England saw prolonged conflict between Native Americans and an ever-expanding Puritan population. The Puritans believed they had divine justification for their jurisdiction over Indian affairs. The Chesapeake Colonies were also marked by Indian-colonist hostilities, as the plantation economy fueled the demand for more farmland. In the less-settled Southern Colonies, relations with the Indians centered on trade, especially for furs. Still, the land requirements of plantation agriculture, as well as colonial abuses of the Native Americans, sparked several Indian rebellions.

Following its conquest of New France in the Seven Years' War, the British Crown issued the Proclamation of 1763 setting aside the territory west of the Appalachians as Indian Country. A line running down the mountains from Maine to Georgia constituted the boundary between Indian and white lands. Enforcement of the proclamation proved futile, as colonists disregarded its provisions and continued to press across the Appalachians. British-colonial conflict over settlement of the western frontier soon was subsumed in the events leading to the American Revolution. After independence, the British concepts of reservations, centralized Indian departments, and Indian Country became part of U.S. Indian policy.

SLAVERY

Land was at the core of the forced migration of hundreds of thousands of Africans to colonial America. In the Chesapeake and Southern colonies, climate and fertile soil made possible large-scale agriculture. On huge estates known as plantations, crops were produced for export to British and other European markets. By the late 1600s, the flow of indentured servants was inadequate to meet the burgeoning labor demands of the Southern plantations. Southern planters found the answer to a steady source of agricultural laborers in the African slave trade.

The first Africans landed in British America in 1619, with the arrival of 20 blacks at Jamestown aboard a Dutch warship. The Dutch captain sold the Africans, captured from a Spanish ship, as bound servants. Over the following decades small numbers of blacks trickled into the colonies. Most were imported via the intercolonial trade between the Chesapeake Colonies and Britain's Caribbean possessions. The Africans' legal status was at first unclear as there were no colonial laws governing slavery. Many blacks early on were considered bound laborers similar to white indentured servants. Distinctions between black and white bonded laborers quickly emerged, however. While a small percentage of Africans gained their freedom, most were bound to servitude for life. They were slaves in fact, if not in law.

In the 1660s Virginia and Maryland moved to institutionalize black slavery. Laws known as Black Codes were enacted governing every aspect of the nascent slave system. Slaves were defined as chattel, or property, that could be bought or sold. Most importantly, slavery became a perpetual condition as slave offspring inherited their parents' status. Faced with a growing number of children with white fathers and black mothers, the Virginia colonial assembly reversed the long-standing tradition in English common law that children bore the status of their fathers. The assembly passed a new law stipulating that such children inherited the status of their mothers. Thus, the offspring of a female slave and a free white man, frequently her owner, were also slaves. Other laws prohibited intermarriage between black and white.

The slave codes were rooted in a growing racism. Slavery was deemed the rightful condition for Africans, who were characterized as savage and inferior. Early on the English rationalized their enslavement of blacks on religious grounds, maintaining that the "heathen" Africans, as non-Christians, were subject to servitude. Later, with growing numbers of blacks converting to Christianity, economic interest took precedence over religious conviction. In the late 1600s one colony after another adopted laws ensuring that black Christians could be held as slaves.

The British crown never enacted a royal slave code. Instead, each colony passed its own slave laws. By the mid-1700s slavery was legally established in all the colonies and deeply entrenched in the South.

As late as 1680, at most only several hundred slaves were entering the British colonies each year. Virginia's 3,000 slaves in 1680 were less than 7% of its population. After 1690, slave importations mounted sharply. Virginia by 1700 was almost 30% black. The volume of the slave trade surpassed 1,000 annually by 1730 and thereafter increased to more than four times that level. In the 45 years before the American Revolution, some 200,000 African slaves

were brought to the colonies. Most found themselves on southern plantations.

By the early 18th century the British had surpassed the Portuguese, Spanish, and Dutch to become the preeminent slaving power. A fleet of more than 1,000 ships in the mid-1700s transported between 5,000 and 15,000 slaves a year to the New World.

The British concentrated their slaving efforts on the Gold Coast (along the Gulf of Guinea) and on the stretch of coast to its east between the Volta and Niger rivers that became known as the Slave Coast. Most of the slaves taken by the British came from the present-day countries of Ghana, Togo, Benin, Nigeria, and Cameroon. Roughly half the slaves brought to British America were from the Gold and Slave coasts. About one-quarter each came from the slaving regions above Sierra Leone and along the Congo and Angolan coast. Numerous different ethnic groups or tribes were represented in the flow of Africans to the colonies. The human tide included large numbers of Yorubas, Ibos, Gabons, Congos, and Angolas.

The importation of slaves to the British colonies was part of a much larger African slave trade that itself was part of a vast Atlantic maritime commerce. The approxi-

VOLUME OF AFRICAN SLAVE TRADE

Exact figures on the number of Africans brought to America in bondage are not available. It is estimated that a few hundred African slaves entered North American ports each year in the 1600s. This number rose to about 1,000 slaves annually in the first three decades of the 1700s. The volume of the African slave trade increased substantially after 1730 and did not subside until federal law banned the importation of slaves into the United States after 1807.

Decade	Estimated Annual Slave Imports
1731–1740	4,050
1741–1750	5,850
1751–1760	4,190
1761–1770	4,380
1771–1780	3,300
1781–1790	1,770
1791–1800	7,660
1801–1807	11,800

Source: *Encyclopedia of the North American Colonies*

African Slave Coast

mately 450,000 slaves brought to the present-day United States over the course of the slave trade represented only about 5 percent of the more than 10 million Africans forcibly transported to the New World. Most ended up on the sugar plantations of the Caribbean.

Those involved in the lucrative slave trade saw the slaves as commodities, even referring to them as "black gold." The slave trade became a key leg in the larger exchange of goods across the Atlantic. The principal maritime commerce that developed in colonial times is often called the Rectangular Trade, a name derived from the rough shape formed by the trade routes involved. The base leg of the rectangle was the long voyage made by the slave ships from Africa to the West Indies. This trek, during which the Africans suffered under horrid conditions, became known as the Middle Passage. In the West Indies, the

African Slave Trade

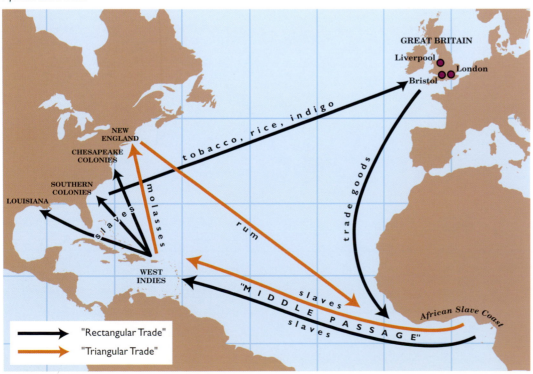

THE MIDDLE PASSAGE

The African slave's long journey into captivity in America began with an often brutal trek to one of the European settlements along the West African coast. There, European traders operated depots where slaves were branded with an identifying mark and held in compounds pending embarkation aboard a slave ship. The compounds were terrifying places where the Africans, already suffering from dislocation and despair, were abused by their captors.

When the time for embarkation came, the slaves were transported by canoes to deeper water, where the slaver rode at anchor. Many Africans chose death over the fate that awaited them. The captain of the slave ship *Hannibal* later recounted how Africans were "so loth to leave their own country, that they have often leaped out of the canoes . . . and kept under water till they were drowned, to avoid being taken up and saved by our boats, which pursued them."

Captains of slave vessels were paid according to the number of slaves delivered. Thus there was a powerful financial inducement to pack as many slaves into a single ship as possible. Slaves, shackled two by two, were crammed into holds often no more than four feet high. Conditions were unbelievably cruel and inhuman. Many suffocated to death in the foul air or were killed by the diseases easily spread in the filthy, fetid holds.

Forced to crouch in the tight quarters, the slaves normally were allowed to stretch on deck once a day to prevent circulation problems. Rations were a meager diet of corn flour porridge and beans. Tortured by thirst, captives had to make do with a pint of water a day. Many, overcome with despair, were prone to a condition slave traders called "fixed melancholy," staring into space, refusing food, and even jumping overboard to take their own lives. Others, when able, tried to resist more directly. Any hint of slave revolt, though, was violently suppressed.

Africans were first "broken" or trained for enslavement. From the Caribbean, slaves were shipped periodically to the British colonies. On depositing their human cargo, the ships loaded up with tobacco, rice, or indigo for transport to British and other European ports. The vessels then returned to West Africa with trade goods for use in the barter for slaves and the cycle began anew.

The Europeans built settlements along the West African coast that served as depots for the slave trade. Slaves were obtained in two basic ways. European agents, known as factors, established trade relations with local African rulers and merchants. Iron utensils, pewterware, cloth, and other goods were exchanged for human captives. Slavery was already practiced in Africa, as various ethnic groups enslaved prisoners of war. It was a simple progression for African chieftains to sell their captives to Europeans. In a tragic irony, Africans were drawn into the huge slave industry that ultimately constituted the largest forced migration in history.

To gain additional captives for trade, Africans resorted to slaving raids against other tribal groups. Europeans also obtained slaves by force. As the supply of slaves on the coast dwindled, slaving parties raided ever farther into the interior. Virtually every ethnic group in West Africa was affected by the slave trade. Upward of 100 were completely destroyed.

The development of a maritime industry in New England led to colonial participation in the slave trade. New England merchants plied Atlantic sea routes that became known as the Triangular Trade. From Newport and other ports, colonial ships carried casks of locally distilled rum to West Africa where they were bartered for slaves. The vessels then undertook the Middle Passage to the Caribbean. In the West Indies, the slaves were traded for molasses, a by-product of the sugar industry. The molasses was taken back to New England where it was made into the rum carried to Africa.

Much of the growth in the colonial slave population came through natural increase. Within several generations, the majority of slaves were no longer African migrants but African Americans, born on American soil. At the time of the American Revolution, approximately 20 percent of the inhabitants of the colonies were black slaves. Of these, roughly 80 percent were native born. While the American Revolution brought political independence to whites, it left blacks in bondage.

THE CHESAPEAKE COLONIES

Settlement of the British colonies began along the long, protected shore of Chesapeake Bay. It was initially guided by the London Company, a joint stock company chartered by King James I in 1606 to colonize America. The firm was authorized to settle to the south, while the Plymouth Company, also chartered that same year, was granted license to settle to the north.

The Chesapeake Colonies

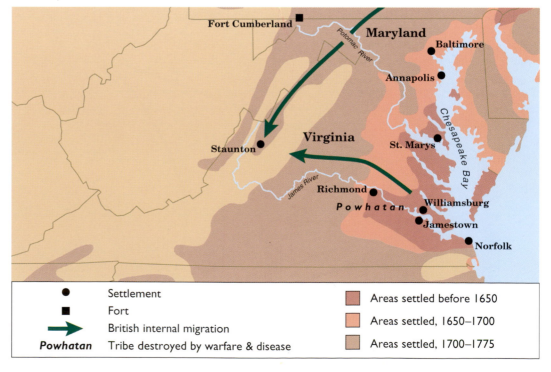

●	Settlement	
■	Fort	
→	British internal migration	
Powhatan	Tribe destroyed by warfare & disease	

▨	Areas settled before 1650
▨	Areas settled, 1650–1700
▨	Areas settled, 1700–1775

In 1607, 104 colonists dispatched by the London Company established an outpost on the James River in present-day southeastern Virginia. They named it Jamestown after the king. Within six months, half of the colonists had died of disease and starvation. Nevertheless, the company proved adept at recruiting new settlers and Jamestown clung to a precarious existence.

The Virginia colony at first was overwhelmingly male. To redress the gender imbalance, the London Company recruited "young and uncorrupt maids." Young working class women in 17th-century England, especially in London's crowded slums, had almost no say over their future. For an adventurous few, Virginia represented the chance for a better marriage and life. Most were promptly married on arrival, and Jamestown's small population was soon bolstered by natural increase.

Tobacco changed Virginia from a struggling outpost to a flourishing colony. The local Indian-grown tobacco had a "byting tast." In 1613 John Rolfe crossed native plants with seeds imported from the West Indies, producing a smooth smoke that captured the European market. Virginia went tobacco wild. A new arrival would have found it growing even in the streets of Jamestown. From 2,500 pounds in 1616, tobacco exports climbed to more than one million pounds in 1628.

Tobacco brought the dispersal of the fledgling colony. The crop depleted the soil and required large tracts of land for its cultivation. By 1630, tobacco plantations extended up the James River 20 miles. Colonists were also reaching out along the Rappahannock and Potomac rivers. Migration inland followed the rivers emptying into Chesapeake Bay as the waterways provided ready routes for the shipment of the tobacco harvest.

The relentless land hunger brought inevitable conflict with Native Americans. Upward of 14,000 Powhatan Indians lived between Chesapeake Bay and the falls farther up the James River at present-day Richmond. At first the colonists maintained an uneasy peace with the Powhatans, but within a decade continuing English advances on their lands triggered violent hostilities. In the long Powhatan War (1622–46), the English crushed further Indian resistance to settlement of Virginia's coastal region.

The cultivation of tobacco was very labor-intensive. Yet Virginia's colonial population by 1630 still numbered only some 2,000. The colony adopted a headright system to encourage settlement, with Englishmen awarded 50 acres for every settler brought over at their own expense. Between 1635 and 1639 alone, 4.1 million acres of land were awarded as headright grants. For much of the 1600s, though, the hands necessary to work the plantations were provided largely by indentured servants. The aggressive recruitment of settlers and indentured servants built Virginia's population to roughly 15,000 in 1650.

Virginia, which became a royal colony in 1624 with the failure of the London Company, was joined by a second English outpost on the Chesapeake in 1633. The architect of this second Chesapeake colony, George Calvert, had been an investor in the London Company. Calvert's colonial venture actually was driven more by religious faith than profit motive. In 1632 King Charles I awarded Calvert, who had a distinguished career of service to the crown, a grant of about seven million acres north of the Potomac River. The king wanted a strategic bulwark against the Dutch colony along the Hudson River.

The Catholic Calvert saw the grant as an opportunity to establish a refuge for countrymen of his faith. Catholics in the early 1600s faced considerable discrimination in Anglican England. They could not bear arms, travel freely, or practice their faith openly. To assuage fears over their allegiance to the pope, Catholics holding public office were required to swear a loyalty oath to the crown. Calvert, who bore the title Lord Baltimore, named his colony Maryland after King Charles I's Catholic wife, Henrietta Maria. When Calvert died later in 1632, it fell to his son Cecilius, better known as the second Lord Baltimore, to settle the colony.

Maryland was the hereditary domain of the Calvert family, thus Lord Baltimore had wide latitude in how it was settled. He foresaw a colony of large estates, a landed Catholic gentry, and a manorial way of life. Lord Baltimore was careful to keep Maryland open to all Christian denominations, though, believing the principle of religious tolerance would benefit Catholics in both America and England. Thus he adopted a headright system under which any gentleman bringing over servants was offered 100 free acres for each. Those bringing the requisite number for 2,000 or more acres were entitled to a manor.

In 1633 the first group of some 200 colonists founded the settlement of St. Mary's just north of the Potomac on the Chesapeake. This first contingent included 17 gentleman investors, most of whom were Catholic, 3 Jesuit priests, and more

The transatlantic voyage, known as the Middle Passage, generally took five to eight weeks depending on the winds. Throughout the colonial period most slave ships made for the West Indies. Over time numbers of slavers sailed directly to American ports. Mortality rates on the slave ships were high. Slave merchants considered a loss of 15% of the human cargo to mistreatment, malnutrition, and disease not out of the ordinary. Those who survived the horrific passage could take little solace as they faced sale in slave markets and lifelong bondage.

than 100 servants, the majority of whom were Protestant. Almost from the start, Lord Baltimore's dream of a semi-feudal Catholic domain was overcome by much greater Protestant than Catholic migration. The area around St. Mary's was settled largely by Catholics. The upper Chesapeake Bay, however, was peopled by Protestants drawn by the ready availability of land and the bountiful shoreline.

By 1660 Maryland had a colonial population of 7,500. The area was sparsely settled by Native Americans and, other than occasional raids by Susquehanna to the north, the colony faced no real resistance to expansion. In 1676, Susquehannocks, driven south into Maryland and Virginia by their Iroquois enemies, were destroyed by the colonists.

Maryland early turned to tobacco cultivation, and its large land holdings soon evolved into plantations. As in Virginia, most laborers in the 1600s were indentured servants. Lord Baltimore opened an office in London to aid in the recruitment of emigrants.

The tidewater or coastal areas of Maryland and Virginia were largely settled by 1700. In the 1600s, the Chesapeake Colonies had a level of immigration eight times greater than that of New England. By century's end, however, the two regions had roughly equal colonial populations, owing to the scant growth of a native-born population in the Chesapeake Colonies. Male indentured servants outnumbered females by more than six to one, and there were too few women to provide for natural population increase. Very high death rates were the most telling factor. Immigrants died in large numbers in the hot, humid, disease-ridden environment. Malaria was rampant in coastal areas. Not until the early 1700s did native-born whites outnumber immigrants.

African slaves replaced indentured servants in the 1700s. The fact that many Africans had an inherited immunity to malaria (connected to the sickle-cell trait) and greater resistance to such diseases as yellow fever reinforced the use of slave labor. Black slaves could better survive in the mosquito-infested tidewater areas. Norfolk and Baltimore became major slave importation ports. In 1700 the Chesapeake Colonies' 13,000 slaves constituted roughly 13% of the population. By 1760 the number of slaves had climbed to 190,000, comprising almost 40% of the population. Slavery followed the spread of plantations along the Chesapeake and its waterways.

The same waterways provided access to the hilly inland area of Virginia known as the Piedmont. Once freed, indentured servants often migrated to the western frontier where land was inexpensive and they could carve out small farms. By 1700 migration up the James River had reached the Blue Ridge Mountains. The Shenandoah valley between the Blue Ridge and Allegheny mountains was explored in 1716. By midcentury the Shenandoah had been peopled by Scotch-Irish and German settlers, who had migrated down the valley from Pennsylvania drawn by cheap land prices.

Internal migration had produced two Virginias by the time of the American Revolution. The Tidewater was a place of landed gentry and large plantations worked by black slaves. The Piedmont was dotted by small family farms and frontier settlements. What is now western Maryland was settled from both the north and east, precipitating a long territorial struggle between Maryland and Pennsylvania. In 1763 surveyors Charles Mason and Jeremiah Dixon were commissioned to establish the boundaries between Maryland, Delaware, Pennsylvania, and Virginia. In future years, the resulting Mason-Dixon Line would divide slave from free states.

NEW ENGLAND

New England was by far the most homogeneous region in British America. It was peopled in an extraordinary burst of Puritan migration between 1630 and 1640 and then, for almost a century, developed independent of any real further immigration. Settlement of New England was spurred by the internal migration of successive generations of Puritan descendants.

Unlike its sister London Company, the Plymouth Company proved unsuccessful at establishing a toehold in North America. In 1607 the company, also a joint stock enterprise, sponsored an expedition of some 120 colonists that founded a settlement at Sagadahoc near the mouth of the Kennebec River in Maine. The outpost failed after one year, discouraging further attempts at colonization. English fishermen continued to frequent the area and, in 1614, the Plymouth Company dispatched Jamestown veteran Captain John Smith to assess the prospects for settlement along the northeastern coast. Smith lent the region its name in his enthusiastic report, *Description of New England*.

It was not Smith's report, however, but chance that brought the first permanent settlement in New England. In the early 1600s English Protestants who believed in separation from the official Anglican Church, with its Catholic elements, were known as Separatists. In 1608 a small group of Separatists fled to the Netherlands to escape religious persecution by English authorities. They settled at Leyden, where they were able to worship in peace, but the community's leaders grew concerned over the corrupting influence of a more worldly Dutch society.

The Leyden Separatists, known to history as the Pilgrims because of their religious-inspired travels, resolved to immigrate to the New World. The Pilgrims saw their contemplated migration in biblical terms. The Jews of the Old Testament had escaped bondage in Egypt and braved the desert wastes of the wilderness to reach Israel, the land promised to them by God. The Pilgrims believed they similarly must flee the oppressive hand of the English crown. With divine providence and protection, they would cross the watery wilderness of the Atlantic to reach their Promised Land, America.

Pilgrim leaders negotiated with the London Company a patent authorizing their settlement near the mouth of the Hudson River. The Pilgrims returned to England where, in September 1620, 41 of their members set sail for America aboard the *Mayflower*. Also among the ship's 102 passengers were 40 other settlers recruited by the London Company and 21 indentured servants and hired hands. Driven off-course by rough weather, the *Mayflower* touched land in November at Cape Cod, some 200 miles north of its intended destination and outside the territory and jurisdiction of the London Company. Thus on their own, the Pilgrims drafted the historic Mayflower Compact providing for their settlement's governance.

The Pilgrims established their New World haven at Plymouth on the Massachusetts coast. As at Jamestown the settlers suffered grievously, with half not surviving the first winter. Their holiday of Thanksgiving partly celebrated the help tendered the struggling Pilgrims by local Indians. The Pilgrims were grateful that Algonquians Samoset and Squanto, who had learned to speak English from English fishermen, taught them how to grow corn and fish Cape Cod Bay. The self-righteous Pilgrims, however, also saw the hand of God in a recent epidemic, introduced by European fishermen, that had struck down thousands of coastal Indians, thus, they believed, clearing the area for their habitation. In 1621 the Pilgrims signed a peace treaty with the Wampanoag chief, Massasoit.

Bolstered by Indian assistance and a steady influx of settlers, the Pilgrim colony took hold. The Pilgrims migrated as families—there were 20 women and 32 children aboard the *Mayflower*—and natural increase soon aided the colony's growth. Plymouth had a population of 300 by 1630, the year the Pilgrims obtained a charter for their colony from the Council for New England, which had replaced the Plymouth Company in 1620.

The Council issued several land patents in the 1620s. Small settlements were established along the New Hampshire and Maine coasts and a trading post was founded at Salem, Massachusetts. The history of New England took a fateful turn in 1627, when a group of Puritans received a charter to settle Massachusetts between the Charles and Merrimack rivers.

The Puritans faced increasing persecution under King Charles I, who had ascended to the English throne in 1625. There was a vigorous Puritan element in Parliament, which provoked the ire of the absolutist king. The Puritans were subjected to harassment, imprisonment, and even branding and mutilation by Anglican authorities. Many Puritans, like the kindred Pilgrims, came to see America as a Promised Land where they could escape religious persecution.

Again, circumstance intervened in the settlement of New England. The charter of the Puritans' Massachusetts Bay Company did not specify the location for its stockholder meetings. Capitalizing on this oversight, Puritan leaders decided to remove not only themselves and their communities to New England but their company as well, thus allowing them to form their own government in the New World. The prospect of a self-governing Puritan Commonwealth precipitated the first mass migration to America.

The Puritan exodus began in 1629 with five ships bearing 300 colonists. By 1634 some 10,000 Puritans had crossed the Atlantic. Settlements were established along the north Massachusetts shore, including Boston, founded in 1630. The Puritan Great Migration continued unabated until the late 1630s, when it was halted by the deepening political and religious conflict in England that culminated in the English Civil War. In all, an estimated 21,000 Puritans had immigrated to New England in little more than a decade.

The Puritan migration never resumed, as first the Puritan victory in the English Civil War and then the development of religious tolerance under the restored Anglican monarchy mitigated the persecution that drove earlier emigration. Puritan New England did not lack for bodies, however, because of a high natural rate of population increase. New England's inhabitants doubled roughly every 27 years.

In the earliest western migration in British America, several groups of Puritans in 1635 journeyed cross-country from Massachusetts to settle the Connecticut River valley at Hartford. Two years later a second contingent established an outpost at New Haven. Soon Puritan settlements spread along the Connecticut River and across Long Island Sound to eastern Long Island. In 1662 Hartford and New Haven formed the nucleus of the newly chartered colony of Connecticut.

The Puritans came to America not only to avoid persecution but also to construct their notion of a godly society. Despite their own history of persecution, the Puritans did not believe in religious tolerance. They brooked no dissent from their fundamentalist religious doctrine. In 1635 the Reverend Roger Williams, whose religious views were more Baptist than Puritan Con-

gregationalist, was banished from Massachusetts. With a small band of fellow exiles, in 1636 he established the settlement of Providence at the head of Narragansett Bay. Two years later, religious leader Anne Hutchinson was similarly banished by Puritan authorities. Hutchinson, the first woman to play a leading public role in the colonies, settled with her followers the island of Aquidneck at the mouth of Narragansett Bay. Newport was founded in 1639. The Narragansett settlements were joined into the colony of Rhode Island in 1644.

Puritan settlements at first retained the form of medieval English villages. The Puritan emphasis on religious community rather than the individual fit naturally with the more ordered social organization of village life. Each village or town was built around the meetinghouse, which doubled as church and town hall. Individual lots, each large enough for a house, garden, and orchard, were laid out around a village green. Surrounding the town were the individual farm plots. Woodlands and pasturelands were held in common.

Colonial New England

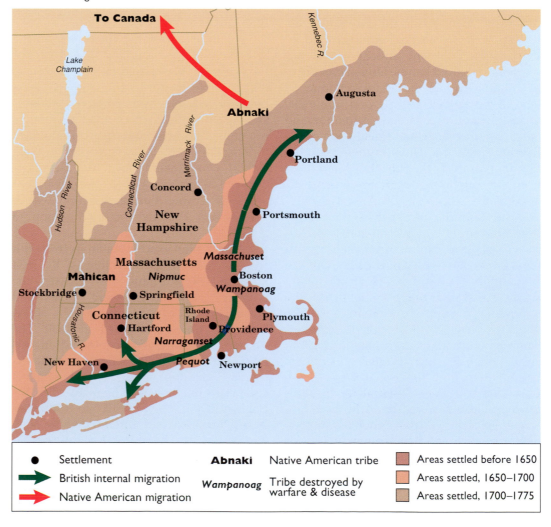

The rapidly expanding population soon propelled the boundaries of Puritan settlement out from the coasts and riverbanks. In general, a family's lands around a Puritan village were large enough to provide plots for two successive generations. By the fourth, or even third generation, however, there was a shortage of available acreage. When a village became too crowded, members would purchase or acquire a tract of unsettled land and venture forth to start a new township.

Between 1660 and 1710, 209 new townships were founded in New England. By the early 18th century the Puritans had settled eastern Massachusetts, the eastern coastal areas of New Hampshire and Maine, and the Connecticut valley as far north as the future Vermont border. New Hampshire became a separate colony in 1680. Maine, part of Massachusetts throughout the colonial period, did not become a separate state until 1820.

In a long series of wars, the Puritans crushed Native American resistance to their expansion. No New England tribe was left unscathed. Most were destroyed. The Puritan attitude toward Native Americans was paternalistic at best and genocidal at worst. In the 1650s Massachusetts, at the urging of the Reverend John Eliot, undertook the conversion of Massachusetts Indians. Eliot established 17 villages where Massachuset Indians were settled and exposed to Puritan religion. Those in the settlements were dubbed Praying Indians. Both Eliot's work and the Massachuset tribe were largely destroyed by King Philip's War (1675–76). The Mahican, who were driven east into the Housatonic valley in 1664 by the Iroquois, became known as the Stockbridge Indians after the adjacent Puritan town. In 1756 some of the Stockbridge Indians migrated to New York where they settled among the Oneidas. This group subsequently acquired the name Brotherton Indians. In 1822 the Brothertons and Stockbridges were removed to Wisconsin where, in 1856, they were granted reservation lands. A handful of Mahicans remained in Connecticut.

In the 1700s the diminution of the Indian threat and continuing land hunger brought the breakup of the traditional Puritan village. Increasingly, individual farms were laid out far from the central town. Puritanism itself evolved into the American Congregationalist and Baptist denominations.

When immigration resumed in the 1700s, it was largely non-English. Between 1714 and 1720, some 54 vessels bearing Scotch-Irish immigrants docked in New England. The Scotch-Irish families came to

NATIVE AMERICAN POPULATION DECLINE ON NANTUCKET AND MARTHA'S VINEYARD

The devastating impact of British colonial migration on Native Americans is dramatically illustrated by the decline of the Wampanoags on Nantucket and Martha's Vineyard. The first English settlers arrived on the two islands off the southeastern coast of Cape Cod in the 1640s. The native Wampanoag inhabitants managed to stay out of King Philip's War (1675–76), which resulted in the virtual extermination of their fellow tribes on the mainland. Instead, European diseases, as so often the case, were the primary killer. A tuberculosis epidemic on Nantucket in 1763–64 claimed 222 of the 358 Indians still on the island. On Martha's Vineyard the remaining Wampanoags in 1711 were confined by English authorities to Gay Head Reservation, one of the first Indian reservations in America. (A small Wampanoag community has survived on the island to this day.)

MARTHA'S VINEYARD (POPULATION)

Dates	From	To
1642–1674	3,000	1,500
1674–1698	1,500	1,000
1698–1720	1,000	800
1720–1764	800	313

NANTUCKET (POPULATION)

1659–1674	3,000	1,500
1674–1698	1,500	1,000
1698–1763	1,000	348
1763–1792	348	20

Source: Russell Thornton, *American Indian Holocaust and Survival: A Population History Since 1492.*

settle along the New England frontier. Western Massachusetts, New Hampshire, and Maine soon had Scotch-Irish settlements.

The Presbyterian Scotch-Irish were not always greeted with open arms. A second wave of Scotch-Irish immigration after 1727 provoked some of the earliest nativism in American history. In 1729 a nativist mob in Boston prevented the landing of a ship carrying Scotch-Irish emigrants. In 1734 a mob destroyed the newly built Presbyterian church at Worcester, Massachusetts. The Scotch-Irish at Worcester encountered such resentment that they moved farther west and established a community at Pelham. By 1775 there were some 70 Scotch-Irish settlements in New England. Still the region's population was overwhelmingly of English stock.

After 1750 New Hampshire began to award land grants west of the Connecticut River in present-day Vermont. Following the defeat of the French in the Seven Years' War, New York moved to assert its control over Vermont, which was part of the colony's original charter. Vermont's New England settlers resisted the influx of New Yorkers from the west, forming irregular military units known as the Green Mountain Boys. New York relinquished its territorial claims in 1789, and Vermont became the 14th state in 1791.

The original Puritan ban on the sale or use of slaves had been set aside by 1650. The primary role New England played in the institution of slavery in America was in the African slave trade. Both shipbuilding and the maritime trade with the West Indies became key regional industries. New England merchants increasingly joined in the lucrative transport of African slaves to the New World. Newport in the 1700s emerged as a major port for colonial slavers.

There were relatively few black slaves in New England, as the region was made up of small towns and family farms. Most slaves were servants or domestics. Small numbers of freed and escaped slaves found refuge in the larger port cities such as Boston.

THE MIDDLE COLONIES

The Middle Colonies were by far the most diverse region in British America. Partly this was the legacy of New Netherland. The

POPULATION OF THE BRITISH COLONIES
(population in thousands)

NEW ENGLAND

Date	White	Black	Total
1610	—	—	—
1620	0.1	—	0.1
1640	13.5	0.2	13.7
1660	32.6	0.6	33.2
1680	68.0	0.5	68.5
1700	90.7	1.7	92.4
1720	166.9	4.0	170.9
1740	281.2	8.5	289.7
1760	436.9	12.7	449.6
1780	698.4	14.4	712.8

MIDDLE COLONIES

White	Black	Total
—	—	—
—	—	—
1.7	0.2	1.9
4.8	0.6	5.5
13.4	1.5	14.9
49.9	3.7	53.5
92.3	10.8	103.1
204.1	16.5	220.5
398.9	29.0	427.9
680.5	42.4	722.9

CHESAPEAKE COLONIES

White	Black	Total
0.3	—	0.3
0.9	—	0.9
8.0	0.1	8.1
24.0	0.9	24.9
55.6	4.3	59.9
85.2	12.9	98.1
128.0	30.6	158.6
212.5	84.0	296.5
312.4	189.6	502.0
482.4	303.6	786.0

SOUTHERN COLONIES

Date	White	Black	Total
1640	—	—	—
1660	1.0	—	1.0
1680	6.2	0.4	6.6
1700	13.6	2.9	16.4
1720	24.8	14.8	39.6
1740	57.8	50.2	108.0
1760	119.6	94.5	214.1
1780	297.4	208.8	506.2

TOTAL POPULATION

Date	White	Black	Total
1610	0.3	—	0.3
1620	1.0	—	1.0
1630	4.6	0.1	4.7
1640	23.2	0.5	23.7
1650	38.7	1.2	39.9
1660	62.4	2.1	64.5
1670	100.5	6.0	106.5
1680	143.2	6.7	149.9
1690	200.2	12.6	212.8
1700	239.4	21.2	260.6
1710	296.0	37.8	333.8
1720	412.0	60.2	472.2
1730	551.9	97.0	648.9
1740	755.6	159.2	914.8
1750	934.3	242.1	1176.4
1760	1267.8	325.8	1593.6
1770	1674.3	456.9	2131.2
1780	2158.7	569.2	2727.9

Source: *Encyclopedia of the North American Colonies.*

English conquest of the Dutch colony in 1664 absorbed the territory of future colonies New York, New Jersey, Pennsylvania, and Delaware into British America. Also absorbed were the Dutch and Swedish settlers along the Hudson and Delaware rivers.

The area seized from the Dutch was the domain of the Duke of York, who in 1685 became King James II. New York was made a colony in 1664. That same year the duke awarded to Sir George Carteret and Lord John Berkeley the region between the Hudson and Delaware rivers, which became the colony of New Jersey.

At the time northeastern New Jersey was inhabited by several hundred Dutch settlers as well as a few hundred Puritan migrants from New England. Several thousand English settlers lived in New York by 1664, having migrated from New England to eastern Long Island and Westchester County north of New York City. To spur settlement of his colony, the Duke of York made free land grants on Long Island and awarded large estates along the Hudson to prominent English families. By 1680 both the Berkeley and Carteret land grants in New Jersey had been subdivided and sold to other proprietors. Small numbers of English emigrants made their way to New York and New Jersey in the late 1600s. New York became a royal colony in 1686, New Jersey in 1702.

The main impetus for settlement of the Middle Colonies came from an English Quaker, William Penn. Son of a renowned admiral, Penn as a young man joined the Society of Friends, a radical Protestant sect founded by George Fox in England around 1650. The Friends, who rejected formal religious creeds or the need for priests, gained the then derisive name Quakers from Fox's admonition to "quake" at the name of the Lord. The Quakers refused to take oaths, bear arms, or pay religious taxes, bringing them into conflict with royal authorities. Quakers faced religious persecution both in England and the colonies.

Penn resolved to create a refuge in the New World for his coreligionists. Despite his Quaker affiliation, he had managed to maintain close family ties to the English Crown. In 1681 he prevailed on King Charles II to award him a vast proprietary grant west of the Delaware River as repayment of royal debts owed his late father. Penn viewed his colonial project as a "Holy Experiment." His object was to build a colony that rested on the Quaker ideals of religious tolerance and the innate goodness of humankind.

Settlement of Pennsylvania began in 1682. Penn journeyed to America to oversee the founding of his colony and its capital, Philadelphia (with its Quaker name from the Greek for "city of brotherly love"). The area around Philadelphia had already been cleared by Swedish farmers, survivors of the short-lived enterprise of New Sweden, and the new colony quickly took root. Most of the initial settlers were English Quakers. They were joined by Welsh Quakers, whose early presence is attested to by the Welsh place names around Philadelphia today. Quakers also immigrated to western New Jersey, across the Delaware River.

Penn proved a masterful promoter of his new colony. In 1682 he published *Some Account of the Province of Pennsylvania*, which, translated into German, Dutch, and French, circulated widely in northern Europe. The pamphlet, which extolled the virtues of Pennsylvania, was part of Penn's aggressive recruitment of settlers, and German settlers in particular. He offered easy terms for land and promised religious liberty to all. The Quaker proprietor was not averse to making a handsome profit on his enterprise, but his primary interest was his Holy Experiment.

German migration to colonial America began in 1683 when a small band of Mennonites under Francis Daniel Pastorious founded the settlement of Germantown just east of the Schuylkill River. The Mennonite sect shared many beliefs with Quakers, including pacifism and the separation of church and state. Over time, as both Germantown and Philadelphia grew, the former was absorbed into the latter.

What began as a trickle of German immigrants soon became a flood. At first most German settlers came for religious freedom. German Baptists journeyed west from Philadelphia to settle Ephrata. Nearby were the Amish, members of the most conservative Mennonite order, who put down roots around Lancaster. German Moravians, or United Brethren, founded Bethlehem northwest of Philadelphia. The Germans, in a mislabeling that endures to this day, became known as Pennsylvania Dutch, from the word *Deutsch*, for German.

After 1700 increasing numbers of German immigrants came for economic reasons. Both colonial landholders and shipping firms sent agents up the Rhine River to recruit German settlers. Peasant farmers in the principalities of Baden, the Palatinate, and Württemberg along the upper Rhine responded to the agents' glowing descriptions of America. Thousands, weary of the grinding poverty brought by heavy taxation

THE WALKING PURCHASE

Few episodes better illustrate the trickery often used by colonists to take Indian lands than the Walking Purchase. In the 1730s Thomas Penn, son of William Penn and second proprietor of Pennsylvania, wanted to sell tracts of land north of Philadelphia to pay off family debts in England. The territory coveted by Penn, however, belonged to the Delaware Indians. He was constrained from just seizing the land by the principle of just compensation in Indian dealings established by his father.

Instead, Penn unearthed an old deed from 1686 by which the Delaware had sold a tract of land at the fork of the Lehigh and Delaware rivers. The vague deed said the tract was bounded on the east by the Delaware River and "doth extend itself back into the woods as far as a man can go in a day and a half." It was not unusual for such deeds to include walking as a measurement of distance understood by Indians. Penn prevailed upon the Delaware to accept the old sale and to agree to a walking of the tract to determine its extent. The Delaware were led to believe by a doctored map that the area would be much smaller than anticipated by Penn.

Unknown to the Indians, Penn hired three of the best walkers in the colony and secretly had a trail cleared so they could cover more ground. A prize of 500 acres was promised to the men who walked the farthest in the allotted time, thus gaining Penn the largest possible tract. On September 19, 1737, the three walkers set forth to the northwest from Wrightstown, across the Delaware from Trenton, at a breakneck pace. They were accompanied by Indian and colonial observers. The Indians soon protested that the walkers were violating the spirit of the deed's language, which meant the distance an average man walked in an average day, but to no avail.

At the end of the first day the two lead walkers had covered 40 miles, reaching a spot near present-day

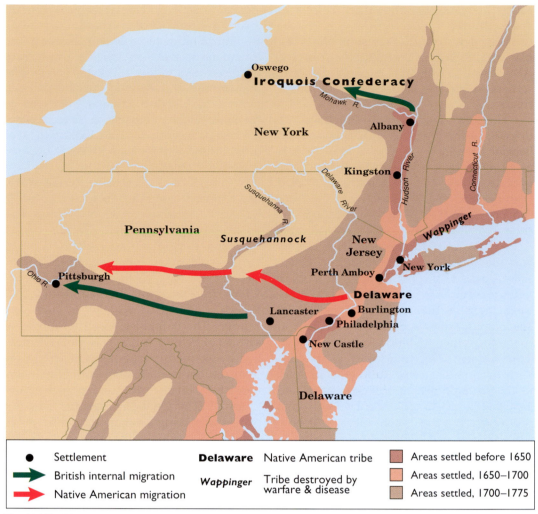

The Middle Colonies

Legend:
- ● Settlement
- → British internal migration (green arrow)
- → Native American migration (red arrow)
- **Delaware** Native American tribe
- *Wappinger* Tribe destroyed by warfare & disease
- ▨ Areas settled before 1650
- ▨ Areas settled, 1650–1700
- ▨ Areas settled, 1700–1775

and the seemingly endless wars that swept across the region, chose to pursue a better life in the New World. Most immigrated to Pennsylvania, but numbers journeyed also to New York as well as the Carolinas and Georgia. Among the boatloads of America-bound migrants heading down the Rhine were German-speaking Swiss farmers from even farther up the river.

Pennsylvania recruiters also found willing immigrants among the poverty-stricken Scotch-Irish of northern Ireland. The Scotch-Irish began arriving in Pennsylvania after 1717. Most settled on the frontier west of the Susquehanna River. Scotch-Irish settlers were also brought to New York, where they carved out farms on the frontier north of Albany. The region's diversity was further heightened by Scottish indentured servants and farmers who, recruited by large landholders in New Jersey, eventually formed a sizable Scottish community in the northeast part of the colony.

The southeastern corner of Pennsylvania was largely settled by the mid-1700s. Lancaster, with some 3,000 inhabitants in 1760, was the largest inland town in British

America. Philadelphia, with a population of almost 19,000, was the largest and most prosperous city in the colonies. Expansion continued in the 1760s as settlers from Connecticut began to move into the upper Susquehanna valley.

The area south of the Delaware River, now the state of Delaware, was acquired by Penn from the Duke of York in 1682. Delaware became a separate colony in 1701, but its settlement remained very much tied to the peopling of Pennsylvania.

Penn's insistence on straightforward dealings with the Native Americans helped produce generally peaceful relations. Still, the burgeoning colonial presence in the Delaware valley compelled the Delaware Indians to migrate westward to the Susquehanna River. In the mid–1700s, with settlers again pushing into their lands, the Delaware once more moved west to settle along the Ohio River. The Susquehannock, driven south by the Iroquois in 1675, were largely destroyed by colonists in Virginia and Maryland. A small number of Susquehannocks remained in Lancaster County where, christianized by Moravian missionaries, they became known as Conestoga Indians.

The arrival of the English in New York brought the final dispersal of the remnants of the Wappinger Indians along the Hudson. The English assiduously courted the Iroquois Confederacy in northern New York. The confederacy, also known as the League of Five Nations, comprised from east to west the Mohawk, Oneida, Onondaga, Cayuga, and Seneca tribes. The confederacy expanded to six tribes in 1722 with the addition of the Tuscarora, who had migrated north to New York from North Carolina after defeat in the Tuscarora War (1711–13). The English viewed the Iroquois tribes as indispensable allies in their long colonial struggle against the French. A small fur-trading settlement was founded at Fort Oswego on Lake Ontario in 1725, but the English were careful not to intrude on Iroquois lands. White encroachment on northwestern New York would wait until after the American Revolution.

Small numbers of black slaves were held in all the Middle Colonies. Most were servants or domestics, although some toiled as agricultural laborers, particularly in New Jersey and Delaware. There were small, free black communities in New York and Philadelphia.

William Penn, for all his vaunted humanism, was a slaveholder. By the mid-1700s, though, the Quakers had condemned slavery and forbidden slave ownership to their members. Quakers assumed a leading position in the fight against slavery that they would hold until its abolition in the Civil War. The first antislavery society in America was organized by Quakers in 1775.

THE SOUTHERN COLONIES

Settlement of the Carolinas began in 1653, when former indentured servants and other poor farmers from Virginia migrated south to the area around Albemarle Sound in present-day northeastern North Carolina. Aided by land grants from the Virginia assembly, eager to secure the young colony's southern frontier, they hewed out small farms and grew tobacco.

In 1663 King Charles II favored a group of eight prominent English figures, all aspiring New World proprietors, with the grant of a charter to Carolina, then defined as the area between Virginia and Spanish Florida. Charleston (named after the king) was founded in 1670. Many of the early settlers came from the English colony of Barbados. The small Caribbean island, by dint

of its lucrative sugar crop, had become overcrowded. Other early colonists included French Huguenots fleeing persecution in France, as well as settlers emigrating directly from England.

Charleston remained a struggling outpost until 1685 when Captain John Thurber brought his ship into the port for repairs. Thurber gave some of the Madagascar seed rice in his cargo to a local inhabitant, Henry Woodward, who planted it. The crop proved ideally suited to the Carolina lowland climate and geography. Within 10 years the blossoming colony was exporting more than 300 tons of rice a year, and soon after the annual volume would be in the millions.

The settlers from Barbados had brought with them their island's slave system, which they applied to the burgeoning rice cultivation. When Native Americans proved ill-suited for slave labor, African slaves were imported from the Caribbean. Charleston became a major slave port and rice became a key crop in the transatlantic slave trade. By 1708, the plantation-based colony along the Carolina coast had about 4,000 settlers and an equal number of black slaves.

By 1740 South Carolina had 25,000 colonists, including a class of wealthy planters who owned upward of 40,000 black slaves. Settlement of the piedmont would dramatically increase the white population in coming decades, but South Carolina's slave character was fixed. The dependency on slavery deepened in 1742 when Eliza Lucas, who oversaw a plantation for her father, succeeded in her efforts to grow indigo (used in dying clothes). Known as "blue gold" after the color of its dye, the crop could be cultivated away from the coast, and slavery moved inland with the indigo plantations.

In 1710 Baron Graffenried of Bern, awarded a Carolina land grant, brought over some 1,000 German and Swiss settlers and founded New Bern. The arrival of the colonists helped trigger the Tuscarora War (1711–13). The decimation of the Tuscarora Indians opened the piedmont of North Carolina, which became a separate colony in 1712, to settlement. The destruction of the Yamasee in 1715 accomplished the same in South Carolina.

The up-country region of North Carolina underwent rapid growth after 1713, as the area drew prospective small farmers unable to compete for land with the great slave plantations of Virginia. The availability of land attracted diverse emigrants. German Moravians settled Salem and its

Allentown. The following morning frontiersman Edward Marshall raced another 20 miles up the Lehigh River to win the 500-acre prize. When a line was surveyed from the point where Marshall stopped back to the Delaware River, Thomas Penn had acquired a half-million acres of Delaware land. The Delaware were powerless to reverse Penn's chicanery. (In an ironic twist, Marshall was also cheated, never receiving his 500 acres.) Resentment over what became known as the Walking Purchase led many Delaware to side with the French in the Seven Years' War.

environs. Scottish Highlanders migrated to the area around present-day Fayetteville. Scotch-Irish and German families from Virginia and Pennsylvania journeyed down the Great Wagon Road to settle in the piedmont region of both Carolinas. Settlers in the South Carolina back country pursued a vigorous trade with Native Americans. Goods and trinkets were exchanged for deerskins, most of which eventually were exported to Europe. This trade was primarily with the Creek, but frontiersmen trekked as far as the Mississippi to barter with the Chickasaw.

The final British colony was the inspiration of soldier and statesman James Edward Oglethorpe. A member of Parliament since 1722, he became interested in the lot of poor debtors, who under the laws of the time were often confined to prison indefinitely. Oglethorpe conceived the idea of a New World colony where debtors could get a fresh start. In 1732 he prevailed on King George II to grant him and 19 associates a charter to the land between the Savannah and Altamaha rivers. While social reform had replaced religious dissidence and the profit motive as the impulse behind colonization, the king was still thinking in strategic terms. His namesake colony, Georgia, would be a bulwark against Spanish Florida to the south.

Oglethorpe and his fellow charter holders, known as the Trustees, offered free Atlantic passage and 50 acres of land to impoverished settlers. Sailing with the first group of colonists, Oglethorpe founded Savannah in 1733. Over the next eight years, the Trustees sent over to Georgia some 1,800 freed debtors and other destitute poor. Another 1,000 colonists came at their own expense.

After 1734 German Lutherans from Salzburg settled New Ebenezer (now Red Bluff) farther up the Savannah River. Scottish Highlanders carved out small farms on

The Southern Colonies

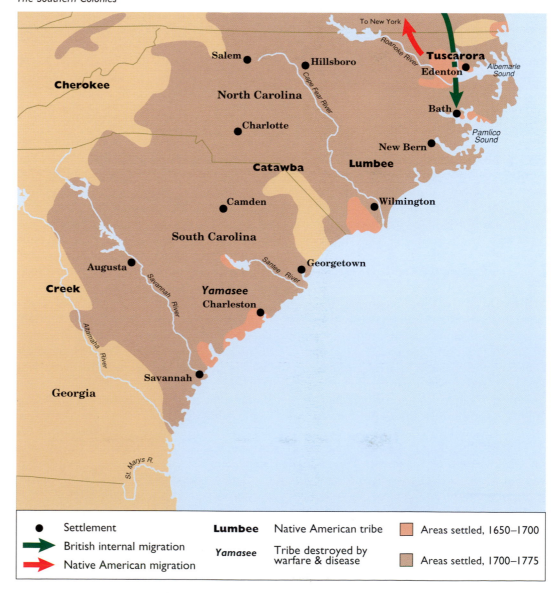

	Settlement	**Lumbee**	Native American tribe		Areas settled, 1650–1700
→	British internal migration	*Yamasee*	Tribe destroyed by warfare & disease		Areas settled, 1700–1775
→	Native American migration				

the Altamaha River below Savannah. Settlement of Georgia was hindered, however, by the Trustees' ban on slavery. South Carolina, with its greater potential wealth from rice and indigo, remained a more powerful lure to colonists.

In 1750 the Trustees rescinded the antislavery law. Two years later they relinquished their charter and Georgia became a royal domain. By 1760 the colony was peopled by 6,000 settlers and 3,600 slaves.

THE WESTERN FRONTIER

The pattern of westward migration that eventually would carry the United States across the continent began in the colonial period. For the first 150 years the British colonies were confined to the coastal strip between the Atlantic Ocean and the Appalachian Mountains. British settlement constantly pushed from the coast inland. What became known as the frontier was the western edge of this expansion. The frontier later would assume an almost mythic place in American lore, becoming ultimately a national metaphor. In simple demographic terms, though, the frontier has generally been defined as an area with not less than two nor more than six inhabitants per square mile.

By 1750 westward expansion had reached the natural barrier of the Appalachians. British colonists soon found their way through the mountains, following the four major natural passages that later would be transited by generations of American settlers. The first route ran along the Mohawk River to Lake Ontario in northern New York. In southern Pennsylvania the Susquehanna and Monongahela valleys helped form a cut in the Appalachians that opened on the future site of Pittsburgh. Just to the south was another natural passage to Pittsburgh along the Potomac and Monongahela rivers. Much farther south the Cum-

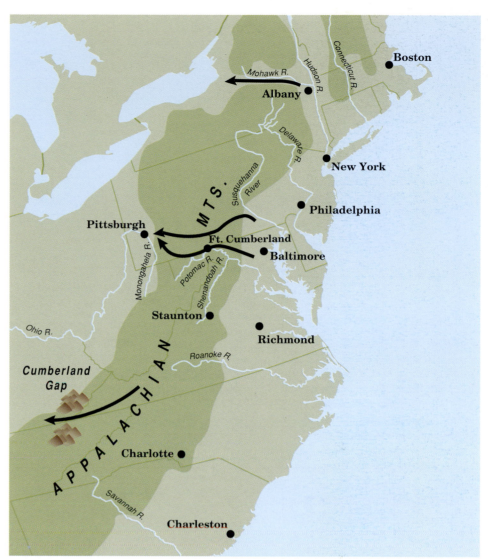

Early Natural Routes West

berland Gap provided a gateway to Kentucky and Tennessee.

The British western frontier crossed the Appalachians in the two decades before the American Revolution. In the late 1740s land companies had been formed to exploit the Ohio valley region. Defeat of the French in the Seven Years' War opened the valley to British settlement. Fort Duquesne, built by

URBAN POPULATION TRENDS IN THE BRITISH COLONIES

Date	New York (1624*)	Boston (1630)	Charleston (1680)	Philadelphia (1682)	Baltimore (1730)
1700	5,000	7,000	2,000	2,000	—
1730	8,500	13,000	4,000	8,500	—
1750	13,300	15,731	8000	13,400	100
1770	21,000	15,520	10,863	28,000	5,000

* Year founded

Sources: *Encyclopedia of American History; Encyclopedia of the North American Colonies*

ABOARD THE *OSGOOD*

Gottlieb Mittelberger joined the great surge of more than 30,000 German settlers who came to Pennsylvania between 1749 and 1754. The young organist and schoolteacher arrived in Philadelphia in 1750, one of almost 500 passengers aboard the ship *Osgood*. Mittelberger was deeply affected by the miseries he witnessed during the long voyage. In 1756 he published an account of his passage, *Journey to Pennsylvania*, that gave an unvarnished portrayal of the hardships faced by German emigrants crossing to America.

Mittelberger recounted how prospective German immigrants first journeyed down the Rhine River to the Dutch seaports of Rotterdam and Amsterdam. There they boarded the *Osgood* and other ships bound for America. The crowding was terrible. Mittelberger described how "the people are packed into the big boats as closely as herring, so to speak. The bedstead of one person is hardly two feet across and six feet long, since many of the boats carry from four to six hundred passengers."

The voyage to Philadelphia took from eight to fifteen weeks. "During the journey," Mittelberger recalled, "the ship is full of pitiful signs of distress— smells, fumes, horrors, vomiting, various kinds of sea sickness, fever, dysentery, headaches, heat, constipation, boils, scurvy, cancer, mouth-rot, and similar afflictions, all of them caused by the age and the highly-salted state of the food, especially of the meat, as well as by the very bad and filthy water, which brings about the miserable destruction and death of many. Add to all that shortage of food, hunger, thirst, frost, heat, dampness, fear, misery, vexation, and lamentation as well as other troubles."

Many were stricken by the diseases that spread in the unsanitary conditions. Mortality rates were especially high among the young. "Children between the ages of one and seven seldom survive the sea voyage; and parents must often watch their offspring suffer miserably, die,

The British Western Frontier

the French at the confluence of the Ohio, Monongahela, and Allegheny rivers, was seized in 1758 and renamed Pittsburgh. During the war British forces built roads along the natural passages through the Appalachians leading to Pittsburgh. Settlers from Virginia and Pennsylvania were soon pouring over these roads into the adjacent valleys. When a land office opened at Pittsburgh in 1769, it was stormed by 3,000 buyers on the first day. By 1770 western Pennsylvania had already been peopled by some 10,000 families.

Tennessee and Kentucky were first settled at the very end of British rule. In the early 1770s colonists from western North Carolina began to move into the environs of the Watauga River in present-day northeastern Tennessee. The Watauga settlements quickly gained several thousand inhabitants. In 1775 frontiersman Daniel Boone, sponsored by the Transylvania Company, an association of North Carolina

land speculators, blazed a trail through the Cumberland Gap to the bluegrass country of Kentucky. Boone founded a small settlement at Boonesborough on April 6, two weeks before the battles of Lexington and Concord launched the American Revolution. The budding migration westward continued during the war. Most of the conflict along the frontier during the Revolution was between British-supported Indian tribes and American colonists. The major campaigns of the war, fought mainly along the coast, rarely had a direct impact on the distant frontier.

COLONIAL TRAVEL

It is hard today to comprehend how difficult it was to travel in colonial times. We are accustomed to a world where we can drive from New York to Philadelphia in several hours. In 1756 the same trip, traveling by coach 18 hours a day (on one of the best roads in the colonies), took 3 days. While colonial-era transportation systems saw steady improvement, often spurred by the vast numbers seeking to migrate, the ability to move from one place to another still depended on wind, water, and, quite literally, horsepower.

The voyage across the Atlantic for prospective immigrants was arduous and often harrowing. Except for those few who could afford private quarters, most sailed in steerage, on the narrow decks below the main deck. Headroom was seldom more than five feet. Conditions were cramped, unsanitary, and there was little recourse against the stifling heat in summer or the bitter cold in winter. Drinking water, often contaminated, was severely rationed. The meager diet, most often biscuits, salt pork, and oatmeal, left passengers weak and depleted. Scurvy and malnutrition were common and more serious diseases were always a threat.

The *Mayflower* was typical of oceangoing ships in the early 1600s. She was 96 feet long at the waterline by 25 feet wide, had three masts, and displaced some 200 tons. As in the famous voyage of the Pilgrims, she carried about 100 passengers crammed into her hold. Much larger ships were developed over the next 150 years. Constructed with multiple decks and displacing over 400 tons, they could transport upward of 500 passengers. Still, these three-masted vessels could average only two to five knots per hour, depending on the winds. The transatlantic crossing took the same time, about nine weeks, in 1770 that it had in 1680. Colonial-era ships were very seaworthy and very few were actually lost at sea.

Navigation also improved in the colonial period. Sea compasses and ship logs were refined and more precise instruments for measuring latitude (position north or south) were devised. Longitude (position east and west) remained a problem. It was not until the 1760s that accurate shipboard chronometers were developed, allowing the determination of longitude and, by extension, a ship's exact location at sea.

Much of the travel within colonial America was along rivers. Canoes, dugouts, rafts, barges, and small boats of various types were used. The first roads were based on Indian trails. Settlers moved by foot, horseback, and cart. By the early 1700s limited road networks were emerging that connected the major towns. Roads in colonial America were of varied quality, ranging from little more than frontier trails

to coach-bearing turnpikes, but all were built of dirt and sand, with the better routes reinforced at times with wooden logs. By the 1770s there were several major long roads in the colonies. The Great Eastern Road ran from New York City to Portsmouth, New Hampshire. The Great Wagon Road (essentially following old Indian trails) extended from Philadelphia through the back country of Virginia and the Carolinas to Augusta, Georgia.

The greater availability of roads led to the growing presence of wagons. The Conestoga wagon, developed by German settlers around Lancaster, gained widespread use in Pennsylvania, as well as Virginia and the Carolinas. The covered, high-wheeled, boat-shaped Conestoga could haul more than any other wagon. Still, a fully loaded Conestoga, drawn by a team of four to sev-

and be thrown into the ocean, from want, hunger, thirst, and the like. I myself, alas, saw such a pitiful fate overtake thirty-two children on board our vessel, all of whom were finally thrown into the sea."

In a description that would echo in the arrival of countless immigrant ships over the next 170 years, Mittelberger captured the relief and joy felt by the haggard passengers at the end of their ordeal. "When at last after the long and difficult voyage the ships finally approach land, when one gets to see the headlands for the sight of which the people on board had longed so passionately, then everyone crawls from below to the deck, in order to look at the land from afar. And people cry for joy, pray, and sing praises and thanks to God."

Major Colonial Trails and Roads

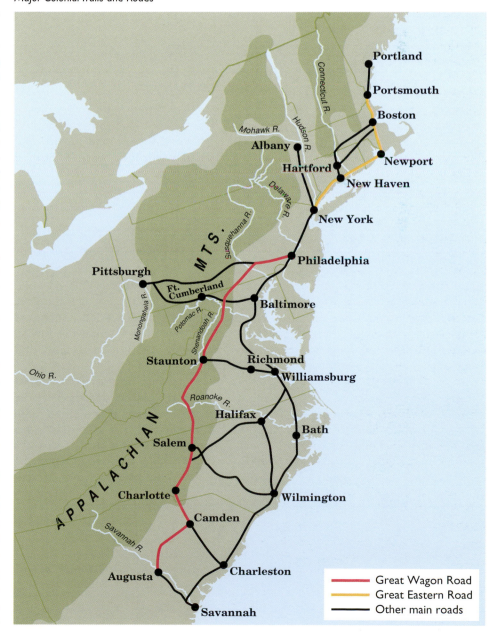

Great Wagon Road
Great Eastern Road
Other main roads

EUROPEAN ANCESTRY OF THE U.S. POPULATION IN 1790

STATE	NATIONAL OR LINGUISTIC STOCK AS % OF POPULATION								
	English	Welsh	Scotch-Irish	Scottish	Irish	German	Dutch	French	Swedish
Maine	77.6	2.2	8.4	4.2	4.8	1.2	—	1.6	—
New Hampshire	81.4	2.3	8.0	4.0	3.7	0.1	—	0.5	—
Vermont	81.4	3.5	7.3	3.6	3.6	0.2	0.2	0.2	—
Massachusets	84.4	5.3	5.3	2.7	2.5	0.3	0.1	1.2	—
Rhode Island	79.9	2.3	7.0	3.5	2.6	0.1	—	4.6	—
Connecticut	87.1	3.1	4.5	2.2	2.1	0.4	0.1	0.5	—
New York	50.3	3.4	8.7	4.3	4.1	9.1	15.9	4.2	—
New Jersey	50.6	3.6	6.8	3.4	4.1	6.5	20.1	3.8	1.1
Pennsylvania	25.8	3.6	15.1	7.6	7.1	38.0	1.3	0.9	0.6
Delaware	63.3	5.5	9.2	4.6	8.0	2.6	1.3	1.7	3.8
Maryland	52.5	4.6	10.4	5.2	10.9	12.7	0.4	3.0	0.3
Virginia	61.3	6.5	11.7	5.9	6.8	4.5	0.7	2.4	0.2
North Carolina	53.2	6.2	15.8	7.9	8.6	5.1	0.4	2.5	0.3
South Carolina	47.6	6.2	18.9	9.4	8.2	5.5	0.2	3.7	0.3
Georgia	58.6	7.9	12.2	6.1	8.6	3.5	0.1	2.6	0.4
Kentucky	54.8	3.6	16.5	8.3	9.0	4.9	1.2	1.5	0.2
Tennessee	50.6	4.8	17.8	8.9	8.7	6.6	1.3	0.9	0.4
United States	59.7	4.3	10.5	5.3	5.8	8.9	3.1	2.1	0.3

Sources: *Encyclopedia of American History; Encyclopedia of the North American Colonies*

en horses, was fortunate to make 30 miles in a day. The Conestoga's impact would extend far beyond the colonial period, as it was the precursor for the covered wagon of Oregon Trail fame.

AMERICAN INDEPENDENCE

The American Revolution (1775–83) had many causes. Among these was migration. The Declaration of Independence included in its list of grievances against the British crown royal emigration, western land, and Indian policies.

The war stopped migration to America. It also briefly halted the slave trade. Most Native Americans tribes sided with the British, seeing in the colonists a far greater threat to their own lands and ways of life. The notable exception were the Delaware, who became the first Indian tribe to sign a treaty with the new American government in 1778. A separate American Indian policy began in 1775 when the Continental Congress formed an Indian Department, patterned on the similar British institution.

Thousands of colonists, known as Loyalists, remained obedient to the British crown during the Revolution. During and just after the war some 100,000 left America for Canada, Florida (then under British control), and Europe. Most departed voluntarily, but the hostility faced by Loyalists in the war's aftermath could not help but spur the decision to leave.

Under the Treaty of Paris (1783) ending the American Revolution, the United States not only won its independence, but also took possession of all British territory running west to the Mississippi and stretching from Canada to Florida. This vast territorial acquisition .would profoundly shape American migration in coming years.

OPEN DOOR AND ENDLESS ROOM
Migration, 1783 to 1845

The United States from the first was an experiment. The fledgling nation would test the revolutionary idea that "we the people" were capable of self-government. Migration soon would make this experiment even more complex and challenging. In 1782 Congress adopted as the motto on the newly designed seal of the United States the Latin phrase *E Pluribus Unum* (one out of many). The motto at the time was understood to signify the formation of a single nation out of the 13 original states. Later, as migration made the nation ever more diverse, the motto came to embody America's struggle to build a pluralistic society.

The American Revolution contributed to the sense of a unique national identity emerging in the United States. America, the first New World nation, was seen as different from and better than the Old World of Europe. Europe represented continued political despotism, religious intolerance, and a large peasantry locked at the bottom of a class society. America in contrast was a noble experiment in freedom, whose liberty and opportunity should be shared by all coming to its shores. The idea of the United States as a sanctuary for the world's oppressed would become a central part of the nation's self-image.

U.S. migration policy during the years 1789 to 1845 encouraged both immigration and westward expansion. America's door was wide open to prospective immigrants. Also wide open was the Western frontier. America was a place of seemingly endless room, made even more so by the addition of the Louisiana Purchase in 1803.

drafted for the purpose of forming, as its preamble states, "a more perfect union."

The Constitution, which took effect in 1789, had a profound impact on American migration. Most significant was its implicit guarantee of the right of internal migration. Today, Americans take for granted the ability to move wherever they want in the United States. This freedom was by no means assured in the 18th century. The Constitution's "privileges and immunities" clause ensured that no state could erect legal, religious, or other barriers to the migration of citizens from other states. On this provision has rested the historic mobility of Americans.

For one group there was no freedom of movement. The Constitution left slavery intact. It would take a civil war to begin to fulfill the promise of a more perfect union for millions of African Americans.

The Constitution assigned several specific powers affecting migration to the newly invigorated federal government. It was given control over all territories belonging to the United States. It also received responsibility for Indian affairs, the admission of new states, and naturalization.

Since the Constitution did not specifically delegate the power to control immigration to the federal government, supervision was left largely to the states for almost a century. A growing number of immigrants and the need for national immigration procedures brought federal control over immigration starting in the 1870s. Federal administration was justified under the regulation of foreign commerce clause.

A MORE PERFECT UNION

In 1781 the Continental Congress adopted the Articles of Confederation to provide a formal framework for the governance of the United States. Under the articles the various state governments remained dominant, with a weak federal government embodied in a Confederation Congress. By 1787 it was clear that the articles were unequal to building a new nation and the Constitution was

THE OPEN DOOR

The United States had a basic policy of free or open immigration throughout its first century. The nation's ports and borders were completely open. Anyone could come. Anyone could stay. No formal records of immigration were kept until 1820, following passage of the federal Steerage Act requiring the listing of all arriving ship passengers by country of origin.

The Northwest Ordinance (1787) contained land and other provisions intended to attract foreigners to the Northwest Territory. Subsequent federal land policies continued to communicate American openness to immigrants. Liberal naturalization laws held out the promise of full citizenship. The Constitution made every elective office but the presidency available to naturalized citizens.

Immigrants were actively recruited. Many states sent representatives to Europe to enlist prospective settlers. Shipping lines, railroads, and major industries also became active in immigrant recruitment. Immigrants came for the most basic human reasons—political or religious freedom, economic opportunity, the chance for a better life. Many fled famine, the ravages of war, or the dislocations brought by industrialization. Various European governments at times encouraged emigration to alleviate their own overcrowding.

The metaphor of a door has long been used to describe U.S. immigration policy. Since America's portals were wide open, its initial embrace of immigration became known as the Open Door policy. The Open Door era extended from 1783 to 1875, when the first federal measure restricting immigration was enacted.

NATURALIZATION

The first Congress convened under the Constitution did not wait long to exercise its authority over naturalization. The Naturalization Act of 1790 established uniform national rules governing how aliens could become U.S. citizens. The measure signaled the young republic's openness to immigration, setting a two-year residency requirement for naturalization. The law limited naturalization to "free white persons," manifesting an institutional racism that would mar U.S. immigration policy for almost two centuries.

The Naturalization Act of 1795 extended the residency requirement to five years. This was increased to 14 years by the Naturalization Act of 1798. The law was one of the four Alien and Sedition Acts passed during a period of worsening relations with France. The acts, which reflected concern over possible divided loyalties among newly arriving Europeans who might be sympathetic to France, allowed the president to deport or detain aliens deemed a threat to the nation's safety. Following the resolution of tensions with France in 1800, the acts were repealed or allowed to lapse. Under the Naturalization Act of 1802, the residency period reverted to five years, which has

remained the basic time requirement ever since.

U.S. IMMIGRATION 1790–1819

Official U.S. immigration statistics date from 1820, when public authorities began maintaining records of alien passenger arrivals. Approximate figures for immigration prior to 1820 were reconstructed by the Census Bureau in 1860, based on a "survey of the irregular data previous to 1819" (ship logs, passenger manifests, court records, etc.).

Years	Total # Immigrants	% of Total Population
1790–1799	42,750	0.8
1800–1809	59,850	0.8
1810–1819	97,470	1.0

Sources: *Encyclopedia of American History; Historical Statistics of the United States*

EARLY IMMIGRATION

Although America's door was open, the volume of immigrants actually crossing the threshold remained comparatively light until after 1820. Perhaps somewhere on the order of 30,000 came in the 1780s. Estimates of the total number of immigrants arriving between 1789 and 1820, when official statistics were first kept, range from 200,000 to 250,000. Almost all were from northwestern Europe.

Several factors worked to limit immigration in America's first decades. Foremost were the French Revolutionary Wars (1792–1802) and Napoleonic Wars (1803–15), which convulsed most of Europe. The wars also curtailed transatlantic shipping.

Both Great Britain and France, concerned over the loss of population, actively discouraged emigration. British migration policy after 1783 aimed at preventing the United States from developing into an industrial rival. However, measures enacted in 1783 and 1795 barring the departure of skilled workers were easily circumvented by determined emigrants. Much more effective was the Passenger Act of 1803. Mandating improvements in sanitary and other conditions, it served to limit the number of passengers British vessels could carry.

The overwhelming majority of the early immigrants were Scotch-Irish. Throughout the 1780s and 1790s, an average of about 5,000 Scotch-Irish a year set sail for American ports. Many were artisans or craftsmen, especially weavers. Most were fare-paying passengers rather than indentured servants. The Scotch-Irish servant trade, which had begun to decline before the American Revolution, had ceased entirely by 1800. British restrictions during the first decade of the 19th century significantly limited Scotch-Irish emigration, which dropped to around 1,000 annually. By 1811, with growing numbers of U.S. ships calling at Irish ports in search of passengers, annual Scotch-Irish emigration had again climbed above 5,000. Both the increasing size of ships and the easing of British migration policy after 1815 would facilitate the surge of Irish migration to America that began in the 1820s. The Scotch-Irish, as the Protestants from northern Ireland were known in America, would continue to dominate Irish immigration until the mid-1830s, after which Irish Catholics came to predominate.

Many of the roughly 150,000 Scotch-Irish who arrived before 1819 joined the Scotch-Irish settlements on the frontiers of Pennsylvania, Virginia, and the Carolinas. Substantial numbers settled in the cities of New York, Baltimore, Philadelphia, and Pittsburgh, which became a Scotch-Irish stronghold.

Much smaller numbers of English, French, and Germans also made their way to America. Continuing U.S.-British antagonisms after the American Revolution limited the number of English newcomers through the War of 1812. What had been a sustained German migration to colonial America in the mid-1700s also fell to low levels during these years. Both English and German immigration would take dramatic upturns after 1815.

WESTWARD EXPANSION

Many early immigrants, like generations of native-born settlers, headed west. Westward expansion became the dominant feature of American migration in the nation's first half-century. By 1845, American settlers had peopled the Old Northwest and Old Southwest, surged across the Mississippi valley, and joined Texas to the Union. The relentless push of the United States across the continent raised the vexatious issue of the extension of slavery, eventually precipitating the Civil War. It also doomed innumerable Native Americans to destruction or forced relocation on reservations.

The United States in 1783 still hugged the Atlantic seaboard. Americans saw the continent stretching to their west as a savage, virgin wilderness awaiting their taming and development. The frontier was the western edge of settlement, "the meeting point," in the words of historian Frederick Jackson Turner, "between savagery and civilization." American settlement moved across the continent in a series of regional frontiers. These frontiers overlapped in both geography and time. Before one had been fully occupied, another was being opened by fur trappers, miners, or cattlemen.

First penetrated was the Appalachian frontier (1783–1815), reaching from the Appalachians to the Mississippi. The Louisiana Purchase extended America's boundaries across the river, spurring settlement of the Mississippi valley frontier (1803–45). With the discovery of passable routes west through the Rocky Mountains, new waves of settlers continued on to the Far Western frontier (1825–65). Last subdued was the Great Plains frontier (1865–90), the arid, treeless expanse between the Mississippi and Rockies initially deemed uninhabitable.

Settlement of the frontier was not a single mass movement from east to west, but more a human tide that crept across the continent. At times this tide surged forward almost irresistibly. Between 1800 and

U.S. Territorial Expansion

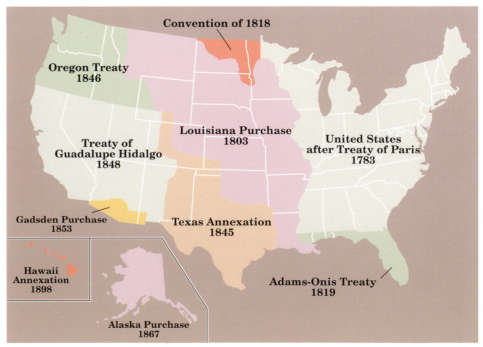

1860, the frontier advanced steadily westward at an average rate of 17 miles a year. While the ranks of pioneers were constantly replenished by easterners and immigrants, over time many westward-heading migrants were the offspring of earlier pioneers who had settled on what was then the frontier. Often, families moved more than once. The experience of Abraham Lincoln (whose frontier background figured in his 1860 presidential campaign) was not uncommon. Born in Kentucky in 1809, Lincoln moved with his family to Indiana in 1816, and then to Illinois in 1830.

Millions joined in the movement westward, which dwarfed earlier American migrations. Most were family farmers, eager for a small plot of land. More often than not, they followed on the heels of earlier pioneers. The frontier generally was peopled in stages. First into the wilderness were hunters, trappers, and fur traders. In the Far West especially, miners were also often in the vanguard, as the discovery of gold or other valuable minerals would bring a rush of prospectors into unsettled areas. Cattlemen pioneered the open ranges of the Great Plains. Behind the trappers, miners, and ranchers came the farmers. The arrival of town dwellers and the development of urban life marked the final passage from frontier to settlement.

Americans for generations subscribed to a history of westward expansion as the story of everyday pioneers struggling to subdue an unruly but bountiful wilderness. More recently, we have come to recognize that this traditional version was incomplete. Much had been omitted. The West was largely wilderness, but it was not uninhabited. Instead, it was home to scores of Native American tribes. Spanish settlers had lived in the Southwest since the 1500s. America's westward migration was as much conquest as it was the taming of "a golden land." The word pioneer, tellingly, derives from the Old French *peonier*, for foot soldier.

The West was a diverse place. Left out of most historical accounts until only recently was the role of African Americans on the frontier. The human tide that flowed into the West came from the Pacific as well as the Atlantic. Historian Patricia Nelson Limerick has recast Turner's classic formulation of the meeting place between savagery and civilization. "The American West was an important meeting ground, the point where Indian America, Latin America, Anglo-America, Afro-America, and Asia intersected."

PUBLIC LAND POLICY

The West, whether wilderness or meeting ground, was a fabulously large expanse of land that for early Americans seemed to stretch forever beyond the Appalachians. The frontier raised basic questions. Who owned this land? How would it be surveyed, sold, settled? How would it be governed? Many factors—from geography and climate to politics, economics, and religion—influenced the flow of people westward. None had a more central or enduring impact than public land policy.

The disposition of the West dominated the Confederation Congress through its brief tenure. It was in public land policy that the largely ineffectual government made its only real mark. The need for action was manifest. The Continental Congress had promised land bounties of 100 to 500 acres to all soldiers who would serve in the Continental Army. Similar tracts had been pledged by various states. With the end of hostilities in 1783, veterans were clamoring for land grants in the unsettled tracts beyond the Appalachians.

The desperate need for revenue also spurred political organization of the West. The sale of public lands offered the Confederation Congress, beset by heavy war debts, its only real source of potential funds. Even as the weak national government turned its attention to the West, settlers were taking matters into their own hands. In 1784 George Washington traveled to the Ohio valley to check on prewar landholdings. Everywhere he found cleared fields, rows of corn, herds of cattle, and settlers homesteading on small farms. In a correspondence to the Confederation Congress, Washington observed "The spirit for emigration is great, and tho' you cannot stop the road, it is yet in your power to mark the way; a little while and you will not be able to do either."

The same year a congressional committee under Thomas Jefferson drafted a plan for settlement of the West. Jefferson was the apostle of an American democracy based on an agrarian society of independent, small farmers. The draft plan, which served as the basis for the historic Confederation land ordinances, reflected Jefferson's belief that the West was "an immensity of land courting the industry of the husbandman." The plan called for carving new, coequal states out of the Western domain. Most importantly, it proposed the division of Western lands into small townships of individual-sized lots so as to favor settlement by family farmers.

The Land Ordinance of 1785 established the basic procedures that would govern the distribution of Western lands for more than a century. Public lands were to be surveyed in townships six miles square. Each township would be divided into 36 numbered sections of 640 acres each. Surveying would follow a rectangular system, as the townships were to be measured off in north-south rows known as ranges. The principle of rectangular survey prior to sale derived from the more egalitarian village land system of colonial New England, in contrast to the "indiscriminate location" system that permitted the larger estates of the plantation South.

The ordinance foresaw a Jeffersonian nation of small landowners. Land was to be sold at public auction, making it as available to individual settlers as to large land companies or speculators. The minimum-sized purchase of a 640-acre section, at $1 an acre, likewise was intended for individual buyers. A stipulation that the revenue from one section in each township be set aside for a school reflected an early commitment to public education. In the coming decades, Congress would change the minimum acreage, purchase price, and credit terms, but the fundamental tenets guiding the sale of public lands would hold.

Surveying began in 1785 in the area of present-day eastern Ohio. By 1786 all state claims to land north of the Ohio River had been formally ceded, finalizing the transfer of the area to the national domain. The region between the Ohio and Mississippi rivers and the Great Lakes became known as the Old Northwest. In 1787 the Ohio Company, a land company formed by war veterans, offered to purchase 1.5 million acres in Ohio. The normally lethargic Confederation Congress was quick to respond, strapped as it was for funds. The proposed sale underscored the need for the political organization of the West. The Land Ordinance of 1785 had provided for the distribution of western lands, but not for their governance.

The landmark Northwest Ordinance, enacted in 1787, established the Old Northwest as the Northwest Territory and outlined provisions for its government. Ultimately, from three to five states were to be created out of the vast domain. Newly settled areas would be called territories until they qualified for statehood. Territories could petition for admission to the Union, "on a equal footing with the original states," on attaining a population of 60,000. Until statehood, territories were to be administered by federally appointed gover-

MAJOR LAND LEGISLATION

LAND ORDINANCE OF 1785 Basic land ordinance that established the rectangular system used in the surveying of the American West. Public lands were to be divided into townships 6 miles square, which in turn would be subdivided into 36 lots of 640 acres each. The minimum-sized piece of land that could be purchased was 640 acres, while the price of land was set at $1 an acre.

LAND ACT OF 1796 Raised the minimum price of government land to $2 an acre. Although a credit system was established that allowed up to one year for payment, the high price of land favored speculators over settlers.

HARRISON LAND ACT (1800) Revision of federal land sale policies intended to make it easier for settlers to acquire land. It reduced the size of the minimum lot that could be purchased to 320 acres and authorized credit terms of up to four years.

LAND ACT OF 1804 Further reduced the size of the minimum lot for sale to 160 acres and lowered the price of land to $1.64 an acre.

LAND ACT OF 1820 Abolished the credit system for land purchases. To counterbalance the impact on individual settlers, the minimum lot for sale was reduced to 80 acres and the price of land was fixed at $1.25 an acre.

PREEMPTION ACT OF 1841 Endorsed the principle of preemption, under which squatters had prior rights to public lands. Many settlers moved west ahead of government surveyors and occupied parts of the public domain as squatters. The act authorized squatters to stake claims to newly surveyed lands and to purchase up to 160 acres at $1.25 an acre.

GRADUATION ACT OF 1854 Authorized the sale of less desirable public lands at lower prices. Lands that had remained unsold for 10 years or more were to be offered at decreasing prices, with a base price of 12 1/2 cents an acre for lots on the market more than 30 years.

HOMESTEAD ACT (1862) Implemented the free-soil principle that the government should provide land to those willing to settle and cultivate it. The law offered free homesteads of 160 acres to settlers who lived on the land at least five years.

DESERT LAND ACT (1877) Authorized individuals to acquire up to 640 acres in desert parts of the West at 25 cents an acre, provided the land was irrigated within three years.

FOREST RESERVE ACT (1891) First federal land conservation legislation, it permitted the president to close timber areas to settlement and to establish them as national parks.

NATIONAL RECLAMATION ACT (1902) Set aside the revenue from land sales in 16 western states for irrigation projects. The law was intended to facilitate settlement in arid areas by making low-cost water available.

ENLARGED HOMESTEAD ACT (1909) Increased the size of free homesteads in selected western states to 320 acres. This was done largely to satisfy Western cattle interests seeking grazing lands.

STOCK-RAISING HOMESTEAD ACT (1916) Permitted homesteads of 640 acres in parts of the West when the land was to be used for grazing or forage.

TAYLOR GRAZING ACT (1934) Provided for 80 million acres (later increased to 142 million acres) of federally held grazing lands under the administration of the Interior Department.

ROOSEVELT EXECUTIVE ORDER (1935) Withdrew the remaining public domain from private entry for purposes of conservation. The action ended homesteading on public lands.

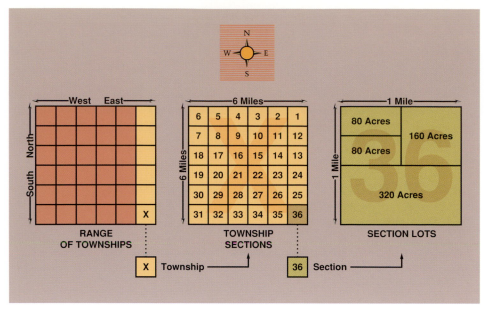

Range and Township System

from Western plantations. This article would have far-reaching consequences for the emerging sectional political struggle over slavery's extension as the United States expanded territorially.

Both of the Confederation ordinances remained in effect following enactment of the new federal Constitution in 1789. The Northwest Ordinance, excepting its ban on slavery, would serve as the framework for the extension of American governance to other western territories.

While Jefferson was envisioning a land of small farmers, Alexander Hamilton, the first secretary of the treasury, had a very different vision of America. Hamilton believed that the United States's future stability and prosperity lay in a strong national government and dynamic capitalist growth. For Hamilton, the West represented an opportunity for economic development as well as a source of government revenue.

Hamilton's fiscal policies put the United States on a firm financial footing. The sale of public lands remained a key source of revenue. In 1796 Congress increased the price of land to $2 an acre. The higher price

nors. The ordinance, which effectively opened the Northwest Territory to settlement, guaranteed freedom of worship and public education to prospective inhabitants. It also prohibited slavery in the territory, as Southern states did not want competition

ADDING STARS TO THE BARS

The first U.S. flag, designed in 1777, had 13 stripes and 13 stars, signifying the 13 newly independent colonies. Beginning with the admission of Vermont and Kentucky to the Union in the early 1790s, additional stars and stripes were added to represent the new states. As the number of states quickly grew, it became evident that the flag would become burdened with stripes, or bars. In 1818 Congress ordered that the flag henceforth should have 13 stripes, symbolizing the 13 original states, and one star for each current and new state.

American migration can be tracked in the addition of stars to the bars. Both territorial status and statehood were contingent on population. All but six new states went through the territorial process first outlined in the Northwest Ordinance. Vermont and Kentucky, already settled by the 1790s, were added directly to the Union. Maine was separated from Massachusetts and West Virginia from Virginia. Texas was admitted after a decade as an independent republic and California gained statehood after acquisition from Mexico.

Settlement of the United States did not advance directly across the American continent. The Old Northwest and Old Southwest were populated first, but after settlement of Texas and the Mississippi valley, pioneers crossed through the Great Plains and Rockies to reach Oregon Country and California. America was then peopled from the coasts inward, as settlers gradually filled up the Great Plains. Last settled was the Southwest.

	Territory	State
Vermont		1791
Kentucky		1792
Tennessee	1790	1796
Ohio	1787	1802
Louisiana	1805	1812
Indiana	1800	1816
Mississippi	1798	1817
Illinois	1809	1818

in practice favored land speculators over actual settlers, most of whom could not afford a 640-acre plot. The 1796 law also began a tradition of locating land offices in the West, near the actual tracts for sale. From initial sites at Pittsburgh and Cincinnati, federal land offices would move across the continent with the tide of American expansion.

High land prices were increasingly subject to pressures created by the desire of ever larger numbers to move westward. A popular political clamor would lead the Congress to make western lands ever more available to ordinary settlers. Many in Congress also favored measures to encourage westward migration as part of a larger policy of national expansion. By 1820 the minimum lot for sale had been reduced to 80 acres, at $1.25 an acre. The practice of awarding land bounties to veterans continued. Many Revolutionary War veterans had received land grants in Ohio. After the War of 1812, land was set aside for veterans in Michigan, Illinois, and Missouri.

Often the press of settlers heading west pushed beyond the government surveyors and land offices into unsurveyed areas.

Those who settled on unsurveyed lands (and thus did not pay for them) became known as "squatters." Later, when the lands were surveyed and put up for sale, the squatters would insist they had prior rights. Their position drew considerable support among an American public that widely embraced the image of the hardy pioneer carving out a homestead in the West. In 1841 Congress recognized the rights of squatters, permitting them to purchase up to 160 acres of already settled land at the time of survey.

OLD NORTHWEST

In 1790 the American frontier stretched from western New York down through the Ohio valley to Tennessee. The first census that year revealed that the United States had a population of almost four million spread out along the Atlantic seaboard in a largely rural, agrarian society. Almost all the arable land east of the Appalachians had been cultivated. This pressure on the soil was the primary impetus for the

	Territory	State
Alabama	1817	1819
Maine		1820
Missouri	1812	1821
Arkansas	1819	1836
Michigan	1805	1837
Florida	1822	1845
Texas		1845
Iowa	1838	1846
Wisconsin	1836	1848
California		1850
Minnesota	1849	1858
Oregon	1848	1859
Kansas	1854	1861
West Virginia		1863
Nevada	1861	1864
Nebraska	1854	1867
Colorado	1861	1876
North Dakota	1861	1889
South Dakota	1861	1889
Montana	1864	1889
Washington	1853	1889
Idaho	1863	1890
Wyoming	1868	1890
Utah	1850	1896
Oklahoma	1890	1907
New Mexico	1850	1912
Arizona	1863	1912
Alaska	1912	1959
Hawaii	1900	1959

spillover of American settlers into the undeveloped lands to the west.

In the North the dominant westward migration in the late 1700s was toward western New York. The Iroquois Confederacy, which largely sided with the British during the Revolution, had been broken by American forces. The plight of the Confederacy opened Iroquois tribal lands to white settlement. In the 1790s settlers from New England poured into the Genesee valley region of western New York. The rush of migrants soon became known as "Genesee Fever." The Mohawk River provided the key route west. At the fever's peak in 1795, an average 20 boats a day passed Albany on their way upriver. The flow was not halted by winter, as settlers moved west on sleighs.

The surge of migrants from New England continued into Ohio. American penetration of the Old Northwest had begun in 1788, when the Ohio Company established the settlement of Marietta just across the Ohio River.

The Old Northwest was not unknown territory. The area had been part of New France prior to 1763, and several hundred French families lived in and around Vincennes and Kaskaskia in what was then known as Illinois Country. In 1788 the U.S. government recognized the land holdings of the French, most of whom were farmers.

The British, who had remained in the Old Northwest in violation of Revolutionary War peace terms, represented one of two main barriers to American westward expansion. The other, the Native Americans, were aided and abetted by the British in their struggle to keep their lands. British motives were twofold: to check American growth and to retain control of the fur trade. In 1794 U.S. forces crushed Indian resistance in the Ohio region at the Battle of Fallen Timbers near present-day Toledo. The same year the British finally agreed in Jay's Treaty to evacuate their military posts in the Old Northwest. Tensions over the U.S.-Canadian border would persist for decades.

Settlement of Ohio accelerated rapidly after 1794. In 1800 the population had reached more than 45,000. New Englanders predominated in the north. The northeastern corner of Ohio, known as the Western Reserve, was largely occupied by settlers from Connecticut. Southern Ohio was first peopled by frontier farmers from Virginia and Kentucky. A large swath of southwestern Ohio was reserved for Revolutionary War veterans from Virginia. In a pattern repeated across the West, most Ohioan

Settlement of the Old Northwest

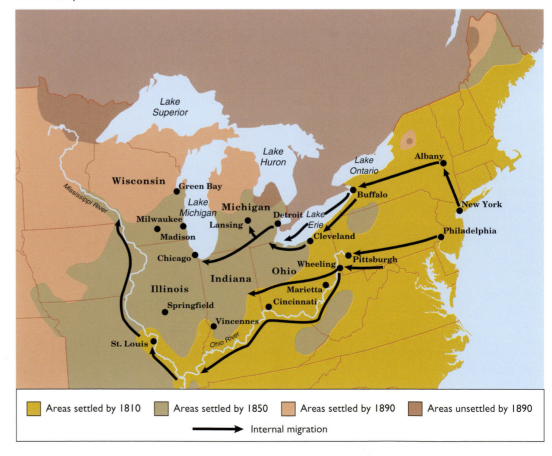

Areas settled by 1810   Areas settled by 1850   Areas settled by 1890   Areas unsettled by 1890

Internal migration

lands were acquired by individual settlers. About 5 percent went to land companies. Many early pioneers were of Scotch-Irish or Pennsylvania German stock. After 1830 the ranks of settlers throughout the Old Northwest included growing numbers of emigrants from Ireland and Germany.

In 1803 Ohio became the first of five states ultimately formed out of the Northwest Territory. The advance of American settlers into Indiana provoked violent opposition by an alliance of Northwest Indian tribes, again backed by the British in Canada. U.S. defeat of the Northwest tribes in 1811 at the Battle of Tippecanoe near present-day Lafayette began the final destruction of Indian resistance to American settlement of the Old Northwest. Competing Anglo-American claims to control of the Great Lakes region flared into open conflict during the War of 1812. Conclusion of the war in 1815 marked the end of British efforts to stem American expansion in the Old Northwest. Remaining Indian opposition to white encroachment into Illinois and Wisconsin was routed in the brief, and one-sided, Black Hawk War (1832).

Both Indiana and Illinois were settled from south to north. The Ohio River served as a great highway bringing pioneers from the states to the south and southeast—Kentucky, Virginia, the Carolinas, and Tennessee. On their heels came settlers from Ohio, Pennsylvania, New York, and, to a lesser degree, New England. The attraction in both states was the abundance of fertile land.

American movement into Michigan began in 1796 when U.S. troops took possession of Detroit from the British. Settlement of Michigan took hold after the War of 1812 and increased steadily in the 1820s as the fur trade gradually was supplanted by farming. At the same time the discovery of lead deposits in southwestern Wisconsin brought American settlers into the Upper Mississippi valley. Early miners who dug caves in the hillsides to survive the harsh winters were called "badgers." Thus was born the popular nickname associated ever since with Wisconsin. The mining of copper and iron likewise underlay the penetration of Michigan's Upper Peninsula in the 1840s. In both Michigan and Wisconsin, lumbering spurred the development of the northern frontier. Northern Wisconsin and Minnesota became known as the Lumbering Frontier.

Access to southern Wisconsin was provided by the Mississippi River. Development of much of northern Wisconsin would await the arrival of the railroad in the early 1850s. Settlement of its northern frontier would continue until the end of the century, but by the mid-1800s the dominant population movement in the Old Northwest involved the rapid emergence of urban centers.

OLD SOUTHWEST

In the South early western migration was also driven by small farmers, most from the backwoods of Virginia and the Carolinas, lured by the promise of inexpensive homesteads beyond the Appalachians. By 1800, though, the character of migration in the South would differ fundamentally from the westward movement of northern free farmers, as settlement of the Old Southwest increasingly rested on the extension of slavery.

The Old Southwest encompassed the area between the Appalachians and the Mississippi from the Ohio River south to Florida. Westward migration into Kentucky and Tennessee had begun in the early 1700s. Settlers crossing the Appalachians through the Cumberland Gap had raised Kentucky's population to 20,000 by 1780. The territory between the Cumberland and Ohio rivers was a hunting ground for various Native American tribes, but home to none, and the influx of American pioneers into Kentucky continued unimpeded throughout the 1780s. Many of the settlers came from Virginia, which considered Kentucky part of its domain. By 1790 Kentucky had some 73,000 inhabitants, including 12,500 slaves. With Virginia foregoing its claim to western lands south of the Ohio River, Kentucky became the first western state in 1792. West Virginia, settled in the drive into the Ohio valley in the late 1700s, remained a part of Virginia until the Civil War.

In 1790 Congress designated the area south of Kentucky the Southwest Territory. Settlement would be similar to the Northwest Territory, except that there was no ban on slavery. Tennessee had a population of about 6,000 backwoods farmers in 1790, concentrated along the Watauga River in the northwest. By 1795 the mounting tide of settlers pouring into the territory had spread across the eastern Tennessee and Cumberland valleys. With a population of more than 60,000, Tennessee became a state in 1796. The Cherokee in the east and the Chickasaw in the west presented minimal resistance to the American advance, surrendering their lands through unequal treaties and land sales. Under the Indian Removal

Policy, both tribes were forcibly relocated to the West in the late 1830s.

The invention in 1793 of the cotton gin, which separated cotton fibers from the seeds, made the mass cultivation of cotton not only possible but also highly profitable. Almost overnight, cotton became the main crop of the Deep South. The production of cotton was labor intensive. In a world where the use of black slaves on tobacco and indigo plantations was already deeply entrenched, cotton planters turned readily to slave labor.

Cotton plantations became a fixture in southern Tennessee. Because cotton was so lucrative, and its soil-depleting cultivation required large tracts of land, the crop spurred settlement of the final two states carved out of the Southwest Territory.

At the dawn of the Early National Period following American independence, the United States and Spain asserted competing territorial prerogatives in the Old Southwest. Spain, having reacquired Florida from Great Britain in 1783, laid claim to a wide swath of territory running north from the Gulf of Mexico. U.S.-Spanish territorial rivalry was resolved through Pinckney's Treaty in 1795. The agreement set the northern boundary of Spanish Florida at the 31st parallel and assured unrestricted U.S. navigation of the Mississippi River through the Spanish-controlled port of New Orleans. Spain's concession on access to the Mississippi was crucial to America's western settlements, whose economic life depended increasingly on free navigation of the river. In 1803 the United States took possession of what had been Spanish Louisiana, opening the Lower Mississippi valley to American settlement.

Cotton plantations quickly spread across southern Mississippi. In 1814 Creek resistance to American penetration of Alabama was dealt a fatal blow at the Battle of Horseshoe Bend on the Tallapoosa River. After the War of 1812, settlers flooded into central Alabama. Known as the Black Belt

Settlement of the Old Southwest

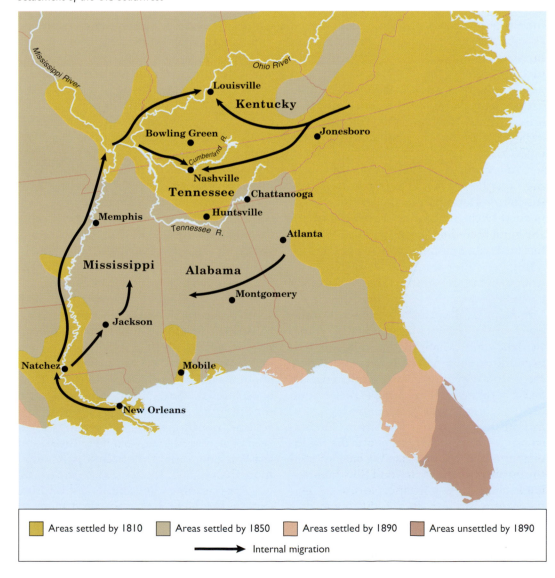

▨ Areas settled by 1810	▨ Areas settled by 1850	▨ Areas settled by 1890	▨ Areas unsettled by 1890

→ Internal migration

because of its rich dark soil, the area became the heart of the South's Cotton Kingdom.

In the 1830s both the Creek in Alabama and the Choctaw in Mississippi were removed to the West. Both states were fully settled by 1850. Interspersed among the cotton plantations were small farms and towns and a handful of modest cities. The Deep South would remain largely rural until well after the Civil War.

LOUISIANA PURCHASE

Twenty years after he helped devise the plan for settlement of the West, President Thomas Jefferson again assumed a central role in America's national expansion. In 1803 the Jefferson administration was able to negotiate the purchase of Louisiana from the French for $12 million.

The acquisition of Louisiana, covering some 828,000 square miles between the Mississippi and Rocky Mountains, roughly doubled the size of the United States. Jefferson's purchase opened the area beyond the Mississippi to American settlement and set the United States on an inevitable course of continental expansion. For Americans, the Louisiana Territory deeply reinforced the sense of the West as a place of endless room.

The purchase treaty left unclear Louisiana's northern and southern boundaries. In the Convention of 1818 the United States and Great Britain defined the northern boundary when they agreed to extend the U.S.–Canadian border from the Lake of the Woods west along the 49th parallel to the Rocky Mountains. As American settlers headed west, disputes over Louisiana's southern boundary would flare into hostilities first with Spain and then with Mexico.

WESTERN EXPLORATION

In 1803 Jefferson already was planning an expedition in search of an overland route to the Pacific Ocean. With the Louisiana Purchase, he expanded the prospective expedition to include exploration of the newly acquired territory. From 1804 to 1806, a small party under Army officers Meriwether Lewis and William Clark crossed the northern Great Plains and Rocky Mountains to reach the Pacific Northwest and then found its way back to St. Louis. The Lewis and Clark Expedition, in addition to proving the feasibility of an overland route across the continent, helped stake the

MAJOR TERRITORIAL ACQUISITIONS

Year	Acquisition	# Acres
1803	Louisiana Purchase	529,911,680
1818	Red River Basin	29,601,920
1819	Spanish Florida	46,144,640
1845	Texas Annexation	249,066,240
1846	Oregon Country	183,386,240
1848	Mexican Cession	338,680,960
1853	Gadsden Purchase	18,988,800
1867	Alaskan Purchase	375,296,000

Source: *Historical Statistics of the United States*

American claim to Oregon Country, opened the Rockies to the fur trade, and stimulated interest in the trans-Mississippi West and its settlement.

Further exploration of the Louisiana Purchase was soon to follow. American reconnaissance of the West was accomplished by government-sponsored expeditions and by independent fur trappers and traders. This exploration served more to influence and shape migration across the continent than it did to chart unknown lands whose basic contours were already known.

In 1806 Lieutenant Zebulon Pike led a small band in search of the sources of the Arkansas and Red rivers. After sighting what later would be known as Pikes Peak, the expedition headed south toward the Red River. Pike and his men soon were imprisoned and detained for several months by Spanish authorities for having crossed illegally into Spanish territory in northern New Mexico. Pike's detention was a harbinger of the impending clash between American expansionist ambitions and Spanish—and then Mexican—territorial claims.

In his 1810 report on the expedition, Pike described the southern Plains as too arid for settlement—an observation repeated by explorer Stephen Long, who in 1820 traversed the region. Long referred to the southern Plains as the "Great American Desert." His description helped dissuade settlement of present-day Nebraska, Kansas, and Oklahoma until the 1850s. The seemingly forbidding terrain of the southern Plains was set aside as Indian Territory in the 1830s.

Fur-trading mountain men first explored much of the northern Rockies and Pacific Northwest. Although a much more formidable barrier than the Appalachians, the Rockies soon yielded passable routes to

THE PATHFINDER

His life touched virtually every aspect of 19th-century American migration. The son of a French immigrant, he helped open the West to settlement, aided in the relocation of Native Americans under the Indian Removal policy, played a prominent role in the great national debate over slavery, and promoted the development of continent-linking railroads.

John C. Frémont was born in Savannah, Georgia, in 1813. After studies at Charleston College, he joined the U.S. Topographical Corps in 1835, where he earned a commission as a second lieutenant. Early on he assisted in the survey of a projected railway line from Charleston to Cincinnati and formed a strong taste for wilderness exploration. He was also part of a Topographical Corps reconnaissance of Cherokee lands in Georgia, undertaken in preparation for the forced removal of the tribe.

Frémont's interest in the western frontier was further whetted as a member of the expedition of noted scientist Joseph N. Nicollet, which explored the region between the upper Mississippi and Missouri rivers in 1838. In 1841, in charge of his own expedition, Frémont mapped much of Iowa Territory. The same year he married Jesse Benton, daughter of Missouri Senator Thomas Hart Benton. The backing of his powerful father-in-law, a leading advocate of U.S. continental expansion, launched Frémont on his renowned career.

He became a famed explorer, heading three major expeditions to the West that earned him the sobriquet "the Pathfinder," after James Fenimore Cooper's hero of the same name. In 1842 he journeyed along the still-faint Oregon Trail into present-day Wyoming and charted the location of South Pass. His second expedition, from 1843 to 1844, explored the Great Basin between the Rocky and Sierra Nevada mountains. Frémont's third expedition, begun in 1845, placed him in California, then a Mexican province, on the eve of the Mexican War. In 1846 he

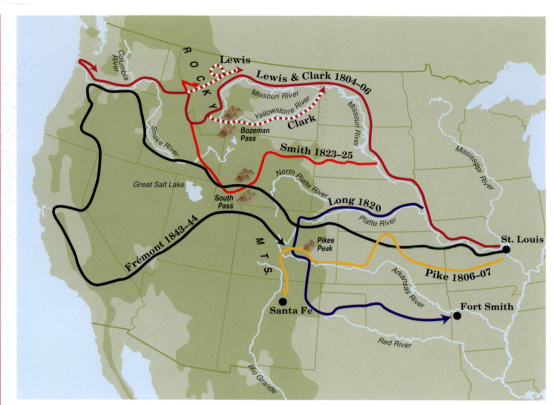

American Exploration of the West

the Far West. Mountain man Jedediah Smith is credited with the discovery in 1824 of South Pass—which he actually learned of from Native Americans—in present-day Wyoming. The pass soon would be used by the Oregon Trail.

American reconnaissance of the West culminated in the 1840s with the government-backed expeditions of John C. Frémont. More detailed exploration would continue for decades, but a basic picture of the West had been drawn. By the 1840s the role of American explorers as the vanguard for future settlers was manifest. Frémont assured his lasting impact on the settlement of the West with his stirring and widely read accounts of his travels, which prompted many Easterners to head westward. His reports first dispelled Long's myth of a midwestern Great American Desert.

THE FLORIDAS

The Louisiana Purchase isolated Spanish Florida from the Spanish provinces in Texas and the Southwest. American attempts to purchase Florida were rebuffed by Spain in 1803 and 1805. Expansionist-minded settlers, though, would lead the United States to seize Florida, which Spain had divided into two provinces, in bits and pieces.

In the early 1800s hundreds of American settlers capitalized on loosened Spanish immigration and land laws to migrate into West Florida, the area from the Apalachicola River to the Mississippi. In 1810 American planters around Baton Rouge rebelled against Spanish rule and proclaimed the independent Republic of West Florida. The same year President James Madison issued a proclamation declaring U.S. control over West Florida between the Mississippi and the Perdido rivers, whereupon American troops took actual possession of West Florida as far east as the Pearl River. U.S. forces seized the area between the Pearl and Perdido rivers in 1813. These territories were incorporated into Louisiana, Mississippi, and Alabama.

In 1818 General Andrew Jackson led 3,000 American troops into Florida as part of a campaign in the First Seminole War (1817–18) to suppress Seminole attacks on American settlers from Spanish soil. U.S. forces quickly occupied the remaining Spanish territory of West Florida and virtually conquered East Florida, the area from the Atlantic to the Apalachicola River. Spain protested the invasion but, bowing to the inevitable, relinquished Florida to the United States in the Adams-Onis Treaty. This 1819 treaty also resolved the southern boundary of the Louisiana Purchase. The agreed U.S.-Spanish border in the West ran in a northwesterly line along the Sabine,

Red, and Arkansas rivers and then due west along the 42nd parallel to the Pacific Ocean. This line became the U.S.-Mexican border upon Mexican independence in 1821.

A territorial capital was established at Tallahassee in 1824. Florida's population grew rapidly as settlers from Georgia and Alabama poured into the northern parts of the territory. Cotton plantations were laid out in the middle counties of the Florida peninsula and around Tallahassee. With the Southern plantation system came slavery. Blacks made up half of Florida's 54,000 inhabitants in 1840. About one-third of white families owned slaves. The bulk of the white population were subsistence farmers in scattered small communities.

American migration down the Florida peninsula was blocked by fierce Seminole resistance. The Seminoles were crushed in the Second Seminole War (1835–42) and most were removed to the West. Florida became a state in 1845.

THE WAY WEST

Early American settlers headed west by foot, by wagon, and by boat. As in colonial times, the first routes into the trans-Appalachian West followed Indian trails and footpaths. Native Americans had long traversed the natural pathway through the Appalachians formed by the Mohawk River valley. The Mohawk Trail, also called the Iroquois Trail, ran from Albany west to Buffalo and then south along the Erie to the interior.

The trail became a major route for pioneers streaming into the Old Northwest. Gradually the trail was improved into a rough wilderness road passable to wagons. The section from Albany to Buffalo became the Genesee Road in 1797, with log bridges and a log- and gravel-reinforced roadway. By 1810 some 200,000 settlers had journeyed west along the ancient trail.

In the Old Southwest the Warrior's Path through the Cumberland Gap became the Wilderness Road. In 1795 it opened to wagon traffic. With its eventual terminus at Louisville, Kentucky, the road spurred settlement of the lower Ohio Valley.

The Indian Tennessee Path crossing the Appalachians south of the Cumberland Gap likewise was developed. By 1795 the section from the Wilderness Road to Knoxville had become the Knoxville Road and from Knoxville to Nashville the Old Walton Road. The Indian trail known as the Natchez Trace, running from Nashville south to Natchez, by 1808 had been upgraded into a wagon road.

The condition of American roads in the late 1700s was generally abysmal. Most were little more than rough tracks through the woods. The need for roads to accommodate the swelling numbers of pioneers striking out for western regions, and the immense costs associated with road construction, led to experimentation with the

participated in the Bear Flag Revolt by American settlers against Mexican rule and then assisted in the final U.S. conquest of California the following year.

Frémont amassed a fortune during the California Gold Rush when it was discovered that his Sierra foothills estate harbored rich gold mines. He entered politics as a senator from California and emerged as a foe of slavery's extension. In 1856 he was the first presidential standard-bearer of the newly formed Republican Party. Running on an antislavery platform, he lost the election when he failed to carry any slave states.

Following the outbreak of the Civil War, Frémont was appointed a major general and given command of the Department of the West, headquartered in St. Louis. In August 1861 he issued an order emancipating all slaves in Missouri. His proclamation was rescinded by President Lincoln, who believed it premature. Reassigned to West Virginia, Frémont resigned his commission in 1862.

After the war he became involved in western railroad ventures, but proved unsuited for business and lost most of his remaining wealth. From 1878 to 1883 he served as territorial governor of Arizona. Frémont died in 1890, the year the frontier was officially closed.

Acquisition and Settlement of Florida

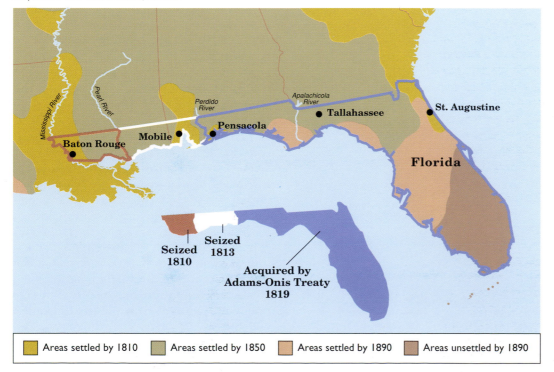

▢ Areas settled by 1810	▢ Areas settled by 1850	▢ Areas settled by 1890	▢ Areas unsettled by 1890

building of turnpikes, or toll roads, which were paid for by the users rather than the general public. During the first half of the 19th century, private companies as well as local governments built over 10,000 miles of turnpike.

The surge of western migrants in the early 1800s put pressure on the federal government to build a major road linking the Atlantic coast and the Mississippi. In 1806 Congress voted to build a broad, wagon-bearing road from Cumberland, Maryland, to Wheeling on the Ohio River and then across the Old Northwest. The first leg of the National Road to Wheeling was completed in 1818. The road would reach

Columbus, Ohio, in 1833 and its final terminus at Vandalia, Illinois, in 1852. By then railroads had replaced roads as the principal means of travel in the trans-Appalachian West.

THE ERIE CANAL

Rivers outranked mountains as the most important topographical feature in early migration westward. Rivers were the early highways. Settlers could move much more easily, and much quicker, by water, thus sparing themselves the arduous ordeal of fighting their way along wilderness roads. The Ohio and the Mississippi, in effect, were the first interstates.

Americans soon conceived of linking the Atlantic seaboard with the trans-Appalachian West by water. By the early 1800s existing construction techniques made feasible the idea of a canal—essentially a manmade river—connecting the Hudson River and Lake Erie. In 1815 New York political leader DeWitt Clinton began a concerted campaign to build the inland waterway. Following authorization of the project by the state legislature, construction began on the Erie Canal in 1817. Much of the backbreaking labor was provided by Irish immigrants. The canal, completed in 1825, paralleled first the Mohawk River and then the Mohawk Trail for 363 miles from Albany to Buffalo.

With its new link to the interior, New York City became the nation's most important port almost overnight. The village of Buffalo emerged as a boomtown. The canal permitted a much greater movement of goods and people. Thousands of Germans and other immigrants traveled along the waterway to the Great Lakes region. The increased traffic made Cleveland and Toledo major ports on Lake Erie.

The commercial success of the toll-charging Erie Canal led to construction of some 3,000 miles of inland waterway by the 1840s. Canals connected New York's harbor to the Delaware River, Lake Erie to the Ohio and Wabash rivers, and Chicago to the Mississippi River system. The Pennsylvania Canal, from Philadelphia to Pittsburgh, included two early railroad links. Canals contributed greatly not only to westward expansion but also to the economic growth that drove industrialization and the rise of cities. Their heyday lasted until about 1850, after which they were supplanted by railroads.

Eastern Trails and Roads

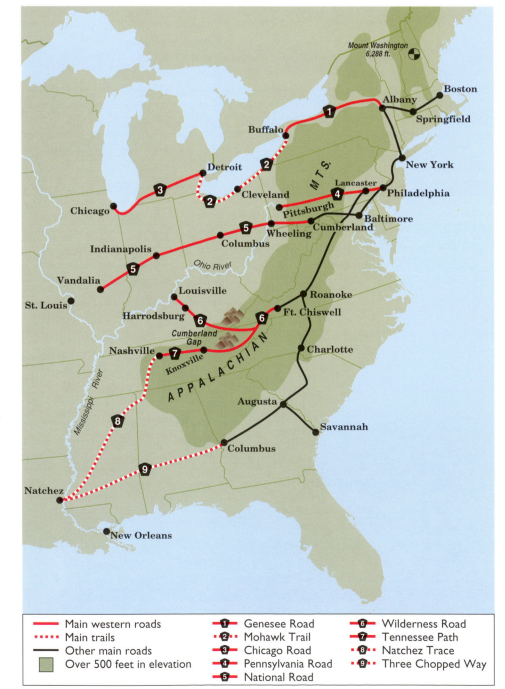

▬▬ Main western roads	❶ Genesee Road ❻ Wilderness Road
▪▪▪▪ Main trails	❷ Mohawk Trail ❼ Tennessee Path
▬▬ Other main roads	❸ Chicago Road ❽ Natchez Trace
▪ Over 500 feet in elevation	❹ Pennsylvania Road ❾ Three Chopped Way
	❺ National Road

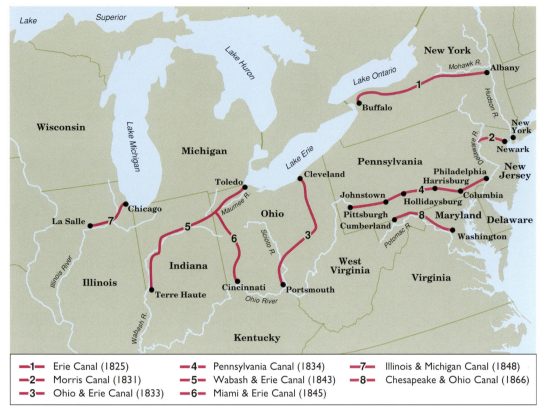

Westward By Canal

1 Erie Canal (1825)	**4** Pennsylvania Canal (1834)	**7** Illinois & Michigan Canal (1848)
2 Morris Canal (1831)	**5** Wabash & Erie Canal (1843)	**8** Chesapeake & Ohio Canal (1866)
3 Ohio & Erie Canal (1833)	**6** Miami & Erie Canal (1845)	

ACROSS THE MISSISSIPPI

The American frontier had extended westward beyond the Mississippi before the Louisiana Purchase. The French and then the Spanish had only sparsely settled the Mississippi valley. In 1790 Spanish Louisiana had a population of some 40,000. The faint Spanish presence up the Mississippi River was anchored on the village of St. Louis, founded in 1763. To encourage settlement of the western Mississippi valley, and forestall American expansion, Spanish authorities offered free land grants to foreign immigrants willing to pay allegiance to Spanish authority. After 1795 American settlers from Kentucky and Tennessee crossed the Mississippi into Missouri. By 1803, when the territory passed to

The Erie Canal, c. 1838   (Buffalo and Erie County Historical Society)

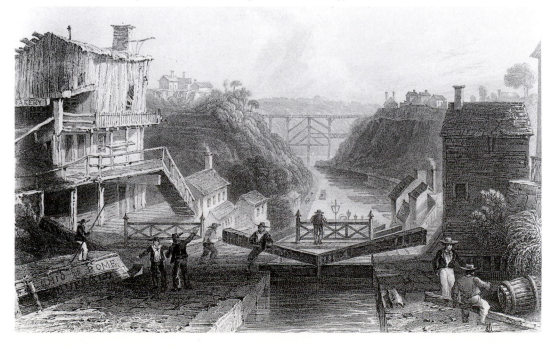

CLIPPERS AND STEAMERS

The 19th century saw the development of some of the most distinctive vessels in maritime history. Advances in shipbuilding made migration faster, easier, and more affordable.

By the late 18th century the refinement of sailing ships and methods had reached a point where little margin remained for further real change. Oceangoing vessels had attained a maximum feasible size of several thousand tons. Sailing schedules, moreover, were subject to the caprices of transoceanic wind patterns. Until the early 1800s, most commercial ships were tramps, sailing haphazard schedules based on the availability of cargo or passengers and the prevailing winds. The first regular transatlantic shipping line, between the United States and Great Britain, was not established until 1818.

The China tea trade, with its extended distances, put a new premium on speed. American shipyards in the 1840s began to build streamlined, heavily rigged vessels whose "bows turned inside out" enabled them to cut through the waves. Over the next 30 years these famed clipper ships would set innumerable speed records. During the California Gold Rush, clippers—even when they sailed around South America—provided the fastest transport for "49ers" rushing out to San Francisco. But clippers, like other sailing vessels, could go only as fast as the wind took them.

The Industrial Revolution and the steam engine would change the maritime world forever. In 1807 Robert Fulton sailed the first fully functional steamboat up the Hudson River from New York to Albany. The *Clermont's* voyage took 32 hours, compared to the four days required by the average sailboat. Paddle-driven, steam-powered vessels soon were plying America's rivers and lakes. By 1811 steamboats were journeying from Pittsburgh to New Orleans. The first Mississippi riverboat of Mark Twain

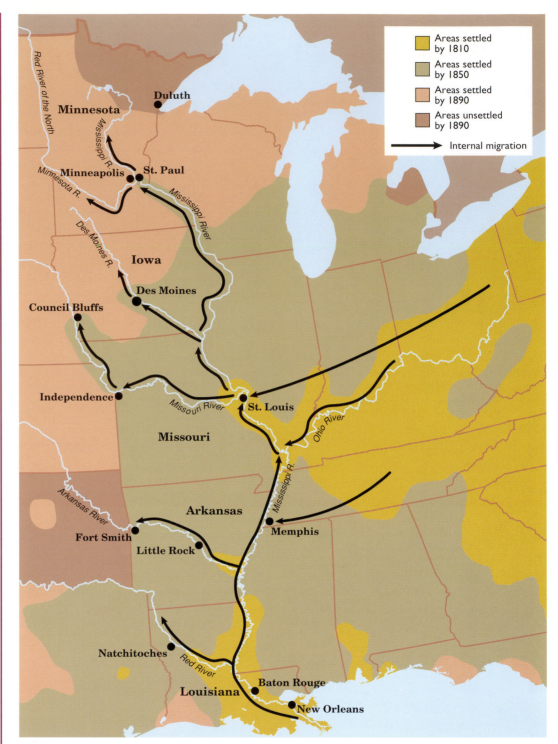

Settlement of the Mississippi Valley Frontier

U.S. ownership under the Louisiana Purchase, Americans formed the majority of Missouri's 10,000 residents.

Within another 50 years, American farmers had brought under cultivation the rich soil of the western Mississippi valley. By the Civil War five states had been carved out of the Louisiana Purchase along the west bank of the Mississippi. American migration first surged across the river to the south. Cotton and sugar plantations rapidly spanned Louisiana, swelling the territory's population to upward of 78,000 in 1810. The French had introduced slavery to Louisiana

and the institution continued under American sovereignty, becoming the labor mainstay of plantation agriculture. Louisiana was admitted to the Union as a slave state in 1812. The steamboat and the burgeoning Mississippi River commerce spurred the state's continued growth, such that by 1840 New Orleans was the nation's fourth largest city.

Migration into Missouri followed the Missouri River. Central Missouri soon was producing hemp and tobacco. Southern newcomers to the territory brought slaves with them to work the fields. St. Louis, locat-

Mississippi steamboat, 1849   (Courtesy of the Cincinnati Historical Society Library, B-83-18)

fame, with flat bottom and three decks, was introduced in 1817.

Steamboats, as the vessels became known, proved invaluable allies in America's westward expansion and industrial growth. Greater numbers of passengers could be carried; travel times were cut dramatically. The entire Mississippi valley was made accessible. Steamboats gradually were replaced by railroads, although many freight-heavy lines endured until just before World War II and the advent of trucking.

The term *steamship* was attached to oceangoing vessels. The first steam-powered vessel to cross the Atlantic was the American-built *Savannah* in 1819. Britain began regular transatlantic steamship service in 1838. Both the screw propeller, which replaced the paddle wheel, and the iron hull had been developed by 1843. One steamship of 1,000-odd tons had four times the capacity of the largest sailing craft. Sailing ships never exceeded 5,000 tons—the starting point for steamers. Steamships would bring to America the massive wave of New Immigrants between 1890 and 1920. By the early 20th century, the largest oceangoing liners could carry several thousand passengers.

ed at the junction of the Missouri and Mississippi rivers, emerged as a fur-trading center and gateway to the West. Both the Oregon and Santa Fe Trails embarked from Independence, farther up the Missouri River. By 1820 St. Louis's 5,000 residents had helped push Missouri's population above 60,000.

Missouri's petition for admission as a slave state in 1820 precipitated an intense sectional debate in the Congress between Northern foes and Southern supporters of slavery. At issue was the extension of the institution into the Louisiana Purchase. The United States at the time comprised 11 free and 11 slave states. For the South, which with its smaller population held fewer seats in the House of Representatives, the preservation of a sectional balance in the Senate was crucial to blocking federal efforts to curtail or even abolish slavery. If the Louisiana Purchase yielded only free states, the South feared, then eventually Northern opponents of slavery could gain a Senate majority and with it the power to legislate against the Southern slave interest. Under what became known as the Missouri Compromise, reached in 1820, Missouri was admitted as a slave state and Maine as a free state. The further extension of slavery in the Louisiana Purchase was banned north of the latitude 36° 30′ (Missouri's southern boundary).

The Missouri Compromise paved the way for admission of Arkansas as a slave state in 1836. Settlement of Arkansas was slowed by the vast swamp in the eastern part of the state, which was not fully remedied by levees and drainage until the late 1800s. The entire territory of Arkansas had only 1,062 inhabitants in the 1810 census. By 1840 slaveholding settlers from Mississippi, Tennessee, and Missouri had developed the state into a cotton-growing center with about 100,000 inhabitants.

In the manner typical of westward expansion, the Native Americans were swept before the inexorable American tide. The Caddo after 1803 were forced to cede their lands in western Louisiana and move to Texas. By the 1830s the Quapaw and Osage had been relocated from Arkansas and Missouri to Indian Territory farther west. The Missouri moved northwest in 1829 and united with the Oto in Nebraska. Defeat of the Sauk and Fox in the Black Hawk War (1832) opened eastern Iowa to settlement. The subsequent influx of pioneers and demand for farmland led to the removal of the Iowa Indians in 1836. Within another 15 years, Iowa had a population of almost 200,000. The new state developed an enduring agricultural identity, becoming by 1890 the nation's leading corn producer.

Vast timber riches drove early migration into Minnesota. An 1837 treaty with the Sioux cleared the way for lumbering in the upper Mississippi valley. St. Paul was founded in 1841 and Minneapolis in 1847. Still, in 1850 Minnesota had only slightly more than 5,000 settlers. Aggressive recruitment by the territorial government of European immigrants, especially Germans and Irish, built the population to more than 150,000 in 1858, when Minnesota gained statehood. Annihilation of the Sioux in western Minnesota in Little Crow's War (1862–64) marked final American penetration of the Mississippi valley frontier. After the Civil War, immigration again propelled Minnesota's rapid growth. Settlement of northern Minnesota was largely completed by Scandinavian immigrants in the 1870s and 1880s.

THE MEXICAN SOUTHWEST

Over the centuries the fusion of Spanish and Central American Indian cultures produced a new and distinct Mexican identity. In 1821, after more than a decade of bloody revolt, Mexico gained its independence from Spain. The new nation inherited the Spanish frontier provinces in the American Southwest.

The Southwest would not remain Mexican for long. By annexation, conquest, and purchase, the United States within 30 years had acquired all of northern Mexico from Texas to California. Migration as much as any factor sealed the fate of the Mexican Southwest. The relentless westward push of the American frontier made inevitable U.S. occupation and absorption of the sparsely settled area.

Acquisition and Settlement of Texas

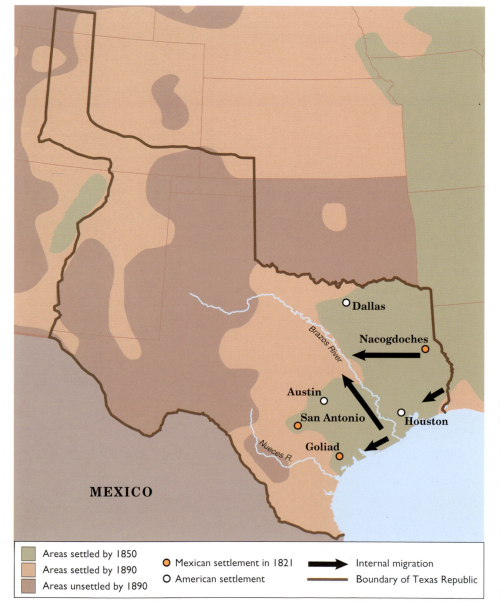

	Areas settled by 1850
	Areas settled by 1890
	Areas unsettled by 1890

○ Mexican settlement in 1821

○ American settlement

→ Internal migration

— Boundary of Texas Republic

LONE STAR REPUBLIC

After the Louisiana Purchase placed the United States at the doorstep of its Southwest Borderlands, Spain aimed to bolster the population of Texas as a bulwark against American expansionism. Efforts by Spanish authorities to spur Mexican migration into Texas foundered. Texas was too far from the center of Mexican population around Mexico City and there was scant tradition in the more hierarchical Mexican social order of the independent small farmers needed. In desperation the Spanish government opened Texas to foreign immigrants, including Americans, willing to live under Spanish rule. The Spanish mistakenly assumed American settlers would assimilate into a Spanish-American society much as European migrants did in the United States.

In 1821 Spanish authorities granted a permit to Missourian Moses Austin to settle 300 families in the Brazos River area of eastern Texas. Austin, who had been a citizen of Spanish Louisiana and had dealt extensively with Spanish officials, was trusted to conform to Spanish governance. After Austin's death the same year, the newly independent Mexican government reconfirmed the grant to his son, Stephen F. Austin. He was designated first in a series of *empresarios*, or land agents, permitted to recruit and settle Americans in Texas.

By 1830 Austin had brought 5,000 settlers to his extensive land holdings on the Brazos. Generous Mexican land policies encouraged American immigration. Most of the early settlers were from the South and many were accompanied by black slaves. While the importation of slaves was technically forbidden by Mexico, which outlawed slavery in 1829, it was tacitly allowed. There were more than 20,000 American settlers in Texas by 1835, as well as some 4,000 slaves.

Upon realizing that American settlers were not learning Spanish, converting to Catholicism, assuming Mexican citizenship, or otherwise assimilating into Mexican society as promised, the Mexican government moved to halt the American influx after 1830. Measures to discourage further immigration had little impact and served only to exacerbate tensions between American settlers and Mexican authorities. A dispute over customs duties flared into open rebellion by the Americans in late 1835. By April 1836 the American settlers had defeated Mexican forces sent to suppress their revolt and established the independent Republic of Texas.

The United States recognized the Republic of Texas in 1837. But fearful of provoking Mexico, which refused to concede the loss of Texas, the U.S. government declined a Texan petition for statehood the same year. Texas struggled to survive as an independent country for almost a decade. Settlements were founded at Houston in 1836 and Dallas in 1841. With a more aggressively expansionist attitude gaining

sway in Washington during the mid-1840s, Texas was annexed in 1845 as a slave state. U.S. victory in the Mexican-American War (1846–48) fixed Texas's southern border at the Rio Grande. Its western boundary was set by Congress in 1850 as part of the division of the massive territory acquired from Mexico after the war.

Texas's population increased dramatically in the period between annexation and the Civil War. A cotton-and-slave culture came to predominate in the eastern part of the state as settlers from the South poured into the area. The Tonkawa and other local Native American tribes were confined to reservations on the Brazos River in 1858. The Tonkawa, as well as the Caddo along the Red River to the north, were removed to Indian Territory in 1859. The Wichita, who had moved north from the Red River into Oklahoma in 1850, were also relocated onto a reservation.

GREAT IRISH AND GERMAN MIGRATION

Immigration to the United States began to build after 1820. The first to come in large numbers were the Irish, whose surging population (growing from less than 7 million to more than 8 million between 1820 and 1840) exerted unbearable pressure on

Irish immigrants   (Boston Public Library, Print Department)

Ireland's overtaxed land. The overcrowding spawned a crisis that defied a domestic solution. The Irish tradition of subdividing the average family's small plot to accommodate successive generations proved inadequate to the population explosion; and Ireland's nascent industry was not generating enough work to absorb the surplus agrarian populace. Protestant Irish from Ulster, the most densely populated province, led the great surge of migrants to America. Some 500,000 departed between 1815 and 1845, driven by economic necessity. This flow soon became a torrent with the exodus of Irish Catholics, who were equally affected by the mounting pressures of overpopulation and economic change. Many Catholics were also eager to escape religious and political persecution under British rule.

After 1840, Catholics made up more than 90 percent of Irish immigrants to America. The complete destruction of the potato crop in 1845 and 1846 by blight disease left the mostly rural Catholic Irish with a stark choice—emigrate or starve. The Great Famine produced a massive outpouring of desperate Irish peasants. In what became known as the Great Migration, some 1.3 million Irish journeyed to America between 1845 and 1854.

The Irish emigration coincided with the development of transatlantic shipping lines. Once in America, Irish immigrants would save enough money to pay for the subsequent passage of relatives back in the homeland; this practice represented an early form of so-called chain migration. The majority of immigrants were under 35 and, although family ties were important, most were unmarried. Their numbers were almost equally split between men and women. Too poor to travel further or buy land, the Irish settled in the cities of the Atlantic seaboard. Large Irish communities formed in Boston, New York, Philadelphia, and Baltimore. The thousands of Irish immigrants pouring into the cities each year contributed to the rapid urbanization then underway. Irish workers provided much of the manual labor in the building and related trades of the explosively expanding cities. Smaller numbers of Irish headed west as members of construction gangs on roads, canals, and railroads.

The heavy German emigration of the colonial period was halted for some 50 years by the American Revolution and then by the Napoleonic Wars engulfing Europe. German emigration resumed in force in the 1830s, with the displacement of agricultural workers by the Industrial Revolution. The severe failure of potato crops in the mid-1840s drove some 900,000 Germans to join the Great Migration to America in the decade after 1845. The collapse in Germany of the liberal revolution of 1848, moreover, prompted thousands of its supporters, soon known as "48ers," to flee to America. Still, the vast majority of Germans came for economic rather than political reasons.

The Germans migrated overwhelmingly as families. The advent of larger, steam-powered ships and regular passenger lines resulted in much lower transatlantic fares that were accessible to thousands of prospective emigrants. At first, most emigrants came from areas along the Rhine River, but as the German states gradually united into the German Empire (pro-

IRISH AND GERMAN IMMIGRANTS

The 2.2 million Irish and Germans that came between 1845 and 1854 were equal to 10% of the U.S. population in 1850. To gain some idea of the magnitude of this migration, a comparable influx between 1985 and 1994 would have involved some 25 million immigrants.

	NUMBER OF IMMIGRANTS		PERCENTAGE OF TOTAL IMMIGRATION	
	Irish	German	Irish	German
1821–30	50,724	6,761	6	5
1831–40	207,381	152,454	35	25
1841–50	780,719	434,626	46	25
1851–60	914,119	951,667	35	37
1861–70	435,778	787,468	19	34
1871–80	436,871	718,182	16	26
1881–90	655,482	1,452,970	13	28

Source: *Immigration and Naturalization Service*

claimed in 1871), small farmers, artisans, and laborers from across the country embarked for America.

The Germans made principally for the Old Northwest, mostly because of the ready availability of land. The German immigrants found homes on farms and in cities. German farm families soon dotted the Ohio valley, while substantial German populations emerged in Buffalo, Detroit, Louisville, Cincinnati, and Chicago. In the 1830s German settlers traveled up the Mississippi from New Orleans to put down roots in Missouri. By the 1840s, this migration had advanced up the Mississippi and across the Great Lakes to Wisconsin, where Milwaukee became the most German of American cities. Smaller number of Germans established agricultural settlements along the Brazos River in Texas.

The German influx continued through the 1850s as shipping lines, railroads, manufacturers, and state governments all recruited immigrants. From Wisconsin, German settlers moved into Minnesota. By the end of the decade the great swath of land stretching from New York west to St. Louis and north to Minneapolis was known as the "German belt."

Irish and German migrants largely defined the face of American immigration between 1820 and 1860. They comprised over 40% of immigrants in the 1820s; some 60% in the 1830s; and more than 70% in the 1840s and 1850s. Both German and Irish immigration were slowed by the Civil War but would continue in strength throughout the century. By the late 1800s German and Irish newcomers were being referred to as Old Immigrants, to distinguish them from the tide of New Immigrants from southern and eastern Europe. This shift in designation underscored the rapidly changing nature of 19th-century migration to America.

THE NATIVIST RESPONSE

The Great Migration sparked the first real wave of anti-immigrant fervor in the United States. Nativism, the favoring of the

German and Irish Immigrants

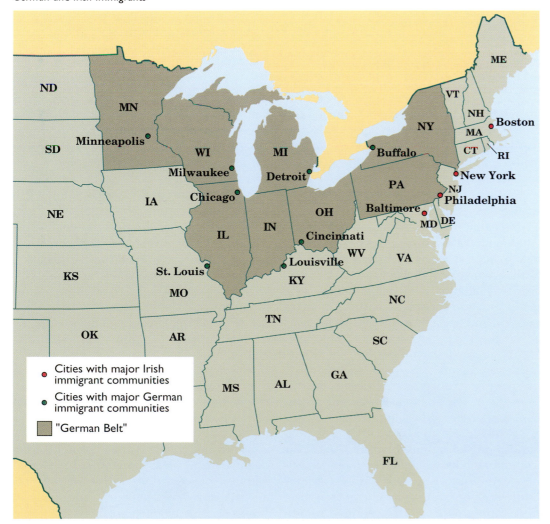

native-born over immigrants, had long smoldered in American culture, but it flared into the open in the 1830s and 1840s with the massive Irish and German influx. Nativist sentiments took one of two basic forms.

First was a general opposition to immigration. As has so often been the case since, economic hard times fueled anti-immigrant feelings. Collapsing land values in 1836 brought about the financial crisis known as the Panic of 1837, which in turn precipitated an economic depression that gripped the nation until 1843. Anti-immigrant sentiment ran strongest in northeastern cities, where unemployment rates soared, wages fell, and the essentials of food, rent, and fuel became virtually unaffordable to the poor. The sheer volume of Irish migration in particular alarmed many working-class Americans concerned for their own livelihoods. Although no organized movement to halt immigration materialized (partly because immigration was still largely seen as a state matter), frictions between immigrants and native workers persisted through the 1840s as recovery from the depression proceeded slowly after 1843. Tensions eased with the growing prosperity of the 1850s, spurred in part by the discovery of gold in California in 1848.

THE CHURCH BURNERS

It was the second and more incendiary form of nativism that especially fanned the flames of anti-immigrant hostility well into the 1850s. This nativism was narrow in focus, manifesting itself in opposition to specific immigrant groups.

Many German as well as most Irish immigrants were Catholic. They arrived in a United States whose population was overwhelmingly Protestant. Many Americans had an intense, visceral fear and loathing of Catholicism. Most believed that Catholicism's allegiance to papal authority rendered it incompatible with American political and social institutions, which rested on the separation of church and state. Many indulged stereotypes of Catholics as uneducated, superstitious peasants, under the sway of a conspiratorial clergy and still prone to the use of dungeons, torture chambers, and other medieval practices.

While forced to overcome considerable opposition and hostility, the German Catholics tended to assimilate more readily into American society. The German Catholic clergy were more liberal than their Irish counterparts and served as a bridge

rather than a barrier to the larger community. The Germans embraced public education for their children and generally aligned themselves with the prevailing Whig and then Republican politics of their Northern neighbors. Of key importance was the fact that most German immigrants, while still poor, had greater means for starting a new life in America than the even more impoverished Irish.

The Irish Catholic experience was very different. Virtual destitution on arrival meant most Irish immigrants ended up in ethnic enclaves in Northern port cities. Barriers of prejudice as well as poverty often prevented Irish dispersion and advancement in the larger society. So too did Irish reluctance to assimilate into Protestant America. Irish priests more often than not were only too happy to see their flocks kept separate from Protestant influences. Many Irish harbored understandably anti-British feelings, and were thus put off by British cultural influences in American society. Irish skepticism toward the Protestant-oriented public education system compounded nativist fears of a Catholic "menace," since most Americans deemed this system key to the assimilation of new immigrant groups. The Irish were often politically alienated in the North by their broad support for the anti-abolition and anti-free-black positions of the Southern-dominated Democratic Party.

The Irish were the first to face overt job discrimination. The line "No Irish Need Apply" was not uncommon in classified advertisements in Boston, New York, and other eastern cities. Beginning in the 1830s, nativist warnings of a Catholic plot to subvert America appeared regularly in newspapers and periodicals. In 1834 Samuel F.B. Morse, future inventor of the telegraph, published a series of letters entitled *A Foreign Conspiracy Against the Liberties of the United States*. Ironically, Morse's invention would do much to speed the rapid industrialization that brought ever more immigrants to America.

A nativist political movement emerged during the late 1830s and early 1840s. The Native American Association was formed in Washington in 1837. Adherents chose the term Native American (at a time when few if any thought of Indians as the original Native Americans) to convey their opposition to Catholic immigrants, who purportedly did not fit the American mold. Irish demands for public funds to aid parochial schools and objections to use of the Protestant King James version of the Bible in public schools heightened nativist antagonisms. The American Republican Party, founded in New York in 1843, advocated barring Catholics and foreigners from voting or holding public office.

Violent confrontations between nativists and Irish immigrants plagued Northern cities in the 1840s. The worst religious riot in American history occurred, poignantly enough, in the City of Brotherly Love in 1844. After the Philadelphia school board authorized use of the Douay version of the Bible by Catholic students, nativists staged rallies in the Irish Kensington district of the city, triggering armed clashes between Protestants and Catholics. Before the state militia could restore order, more than 30 persons had been killed, 150 lay wounded, and two Catholic churches had been burned to the ground. Although a national Native America Party was established in 1845, the Philadelphia violence had discredited nativists, who were tagged with the pejorative name "church burners." The nativist appeal briefly faded and the increasingly secretive movement went largely underground.

THE KNOW NOTHINGS

Formation of the Order of the Star Spangled Banner in New York in 1849 presaged a public resurgence of nativism in the 1850s. By 1854 nativist groups had founded the American Party. The secretive body, whose platform called for the exclusion of Catholics and immigrants from public office and a 21-year naturalization requirement, soon became known as the Know-Nothing Party, because its members answered all questions about the organization with an evasive "I know nothing." The party gained a strong national following in 1854 and 1855, but just as quickly its influence waned as the nation's attention was dominated by the deepening sectional conflict over slavery.

The nativist movement had petered out by the late 1850s, deflated not only by the impending Civil War but also by the growing demands of the Industrial Revolution for immigrant labor. Still, American nativism based on religious, racial, or ethnic prejudice had not died, but rather gone into hibernation. It would reawaken later in the century to oppose the immigration of Asians and southern and eastern Europeans. Ironically, the often-nativist North's much larger immigrant population proved a decided advantage in its victory in the Civil War. Both German-American and Irish-American regiments would fight in the Union Army to end the scourge of slavery.

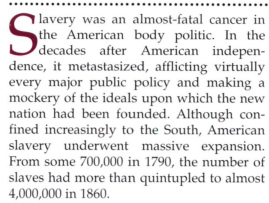

MIGRATION IN CHAINS
American Slavery

Slavery was an almost-fatal cancer in the American body politic. In the decades after American independence, it metastasized, afflicting virtually every major public policy and making a mockery of the ideals upon which the new nation had been founded. Although confined increasingly to the South, American slavery underwent massive expansion. From some 700,000 in 1790, the number of slaves had more than quintupled to almost 4,000,000 in 1860.

The African slave trade was stopped in 1808, only to be supplanted by an equally horrific domestic slave trade. Hundreds of thousands of black Americans were taken west in irons to sustain the growth of a vast Southern empire based on slave labor. By 1860 slavery had spread to nine new states and extended more than halfway across the continent into Texas. The malignant institution was so virulent and pervasive that the only cure was an all-consuming conflict that nearly destroyed the United States before saving it.

ALL OTHER PERSONS

African Americans had been in the British colonies since before the *Mayflower*. At the time of the American Revolution, slavery was already deeply entrenched in the South, with slaves found in every state. Many slaves saw the Revolution not as a fight of freedom against tyranny, but as an opportunity to escape from bondage. During the upheaval surrounding the war, thousands fled their plantations, sometimes to wilderness refuges, but more often to British-controlled areas, where they had been promised freedom as part of an effort to undermine the rebellion. When British forces evacuated America after the war, they took with them at least 10,000 escaped slaves. Some gained their freedom; many wound up in slavery in the British West Indies.

Other black Americans, both free and slave (again on a promise of freedom), fought for the rebel cause. In victory, though, the ringing ideals of the Declaration of Independence did not apply to all.

More than a few of the Founding Fathers were troubled by slavery, but they were not prepared to extend the inalienable rights of "life, liberty, and the pursuit of happiness" to black slaves. A small minority of white Americans in the 1780s opposed human bondage on moral grounds, mostly owing to Christian beliefs about the equality of all souls before God. Human knowledge had not progressed to the point, however, where slavery was understood to be inherently wrong.

Most of the misgivings about slavery were practical ones. Thomas Jefferson expanded a view held by many of his fellow slave owners that slavery degraded society at large, lowering the manners, morals, and work habits of blacks and whites alike. The steady decline in the tobacco economy of Jefferson's Virginia and the other states of the upper South raised questions about the actual efficiency of slavery as a system of production. Planters wondered if free labor would allow for a more productive use of land and other resources. The first stirrings of a market economy, especially in the North, led to a growing perception of slavery as a violation of such basic capitalist principles as the free movement of workers in the marketplace. Only in the slave-dependent lower South did strong sentiment exist for slavery's preservation.

Although deemed too essential to the lower South to abolish outright, slavery seemed to have no real future. Many believed the institution, if properly curtailed, would gradually wither and die. Few if any of America's early political leaders saw blacks as other than inferior, if not innately suited to slavery. Still, there was an emerging awareness that blacks, once freed from bondage, would no longer act like slaves and were capable of advancement.

While the Articles of Confederation did not address slavery, implicitly keeping the institution as it was, the 1780s witnessed the first American social and political movements to manumit (free) slaves and outlaw slavery. The New York Society for Promoting Manumission, established in 1785, inspired similar antislavery societies in other states from Massachusetts to Virginia. Quakers in Pennsylvania had long opposed slavery, and that state in 1780 became the first to enact legislation gradually abolishing the practice. New Hampshire followed suit in 1783, Connecticut and Rhode Island in 1784, New York in 1785, and New Jersey in 1786. In the first judicial ruling against slavery, Massachusetts's highest court held in 1783 that the state's 1780 constitution prohibited enslavement.

The Northwest Ordinance in 1787 managed to accommodate the conflicting impulses of the time. It barred slavery in the Northwest Territory, but did so partly to protect the slave economies of the upper South. It also included a provision forbidding the harboring of fugitive slaves in the territory.

The Constitution reflected the deep unease of its framers about slavery. The document made euphemistic but unmistakable reference to slavery in three separate places, avoiding mention of the institution by name. In the infamous clause that provided for counting three-fifths of a state's slave population for electoral purposes, slaves were referred to only as "all other persons."

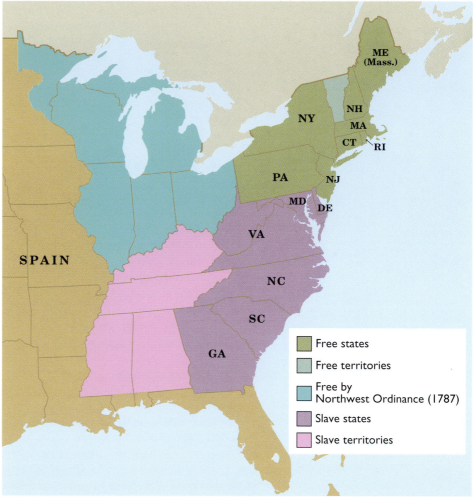

Slavery in 1790

SLAVE DISTRIBUTION IN 1790

North	
New Hampshire	157
Rhode Island	958
Connecticut	2,648
New York	21,193
New Jersey	11,423
Pennsylvania	3,707
Total	**40,086**
Upper South	
Delaware	8,887
Maryland	103,036
Virginia	292,627
North Carolina	100,783
Kentucky	12,430
Tennessee	3,417
Total	**521,180**
Deep South	
South Carolina	107,094
Georgia	29,264
Total	**136,358**
Grand Total	**697,624**

Source: *Historical Statistics of the United States*

The Constitution left slavery in place. If anything, it seemed to have reinforced the institution. In a clause that would serve as the basis for future fugitive slave acts, it made enslavement a permanent status that could not be escaped by flight from slave to free state. Another clause, again in deference to the lower South, barred federal interference in the importation of slaves until 1808. Yet the need to constitutionally protect slavery also conveyed the institution's duress. The Constitution in reality anticipated slavery's eventual demise, with the banning of the African slave trade part of its final denouement.

THE EXECRABLE COMMERCE
....

Jefferson had tried unsuccessfully to condemn the African slave trade in the Declaration of Independence, calling it an "execrable commerce" in a line stricken from the draft document at the insistence of Southern delegates to the Continental Congress. Jefferson could not foresee that he would preside over the formal termination of the odious trade three decades later as president. He also could not foresee that it would be replaced by another execrable commerce, a domestic slave trade that would make his native Virginia the center of a massive slave-breeding and trafficking enterprise.

AFRICAN SLAVE TRADE

American slavery in 1790 seemed destined for a gradual and peaceful death. All of the Northern states had begun to eliminate the institution, and its extension westward into the Northwest Territory had been blocked. The continuing downturn in tobacco production in the Chesapeake area meant there was a dwindling demand for slave labor in the upper South. Only in the low country of the Carolinas and Georgia, with its rice and cotton plantations, was there a need for additional slaves, mostly to replenish existing numbers. Rice and cotton cultivation were then confined to coastal areas, and there was little sense of an impending growth of slavery in the region.

Strong antislavery sentiments were voiced in a majority of the states. In 1793 Congress passed the first fugitive slave law, but the wide expectation was that the African slave trade would be halted when first allowed under the Constitution in 1808.

Anticipation of the trade's end was one of two factors spurring an upsurge in slave importations after 1790. Slave traders, seeking to maximize their business while still able, imported some 8,000 slaves each year in the 1790s. This number climbed to almost 12,000 annually between 1801 and 1807, roughly double the highest level in colonial times.

The other factor was the invention by Eli Whitney in 1793 of the cotton gin. The introduction of steam power in British industry in the late 1700s had greatly speeded the process of spinning and weaving cotton into fabric. The sharply lowered costs of this production in turn had created a burgeoning demand for American cotton. Southern planters had responded by increasing the cultivation of cotton along the coast of South Carolina and Georgia.

The problem was that the long-staple cotton raised in the low country could not flourish inland. Short-staple cotton, which could, required much more time and effort to manually separate the seeds from its fabric. Whitney's cotton gin mechanically extracted the seeds, increasing by fiftyfold the average daily output of clean short-sta-

ple cotton. The sudden profitability of short-staple cotton meant that cotton cultivation could rapidly expand inland. It also meant that American slavery would not slowly fade away on the coasts of the lower South, but instead would undergo an explosive resurgence in the movement westward of a Southern Cotton Kingdom.

Annual cotton production rose from 3,000 bales in 1790 to 178,000 in 1810. In the South, cotton and slavery were inextricably intertwined. Still, educated opinion in both the United States and Europe by the early 1800s had confronted the indefensible nature of the African slave trade. Growing international condemnation of the heinous commerce, led by Great Britain, fortified American leaders in their inclination to abolish it. At President Jefferson's recommendation, Congress passed legislation in 1807 forbidding slave importations into the United States after January 1, 1808.

The law provided for the forfeiture of seized slave vessels and their human cargoes. In 1820 Congress declared participation in the African slave trade an act of piracy, punishable by death. Despite the prohibitions, the trade continued. Most of the increasing manpower demands of plantation agriculture were met by the domestic slave trade, but strong economic incentives for slave smuggling remained. Between 1808 and 1860 an estimated 250,000 African slaves were brought illegally into the American South. Many were smuggled in through Cuba.

The measures barring the illegal commerce were not enforced by southern authorities. In 1842 the United States agreed to assist British naval forces in interdicting the illegal slave traffic along the African coast, but successive Democratic administrations, sympathetic to Southern slave interests, never dispatched more than a few frigates and the joint action had no tangible impact. In the 1850s the foreign slave trade emerged as an issue in the deepening sectional conflict in America over slavery. Southern calls for the repeal of U.S. laws prohibiting the international slave traffic mounted in the years before the Civil War. The Union blockade of the South during the war, together with the abolition of slavery, finally ended the importation of slaves to American soil.

DOMESTIC SLAVE TRADE

In the half-century after the legal termination of the African slave trade, the slave population of the United States first sur-

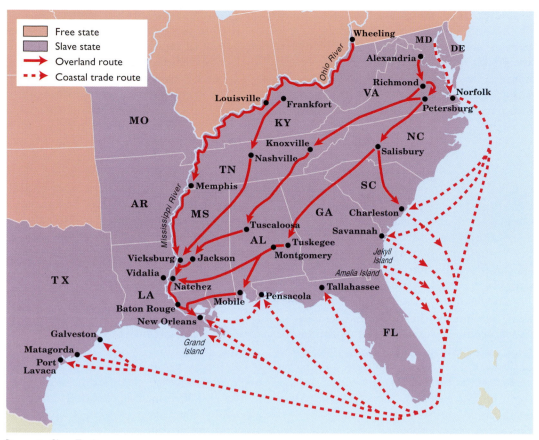

Domestic Slave Trade

SLAVE AUCTION

In 1861 escaped slave Harriet Jacobs, then in Boston, wrote an account of her life in bondage in Virginia. In her renowned slave narrative, *Incidents in the Life of a Slave Girl,* she recalled the impact of the annual slave auction, held on New Year's Day, on a local slave woman. Jacobs also recounted how the horrifying fate of the auction extended to the old as well as the young.

... to the slave mother New Year's day comes laden with peculiar sorrows. She sits on her cold cabin floor, watching the children who may all be torn from her the next morning; and often does she wish that she and they might die before the day dawns. She may be an ignorant creature, degraded by the system that has brutalized her from childhood; but she has a mother's instincts, and is capable of feeling a mother's agonies.

On one of these sale days, I saw a mother lead seven children to the auction-block. She knew that some of them would be taken from her; but they took *all.* The children were sold to a slave-trader, and their mother was bought by a man in her own town. Before night her children were all far away. She begged the trader to tell her where he intended to take them; this he refused to do. How *could* he, when he knew he would sell them, one by one, wherever he could command the highest price? I met that mother in the street, and her wild, haggard face lives to-day in my mind. She wrung her hands in anguish, and exclaimed, "Gone! all gone! Why *don't* God kill me?" I had no words wherewith to comfort her. Instances of this kind are of daily, yea, of hourly occurrence.

Slaveholders have a method, peculiar to their institution, of getting rid of *old* slaves, whose lives have been worn out in their service. I knew an old woman, who for seventy years faithfully served her master. She had become almost helpless, from hard labor and disease. Her owners moved to Alabama, and the old black woman was left to be sold to any body who would give twenty dollars for her.

passed that of any other country in the New World and then went on to exceed that of all the other American countries combined. This growth was due almost entirely to natural increase, as the number of slaves smuggled into the United States roughly equaled the number gaining their freedom through manumission or escape.

There were several reasons for the much higher growth rate in the United States. The generally healthy and mild climate of the South kept slaves from succumbing to the kinds of diseases more prevalent in the tropics. Work as a field hand was an unremitting ordeal, but the cultivation of cotton and tobacco was less physically demanding than that of sugar or coffee. Most important, though, was that slaves themselves became the crop.

Cotton cultivation, which required a minimum growing season of 200 frostless days, was confined to the lower South. The rapid expansion of cotton plantations across the Deep South created an intense demand for slave labor. Slave owners in the upper South quickly realized that their "surplus" slaves were a valuable commodity. With the decline in tobacco production, it was a commodity the Chesapeake states, and Virginia in particular, had in abundance. By 1800 a domestic slave trade had developed, with slave traders purchasing

excess slaves in non-cotton producing states and then moving them to cotton producing states for sale. This domestic commerce had already reached the point in 1808 where it could readily replace the newly closed African slave trade as the regular source of slaves.

The Deep South's cotton boom, combined with the ban on slave importations, kept the domestic slave trade a lucrative business throughout the antebellum period. The price of a field hand eventually rose from about $300 in 1795 to between $1,200 and $1,800 in 1860. It was not unusual for the average trader's annual rate of return to reach 30 percent. Such profits bound the South together in a terrible slave economy.

As cotton cultivation moved westward into Alabama, Mississippi, Louisiana, and Texas, so did the domestic slave trade. It is estimated about one million slaves were taken west between 1790 and 1860. Many accompanied masters who left home in search of new opportunities. This was the case with the majority of the early black migrants into Kentucky and Tennessee, as many of the states' first settlers were slave owners from Virginia and North Carolina. Later in the Deep South entire plantation staffs would be moved westward by slave-owning families relocating or expanding their holdings.

After 1815 the domestic slave trade predominated in the forced internal migration of slaves. Eventually the commerce accounted for as much as 70 percent of the massive transfer of slaves westward. In doing so it replicated many of the horrors of the African slave trade; it also created new ones.

One of these was the virtual breeding of slaves. Almost all the blacks relocated by the domestic trade came from the more northern slave states and almost all went to the cotton-producing tier of states along the Gulf of Mexico. Maryland, North Carolina, and Kentucky all had active slave markets, but Virginia was by far the biggest provider, sending roughly 300,000 slaves to the Gulf states between 1830 and 1860.

To ensure a steady supply of slaves, slave owners in the upper South took to guaranteeing the constant replenishment of their slave populations through the most basic means of human reproduction. Some chose mates for young slaves and forced them to live together. More often, owners encouraged slaves to marry, and thus to procreate, at an early age.

When it came time to sell, however, there was little or no respect for slave marriages, much less for slave families. In another especially repugnant aspect of the domestic commerce in human beings, slaves were sold and moved without regard for family ties. In the upper South, about one in three first marriages was broken by the slave trade and close to half of all children were sold away from at least one parent. Most sellers kept children with their mothers until about age 13, at which point they were deemed capable of work and thus ready for market.

Slaves were normally bought and sold at auction like cattle. Most in demand, not surprisingly, were prime field hands, ranging in age from 15 to 30. Next in order of value were slaves capable of household and industrial tasks. A disproportionate share of the slaves sent west were young adults between the ages of 15 and 25. Both men and women toiled as field hands. Except to Louisiana, where the premium was on young men for the backbreaking work in the sugar fields, slave merchants shipped roughly equal numbers of males and females.

It was not uncommon for a young female slave in Virginia to find herself suddenly torn from her family and transported hundreds of miles to a strange new plantation in Mississippi. Separation from relatives and friends was probably the most devastating experience endured by slaves.

The physical ordeal of the journey west was made even worse by the psychological cruelty involved in the permanent forced parting from loved ones.

Most of the domestic slave trade moved overland. Slaves were formed into coffles, or chain gangs, and marched under guard into the Deep South. Others were jammed into boats that plied the coastal waters from Virginia to Texas. Major marketing and distribution points included Richmond, Norfolk, and Louisville in the slave-sending upper South and Charleston, Mobile, and New Orleans in the slave-receiving lower South. The trade was relentless, with at least 100,000 slaves taken west every decade between 1810 and 1860.

COTTON KINGDOM

Slavery was in the vanguard of American expansion across the South. Kentucky joined the Union as a slave state in 1792, followed by Tennessee in 1796. Cotton was soon the staple crop in southern Tennessee. U.S. victory in the War of 1812 opened Alabama and Mississippi to the surge of cotton plantations across the Deep South.

Everywhere expansion, slavery, and, most often, cotton were linked together. The French had introduced slavery to Louisiana in colonial times, and the institution was perpetuated there under Spanish rule and, after 1803, by American governance. American planters added extensive cotton cultivation to Louisiana's prodigious sugar output. Florida was made slave territory on its acquisition from Spain in 1819, and the seemingly ubiquitous cotton was grown in its northern parts.

Alabama, Mississippi, and Louisiana, with their rich soil and hot, sunny climate,

GROWTH OF SLAVE POPULATION, 1790–1860	
1790	697,624
1800	893,602
1810	1,191,362
1820	1,538,022
1830	2,009,043
1840	2,487,355
1850	3,204,313
1860	3,953,760

Source: *Historical Statistics of the United States*

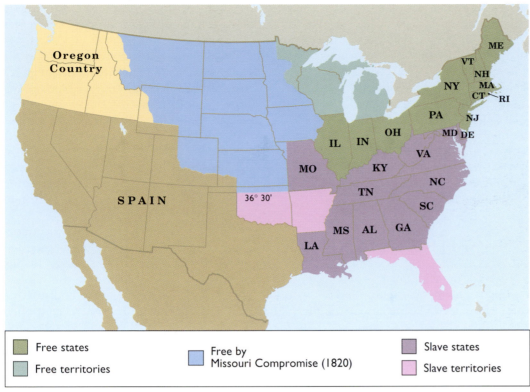

Slavery's Westward Migration after 1820

were ideal for cotton cultivation. They were the locus of an extraordinary cotton boom that increased U.S. production of the crop more than twentyfold from 1810 to 1860, when the annual harvest exceeded 4 million bales. Cotton, and by extension slavery, was the Southern economy. It also was a vital part of the American economy as a whole. Cotton was the leading U.S. export throughout the antebellum period, often surpassing the value of all other exports combined. Cotton cloth manufacture spurred the first real growth of a factory system in New England, contributing to the industrialization that heightened emerging sectional differences between North and South.

Key among these was the budding debate over slavery. Antislavery sentiment in the South faded after 1815 as cotton threaded its way into every aspect of the region's thriving economy. Even those opposed to slavery found it increasingly difficult to argue against its essential role in the region. It was a bad system, they acknowledged, but on practical grounds it could not be eliminated. In 1820 an aging Jefferson captured the South's dilemma. "We have the wolf by the ears, and we can neither hold him, nor safely let him go. Justice is in one scale, and self-preservation in the other."

Growing numbers in the North were not so ambivalent. At the least they did not want Jefferson's wolf ranging any farther into the western territories acquired through the Louisiana Purchase. Slavery had crossed the Mississippi River above Louisiana with the first American settlers into Arkansas and Missouri. Louisiana had been admitted as a slave state in 1812 and Arkansas organized as slave territory in 1819. Missouri's application for statehood that same year, as slave soil, set off the first open sectional conflict over slavery.

Aware of mounting Northern unease over slavery, the South after 1802 had insisted on maintaining a balance in the Senate between free and slave states. The more populous North held a majority of the seats in the House of Representatives, but in the Senate, where each state had two votes, the South could block federal antislavery legislation. A tradition of alternately admitting slave and free states had resulted in 11 of each by 1819. When Northern legislators proposed barring slavery in Missouri, Southern members responded indignantly. In fierce debate Congress in 1820 hammered out what became known as the Missouri Compromise. Missouri was to be admitted as a slave state and Maine as a free state, preserving the sectional balance. Slavery was excluded from the Louisiana Purchase above the latitude 36°30'. At the time the compromise meant slavery could extend no farther west, as the territory below the Louisiana Purchase was part of

BACK TO AFRICA

Those advocating the manumission of slaves faced a difficult question—what to do with the hundreds of thousands of freed blacks that would result? From the 1780s on, most American leaders believed large numbers of freed blacks could not be absorbed into white society.

As early as 1776 Thomas Jefferson proposed a plan for the colonization of American blacks in Africa. The idea of returning freed slaves gained favor in the 1790s, especially in Virginia and the other tobacco states of the upper South. As tobacco production declined, planters contemplated having large numbers of excess slaves. African colonization seemed a sensible solution, but somehow overlooked was the fact that most slaves could not "return" to Africa as they had been born on American soil.

Various colonization proposals were floated in the early 1800s. In 1817, at the urging of President James Madison, Kentucky congressman Henry Clay, and other influential leaders, Robert Finley, a Presbyterian minister from New Jersey, organized the American Colonization Society. Its purpose was to aid the immigration of freed slaves to Africa. The society was headed at various times by such noted figures as Madison, James Monroe, and John Marshall. It was financed by private contributions, mostly from Maryland, Virginia, and Kentucky.

The society purchased a tract of land on the west coast of Africa, just below the British colony of Sierra Leone. The introduction of freed American blacks to the area was not new, as Englishman Granville Sharp in 1787 had settled some 400 former slaves at Freetown in Sierra Leone.

The society's first boatload of freed slaves, led by white missionary Jehudi Ashmun, established the settlement of Monrovia (after President Monroe) in 1822. The society provided advisers, supplies, and other assistance to the colony, which was named Liberia.

Between 1822 and 1860, the society helped move about 6,000 black settlers to Liberia. Perhaps another

Spanish Mexico. Southern senators accepted the compromise in part because they believed the soil and climate of the territory above 36°30′ unsuited for slave-cultivated crops.

The compromise also paved the way for Arkansas to join the ranks of cotton-growing states. By the 1830s cotton's hold on the South was complete. As the expression went, cotton was king. What became known as the Cotton Kingdom stretched across the Deep South from South Carolina to Arkansas.

SLAVE FLIGHT AND REVOLT

The kingdom metaphor was only too apt, as Southern planters became a kind of aristocracy. Many affected the chivalrous lifestyle immortalized by the movie *Gone With the Wind*. Most were blind to the contradictions between their codes of honor and the inhumane system of bondage on which their world depended. In their kingdom, many of the inhabitants were not loyal subjects, but desperate and angry slaves.

Most slaves dreamed of escape, but there were few possibilities. Most often the greatest opportunities for flight were along the frontier, where blacks could slip away into the wilderness and find haven with either Native Americans or other runaway slaves. Escaping slaves in Texas could make for Mexico, which had abolished slavery in 1829. Small numbers of slaves in Georgia and Alabama managed to flee to Spanish Florida, but this refuge was lost when Florida became U.S. soil. In the 1830s and 1840s the Seminole Indians welcomed runaway slaves, who could help in the fight against U.S. forces, to their hideaways in the Florida Everglades. From southern Florida, a small number of slaves, stowing away on ships or disguising themselves as sailors, escaped to Andros Island in the Bahamas, where the British eliminated slavery in 1833. The famed black abolitionist Frederick Douglass was among the handful of slaves who escaped to the North by sea. In 1838 Douglass, posing as a sailor, was able to board a ship in Baltimore that carried him to freedom in New York. Most fugitive slaves made for the North, hiding by day and traveling along back trails by night, using the North Star as their guide. Southern slave patrols, however, and the long distances to free states greatly hindered their flight. Only a small percentage of the slave population, numbering in the tens of thousands, ultimately made it to freedom. The majority of slaves never attempted flight,

unwilling to risk recapture and punishment, or to accept separation from relatives and friends.

Many runaway slaves remained in the South. A few made their way to the region's cities and blended into the free black population. Small groups of slaves known as maroons hid out in unsettled areas such as the Great Dismal Swamp along the border between Virginia and North Carolina. Most fugitive slaves in the South never enjoyed more than a short freedom before suffering capture, brutal whipping, and return to servitude.

Other slaves dreamed of retribution. Though infrequent, and closely guarded against by local authorities, slave revolts were a searing reminder of the violent antagonisms simmering just beneath the surface of the South's tightly controlled slave system. In 1800 Gabriel Prosser secretly organized over 1,000 fellow slaves on Virginia plantations for an armed attack on neighboring Richmond. Prosser, who had learned to read and had studied the Bible, believed himself a Samson-like figure destined to free his people. Once Richmond was taken, he planned to liberate all of Virginia and make it a freed-slave kingdom. If the plan failed, the slaves were to go into the mountains and fight from there.

Prosser's uprising was revealed to authorities by other slaves the day before it was to occur. With the element of surprise gone, the slave rebellion dissolved before it got started. Prosser was caught and hanged, along with 40 other leaders of the abortive revolt.

The successful slave revolt in French colonial Haiti in 1791 inspired Denmark Vesey, a former slave and free black living in Charleston, to contemplate a similar uprising in South Carolina. By 1821 Vesey had organized a secret network that would mobilize some 9,000 slaves for an assault on Charleston. The revolt was set for July 1821 but again authorities learned of the plot through other slaves. The uprising was thwarted and 37 black rebels, including Vesey and other ringleaders, were executed.

The Vesey plot terrified the local white populace and alarmed slave owners throughout the South. In its wake, the "black codes" governing slavery were tightened to curb the mobility of slaves, limit their attendance at meetings, and restrict their education. Slaves were forbidden to circulate after curfew and nightly road patrols were established by local authorities. In every slave state except Maryland, Kentucky, and Tennessee, laws prohibited teaching slaves to read and write. Additional restrictions were also placed on free blacks.

A widespread slave rebellion in the South was never feasible, and the Southern slave regime was never seriously threatened. Still, white fears were raised to a fever pitch by the renowned revolt led by Nat Turner in Southampton County, Virginia, in 1831. In the "Southampton Insurrection," 60 to 80 fellow slaves inspired by the charismatic Turner went on a rampage against local slave owners, believing it their only chance at freedom. In two days they killed 57 whites, sowing panic throughout the area before they were suppressed by state and federal forces. A sensational manhunt led to the capture of the fugitive Turner, who was subsequently hanged. In all as many as 100 blacks were killed.

The Turner insurrection was the last notable slave revolt, as it brought even more stringent controls that precluded further rebellions. It also hardened Southern resistance to the elimination of slavery. After 1831, there was little or no sentiment in favor of manumission in the South. By 1860, 10 states had enacted provisions curbing both the statutory and voluntary emancipation of slaves. Southern attitudes coalesced around the belief that slavery was indispensable not only to the region's economy but also to its social order and way of life.

THE PECULIAR INSTITUTION

From the 1830s slavery in the Western Hemisphere became more and more unique, or peculiar, to the American South. Ultimately it became known as the South's "peculiar institution." Great Britain ended bondage in its New World colonies in 1833; France did the same in 1848. The Spanish American republics abolished slavery as they became independent. When Peru issued an emancipation proclamation in 1854, slavery in the Western Hemisphere was legal only in Brazil, the Spanish islands of Puerto Rico and Cuba, and the United States.

By 1840 virtually all the blacks in the North were free. Faced with increasing isolation, the South became more defiant in its defense of slavery. It also became more zealous. Slavery went from being a necessary evil to a positive good. Southerners advanced many specious arguments to justify their peculiar institution. It was a superior economic system to free labor; it was

sanctioned by the Bible; it was the appropriate condition for an inferior black race unable to fend for itself. Racism was prevalent in the North, but in the South it was used to justify slavery. Blacks were portrayed as better cared for and more contented under slavery. "The Negro slaves of the South are the happiest, and in some cases, the freest people in the world," wrote George Fitzhugh, one of the better-known Southern apostles of slavery.

THE UNDERGROUND RAILROAD

Black flight put the lie to Fitzhugh's absurd, but commonly endorsed, depiction of the happy slave. After 1831, with the further tightening of harsh slave codes, runaway slaves fled north in larger numbers. Many made their way along the Underground Railroad. This was a secret and shifting network of hiding places and routes for helping slaves escape to the North or Canada.

3,000 were sent through the efforts of other short-lived colonization groups. The numbers were small as most freed slaves resisted entreaties to immigrate to Africa, preferring to remain in their native America, however flawed it might be.

Support for manumission, and by extension for colonization, waned in the South after 1820. In the upper South, surplus slaves were funneled into the domestic slave trade. By 1830 it was clear to most Americans that colonization could not resolve the slavery question. Colonization activities gradually declined in the decades before the Civil War.

In 1847 black settlers in Liberia issued a Declaration of Independence, severed their ties with the American Colonization Society, and established Africa's first independent republic. From 1865 to its demise in 1912, the American Colonization Society functioned chiefly as adviser to the Liberian government.

Slave Revolt and Flight

Underground Railroad

journey was in the South. Once in the North, however, runaway slaves were not necessarily safe because of fugitive slave laws. As many as 50,000 escaped slaves fled to Canada, where they were protected by a British government that rejected demands for their extradition by U.S. authorities. The most favored routes to Canada were through Pennsylvania and Ohio, as Quaker communities in both states readily provided refuge to escaped slaves. After the Civil War some 30,000 blacks returned from Canada to the United States.

Southern slave patrols made travel on the Underground Railroad both dangerous and difficult. Slaves would move through swamps and along streams to throw off the scent of pursuing bloodhounds. Given the hazards and physical challenges, a majority of the slaves escaping were young males from the border states of Maryland, Virginia, Kentucky, and Missouri. Volume on the railroad was never heavy. In the peak years, after 1850, perhaps several thousand slaves a year managed to reach the North. In all, an estimated 75,000 slaves fled along the railroad to freedom.

FREE BLACKS NORTH AND SOUTH

Both fugitive slaves and free blacks in the North were at risk of forcible removal to the South by professional slavecatchers, who were not particularly careful about the status of those they seized. Antipathy for the entire practice of slavecatching led Pennsylvania and other Northern states after 1825 to pass personal liberty laws that protected free blacks and impeded enforcement of the federal fugitive slave law. Fugitive blacks, though legally still slaves, could find safety in Northern free black communities.

The free black population in the North had grown from about 27,000 in 1790 to just over 170,000 in 1840. Almost all were manumitted slaves or their descendants. Though free, Northern blacks faced both legal discrimination and considerable hostility. They were excluded from schools, denied the right to vote, and attacked by whites who refused to live or work near them. Their de facto confinement to segregated enclaves meant free blacks were much more likely than other Northerners to be urban dwellers. More than 60 percent of free blacks lived in Boston, New York, Philadelphia, and other cities.

There were actually more free blacks in the South, although they never constituted more than 10 percent of the region's total

THE WOMAN CALLED MOSES

The runaway slave Harriet Tubman is remembered to posterity as the greatest "conductor" on the Underground Railroad. Tubman was born at a plantation on the eastern shore of Maryland around 1821. She received no schooling, as was customary for slaves, and was put to work from an early age in the fields. In 1844 she wed John Tubman in an arranged marriage. Though he was a free black, by law she remained a slave.

Harriet Tubman first displayed the extraordinary independence and fortitude that would mark her life in resolved to escape. Fleeing north on

Its name dated from an 1831 episode in which a Kentucky slave owner pursued Tice Davis, a runaway slave, across the Ohio River. When the owner lost track of Davis, he remarked that the slave "must have gone off on an underground road." The name Underground Road soon evolved into Underground Railroad, reflecting the dominant movement image of the time. Safe houses and other stops were called "stations," and those guiding slaves to freedom "conductors."

More than 3,000 persons, both black and white, in both the South and North, helped "run" the railroad at various times, but there was never any formal organization. Networks to guide and assist fugitive slaves existed in the South as early as 1786 and spread onto the free soil of the Northwest Territory after 1815. Branches of the railroad extended into the northeastern states after 1830.

Often slaves made their own way along the railroad; other times they were aided by conductors. The most dangerous part of the

FREE BLACK POPULATION, 1790–1860

	UNITED STATES		NORTH		SOUTH	
	# Free Blacks	% Total Black Population	# Free Blacks	% Total Black Population	# Free Blacks	% Total Black Population
1790	59,466	7.9	27,109	40.2	32,357	4.7
1810	186,446	13.5	78,181	74.0	108,265	8.5
1840	386,303	13.4	170,728	99.3	215,575	8.0
1860	488,070	11.0	226,152	100	261,918	6.2

Source: Peter Kolchin, *American Slavery 1619–1877*

black population. There was also a marked contrast between the free black populations of the upper and lower South. Of the South's approximately 215,000 free blacks in 1840, 175,000 were in the upper South, and only 40,000 in the Deep South.

Most Southern free blacks were also former slaves or their descendants. Almost all the manumissions in the South occurred before 1810, and most were in the upper South. Augmenting the upper South's free black numbers were the two exceptions on manumission, Delaware and Maryland, where slaves were freed in significant numbers throughout the antebellum period.

Although there were relatively few free blacks in the Deep South, their situation was, in general, better than that of those in the upper South. The Deep South's free blacks were overwhelmingly light-skinned. Many were of mixed parentage and often were referred to as mulattoes rather than blacks. Along the Gulf of Mexico, free blacks with French or Spanish ancestry called themselves Creoles.

Terms such as *mulatto* and *Creole* separated the light-skinned free blacks from enslaved blacks. In the predominantly rural Deep South, a majority of the free blacks were urban dwellers. Many occupied skilled positions and attained a certain social status, despite the pervasive white racism. Creoles in Pensacola, Mobile, and especially New Orleans prided themselves on their distinctive heritage and culture. So did the hundreds of free, light-skinned refugees from violence-racked Hispaniola (the island comprising Haiti and Santo Domingo) who settled in Charleston, Savannah, and New Orleans around 1800.

The upper South's free blacks were darker, poorer, less educated, and more rural. Most lived on the edges of white society, surviving as farmhands and day laborers. A few owned and tilled small plots. About one-third lived in cities, with most residing in Baltimore and Washington, D.C.

BLEEDING KANSAS

Slavery was in force in the nation's capital until 1850. Most in the North opposed the extension of slavery into new territories, but few were prepared to call for its elimination where it already existed. A strong abolitionist movement emerged only slowly. The first issue of the abolitionist newspaper *The Liberator* was published by William Lloyd Garrison in 1831. Two years later he helped form the American Anti-Slavery Society. In the decades leading to the Civil War, Garrison; Theodore Weld; former slaves Sojourner Truth and Frederick Douglass; Harriet Beecher Stowe, author of *Uncle Tom's Cabin*; and others would agitate forcefully against slavery

After the Missouri Compromise, the issue of slavery's extension lay largely dormant until 1837, when a newly independent Texas petitioned for admission to the Union as a slave state. Northern antislavery legislators, led by John Quincy Adams, blocked Texas's annexation. Their Southern proslavery counterparts were enraged, but remained determined to add Texas to the Cotton Kingdom. Eight years later they capitalized on a growing national sense of America's transcontinental "manifest destiny" to garner enough votes in Congress to annex Texas as slave soil.

Annexation of Texas helped trigger the Mexican War (1846–48), which gained the United States a giant swath of Mexico stretching across the Southwest from New Mexico and Colorado to California. The Mexican Cession precipitated the last great sectional crisis that culminated in the Civil War.

The South, worried that it would be outnumbered in the Senate by free states carved from western territories, no longer supported the prohibition on slavery above 36°30'. Many Southerners saw the Southwest, and especially southern California, with its temperate climate and arable soil,

1849. Fearful on her master's death that the plantation's slaves would be sold into the Deep South, she resolved to escape. Fleeing north on the Underground Railroad, she reached Philadelphia, then an abolitionist center, where she was able to live as a free woman.

As a runaway slave Tubman faced severe penalties if ever caught, but two years later she slipped back into Maryland to help her endangered former husband, since remarried to another woman, to escape to the North. The trip was the first of many on the Underground Railroad. Tubman made as many as 20 forays into the South and brought some 300 slaves back to freedom.

She became known as Moses for guiding her people out of slavery, as the Old Testament figure had led the Jewish people from bondage in Egypt. Eventually Southerners offered a $40,000 reward for her arrest—dead or alive. Undeterred, the intrepid Tubman would brook no fear among her "passengers." If any showed signs of faltering, afraid of the beatings they faced if captured, she would point her shotgun at them, saying "Live North or die here."

To support herself, Tubman worked intermittently as a seamstress, laundress, and cook. The Civil War finally let her fight directly against slavery, and she served as nurse, scout, and spy for the Union Army. After the war she was active in temperance and women's movements.

Tubman slowly gained public recognition of her exploits. In her later years Congress voted her a small pension for her wartime services. On her death in 1913, full military honors were rendered at her funeral. In 1978 the U.S. government commemorated the Moses of the Underground Railroad with a Harriet Tubman stamp.

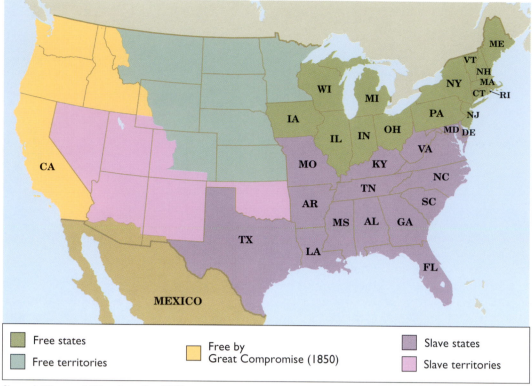

Slavery's Westward Migration after 1850

as a natural addition to their slave empire. In the North, groups opposed to any extension of slavery formed the Free Soil Party, with the motto "free soil, free speech, free labor, and free men."

California's application to become a free state, strongly supported in the North,

produced an uproar in the Congress. Southerners felt their peculiar institution under attack and demanded its protection. After bitter debate, Congress enacted a series of measures in 1850 that collectively were dubbed the Great Compromise. The North gained the immediate admission of Califor-

Slavery's Westward Migration after 1854

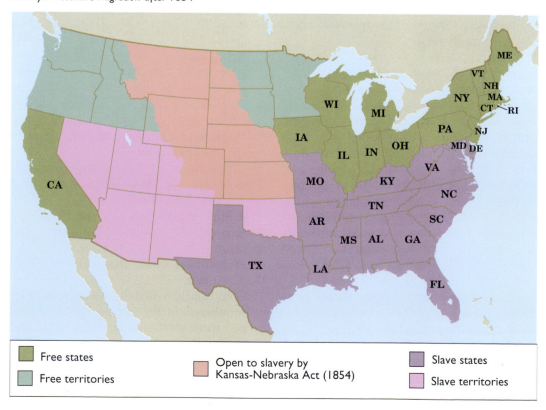

nia as a free state and termination of the domestic slave trade in the District of Columbia. The South won the opening of the newly formed New Mexico and Utah territories to slavery and a new and more stringent fugitive slave law.

Acquisition of California intensified planning for a transcontinental railroad. In 1854 Illinois Senator Stephen A. Douglas introduced a bill to organize the Kansas and Nebraska territories out of the northern part of Indian Territory, thus allowing the proposed railroad to follow a central route across the Great Plains. When Southern legislators hinged their support on repeal of the 36°30′ restriction on slavery, Douglas acceded. The Kansas-Nebraska Act introduced a new doctrine of "popular sovereignty," which left it to the residents of Kansas, Nebraska, and other territories to decide for themselves whether to be free or slave soil.

The Fugitive Slave Act, which made aiding a runaway slave a crime, had stoked antislavery passions in the North. The Kansas-Nebraska Act fanned the flame. The Republican Party was formed the same year on a platform calling for the repeal of both measures and the prohibition of any extension of slavery into the territories.

Both Northern and Southern groups rushed settlers into Kansas in an effort to influence the territory's vote on slavery. Fighting between the two sides soon gave the territory the name Bleeding Kansas. The free-soil forces prevailed, but Kansas remained an open wound until the Civil War.

In its infamous *Dred Scott* decision in 1857, the Supreme Court endorsed a Southern view of slavery. The Court first held that black slaves were property, not persons, under the law. It then found that federal restrictions on slavery in the territories were unconstitutional, in that they deprived slave-owning citizens of their property without due process of law. Under the ruling, slavery could be extended to the Oregon Territory or even, by implication, to free states. The decision heartened the South but converted many previously moderate Northerners to the antislavery cause. In 1858 Abraham Lincoln captured the essence of the sectional conflict then spinning out of control, predicting the nation could not endure "half slave and half free." It had to become "all one thing, or all the other." The Republican Lincoln's election as president in 1860 set in motion the South's secession from the Union, which in turn precipitated the Civil War.

SLAVE DISTRIBUTION IN 1860

North	64
Upper South	
Delaware	1,798
Maryland*	90,374
Virginia	490,865
North Carolina	331,059
Kentucky	225,483
Tennessee	275,719
Missouri	114,931
Total	1,530,229
Deep South	
South Carolina	402,406
Georgia	462,198
Florida	61,745
Alabama	435,080
Mississippi	436,631
Arkansas	111,115
Louisiana	331,726
Texas	182,566
Total	2,423,467
Grand Total	3,953,760

* includes the District of Columbia

Source: *Historical Statistics of the United States*

A MIGHTY SCOURGE

When Lincoln took office in 1861, slavery had changed the face as well as the character of America. Black Americans were found in sizable numbers in every state of the South. Most were slaves, and almost two-thirds were located in the Deep South. In the heart of the Cotton Kingdom, in Alabama, Mississippi, and Louisiana—states that had not existed in 1790—black slaves constituted roughly half the total population. Slavery extended into Texas and threatened to reach farther westward.

The Civil War (1861–65) was waged first over the expansion of slavery, which the North adamantly opposed and the South considered a fundamental right whose preservation was worth the dissolution of the Union. In 1863 Lincoln issued the Emancipation Proclamation, transforming the war into a fight over the elimination of slavery. In the South slaves never rose in

FATHER OF THE EXODUS

Benjamin Singleton was at the forefront of the two major currents in black migration between the Civil War and World War II—movement from South to North and immigration to Africa. Born in 1809 in Nashville, Tennessee, Singleton tried several times to flee from slavery before finally escaping and making his way to Detroit. There he ran a boardinghouse where other runaway slaves often stayed.

After the Civil War he returned to Tennessee, where he hoped to help former slaves build new, and independent, lives. In the late 1860s Singleton was part of an effort to buy lands for aspiring black small farmers. When white owners would not sell at reasonable prices, preferring to preserve black sharecropping, he encouraged blacks in Tennessee to move to Kansas.

Singleton anticipated the Great Exodus of blacks from the South after Reconstruction ended in 1877. He helped found several black settlements in Kansas and formed a company that assisted hundreds of blacks to relocate there from Tennessee between 1877 and 1879. He actively promoted black migration out of the South and distributed posters about his settlements throughout the region. His efforts helped inspire thousands to leave for Kansas and elsewhere.

The surging black migration caught the attention of Congress, which called Singleton to testify in 1880. His appearance, at which he explained his role in the movement northward, gained him the moniker "Father of the Exodus."

After Southern authorities succeeded in forcibly halting the Great Exodus, Singleton turned his attention to black self-improvement. In 1881 he established an organization called the United Colored Links in a black area of Topeka. The area was known as Tennessee Town because so many Exodusters, as black migrants to Kansas were called, had settled here. The primary aim of the Links was the

armed rebellion in anticipation of freedom, but did undermine the Southern war effort through passive resistance. As Union armies advanced into the Confederacy, slaves would abandon their plantations and flock to the Union lines. Some 180,000 black Americans, from both North and South, served in the Union forces.

In his Second Inaugural Address, Lincoln called the war a "mighty scourge," casting it as a national penance for the sin of slavery, to be fought if necessary until "every drop of blood drawn with the lash, shall be paid by another drawn with the sword." Union victory ended the Southern slave system, at a cost of over 600,000 lives.

FROM RECONSTRUCTION TO JIM CROW

Upon ratification in 1865, the 13th Amendment to the Constitution abolished slavery in the United States. The North imposed martial law on the South and undertook a program of "reconstruction" to transform Southern society. One key aim was assisting newly freed slaves, or freedpersons, to attain the civil and political rights of full citizens. The 14th Amendment in 1868 extended citizenship to all native-born Americans,

including freed blacks, and mandated equal protection under the law to all. The 15th Amendment in 1870 guaranteed all citizens the right to vote.

In the aftermath of the war, there was an initial euphoria as former slaves celebrated their freedom. Many sought out loved ones forcibly separated from them by slavery. Others moved away from the hated memories of their enslavement, contributing to widespread local migration. In anticipation of a better life, almost all the freedpersons remained in the South. They were joined by numbers of free blacks from the North returning to relatives and friends or to take part in Reconstruction.

The federal government undertook to provide freedpersons with new, and theoretically equal, opportunities. It stopped short, however, of furnishing specific assistance to help them surmount the legacy of slavery. Blacks gained access to public schools and to the political system. Various plans to redistribute land to former slaves, though contemplated, were never enacted.

The vast majority of freedpeople remained in the countryside. A small but important number managed to scrape together enough money to acquire their own land. Black landownership climbed from 2 percent of agricultural families possessing farms in 1870 to 21 percent in 1890.

Slavery in 1860

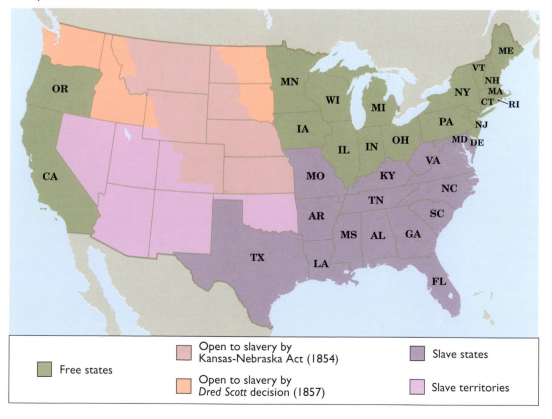

Legend:
- Free states
- Open to slavery by Kansas-Nebraska Act (1854)
- Open to slavery by *Dred Scott* decision (1857)
- Slave states
- Slave territories

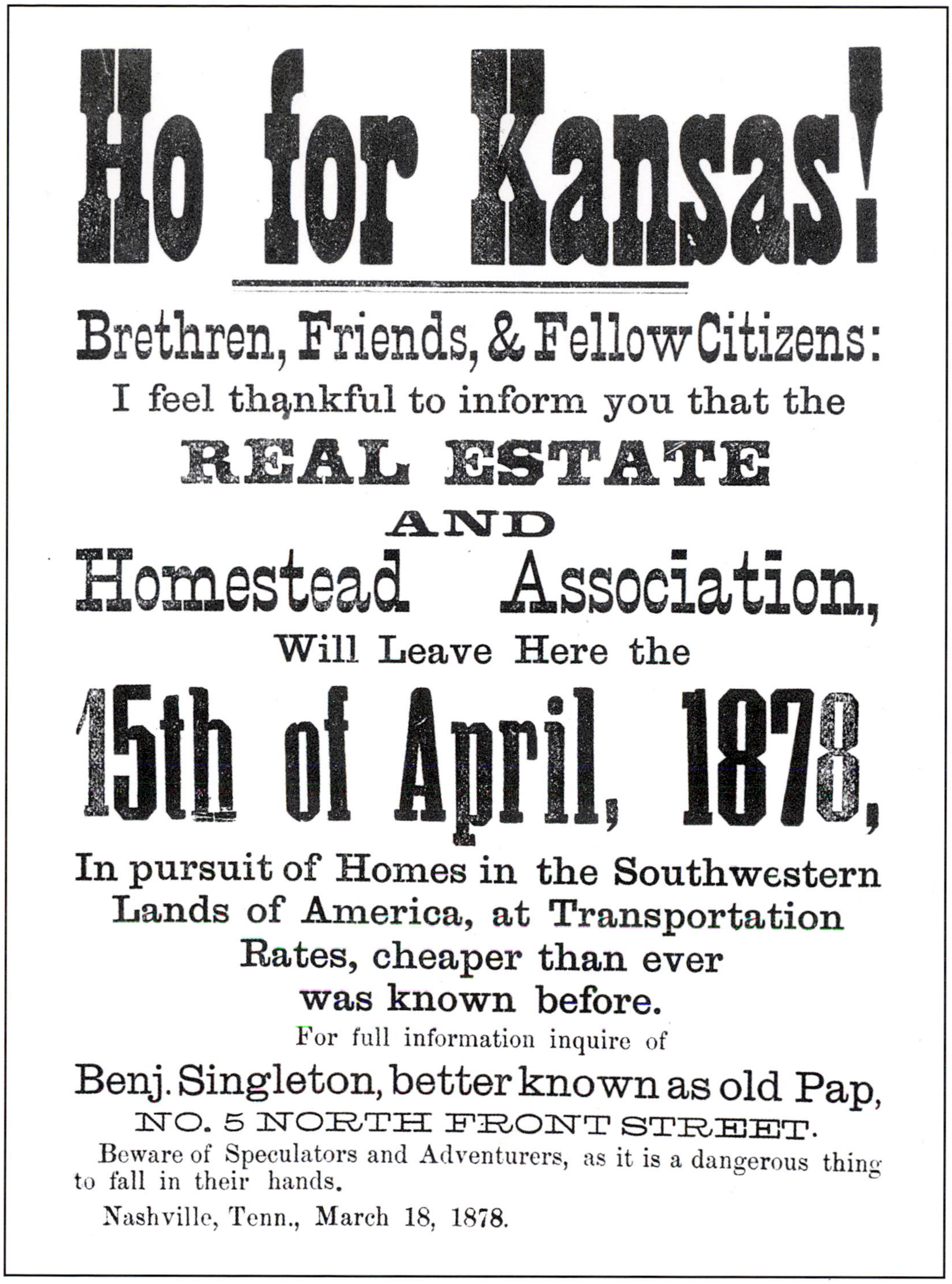

Ho for Kansas!

Brethren, Friends, & Fellow Citizens:

I feel thankful to inform you that the

REAL ESTATE

AND

Homestead Association,

Will Leave Here the

15th of April, 1878,

In pursuit of Homes in the Southwestern Lands of America, at Transportation Rates, cheaper than ever was known before.

For full information inquire of

Benj. Singleton, better known as old Pap,

NO. 5 NORTH FRONT STREET.

Beware of Speculators and Adventurers, as it is a dangerous thing to fall in their hands.

Nashville, Tenn., March 18, 1878.

Advertising African-American settlement in Kansas   (Kansas State Historical Society)

development of black-owned enterprises, but a lack of seed money in the local black community kept them from achieving their goal.

Disheartened by the impediments to black advancement, Singleton conceived of a black exodus from America itself. He came to see Africa as the "fatherland" to which black Americans should return. In 1885 he founded the Trans-Atlantic Society to help blacks emigrate to Africa. His project met with little enthusiasm among African Americans and by 1887 his organization had fallen apart. Singleton died in 1892. His ideas of black self-sufficiency and especially black emigration to Africa would be given new life by Marcus Garvey and others in the 1920s.

Most freedpersons, however, went from slave to sharecropper. Under this arrangement, blacks contracted for the right to live on and work a parcel of land in return for providing a share of the crop to the owner.

Sharecropping began to resemble the social structure of the antebellum South, with white owners presiding over black tenants. Sharecroppers were free, but far from equal. In the 1870s, as Reconstruction governments in the former Confederate states were replaced by local administrations, Southern whites regained political control. White racism was rampant, fueled by perceived Northern favoritism toward blacks. Vigilante violence, aimed at terrorizing blacks into submission, flourished.

THE GREAT EXODUS

The postwar Northern fervor for Reconstruction had subsided by 1877, when Republican Rutherford B. Hayes finally prevailed in the contested 1876 presidential election. The disputed voting results had forced the election into the House of Representatives. To gain the southern votes nec-

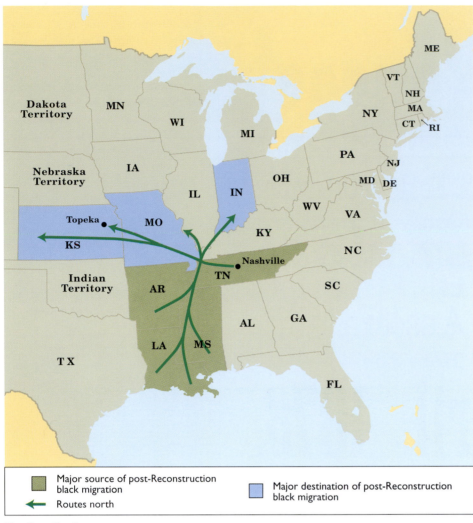

Major source of post-Reconstruction
black migration

Major destination of post-Reconstruction
black migration

Routes north

The Great Exodus

essary to secure his victory, Hayes agreed to withdraw the remaining federal troops from the South. This promise, fulfilled the same year, ended the Reconstruction period and removed the remaining protections against discrimination and oppression for Southern blacks.

In response thousands of blacks fled the South after 1877. By 1880 more than 50,000 had made their way north in what became known as the Great Exodus. Tens of thousands went to Kansas, prompted by reports of readily available land. The outflow reached a level where Southern authorities, concerned over the loss of sharecropping labor, felt compelled to stop it. They posted armed patrols along roads to turn the migrants back and by the end of 1880 the exodus was largely halted.

In the 1880s and 1890s Southern states enacted measures that rolled back black civil and political rights. Blacks were legally segregated from whites and confined to an inferior, subservient status. The term Jim Crow, long derisively applied to blacks, came to stand for this system of segregation. In 1900, 37 years after emancipation, Southern blacks found themselves trapped by Jim Crow laws in second-class citizenship.

TRAILS OF TEARS
Native American Migration

They are the other images of America's triumphant conquest of the frontier—the Cherokee herded west along the Trail of Tears, the Navajo made to endure the Long Walk across New Mexico, the desperate Flight of the Nez Percé from pursuing U.S. troops. The removal of the Native Americans from the path of American transcontinental expansion ranks with slavery as one of the two great involuntary migrations in U.S. history. In 1783 the area between the Appalachian Mountains and the Pacific Ocean was still largely the domain of Indian tribes. Within another century, the Native Americans had been driven from their lands, forced into local reservations, or relocated to what is now Oklahoma. This massive, and often violent, displacement brought the virtual destruction of Native American ways of life and exacted a staggering human toll. From perhaps 800,000 at the time of American independence, the number of Native Americans had dwindled to less than 250,000 when the frontier was declared officially closed in 1890.

INDIAN POLICY

The Native Americans were victims of historical forces far beyond their control. What primarily determined their fate was American Indian policy. While various factors influenced its implementation—the discovery of gold, for example—U.S. Indian policy was consistently guided by two often conflicting goals: fair treatment of the Native Americans and simultaneous promotion of the western movement of American settlers. It is scarcely evident in the way U.S.-Indian relations unfolded, but federal officials from the 1780s on were aware of the mistreatment of Native Americans and often endeavored to fashion policies intended to help or protect Indian tribes. While there was little real appreciation of the Native American plight, there was a widespread desire to keep U.S. Indian policy within the established legal norms of a civilized society. In practice, however, any concern for, or commitment to, Indian rights was invariably subordinated to the overarching objective of opening the West to American settlement. Respect for Indian land rights never stood in the way of the relentless seizure of Indian territory.

Three basic approaches were taken to clearing Indians from the advance of American settlement: removal of tribes to a separate Indian territory; confinement of tribes to designated reservations; and forced assimilation of Indians into American society. The use of these different strategies frequently overlapped. Assimilation, for instance, often entailed the conversion of Indians to farming, which facilitated their placement on smaller reservations.

U.S. Indian policy continued to affect Native American migration well past the final settlement of the West. The long and mostly tragic story of U.S.–Indian relations can be divided into six relatively distinct periods: 1783–89, when Indian lands were treated as "conquered provinces"; 1789–1830, when emphasis was on the purchase of Indian lands as part of a larger policy of trade and intercourse; 1830–1853, which saw the formulation of an official Indian removal policy; 1853–1887, which was marked by development of the reservation system; 1887–1934, when the federal government pursued the final breakup and assimilation of Indian tribes; and 1934 to the present, during which U.S. policies have supported a return of tribal organization and life.

INDIAN TREATIES

The U.S. government relied on treaties to shape and define relations with Indian tribes until 1871. In doing so, the United States continued the practice established by Great Britain in the colonial period of treating tribes as nations and negotiating formal diplomatic agreements with them. However, the United States did not consider Indian tribes to be independent nation states. Rather, the tribes were viewed as essentially separate governments, with limited sovereign powers over their peoples and lands. Eventually the term "domestic dependent nations" was coined to explain the status of

Indian tribes. Although within the territory of the United States, the tribes were long understood to be outside the American polity. Thus treaties were required to govern U.S.–tribal relations.

Some 370 treaties had been formally concluded by 1871, when Congress terminated their use with Indian tribes. Congress's action underscored the growing sentiment that recognition of tribes as independent powers was no longer necessary or appropriate. Thereafter, U.S. envoys made simple agreements with tribes that became federal law on approval by Congress.

The 1871 legislation did not abrogate existing Indian treaties. As it was, most treaties had never been much more than artifice. A complex instrument like a treaty could never really bridge the chasm between Native American and American notions of sovereignty or land rights. Most treaties were imposed on the Indians, with American negotiators often resorting to trickery, deception, or bribery. Many treaties were signed under duress. Additionally, the U.S. record of adherence to the generally one-sided agreements was abysmal. The federal government violated the terms of many treaties and consistently failed to protect Native American treaty rights. Early Indian historian Helen Jackson rightly titled her 1880 study of U.S.-Indian relations *A Century of Dishonor*.

INDIAN LAND CESSIONS

The United States relied on Indian treaties to regulate trade with tribes, establish peace terms following Indian wars, and define the extent of federal control over tribal affairs. The main purpose of the agreements, though, was to arrange for Indian land cessions. Of the 370 formally ratified treaties, 230 addressed land cessions or related territorial matters. Of these, 76 involved the removal of Indians to the West.

Native Americans had no say in U.S. territorial expansion. When the United States acquired the Louisiana Purchase from France in 1803, for example, no consideration was given to the consent of the affected tribes. Indian tribes, denied recognition as nation-states, were not deemed to have sovereign territorial rights. The U.S. government did, however, accept the principle that tribes on American soil held a fundamental title to their lands, based on a right of original occupancy. Such title, in theory, could be taken from tribes only with their assent, as expressed in treaties. In practice, the requirement for Indian consent to land cessions was little more than a formality. Indian tribes along the constantly retreating frontier were forced to relinquish their territories as the pressure of advancing white settlement overpowered their resistance to the loss of their lands. America had gained title

NATIVE AMERICAN ATTRITION, FROM EUROPEAN CONTACT TO 1907

| Region | Date | CHARACTERISTICS AT EUROPEAN CONTACT | | | | CHARACTERISTICS IN 1907 | | | | | |
		Population	Number of Tribes	Mean size	Contact size, %	Population	Number of Tribes	Mean size	Tribes extinct	Tribes nearing extinction	Tribes extinct or near extinction, %
North Atlantic	1600	55,600	24	2,317	39.4	21,900	10	2,190	14	6	83.3
South Atlantic	1600	52,200	35	1,491	4.2	2,170	15	145	20	14	97.1
Gulf States	1650	114,400	39	2,933	54.8	62,700	12	5,225	27	4	79.5
Central States	1650	75,300	12	6,275	61.3	46,126	10	4,613	2	1	25.0
Northern Plains	1780	100,800	20	5,040	50.1	50,477	19	2,804	1	1	10.0
Southern Plains	1690	41,000	12	3,417	7.0	2,861	7	409	5	0	41.7
Columbia Region	1780	88,800	95	935	17.4	15,431	83	211	12	40	54.7
Central Mountains	1845	19,300	6	3,217	59.8	11,544	6	1,924	0	0	0
New Mexico and Arizona	1680	72,000	25	2,880	74.8	53,832	19	2,833	6	1	28.0
California	1769	260,000	45	5,778	7.2	18,797	36	696	9	9	40.0
Total		879,000	313			285,838	217		96	76	
Average	1704			2,712	66.3			1,470			57.5

Source: Russel Thornton, *We Shall Live Again: The 1870 and 1890 Ghost Dance Movements as Demographic Revitalization.*

to all Indian lands east of the Mississippi by 1842, in the Far West by 1873, and in the Southwest and Great Plains by 1889.

INDIAN WARS

The Native Americans did not go gently. Indian tribes were in almost constant conflict with American settlers and soldiers for more than 100 years. War was ultimately how the Native Americans were driven from their lands and forced to settle on reservations. Use of military force became the defining element of U.S. Indian policy until the final suppression of Native American resistance in 1890.

Warfare between Indians and whites followed the pattern of American migration across the continent. Indian tribes east of the Mississippi, with the notable exception of the Seminole, had been pacified by 1832. The tribes of the Far West were subdued between the 1840s and 1870s. In the final, and often most violent, phase of the Indian wars, fighting engulfed the Southwest and Great Plains from the 1860s to the 1880s. Many tribes fought valiantly against inevitable defeat. In later decades, many of the most defiant Indian leaders and their bands were taken into captivity at Fort Sill in Indian Territory. So many Indian warriors are buried in a graveyard at Fort Sill that the cemetery is known as the Indian Arlington after the national military cemetery at Arlington, Virginia.

"CONQUERED PROVINCES"

War was part of the U.S.–Indian experience from the start. Despite the fact that many tribes fought alongside the British during the American Revolution, the Indians were not included in Anglo-American peace negotiations. The war-ending Treaty of Paris made no mention of Native Americans. Yet, under its terms, British-designated Indian Country west of the Appalachians became part of the United States. America was left to conclude its own settlements with the Indian tribes. The U.S. government had little doubt as to the status of tribes then on American soil. In September 1783—the same month the final Treaty of Paris was signed—George Washington referred to Indian lands as "conquered provinces" subject to U.S. seizure, a characterization that encapsulated American attitudes.

Flush with victory, and eager to begin settlement of the Old Northwest, the U.S. government moved to impose peace terms on the Indian tribes. The Articles of Confederation had assigned authority over Indian affairs to the central government, although states retained an ill-defined control over Indian matters within their own borders. In September 1783 the Confederation Congress issued a proclamation explicitly reserving to itself the right to secure title to Indian lands outside existing state jurisdictions. The U.S. government laid claim by so-called right of conquest to all Indian territory from the edge of American settlement west to the Mississippi. This right of conquest rested on the assertion that the Indians, as allies of the defeated British, had forfeited ownership of their lands.

In the spring of 1784 Congress appointed commissioners to negotiate with the Indians. In the Treaty of Fort Stanwix concluded the same year, U.S. negotiators forced the six tribes of the Iroquois Confederacy to surrender their lands in the Ohio valley. U.S. forces had inflicted serious reverses on the Iroquois during the Revolution. The Confederacy itself fell apart when the Oneida and Tuscarora split with the Mohawk, Onondaga, Cayuga, and Seneca and sided with the Americans. The Iroquois were allowed to remain on tribal lands in western and northern New York, where eventually they were confined to eight small state reservations.

Although the Delaware had signed a friendship treaty with the United States in 1778, the tribe after 1782 joined with the British to halt American advances in the Ohio region. In the Treaty of Fort McIntosh in 1785, the Delaware, as well as the Wyandot, Chippewa, and Ottawa, were made to yield their claims to the upper Ohio valley. A similar treaty was signed with the Shawnee in 1786.

Seizure of Indian lands was not limited to the North. The Treaty of Hopewell, also concluded in 1785, compelled extensive Cherokee land cessions in North Carolina and Tennessee. A second Treaty of Hopewell the following year extracted similar concessions from the Choctaw and Chickasaw.

In all the treaties, the U.S. government promised to protect remaining tribal lands from white encroachment. In practice, however, the Confederation Congress proved powerless to control the westward press of settlers and land speculators. In 1786 Congress enacted the Ordinance for the Regulation of Indian Affairs. The measure provided for Indian districts north and south of the Ohio River, each under a super-

INDIAN WARS AND LAND CESSIONS IN THE TRANSAPPALACHIAN WEST

AMERICAN REVOLUTION (1775–83) Most Native Americans supported the British during the Revolution, believing the rebel colonists posed much the greater danger to their tribal lands. An American army in 1779 responded to Iroquois raiding parties by razing the Iroquois homeland in upstate New York, inflicting a mortal blow to the Iroquois Confederacy. Defeat of the Cherokee by American forces the same year further opened Kentucky and Tennessee to settlement. With the end of hostilities the United States took the position that warring Indian tribes, as allies of the defeated British, had forfeited all rights to their lands. In a series of treaties imposed between 1784 and 1786 the U.S. government compelled land cessions from formerly belligerent tribes along the Western frontier.

LITTLE TURTLE'S WAR (1790–94) American settlers advancing into the Old Northwest met mounting Native American resistance. A loose confederation of Ohio valley Indians under the brilliant Miami chief Little Turtle routed American forces sent to pacify the hostile tribes. In 1793 a more formidable American army delivered a crushing blow to Little Turtle's warriors at the Battle of Fallen Timbers in northwestern Ohio. The Ohio valley tribes subsequently were forced to relinquish all of Ohio and eastern Indiana.

TECUMSEH'S REBELLION (1811–12) Shawnee warrior Tecumseh dreamed of creating a single Indian nation that could halt American western expansion. The 1809 Treaty of Fort Wayne, in which territorial governor and future president William Henry Harrison tricked local chiefs into signing away 3 million acres in southern Indiana, prompted Tecumseh to redouble his efforts to form a broad Indian military alliance. In 1811 Harrison marched with an army on Tecumseh's base at Tippecanoe in western Indiana and, after a bloody fight, burned the abandoned village. In the battle's aftermath Tecumseh counseled restraint until a powerful Indian alliance was a reality, but various tribes launched attacks on American settlements across the Ohio valley frontier. The raids, often encouraged by the British in Canada, became a cause of the War of 1812.

WAR OF 1812 (1812–15) When war broke out between the United States and Great Britain in 1812, Tecumseh saw the opportunity to achieve his goal of a separate Indian nation. Tecumseh allied himself and his warriors with the British side, which shared his opposition to American penetration of the Old Northwest. Tecumseh's death in 1813 at the Battle of the Thames in southern Canada spelled the end of effective Anglo-Indian resistance to American preeminence in the Old Northwest. After the war the region's tribes were forced to sign treaties opening the territory below Lake Michigan to American settlement.

CREEK WAR (1813–14) Tecumseh had appealed to Creek leaders to join his proposed Indian confederation. The Creeks split into two factions: the Red Sticks wanted war with the whites; the White Sticks counseled peace. The War of 1812 emboldened the Red Stick faction to attack American settlements along the southern frontier. In 1814 an American army under General Andrew Jackson crushed the Red Stick rebellion at the Battle of Horseshoe Bend in central Alabama. In the Treaty of Fort Jackson signed the same year, the American general forced the Creek to cede 23 million acres in southern Georgia and central and southern Alabama.

SEMINOLE WARS (1817–58) After the War of 1812, tensions along the Georgia-Florida border mounted over the harboring of runaway black slaves by Seminole Indians. U.S. troop forays into Spanish-held Florida to suppress the practice flared into the First Seminole War (1817–18). In 1818 an American army overran northern Florida and drove the Seminole southward into the Florida peninsula. In 1832 the U.S. government prevailed on the Seminole to sign the Treaty of Payne's Landing, stipulating their relocation within three years to Indian Territory. By 1835, however, no Seminole had moved west. U.S efforts to remove the tribe by force triggered the Second Seminole War (1835–42). Despite their fierce resistance, most of the Seminole eventually were removed to Indian Territory. In 1842 U.S. officials abandoned attempts to flush the remaining Seminole out of the swamps and everglades of southern Florida. The subsequent movement of American settlers into the southern everglades precipitated the Third Seminole War (1855–58). The bloody fighting only desisted when a group of Seminole was brought from

Indian Territory to negotiate the removal of their tribal brethren.

KICKAPOO RESISTANCE (1819–24) After the War of 1812, veterans collecting on promised land bounties led the American push into Illinois. Bowing to pressure from federal land agents, the Kickapoo agreed under an 1819 treaty to cede their lands in southern Indiana and Illinois and move across the Mississippi into Missouri. Many small bands of Kickapoo resisted removal and resorted to harassing raids on American settlements. Increasing U.S. military pressure had forced most Kickapoo across the Mississippi by 1824.

WINNEBAGO UPRISING (1826–27) In the 1820s the Winnebago Indians joined in the mining of rich lead deposits in the upper Mississippi country of northwest Illinois and southwest Wisconsin. Tensions flared when U.S. officials moved to halt the Winnebago mining out of concern that the tribe would never relinquish its profitable territory. In 1827, after a series of violent clashes with American miners and settlers pouring into the area, the Winnebago were intimidated by an overwhelming U.S. military force into submitting to confiscation of their lands.

BLACK HAWK WAR (1832) After the War of 1812 the Sauk and Fox, who had sided with the British, were forced to reconfirm a contested 1804 treaty relinquishing their tribal lands in western Illinois and Wisconsin. The Sauk chief Black Hawk and his followers steadfastly refused to depart their homeland in northwestern Illinois. Under U.S. military pressure, Black Hawk fled with his band of 300 warriors and their families across the Mississippi into Iowa in 1830. His continuing opposition to white expansion rallied members of other tribes to his side. Black Hawk and a much larger band of followers crossed back into Illinois in 1832, seeking to reoccupy ceded lands. Met by a superior American force, Black Hawk and his warriors managed to escape north into Wisconsin, where they were routed by another American army at the Battle of Wisconsin Heights. The last war in the Old Northwest ended with the massacre of the remnants of Black Hawk's band as they attempted to flee westward across the Mississippi.

intendent authorized to take necessary steps to protect Indian rights and property. The ordinance from its inception was undermined by inadequate enforcement and open flouting of its provisions. By 1787, Indian anger over forced land cessions and continuing white encroachment engendered mounting hostilities along the frontier, thereby threatening the U.S. goal of a peaceful and orderly westward expansion. The still sparsely settled United States of the 1780s was also far warier of costly Indian wars than the much more populous nation of later decades.

Congress after 1787 abandoned its conquered-province approach to Indian land acquisitions and reverted to the colonial-era practice of negotiating with tribes for the purchase of their lands. The Northwest Ordinance in 1787 reaffirmed Indian title to lands west of the Appalachian Divide. In 1788 Congress went so far as to appropriate monies to reimburse tribes for lands already ceded. Still, the change in policy was one of approach, not of goal. The landmark Northwest Ordinance also made clear the overarching American intention to settle the West, with the inevitable implication that Indian lands would be acquired and their occupants displaced.

TRADE AND INTERCOURSE

Indian matters were on the minds of the Constitution's framers. The Confederation-era principle of federal primacy in Indian affairs was incorporated into the Constitution. Article 1, section 8, clause 3 gave Congress the authority to "regulate commerce . . . with the Indian tribes." This power, from the start, was connected to the treaty-making power vested in the president. The first treaty concluded by the newly constituted U.S. government was with an Indian tribe. The Treaty of New York in 1790 established relations with the Creek Indian Nation and, not surprisingly, arranged for substantial tribal land cessions in Georgia.

Supervision of Indian affairs was assigned to the Department of War. Still, the basic aim of U.S. policy continued to be the maintenance of peaceful, if not friendly, relations with western tribes to facilitate settlement of the frontier and to preclude Indian alliances with the British in the Old Northwest or with the Spanish in the Old Southwest. U.S. officials were also aware of the unscrupulous actions of settlers along the frontier. In 1789 President George Washington told Congress that "the treaty with the Cherokees has been entirely violated by the disorderly white people on the frontiers of North Carolina."

Congress in the 1790s passed a series of laws "to regulate trade and intercourse with the Indian tribes, and to preserve peace on the frontier." The acts provided for the licensing of Indian traders; prohibited the acquisition of Indian lands by individuals unless authorized by public treaty with the United States; defined Indian Country; and set punishments for crimes committed by whites against Indians on Indian lands. These measures, codified in the Trade and Intercourse Act of 1802, served as the foundation for U.S. Indian policy until the 1830s.

THE FACTORY SYSTEM

As Americans pushed westward, fur traders and others were only too ready to fleece the Indians. To prevent such exploitation, which threatened conflict along the frontier, Congress in 1796 established government-owned trading houses, where Indians could get goods at cost.

With American expansion an ever-larger number of tribes came under U.S. control. The network of trading posts, called the factory system after the factors, or agents, in charge of the government stores, was extended across the Mississippi River in 1806 and placed under a superintendent of Indian trade. Opposition by fur companies and frontier merchants led to termination of the factory system in 1822. The void in the management of U.S.-Indian relations was filled in 1824 by creation of the Bureau of Indian Affairs in the War Department. The bureau regulated the Indian trade, administered U.S.-Indian treaties, and later assisted in the removal of tribes to Indian territory and oversaw federal reservations. In 1849 the bureau was transferred to the newly formed Interior Department.

The desire for a more honest Indian trade never extended to a larger respect for Indian rights, particularly land rights. Relentless American pressure forced tribe after tribe to cede its lands along the frontier. In 1809 Indian leader Tecumseh angrily denounced the unending encroachment at a meeting with William Henry Harrison, then governor of Indiana Territory. At one point, as the two men sat alone on a long bench, Tecumseh kept crowding Harrison so that he had to keep moving toward one end. When Harrison complained, the Shawnee chief replied that he was just demonstrating how the whites pushed the Indians off their

Delaware — Tribe removed to Indian Territory
Chippewa — Tribe confined to reservation
⚔ — Battle site

Eastern Native American Tribes, 1775 to 1860

lands. Native Americans resorted to diplomacy, appeasement, alliances with the British and Spanish, and warfare to halt the American advance but all to no avail. By 1830 any meaningful resistance to white settlement east of the Mississippi had been crushed.

INDIAN REMOVAL

American settlement of the West early on raised the difficult question of how Indians and whites could live in close proximity. Tribes squeezed onto ever smaller tracts of land saw their traditional hunting grounds converted to farms by iron tool-armed settlers. The mix of vastly different Indian and white cultures only deepened mutual distrust and misunderstanding. Many settlers, reflecting a brutal frontier hostility to Native Americans, would readily have welcomed their virtual annihilation.

Those responsible for U.S. Indian policy saw the answer in the conversion of Indians to an American small-farm way of life. As early as 1793 Congress appropriated monies "to promote civilization" among Indian tribes, chiefly through the provision of farm tools and livestock. Such efforts were not solely for the betterment of Native Americans. President Thomas Jefferson in 1803 articulated the common view that aiding the adaptation of the Indians to agriculture would not only help pacify the frontier, but also make them more amenable to further land cessions.

Protestant missionary groups set up schools at which Indian children were taught basic English reading and writing as well as the Gospel. In 1819 Congress voted an annual allotment in support of Indian education. By the mid-1820s, there were some 30 missionary-run schools with over 900 Indian students.

Native American culture, however, proved remarkably resilient to white acculturation. By the late 1820s even the most ardent supporters of "civilizing" the Indians acknowledged that little progress had been made. Most tribes clung to their traditional ways, even as contact with whites brought an ever more desperate plight of disease, alcoholism, and starvation.

Even supporters of Indian assimilation began calling for the removal of the remaining eastern tribes to west of the Mississippi River. Some argued such drastic action was necessary to prevent the extinction of the Indians; others, that acculturation could work only gradually and apart from the hostile presence of white settlement.

The idea of Indian removal was not new. It had first been contemplated by Jefferson, who, after the Louisiana Purchase, noted that acquisition of the vast territory made possible the relocation of eastern tribes. Developments surrounding the War of 1812 crowded out further consideration of Indian removal until the presidency of James Monroe. Both Monroe and his successor, John Quincy Adams, favored removal, believing it would benefit not only land-hungry settlers but the "half-civilized" tribes as well. Despite their support for relocation, action in the Congress stalled over the potential cost.

It is ironic that the final impetus for Indian removal stemmed from a dispute over Cherokee lands in Georgia. The Cherokee were by far the most assimilated tribe on American soil. They had developed a written form of the Cherokee language so they could have books, newspapers, and official records like their white neighbors. In 1820 the Cherokee Council adopted a republican form of government patterned on that of the United States. In 1827 the mixed Cherokee John Ross and other tribal leaders founded the Cherokee Nation under a written constitution, with an elected principal chief, senate, and house of representatives. The Cherokee capital was established at New Echota, Georgia, in the heart of U.S. treaty-protected ancestral lands.

The discovery of gold at nearby Dahlonega in 1828, however, spurred long-standing claims to Cherokee lands by the Georgia state government. Georgia was not alone in seeking to abrogate existing treaty terms, as Alabama and Mississippi also coveted Indian lands. The fate of the Cherokee and other eastern tribes was sealed the same year with the election of legendary Indian fighter Andrew Jackson to the presidency. Sharp Knife, as he was known to the Indians, was convinced that tribal enclaves could no longer exist within the states. Either the Indians had to move west or become subject to the laws of the states, which meant the loss of their remaining lands.

The Cherokees resisted federal entreaties either to relocate or accept absorption into Georgia. The fact that they had fought under Jackson against the Creek at the Battle of Horseshoe Bend (1814) did not sway the president in his determination to see Indian removal through. In 1830 he gained passage of the Indian Removal Act. The law authorized the president to set aside unorganized public lands west of the Mississippi and to exchange these districts for Indian-held areas in the East. Emigrating tribes would receive perpetual title to their new lands. The act provided for the cost of relocating the Indians and guaranteed their protection in their new home.

INDIAN TERRITORY

Jackson intended to remove the eastern tribes to an area in Indian Country west of Arkansas and Missouri. Since the 1790s the term Indian Country had been used to designate the territory for which Indians had not ceded their claims to the U.S. government. Early trade and intercourse acts had defined Indian Country only loosely, with its boundary "a line of meter and bounds, variable from time to time by treaties." Indian removal necessitated a more precise definition, which was provided by the Trade and Intercourse Act of 1834. Indian Country became "that part of the United States west of the Mississippi . . . to which the Indian title has not been extinguished." The law, in effect, accepted the relocation of eastern tribes, and the relinquishment of their lands, as an accomplished fact. The part of Indian Country specifically set aside for Indian removal became known as Indian Territory.

At its greatest extent, in 1834, Indian Territory stretched north from the Red River to the Missouri River and ran west from Iowa, Missouri, and Arkansas to the 100th meridian. The semi-arid region, then at the western edge of U.S. territory, was considered unsuited for white settlement. Despite the seemingly inhospitable terrain, and the

Indian Territory in 1834

- Territory
- State
- Indian Territory

promise of perpetual land titles, the tribes relocated to Indian Territory were not long safe from white encroachment. On both Indian removal and Indian Territory the U.S. government "spoke with forked tongue." With railroad interests and then settlers pressing for entry into the central and southern Plains, the United States progressively reduced the size of Indian Territory until its eventual incorporation into Oklahoma in 1907.

DOMESTIC DEPENDENT NATIONS

When Georgia in 1830, in anticipation of Indian removal, extended its control over Cherokee lands, the tribe appealed to the Supreme Court. The Cherokees asserted that as a sovereign nation they were immune from state action. In two landmark decisions that shape Indian affairs to this day, the court ruled first on the legal status of Indian tribes and then on the measure of state authority over Indian areas. In *Cherokee Nation* v. *Georgia* (1831), Chief Justice John Marshall, writing for the majority, held that Indian tribes were not independent in the sense of foreign states, but were "domestic dependent nations" under the sovereignty and protection of the United States. In *Worcester* v. *Georgia* (1832) the Court nullified Georgia's extension of state law over the Cherokees, ruling that the federal government had exclusive jurisdiction over Indian affairs. Again penning the majority opinion, Marshall noted that Indian land rights within treaty-designated boundaries had long been "guaranteed by the United States."

Jackson had no intention of complying with the two decisions, which at least implied Indian removal should be voluntary. He reportedly remarked after *Worcester*, "John Marshall has made his decision. Now let him enforce it." The Jackson administration had set about Indian removal in earnest in 1830. When Indian tribes almost invariably resisted relocation, U.S. emissaries used persuasion, bribery, trickery, and threats to compel acquiescence. The coercion was cloaked in legality, as the tribes were made to sign treaties relinquishing their lands and accepting resettlement. The brutal, involuntary nature of the migration was only too visible, as U.S. Army troops were used to escort the Indians westward.

Trail of Tears   (Woolaroc Museum, Bartlesville, Oklahoma)

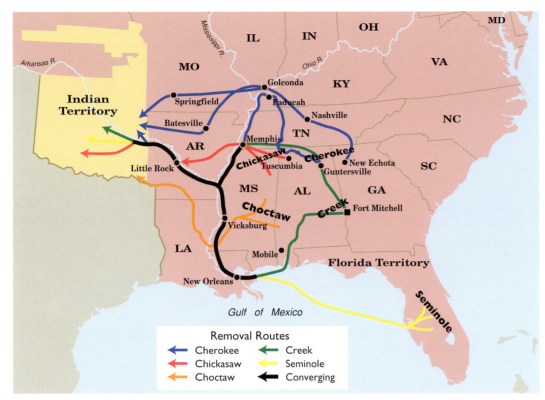

Indian Removal from the Old Southwest

TRAIL OF TEARS

The attention of President Jackson, a Tennessean, was on the major tribes of the Old Southwest. The Choctaw in southern Mississippi, forced to sign the Treaty of Dancing Rabbit Creek in 1830, were the first to go. Between 1831 and 1834, Choctaw men, women, and children were gathered into temporary camps and then herded west on forced marches to the southern reaches of Indian Territory. Conditions were terrible, with shortages of food, blankets, horses, and wagons. As many as a quarter of the 20,000 Choctaw died en route, with disease and starvation claiming still more after their arrival.

A similar fate befell the Creek in Alabama in 1836 and the Chickasaw in northern Mississippi after 1837. The shorter journey made the Chickasaw removal less arduous; still, some 1,000 succumbed on the way westward. Of 17,000 Creeks, 2,000 did not survive the trip and another 3,500 soon perished in Indian Territory.

After Georgia began parceling out their lands by lottery, the Cherokees finally were forced to accept removal. The exodus began in the spring of 1838 as soldiers first confined the Cherokees to stockades and then relentlessly pushed them along an 800-mile trek to Indian Territory. The cruel pace kept the Cherokee from stopping even to bury their dead. A second and final migration followed in the fall and winter of 1838–39. The horrific suffering of this second journey led the displaced Cherokee to call their route west the Trail of Tears. At least 4,000 of the 16,000 Cherokee removed perished in the stockades or on the two long marches.

The Seminole in Florida fought removal. During and after the Second Seminole War (1835–42), some 4,200 Seminole were subdued and sent across the Gulf of Mexico by ship to New Orleans and, from there, to Indian Territory. Small bands of Seminole managed to remain in southern Florida, as did remnants of the Cherokee in western North Carolina and the Choctaw in Mississippi. All three groups eventually were located on reservations.

The Trail of Tears became a metaphor for Indian removal. The ordeal of arduous forced journey to Indian Territory was also endured by northern tribes. U.S. defeat of the Sauk- and Fox-led resistance in the Black Hawk War in 1832 ushered in an active period of Indian removal in the Old Northwest. The Winnebagos and most Potawatomis were made to join the remnants of the Sauk and Fox in what shortly would become Iowa Territory. All three tribes were subsequently relocated to Indian Territory. Other Potawatomis were removed directly to the Indian reserve, as were their Great Lakes neighbors the Ottawa and Wyandot. Also escorted along trails of tears were mixed bands of Delaware, Shawnee, Miami, and Illinois.

INDIAN WARS AND LAND CESSIONS IN THE FAR WEST

CAYUSE WAR (1847–55) The Cayuse Indians along the Columbia River grew increasingly alarmed by the surge of American migration into Oregon in the 1840s. Cayuse attacks triggered widescale warfare with American settlers in 1847. U.S. troops joined the conflict in 1848. After years of sporadic fighting, the war-depleted tribe was finally subdued and forced onto a reservation.

ROGUE RIVER WAR (1855–56) American settlers in southwest Oregon referred to the Tutuni and Takelma tribes along the Rogue River as the Rogue Indians. In 1855 warfare erupted between settlers and Indians over plans to remove the tribes and develop their lands. U.S. troops routed the Rogue Indians in the Battle of Big Meadows in 1856 and the tribes were relocated to reservations on the Pacific Coast.

YAKIMA WAR (1855–58) In 1855 the governor of Washington Territory, Isaac Stevens, prevailed on the Yakima and other tribes along the upper Columbia River to relinquish their lands and move to reservations, where they would be provided homes, schools, horses, and cattle. When Stevens reneged on his promise to delay for at least two years the opening of their lands to white settlement, the Indians repudiated the agreement. The Yakima were first to wage violent resistance to the white encroachment, soon followed by the other Columbia Basin tribes. In 1858 the Native Americans suffered a pivotal defeat at the Battle of Four Lakes. Their power broken, the Columbia Basin tribes were removed to reservations.

SNAKE WAR (1866–68) In the 1860s the Northern Paiutes in Nevada and Oregon carried out numerous raids on the growing numbers of American stagecoaches, mining camps, and ranches in the area. In 1866 U.S. forces under legendary Indian fighter George Crook launched a ruthless campaign against the northernmost of the Paiutes, known as the Snake Indians. Worn down by the constant U.S. pressure, the Snake bands surrendered in 1868 and were settled on a reservation in Oregon.

MODOC WAR (1872–73) In 1864 the Modoc along the Oregon-California border signed a treaty in which they ceded their lands and agreed to live on the Klamath reservation in southern Oregon. Faced with chronic food shortages, a Modoc band slipped away from the reservation in 1870 and established a village in the Lost valley of northern California. U.S. troops moved to return the Modoc to the reservation in 1872, precipitating a bitter conflict. Depleted by war and finally routed at the Battle of Dry Lake in 1873, the surviving Modoc surrendered and were sent to Indian Territory.

NEZ PERCÉ WAR (1877) In 1855 the Nez Percé, whose ancestral lands straddled the junction of Washington, Oregon, and Idaho, agreed to surrender much of their territory to American settlement. In return, they were guaranteed they could keep the heart of their original domain, including the Wallowa valley of northeastern Oregon. In the early 1860s, however, a gold rush brought American settlers into the valley. U.S. promises in 1873 to set aside the Wallowa area as a reservation for the tribe were revoked two years later. Facing relocation to a reservation in Idaho, the Nez Percé resolved to flee to the east and seek a military alliance with the Crow in Montana. From June to October 1877, the Nez Percé trekked some 1700 miles through the wilderness of Idaho, Wyoming, and Montana in a desperate attempt to escape destruction or capture by pursuing U.S. troops. Unable to find refuge among the Crow, the Nez Percé made for Canada but were surrounded by American troops in northern Montana and, at the Battle of Bear Paw, forced to surrender. The Nez Percé were removed to Indian Territory and then to reservations in the Northwest.

UTE WAR (1879) As the American mining frontier moved into western Colorado and eastern Utah in the mid-1800s, the local Ute Indians were pressured into signing away most of their lands. When Colorado became a state in 1876, mining interests lobbied for the removal of the Utes from their remaining tract along the White River. In 1879 the Utes fought back against efforts by U.S. Indian agents to confiscate most of their hunting grounds and convert them to farming. Faced with overwhelming U.S. force, the Utes capitulated and were relocated to reservations in Colorado and Utah.

Land speculation around Buffalo in the 1830s spurred relocation of the area's Senecas. Other New York Indians, most notably Cayugas and Mohawks, were also sent west.

The northern tribes were largely settled in the part of Indian Territory to the west of Missouri. Disease and malnutrition took a terrible toll on the long journeys there. Many groups were unable to complete the trip in one season and suffered horribly in inadequate winter quarters.

A few tribes were spared the tribulations of removal. The Menominee and Chippewa in still sparsely settled northern Wisconsin and Upper Michigan eventually were confined to reservations.

Indian expulsion in the Old Northwest also precipitated the astonishing migration of the Kickapaw. After the Black Hawk War, the remaining Kickapaw in southern Illinois departed for Missouri where they joined fellow tribe members. Some Kickapaw moved on into Kansas in Indian Territory. Others, though, traveled south in search of a homeland. They stayed briefly in southern Texas and then crossed the Rio Grande to settle in northern Mexico, where they became known as the Mexican Kickapaws. During the Civil War, Kickapaws from Kansas tried to join their southern relatives. They were attacked en route by Texas Rangers, sparking Kickapaw raids on Texas border settlements. In 1873 the U.S. Cavalry crossed the Rio Grande, destroyed the main Mexican Kickapaw village, and escorted most survivors to Indian Territory.

Jackson's successors in the White House finished one of the saddest chapters in American history. Removal of the eastern tribes was largely accomplished by 1846. An estimated 75,000 Native Americans had been dispatched to Indian Territory, with as many as a quarter dying in the process.

Indian removal remained a mainstay of U.S. policy as American settlement spread across the continent. By the early 1840s removal had cleared the western Mississippi valley from Iowa to Louisiana of any significant Native American presence. When Texas joined the Union in 1845, it was agreed that its tribes would be relocated to Indian Territory.

THE RESERVATION SYSTEM

The Louisiana Purchase not only made possible Indian Territory, but also added several hundred thousand Indians to the native

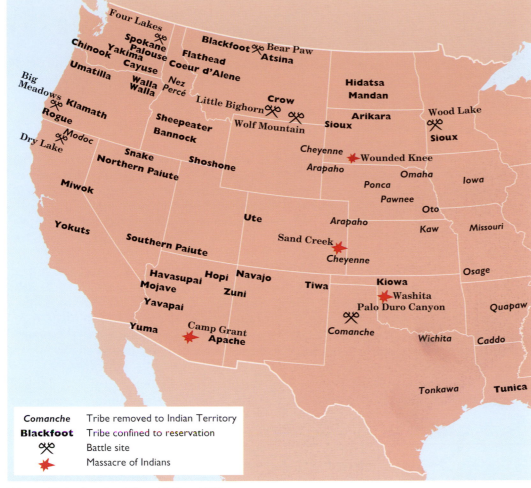

Western Native American Tribes, 1775 to 1890

population within U.S. territory. The lands set aside for the removal of eastern tribes were already inhabited—the Kaw, Omaha, Oto, Pawnee, and Ponca lived in the central Plains. These tribes were assigned ostensibly permanent areas in northern Indian Territory, as were the relocated eastern tribes to their south. All the tribes were subjected to continuing efforts at white acculturation by Indian agents. The Cherokee, Chickasaw, Choctaw, and Creek, already more assimilated, became known, along with the Seminole, as the Five Civilized Tribes.

A basic premise of Indian removal was the confinement of Native Americans to separate areas, out of the way of white settlement, where they gradually would learn "the arts and habits of civilization." The twin goals of isolation and assimilation remained the basic aim of U.S. Indian policy, but developments in the early 1850s led to the advent of reservations as the principal means of achieving them.

Acquisition of Oregon Country and the Mexican Cession between 1845 and 1848 both extended the United States across the continent and brought another 200,000 Native Americans under its sovereignty.

From the far western frontier in 1834, Indian Territory now bestrided the heavily traveled Oregon Trail to the Pacific Northwest and California. The desire to build a transcontinental railroad on a central route, as well as the Southern political interest in extending slave territory to the west, prompted passage of the Kansas-Nebraska Act in 1854. The act reduced Indian Territory to within the boundaries of present-day Oklahoma and established the Kansas and Nebraska territories. The tribes in these territories were consolidated into the newly compressed Indian Territory to the south.

Removal of the numerous tribes across the West became manifestly infeasible. On the other hand, the sheer size of the West made possible the isolation of Native Americans on scattered reserved parcels of land rather than in a single Indian Territory. The idea of lands "reserved" for Indians dated to colonial times, but had been applied only rarely and never systematically. The establishment of formally designated Indian reservations was first tried in California in 1853. In the late 1850s, the Cayuse, Rogue, Yakima, and other tribes in the Pacific Northwest were forced onto reservations to

INDIAN WARS AND LAND CESSIONS IN THE SOUTHWEST

NAVAJO WAR (1860–66) After the United States took possession of the Southwest from Mexico in 1848, the Navajo in northern New Mexico and Arizona soon found their lands under American pressure. In 1860 Navajo warriors almost overran Fort Defiance in northeastern Arizona in an attack meant to halt the grazing of U.S. Army horses in pasturelands long used by the Native Americans. Sporadic fighting between Navajo and Americans continued until 1863, when U.S. forces under Colonel Kit Carson undertook a concerted campaign to pacify the Indians. Carson waged a scorched-earth offensive, destroying Navajo crops and confiscating their livestock. Between 1864 and 1866 some 12,000 Navajo surrendered to Carson's soldiers and were removed to a reservation.

APACHE WARS (1861–86) In 1861 hostilities flared between the U.S. Army and the Chiricahua Apache, led by famed chief Cochise, in southern Arizona. The Apache Uprising (1861–63) soon spread across Arizona and New Mexico to other Apache bands. The Chiricahua eventually fled into the mountains of northern Mexico. The resistance of the Mibreno Apache farther north weakened after the capture and murder of their leader Mangas Coloradas by American forces in 1863. The same year the Mescalero Apache in southern New Mexico were subdued. To prevent further Indian-white conflict, as well as formalize the taking of Apache lands, the federal government in 1872 established several tribal reservations in Arizona. Cochise and the Chiricahua agreed to move to reservation lands in their southern Arizona homeland. In the Tonto Basin Campaign (1872–73), General George Crook pacified the Apache bands of central Arizona, which likewise were settled on reservations.

make way for settlers streaming into the region. Reservations were justified, in part, as places where Indians could be inculcated in white customs and technology, but, as always, the real issue was land.

THE LONG WALK

U.S.–Indian conflict was inevitable in the West. The introduction of reservations became the spark that ignited hostilities across the frontier. In the Southwest the Navajo and Apache fought tenaciously against confinement. U.S. forces in 1864 overran the Navajo stronghold at Canyon de Chelly in the Chuska Mountains of northeastern Arizona. Some 6,000 demoralized and half-starved Navajo were taken prisoner. Most often reservations were carved out of existing tribal lands. The reservation set aside for the Navajo, however, was 300 miles to the east in New Mexico. Soon American soldiers were escorting ragged columns of Navajo across the barren desert. At least several hundred Navajo died on the forced trek. What the Navajo called the Long Walk became an enduring symbol of the merciless subjugation of western tribes. Another 2,000 Navajo perished after arrival at the inhospitable stretch of land chosen for their relocation. The

heartwrenching mistreatment of the Navajo led the U.S. government in 1868 to establish a reservation for them in the Chuska Mountains. In a searing irony, the Navajo returned westward over the trail of the Long Walk to their ancestral homeland.

PEACE POLICY

The return of the Navajo reflected a new phase in U.S. Indian Policy. After the Civil War, American attention turned back to the West and the Indian warfare that in the mid-1860s engulfed the Great Plains from Texas to Montana. Hostilities with the Cheyenne, Apache, and Sioux in particular disrupted links to the Far West and impeded the advance of American settlement. Against a backdrop of calls for the military annihilation of the Plains Indians, Congress in 1867 appointed a special commission to determine the reasons for the outbreak of violence and to find ways to end it. The Indian Peace Commission pinned the costly hostilities on white mistreatment of Native Americans and called for a firm U.S. commitment to honor treaty obligations as part of a strategy to negotiate the peaceful confinement of Plains Indians to reservations. The commission succeeded in negotiating the Medicine Lodge Treaty in 1867, relocating the southern Cheyenne and Arapaho to nearby Indian Territory; and the Fort Laramie Treaty in 1868, establishing reservations in the northern Plains for the northern Cheyenne and Arapaho and the Sioux.

The commission's work underlay the "peace policy" announced by President Ulysses S. Grant in 1869 to guide U.S.-Indian relations. Emphasis was on providing incentives to the Indians to acquire the "self-sustaining habits" of a settled agricultural life. The army would be used, where necessary, to compel Indian acceptance of reservations; Indian Service agents would oversee the provision of tools, supplies, education, and other assistance on the reservations.

The army had the larger role. Some tribes, such as the Arikara, Mandan, and Hidatsa in North Dakota, accepted settlement on reservations. Others did not. The Apache were not forced onto reservations until 1873, the Comanche and Kiowa not until 1875, and the Ute not until 1880. With the designation of reservations for the Atsina, Blackfoot, and Crow in Montana in the 1880s, the confinement of tribes on American soil, if not the confiscation of their lands, had been completed.

FLIGHT OF THE NEZ PERCÉ

It did not take the U.S. government long to go back on its commitment to honor agreements with Indian tribes. The treaty-protected Black Hills on Sioux lands in South Dakota were opened to miners in 1874; the reservation promised to the Nez Percé in Oregon in 1873 was rescinded two years later. Reservation conditions, more often than not, were far less than promised. Native Americans were not authorized to leave their reservations, and the army was tasked with keeping discontented tribes from doing so. Fleeing Modoc and Apache, after recapture, were sent to Indian Territory, which became a prison for rebellious bands, and especially their leaders.

The Nez Percé in 1877 fled rather than accept relocation to a reservation in Idaho. Their epic journey, during which they often evaded or fought off the superior U.S. forces in pursuit, is known to history as the Flight of the Nez Percé. The Nez Percé fled not only confinement, but also the disappearance of their world. At one point they crossed the recently formed Yellowstone National Park, startling the tourists who saw them pass through. The encirclement and capture of the Nez Percé only 30 miles from the U.S. border with Canada, where they hoped to find refuge, came to symbolize the final extinguishing of Native American freedom.

THE VANISHING AMERICAN

Reservation life was a slow death not only for Indian culture but for Indians themselves. Native Americans struggled to retain their tribal identity, organization, and governance. Most successful were the Five Civilized Tribes in Indian Territory. Dispirited and disoriented, many Indians resisted conversion to a settled agricultural life, and tribes were largely dependent on the federal government for rations and supplies. Acculturation was not working and mortality rates were high.

The commissioner of Indian affairs estimated the Native American population had declined from 278,000 in 1870 to 244,000 in 1880. Church groups, reformers, public officials, and others concerned over the desperate plight of the Indian spoke openly of the "vanishing American." The standard solution offered was the assimilation of Indians into white society. This

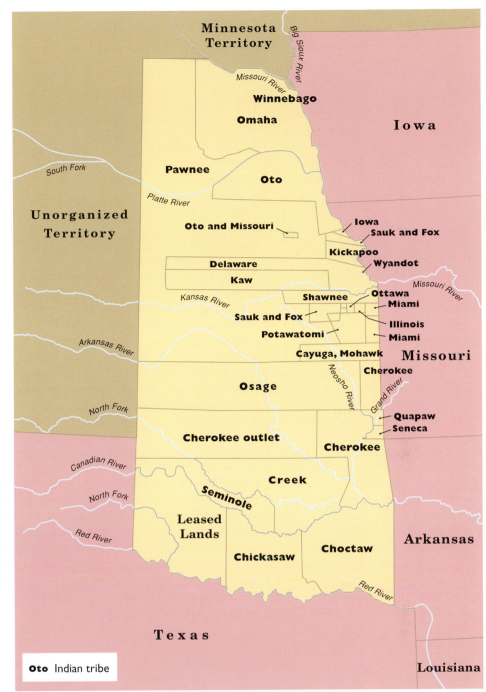

Oto Indian tribe

Indian Territory in 1854

Indian Territory in 1876

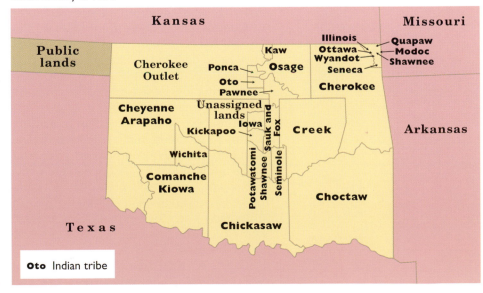

Oto Indian tribe

"I WILL FIGHT NO MORE"

The U.S. Army in 1875 ordered the Nez Percé to move to a reservation. Chief Joseph articulated his tribe's deep resistance to relocation from their homeland.

The earth is my mother ... I cannot consent to sever my affections from the land which bore me. I ask nothing of the President. I am able to take care of myself. I do not desire the Wallowa valley as a reservation, for that would subject me to the will of another and make me dependent on him and subject to laws not of our own making. I am disposed to live peaceably.

Chief Joseph helped lead the brilliant but ultimately futile flight of the Nez Percé. On October 5, 1877, in the Bear Paw Mountains of Montana, he gave a haunting surrender speech on behalf of his tribe to the encircling U.S. Army.

I am tired of fighting. Our chiefs are killed. Looking Glass is dead. The old men are all killed. It is the young men who say yes or no. He who led the young men is dead. It is cold and we have no blankets. The little children are freezing to death. My people, some of them, have run away to the hills and have no blankets, no food; no one knows where they are, perhaps freezing to death. I want time to look for my children and see how many of them I can find. Maybe I shall find them among the dead.

Hear me, my chiefs, I am tired; my heart is sick and sad. From where the sun now stands, I will fight no more forever.

INDIAN WARS AND LAND CESSIONS IN THE GREAT PLAINS

ARIKARA "WAR" CAMPAIGN (1823) The Arikara, reacting to encroachment on their lands along the upper Missouri River by American trappers and traders, launched a bloody raid on a party of fur traders in 1823. In the first American military expedition against Plains Indians, U.S. troops attacked Arikara villages in the Dakotas, driving the tribe to the north and securing the Missouri valley for continued American expansion.

SIOUX WARS (1862–77) The Sioux have come down to modern memory as the most famed of the Plains warriors. The four main branches of the Sioux—the Santee in Minnesota, the Yankton and Yanktonai in the Dakotas, and the Teton in Montana and Wyoming—fought American expansion for almost 20 years. U.S.-Sioux hostilities first escalated into full-scale warfare in August 1862 when the Santee under Chief Little Crow launched an all-out assault to stop settlement of their lands along the Minnesota River. U.S. forces routed the Santee the following month at the Battle of Wood Lake. Many of the surviving Sioux fled northwestward. Little Crow's War (1862–64) dragged on another two years, as U.S. troops pushed into the Dakotas in a punitive expedition that destroyed remaining Santee resistance. In 1865 Red Cloud led an alliance of Teton Sioux and northern Cheyenne and Arapaho in an offensive against the growing American traffic on the newly pioneered Bozeman Trail. Sioux victories over U.S. forces in 1867 at the battles of Hayfield in Montana and Wagon Box in Wyoming convinced American authorities to seek a negotiated settlement to the costly conflict. Red Cloud's War (1864–68) was ended by a treaty signed at Fort Laramie in 1868. The U.S. government pledged to abandon its Bozeman Trail forts on Sioux lands. In return, the Sioux and northern Cheyenne and Arapaho agreed to move to designated reservations by 1876. In the Fort Laramie agreement, the U.S. government guaranteed the sanctity of the Black Hills in South Dakota, an area held sacred by the Sioux. When Americans rushed into the Black Hill region after the discovery of gold there in 1874, Sioux warriors attacked the trespassers and refused to relocate to reservations. War broke out in early 1876 when the U.S. military moved against the defiant Plains Indians. In June 1876 Sioux, Cheyenne, and Arapaho warriors under Teton chieftains Crazy Horse and Sitting Bull annihilated a detachment of more than 200 calvary troops under Lieutenant Colonel George Armstrong Custer at the Battle of Little Bighorn. Custer's Last Stand shocked Americans nationwide and spurred on the military campaign against the Plains Indians. Crazy Horses's defeat at the Battle of Wolf Mountain in January 1877 signaled the end of the Black Hills War (1876–77). The remaining Sioux and their northern Cheyenne and Arapaho allies were escorted to reservations.

---

meant individual land ownership, the elimination of tribal government, and the "Americanization" of Indians into equal citizens in the larger society.

A new period in U.S.–Indian relations was ushered in by the General Allotment Act of 1887. Indian reservations were to be broken up and allotted to individual Indians in 160-acre homesteads. These lands were to be held in trust by the federal government for 25 years, to prevent their unknowing loss or sale by Indians unfamiliar with property ownership. Not coincidentally, "surplus" reservation lands after allotment would be retained by the federal government, with a compensatory fee paid to the applicable tribe, and opened to white settlement. The act also provided for a comprehensive school system under the Bureau of Indian Affairs to stamp out "Indianness" and educate Indians in the ways of white society.

The Five Civilized Tribes alone managed to forestall allotment. After 1889, mil-

lions of supposedly surplus acres were bought in Indian Territory from other tribes (at far below market prices) and

NATIVE AMERICAN POPULATION, 1890–1990

1890	248,000
1900	237,196
1910	276,927
1920	244,437
1930	343,352
1940	345,252
1950	357,499
1960	523,591
1970	792,730
1980	1,366,676
1990	1,959,234

Source: Census Bureau

CHEYENNE-ARAPAHO WAR (1864–69) The Pikes Peak Gold Rush in 1858 brought an onrush of American settlers into Colorado. The southern bands of both the Cheyenne and Arapaho refused to sell their lands and settle on reservations. In 1864 the U.S. territorial military commander Colonel John Chivington launched a campaign of virtual extermination against the Native Americans. The Cheyenne and Arapaho fought back in what is sometimes referred to as the Colorado War (1864–65). Hostilities subsided until 1867, when additional U.S. troops, free to head west after the Civil War, undertook a futile campaign to pacify the Cheyenne and Arapaho. The same year U.S. peace negotiators prevailed on the Native Americans in the Medicine Lodge Treaty to accept reservation lands in Indian Territory. Perceived violations of treaty terms by American officials sparked continuing Indian unrest. In 1868 General Philip Sheridan mounted a major campaign against the Southern Plains Indians. The constant U.S. military pressure took its toll and by 1869 the last of the southern Cheyenne and Arapaho had been confined to Indian Territory.

RED RIVER WAR (1874–75) The Comanche were in almost constant warfare with Americans from the first migration of settlers into Texas in the 1820s. The Comanche and their equally fierce allies, the Kiowa, attacked travelers, settlers, and even soldiers who dared to enter their territory. In 1868 General Philip Sheridan, during his campaign against the Southern Plains tribes, established a combined Comanche-Kiowa reservation just north of the Red River in Indian Territory. Farther west along the upper Red River, Comanche and Kiowa warriors continued to resist subjugation. After 1870 the Comanche and Kiowa fought desperately against the white hunters then depleting the Southern Plains of the buffalo herds on which they depended. In what is also known as the Buffalo War, U.S. forces in September 1874 dealt a devastating blow to the tribes in an attack on their stronghold at Palo Duro Canyon in northwestern Texas. By the following June, the last of the Comanche and Kiowa had surrendered and were confined to Indian Territory.

WOUNDED KNEE (1890) In 1890 U.S. officials banned the Ghost Dance Religion then spreading rapidly among the demoralized and destitute Native American tribes living on reservations across the West. Hundreds of defiant Sioux, adherents of the mystical new religion which emphasized a return to traditional Indian ways, gathered in the northwest corner of the Pine Ridge Reservation in South Dakota. U.S. soldiers sent to disband the gathering surrounded a band of some 300 Sioux at Wounded Knee Creek. In the confusion, a brief firefight quickly escalated into a violent American fusillade. When the smoke cleared, at least 150 Indians had been cut down, including many women and children. The Wounded Knee Massacre, which crushed what was left of the Sioux spirit of resistance, has come to symbolize the bitter end of almost 400 years of warfare between Indians and whites for possession of America.

thrown open to settlers in the Oklahoma land runs. In 1898 the Curtis Act dissolved tribal governments and extended allotment to the Five Civilized Tribes. The destruction of tribal governance made Native Americans, in essence, the wards of a paternalistic, but unresponsive, federal bureaucracy.

Federal seizure of Indian lands proceeded smoothly; allotment and assimilation did not. Many Native Americans were dislocated by tribal dispersement, caught in a no man's land between their traditional culture and a still-alien white culture. Most existed by a combination of subsistence farming and federal support.

After the 25-year trust period ended, many Indians were defrauded of their lands by unscrupulous white speculators. Partly to recognize purported Indian assimilation (and partly to recognize Indian service in World War I), Congress in 1924 conferred full citizenship on all Indians born in the United States. The Native

Indian Territory in 1896

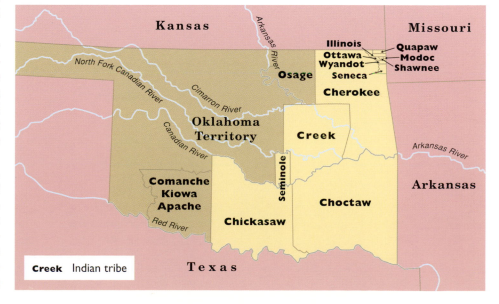

Creek   Indian tribe

American population had slowly grown from an 1890 low of less than 240,000, but by the late 1920s those responsible for Indian affairs could no longer escape recognition that assimilation had been a failure and allotment a great injustice. Native Americans had been dispossessed of nearly two-thirds of the 150 million acres they had held in 1887.

NATIVES AND STRANGERS

The social experimentation spurred in the early 1930s by the Great Depression extended to Indian affairs. In 1934 President Franklin D. Roosevelt signed the Indian Reorganization Act, inaugurating an "Indian New Deal." The act reversed the allotment and assimilation policy. It restored reservations, trust areas, and tribal governance; returned unsold surplus lands to tribes; provided additional resources to raise Indian standards of living; and acknowledged the importance of Indian culture to Indian life.

The law stopped the long, invidious destruction of Indian tribes, but before it could take real effect the nation found itself at war. More than 25,000 Native Americans served in the U.S. military during World War II. Thousands more left reservations to work in war-related industries. For many the wartime experience served to weaken ties to reservation life.

Many returning Indian veterans and workers after the war were dissatisfied by the depressed economic conditions on reservations. Congress responded by enacting new termination and relocation policies in the early 1950s. Termination referred to the withdrawal of the "protective" federal status of reservations so that tribes might better develop their potential resources and wealth. Job training and

Long Walk and Flight

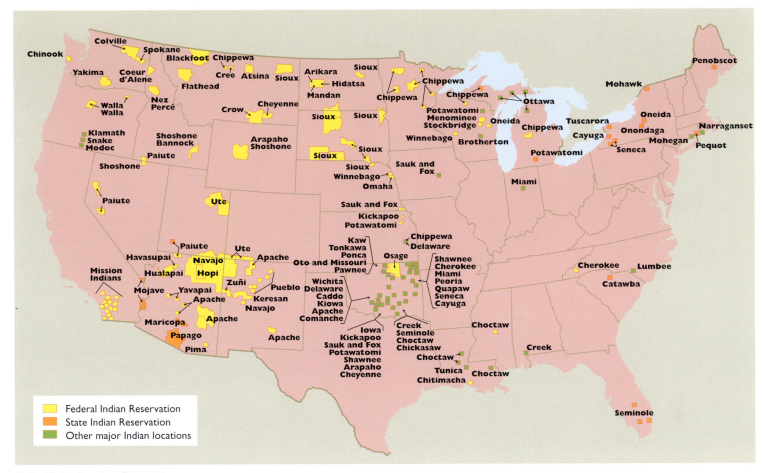

Major Native American Reservations

relocation funds were provided to encourage off-reservation employment. From 1952 to 1957, a federal relocation program moved some 17,000 Indians to such cities as Los Angeles, Oakland, Denver, and Chicago. The years 1945 to 1970 saw a burgeoning Indian migration from reservations to urban areas. Most left, not because of federal assistance, but in search of greater opportunity in the booming postwar economy. This outflow leveled off after 1970.

The ineffectual termination and relocation policies were abandoned in the 1960s. The decade was a period of growing Indian self-awareness and militancy. Demands for long-ignored Native American rights compelled the federal government in the 1970s to adopt the current Indian self-determination policy, emphasizing self-government, cultural renewal, development of tribal resources on restored reservations, and, above all, Indian involvement and choice in the management of their affairs. The 1990 census counted 2,065,000 Native Americans, about 0.8% of the total U.S. population. Roughly half lived on or near reservations; slightly less than half dwelled in urban areas, with small numbers found in rural nonreservation communities.

MANIFEST DESTINY
Migration, 1845 to 1890

8

When Americans looked west in 1845, their gaze extended to the Pacific Ocean. Annexation of Texas the same year evoked for many a vision of American settlement stretching "from sea to shining sea." Thousands of settlers already were streaming into Oregon Country and there was an air of inevitability about American expansion across the continent. Journalist and ardent expansionist John L. O'Sullivan captured the national mood when he asserted America's "manifest destiny to overspread the continent allotted by Providence for the free development of our yearly multiplying millions."

O'Sullivan's prediction was right on both counts. Within three years, the United States had taken possession of the area from the Rockies to the Pacific. Within another 40 years, its population had climbed from 23,000,000 to more than 60,000,000. Millions of settlers surged into every corner of the West. This migration was so massive and pervasive that by 1890 the frontier was declared closed.

Manifest Destiny entered the popular lexicon as a catchphrase for American expansionism. It also conveyed the sense of a nation, and its people, on the move.

Development of the railroad linked a continental America together. It also helped make possible the rapid growth of American cities after 1850. The late 1800s saw two distinct movements. Even as legions of settlers were spreading out across the West, millions of other migrants were congregating in the new urban centers.

OREGON FEVER

American mountain men trapping beaver in the Pacific Northwest were the advance guard of Manifest Destiny. The United States, Great Britain, Russia, and Spain all coveted the region and its fur riches in the early 1800s. After the War of 1812, the United States and Great Britain in 1818 agreed to joint occupation of the area between the Rocky Mountains and the Pacific Ocean from the 42nd parallel north to latitude 54°40'.

American diplomacy under Secretary of State John Quincy Adams worked to exclude the Spanish and Russians from the region. The Adams-Onis Treaty in 1819 set the northern boundary of Spanish California at the 42nd parallel. The Russo-American Treaty of 1824 made 54°40' the southern boundary of Russian Alaska.

After 1824 American fur trappers made their way through the South Pass in the Rockies to what became known as Oregon Country. They competed with their British counterparts in trapping the abundant beaver in mountain streams along the Columbia and Snake river valleys. Trappers called the beaver pelts "hairy money," as they were in much demand back East for the tall gentlemen's hats then in fashion.

On the heels of the mountain men came American missionaries seeking to spread the Christian faith to the area's numerous Native American tribes. Methodist minister

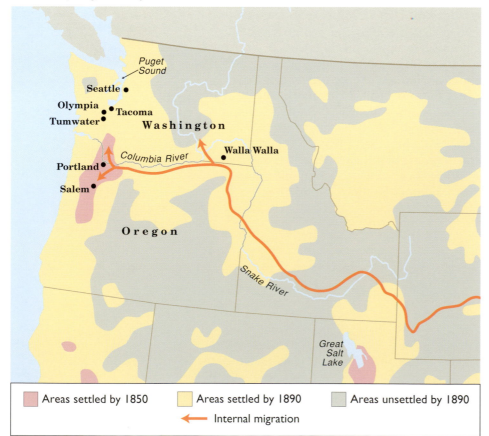

Settlement of Oregon Country

▨ Areas settled by 1850	▨ Areas settled by 1890	▨ Areas unsettled by 1890
← Internal migration	

William Henry Jackson, Wagon Train on the Oregon Trail   (Courtesy of The American Heritage Center, University of Wyoming)

Lee Jason established the first mission, and the first American agricultural settlement, in the Willamette valley near present-day Salem, Oregon, in 1834. Two years later physician and Presbyterian missionary Marcus Whitman founded the Walla Walla mission in what is now southeastern Washington. After 1838 Jesuit missionaries, determined that Catholicism not be left behind, journeyed from St. Louis to proselytize among the Coeur d'Alene Indians at the Columbia's headwaters.

As word of Oregon Country's fertile valleys, majestic fir forests, salmon-laden rivers, and moist, mild climate reached the western edge of American settlement in the Mississippi valley, it set off a veritable "Oregon fever." Settlers along the frontier then had little interest in the treeless prairies or arid high plains to their immediate west. What they wanted, the Pacific Northwest promised in abundance—wood, water, game, and soil. After 1841 the feverish excitement over Oregon swept across Iowa, Missouri, Illinois, and Kentucky. Many pioneer families resolved to set out more than halfway across the continent to make new homes beyond the Rockies.

THE WAGON TRAIN

First mountain men and then missionaries had demonstrated that wagons could cross the Rockies through South Pass. The first organized movement in 1841 of settlers over what became known as the Oregon Trail ushered in the Great Migration to Oregon Country. Every spring pioneers would assemble around Independence, Missouri, the jumping-off point for the journey west. Their canvas-covered wagons, called "Prairie schooners," were not the huge, horse-drawn Conestoga wagons used in the East, but smaller, stronger, lighter, oxen-pulled versions capable of making it through the mountains. The wagons were for hauling food, water, and belongings, and most settlers walked alongside.

Settlers would join together in groups of as many as 100 wagons, select a captain or leader, and hire a guide. Departures began in May, when the grass on the Plains allowed for grazing. The wagon train, with a herd of cattle in tow, would follow the general course of the Platte River across the Great Plains to South Pass and then

"A MOVING VILLAGE"

Narcissa Whitman, wife of missionary Marcus Whitman, was in the first party of white women to cross the Rocky Mountains. In a letter to her sister and brother written while on the Oregon Trail in 1836, she conveyed something of the spectacle their wagon train presented as it moved across the Plains.

We are really a moving village— nearly four hundred animals with ours, mostly mules and seventy men. The Fur Com. has seven wagons and one cart, drawn by six mules each, heavily loaded; the cart drawn by two mules carries a lame man, one of the proprieters of the Com. We have two waggons in our com[pany.] Mr. & Mrs. S. and Husband and myself ride in one, Mr. Gray and the baggage in the other. Our Indian boys drive the cows and Dulin the horses. Young Miles leads our forward horses, four in each team. Now E. if you wish to see the camp in motion, look away ahead and see first the pilot and the Captain Fitzpatrick, just be fore him—next the pack animals, all mules loaded with great packs—soon after you will see the waggons and in the rear our company. We all cover quite a space. The pack mules always string along one after the other just like Indians.

descend down the Snake and Columbia valleys into Oregon Country. At first there was no distinct trail, but soon wagon wheel ruts had carved out a clear route in the sod.

If things went without a hitch, a wagon train leaving in May would reach the Willamette valley before Thanksgiving. The grueling 2,000-mile journey took its toll in hardships endured and in lives lost. Hazards such as an early mountain snow could doom a caravan, but most made it through to their destination.

By 1845 5,000 settlers had traveled the Oregon Trail to the area around Portland, which was founded that year. The American migration forced Great Britain to abandon its proposed division of Oregon Country along the Columbia River. In 1846 the British government acceded to the long-standing American suggestion of extending westward to the Pacific Ocean the 49th parallel boundary between the United States and Canada. Western expansionists in Congress asserted American title up to 54°40', coining the slogan "Fifty-four

Forty or Fight," but President James K. Polk, his attention on impending war with Mexico, wanted the Oregon question resolved and gained Senate approval of the agreed border.

The Pacific Northwest was organized as Oregon Territory in 1848. The covered-wagon migration surged to some 300,000 settlers moving west on the Oregon Trail between 1849 and 1860. More than 200,000 were headed for California. After South Pass they turned onto the California Trail that ran through Donner Pass to the Sacramento valley. Another 40,000 followed the Mormon Trail from South Pass to Salt Lake City in Utah. Around 55,000 continued on to Oregon. By the time the covered-wagon era drew to a close in the late 1860s with the advent of transcontinental railroads, more than 350,000 Americans had sailed their Prairie schooners on the overland routes to the Far West.

Oregon had just over 12,000 inhabitants in 1850. From then until the end of the century the population almost doubled every

Major Western Trails

—O— Oregon Trail	⋯M⋯ Mormon Trail	‑‑T‑‑ Taos Trail
⋯Bz⋯ Bozeman Trail	—so— Southern Overland Trail	—S— Santa Fe Trail
‑C‑ California Trail	‑‑os‑‑ Old Spanish Trail	▨ Over 500 feet in elevation

10 years. Settlement concentrated first in the Willamette and Rogue river valleys along the coast. The Oregon Donation Act in 1850 spurred development of the interior. The federal land measure granted 320 acres to single and 640 acres to married settlers (inspiring not a few marriages). The act gave away land not yet acquired from its Native American owners, helping to incite Indian warfare throughout the Columbia Basin. Most local Native American tribal resistance was suppressed by 1858.

The first American settlement north of the Columbia River was at Tumwater on Puget Sound in 1845. Nearby Olympia was founded in 1848, followed by Seattle in 1851 and Tacoma in 1852. A separate Washington Territory was formed in 1853 and Oregon became a state in 1859. The Idaho gold strikes of the early 1860s brought boom times to eastern Washington and made Walla Walla the largest town in the territory. Idaho became a separate territory in 1863, but its settlement would accompany development of the Mining Frontier.

Because of its remoteness, Washington's population grew only slowly until arrival of the Northern Pacific Railway in 1883. The railroad stimulated industrialization, urbanization, and an influx of new residents in both Washington, which gained statehood in 1889, and Oregon. Washington's population of 75,000 in 1880 soared to 518,000 by 1900. Much of the explosion came with the Alaskan gold rush in the 1890s. Still, their rugged interiors kept Washington and Oregon among the most sparsely settled states at the turn of the century.

THE MORMON EXODUS

Most of the migrants to the Far West were farmers and ranchers looking for a place to settle, merchants and craftsmen capitalizing on new opportunities, or gold-seekers hoping to get rich. Among the throngs were a smaller number of religious migrants known as Mormons. They traveled west to escape persecution or simply to live in their religious settlement in Utah.

Joseph Smith, believed by Mormons to be a prophet, founded the Church of Jesus Christ of Latter-day Saints at Palmyra, New York, in 1830. The charismatic Smith drew many converts to the new denomination. Members were called Mormons, after the fifth-century prophet whose teachings, Smith claimed, had been revealed to him. (Among these teachings was that the Indi-

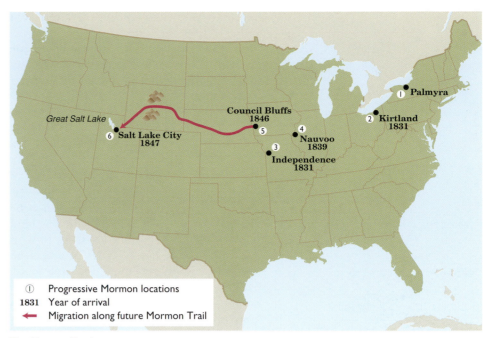

The Mormon Exodus

ans were descended from one of the lost tribes of Israel.)

Faced with local hostility to his new church, Smith moved the Mormons first to Kirtland, Ohio, then to Independence, Missouri, and finally to a place in Illinois he renamed Nauvoo. Mormon missionaries met considerable success in recruiting new members in Northern states as well as northern Europe. By 1844 some 20,000 Mormons lived at Nauvoo, including several thousand immigrant converts from England.

The Mormon practice of polygamy heightened antagonisms among neighboring settlers. In 1844 a mob attacked Nauvoo and killed Smith. When the violence continued, the new Mormon leader Brigham Young, invoking Moses in the Book of Exodus, decided it was time to lead his people out of persecution to their own providentially provided homeland. Young read John C. Frémont's 1845 report on his exploration of the Rockies and noted the explorer's favorable description of the Wasatch Range adjoining the Great Salt Lake.

Young resolved to relocate the Mormons to the remote area in part because it was then Mexican territory and thus beyond the jurisdiction of a persecuting America. The Mormon exodus began in February 1846 when Young led an initial caravan of some 1,800 members and 400 wagons to Council Bluffs, Iowa. Other groups followed behind. After spending the winter near Council Bluffs, Young set out with a small advance party. They blazed a new Mormon Trail along the north bank of the Platte River to South Pass, and then trekked southwest, reaching the Salt Lake valley in July 1847.

In their wake came thousands of Mormons. By the end of 1848, 5,000 had arrived in the new Promised Land that Young named Deseret. Another 11,000 soon followed from Nauvoo. Young called for Mormons to be "gathered to" Deseret, and the flow of migrants from both the East and then northern Europe continued along the Mormon Trail. When wagons were scarce, handcarts were used, adding to the hardships of the trying journey. By 1869, some 85,000 Mormons had made the trek.

The Salt Lake valley, far from flowing with milk and honey, was a sagebrush wasteland. The Mormons, undaunted, settled along the western edge of the Wasatch Range, known as the Wasatch Front. They dug canals to bring water from the mountains and make the desert bloom. By 1860 there were more than 150 self-sustaining settlements, built around intensively cultivated small farms. Salt Lake City, founded in 1847, thrived as the capital of the Mormon Canaan.

The Mexican Cession in 1848 put the Mormons back on American soil. Deseret became part of Utah Territory in 1850. Relations between the Mormons and the territorial government were strained by the issue of polygamy. Federal law forbade the practice in 1862, but the Mormon Church nonetheless clung to it until 1890. The discovery of silver-bearing ores and then completion of the transcontinental railroad in 1869 brought miners and other non-Mormons to Utah. The desert inhospitality of much of the territory kept settlement confined to the Mormon-dominated Wasatch Front. When Utah became a state in 1896, its population of some 250,000 was still overwhelmingly Mormon.

THE MEXICAN CESSION

Not only Utah but the entire expanse from New Mexico and Colorado to California belonged to Mexico in 1846. The arid area had at most only 50,000 inhabitants of Spanish ancestry in 1821, when it became part of a newly independent Mexico. Because of its remoteness from the Mexican heartland, few Mexicans migrated there in the decades after independence. Nonetheless, nationalistic governments in Mexico City rejected several U.S. offers to purchase California.

In 1846 the United States and Mexico went to war over the southern border of Texas, but American leaders, President Polk foremost, also had their sights on California. Manifest Destiny was just one war from fulfillment. In 1848 Polk forced a defeated Mexico to accept what became known as the Mexican Cession. In return for $15 million, Mexico ceded to the United States the vast territory now comprising the Southwest.

THE 49ERS

The prize was California. American whalers and clippers bound for China had long put to port there, and, after 1841, a trickle of settlers had followed fur trappers down the California Trail to the Sacramento valley. In 1848 California's population of some 15,000 included more than 5,000 American traders, trappers, and settlers.

U.S. forces seized California early in the Mexican War. In January 1848 gold was found at the water-powered sawmill of an American settler in the Sacramento valley. Word of the discovery spread along the Pacific Coast in a matter of weeks. Within a few months all of America was enthralled by tales of fortunes to be made in the streambeds of the Sierra Nevada Mountains. Steamships carried the news to Europe. In July California's military governor reported that $50,000 in gold was being panned daily in the area drained by the Sacramento and San Joaquin rivers.

Settlement of the Mexican Cession

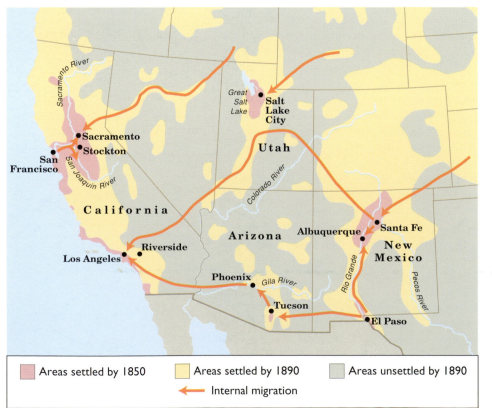

Areas settled by 1850   Areas settled by 1890   Areas unsettled by 1890

← Internal migration

San Francisco, 1860 (California State Library)

By 1849 the great California Gold Rush was on. Tens of thousands of would-be prospectors made for California as fast as they could. The 49ers, as they were soon called, came overland by the Oregon and California trails, around Cape Horn by ship, and even across the Isthmus of Panama, if they could afford the costly shortcut.

Farmers, craftsmen, workers, clerks, and even clergymen dropped everything to race to California and stake their claims. Most were from New England, New York, and Pennsylvania, but numbers came from across America and from Europe. Overnight San Francisco went from a sleepy port to a boomtown of 25,000. Between 1848 and 1853, when the gold fever waned, more than 200,000 aspiring prospectors had poured into California.

A few struck it rich. Most did not, but rather than leave, they stayed and settled. The Gold Rush enabled California to bypass the territorial stage and become a state in 1850. Most of the population was concentrated in the northern valleys and in the boom cities of San Francisco, Sacramento, and Stockton. Southern California remained a thinly populated area of cattle ranchers until after 1870. Throughout the state Native American tribes, already decimated by 80 years of Spanish and Mexican rule, were readily confined to reservations.

California's great distance from the Mississippi valley hindered its growth. At first the only overland communication was provided by the riders of the Butterfield Overland Mail (1858) and the Pony Express (1860). The telegraph reached California in 1861, but it was the first transcontinental railroad in 1869 that linked the state to the rest of the nation.

California's population of 560,000 in 1870 exploded to more than 1,200,000 by 1890. Much of the growth came in the southern third of the state. Irrigation projects after 1870 transformed the Los Angeles Basin. Riverside, just below the San Bernardino Mountains, became the hub of a major citrus fruit industry. A real estate boom in southern California in the 1880s brought the first large migration to the state from the Midwest. Los Angeles County remained the "Queen of the Cow Counties," but the enduring lure of southern California would eventually make the state the most populous in the nation.

THE DESERT FRONTIER

Irrigation would also play an important part in the settlement of the desert Southwest. When the area of what is now New Mexico and Arizona was absorbed into the United States in 1848, there were maybe 35,000 Mexicans located on the upper Rio Grande, mostly around Albuquerque, and at most another 1,000 in the river valleys near Tucson.

As early as 1821 American traders were bringing goods into New Mexico over the Santa Fe Trail. By the late 1840s growing numbers of settlers bound for California were traversing the region on the Santa Fe, Old Spanish, and Southern Overland trails. The first permanent American presence followed organization of the area as the New Mexico Territory in 1850, with the development of farms in the lower Rio Grande and Pecos river valleys.

The availability of water determined the pattern of American settlement. When U.S. surveys showed the natural route for a contemplated railroad from the Deep South to California would run through a region south of the Gila River, Washington acquired another sliver of Mexico for $10 million in 1853. Construction of the railroad would await the Civil War, but the Gadsden Purchase, with its water supply, prompted the first settlement of Arizona, mostly by farmers from Southern states. Cattle ranches spread across the region's southern river valleys.

Arizona became a separate territory in 1863. When pioneers founded Phoenix in 1870, using the ancient Hohokam Indian canals for irrigation, the territory still had only 9,700 inhabitants. New Mexico's population barely topped 90,000.

One reason for the population sparsity was inhospitable terrain; another was the Apache, who fought American encroachment in Arizona and New Mexico with great tenacity and skill. While the Navajo resistance to white settlement in the Southwest had been crushed by 1866, the Apache warred on. A few hundred Apache warriors, masters of guerrilla warfare, tied down thousands of American soldiers for 25 years. The last Apache were not subdued until 1886.

Arrival of the railroad and the discovery of copper and silver deposits spurred the development of both territories after 1880. Newcomers worked in the mines or homesteaded the lands made arable by irrigation projects. Albuquerque became a railroad hub, but neither territory had any real urbanization by the time both became states in 1912. Each remained sparsely settled, with much of its land allocated to Indian reservations or left as undeveloped desert.

THE MINING FRONTIER

There were cowboys and gunslingers in Arizona and New Mexico, but the popular image of the wild frontier West was born in the Rocky Mountains. Settlement of the Rockies progressed through overlapping stages of mining boom times, Indian wars, railroad construction, cattle ranging, lumbering, and farming. It is a history mythologized in countless Hollywood Westerns.

Gold rushes precipitated the development of Rocky Mountain states Colorado, Idaho, and Montana. While no lodes were found in Wyoming, its central location saw it settled as part of the mining boom. Only Mormon Utah in the Rockies was not part of the Mining Frontier, which extended also to neighboring Nevada.

American fur trappers wandered throughout the Rockies in the 1820s and 1830s. The heyday of the mountain men had ended by 1840 with the steady depletion of the once-abundant beaver and the adoption of silk hats as the fashion of choice. After 1840 American settlers passed through Wyoming, Idaho, and Nevada on the way to Oregon and California. In the late 1840s a small number of Spanish-speaking farmers from New Mexico moved into the San Luis valley in southern Colorado, but otherwise the only permanent American presence in the rugged region at mid-century were the isolated outposts along the major western trails.

Discovery of the California Mother Lode in the Sierra Nevadas in 1848 led many frontier argonauts to surmise that the stony peaks of the Rockies also harbored precious metals. In 1858 they were proven right when prospectors struck gold near Pikes Peak in Colorado.

The fortune-hunting hordes of the Pikes Peak Gold Rush were just descending on Colorado in 1859 when the Comstock Lode, with its solid veins of gold and silver, was uncovered on the eastern slope of the Sierra Nevadas in western Nevada. Colorado's gold rushers had journeyed chiefly from the East. In Nevada, the gold seekers simply crossed the Donner Pass from California or detoured off the California Trail.

In a pattern that would be repeated across the Mining Frontier, boomtowns such as Virginia City in Nevada and Denver (initially called Auraria) in Colorado sprung up virtually overnight. Unlike the streambed panning in California, mining in Nevada and the Rockies required digging shafts to follow the veins running deep into the mountains. This necessitated more workers; more equipment and supplies; and, before long, organized ventures to provide the needed capital and expertise.

Colorado had almost 35,000 inhabitants by 1860, Nevada just under 7,000. Both became territories in 1861. Despite its meager population, Nevada was rushed to statehood in 1864, partly because of its great mineral wealth and partly to increase the number of antislavery states during the Civil War.

Discovery of gold in Idaho in 1860 and in Montana in 1862 pushed the Mining Frontier into the northern Rockies. The lawlessness accompanying the resulting gold rush made organized government an imperative. An estimated 70,000 newcomers were in the goldfields of the Clearwater, Salmon, and Boise river valleys when territorial governance was extended to Idaho in 1863. A separate Montana Territory was formed the following year.

Farm settlements took hold in both Idaho and Montana to provision the mining towns. The burgeoning settler traffic in the mid-1860s on the Bozeman Trail from Fort Laramie in Wyoming to Virginia City in the Montana goldfields triggered hostilities with the Sioux that went on until 1877. U.S. troops forcibly cleared the Cheyenne and Apache from eastern Colorado in the 1860s. Discovery of silver in the San Juan Mountains brought confinement of the Utes in western Colorado to reservations.

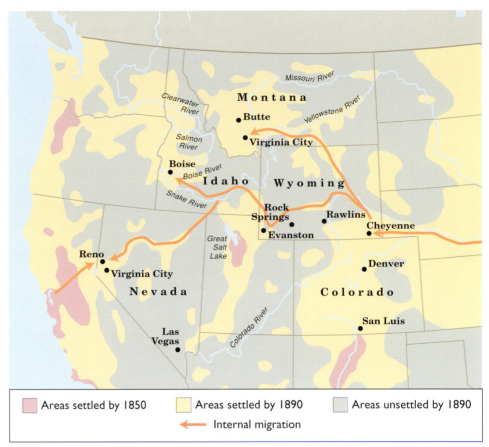

Areas settled by 1850	Areas settled by 1890	Areas unsettled by 1890

⟵ Internal migration

Settlement of the Mining Frontier

The tracklaying crews of the Union Pacific Railroad entered eastern Wyoming in 1867 and had crossed into Utah by 1869. Cheyenne, Rawlins, Rock Springs,

Helena, Montana, 1873   (The Montana Historical Society)

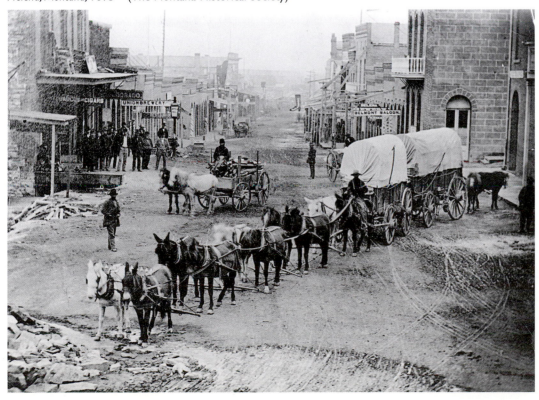

Evanston, and other towns sprang up along its route, leading to the creation of Wyoming Territory in 1868. Many of the early settlers came from Texas and the Midwest. Cheyenne became the destination of massive cattle drives from Texas in the 1870s and 1880s. From Cheyenne the cattle were shipped by rail to the stockyards of Chicago. Ranching flourished in the territory and Wyoming became a "Cattlemen's Commonwealth." Sheep also thrived in the high Plains clime. When Wyoming achieved statehood in 1890, its population of some 63,000 included an important cohort of sheepherders.

Las Vegas and Reno in Nevada also developed as railroad towns. The state's mining boom waned after 1873, when U.S. currency was taken off the silver standard and the precious metal's price plummeted. As the Comstock and other mines petered out, Nevada's population dropped by one-third between 1880 and 1900, to 42,000. The term "ghost town" entered the popular vocabulary to describe deserted frontier settlements such as Virginia City. Mining revived after 1900 with new gold and silver discoveries, as well as federal silver-buying programs, but the desert state's future development would be driven by tourism (with prospectors gambling rather than digging for gold).

The gold rush to Colorado, Idaho, and Montana had subsided by 1870. Important copper deposits were found near Butte, Montana, but gold and silver mining declined, affecting the small mining communities scattered across the Rockies. Idaho's population fell precipitously in the late 1860s.

The railroad in Colorado in the 1870s and in Idaho and Montana in the 1880s brought both economic growth and new migrants. Colorado, made a state in 1876, turned increasingly agricultural, with newcomers cultivating its valleys and raising livestock on its eastern plains.

Farming, ranching, and lumbering guided the slower settlement of Idaho and Montana. Colorado had a shade over 400,000 residents in 1890. Idaho, granted statehood the same year, had barely 90,000. Montana, which gained statehood in 1889, had just 143,000, with much of the recent influx in the eastern Yellowstone Valley.

INDUSTRIAL LANDSCAPES

The railroads that crossed the Mining Frontier were a product of the revolutionary changes in technology and manufacturing inaugurated in the late 1700s. The transformation in centuries-old methods of production began in Great Britain and by the early 1800s had moved to the United States. The catalyst was Scottish engineer James Watt's development of an efficient steam engine in the 1760s. Constantly improved versions of the engine soon were powering newly designed machines that could do faster and better the work previously performed by human hands.

Innovations in machinery were driven by the need for mechanical devices to spin and weave cotton. The development of water-powered textile machinery in the 1780s and 1790s made possible the first industrialization, or use of machine production in large-scale manufacture. The textile machines were made of iron, unlike most machines of the time, which were fashioned out of wood. The potential of such machinery, and its eventual marriage to steam power, depended on the supply of iron. By the late 1700s British mills had mastered the use of coke (a form of coal) and blast furnaces to produce the more malleable wrought iron required for the manufacture of machines.

FIRST INDUSTRIAL REVOLUTION

The sudden synergy among steam power, machinery, and iron production ushered in a new industrial era. This dramatic shift from hand tools to machine production became known as the Industrial Revolution. Once unleashed, technology would progress at a dizzying pace from the cumbersome machines of the early 1800s to the Information Age we live in today. To distinguish it from later developments, the period from 1780 to 1860, dominated by steam power, is often called the First Industrial Revolution. Its final decades, in particular, were marked by extraordinary changes in manufacturing, transportation, and communications.

LOWELL TEXTILE MILLS

The United States embraced the Industrial Revolution. Industrialization shaped American history as much as the frontier. It was not only the technology that was revolutionary, but also its impact on the economy and society. This impact had a profound

New England factory life: Bell Time, Winslow Homer (*Harper's Weekly* July 25, 1868; collection of the Boston Athenaeum)

influence on migration both to and within America.

Industrialization came to America with the Lowell textile mills, which used the new machines developed in Great Britain. In 1813 the Boston Manufacturing Company built the nation's first fully mechanized mill in the town of Waltham, just west of Boston on the Charles River. The facility was the first textile mill to integrate all the operations for converting cotton into cloth in a single building, or factory. The widely adopted use of integrated manufacture became known as the Waltham System.

In 1822 the company constructed a complex of mills on the Merrimack River north of Boston in a town it renamed Lowell in honor of the firm's founder. The Lowell mills made possible a much greater volume of production. They also required a large number of workers. Most of the men in rural New England were needed for farming. In a dramatic departure from traditional social patterns, the company began recruiting young farm girls from the surrounding countryside to work in the mills. To attract female workers, and reassure their families, the women were strictly supervised, housed in well-run dormitories, and paid good wages. Before long, more than 300 young women were laboring in the Lowell mills. Many were barely in their teens, reflecting the time's ready use of child labor. Few stayed more than a few years before returning home to get married,

but a constant flow of new workers kept the mills humming.

This paternalistic approach to management was dubbed the Lowell System. Before industrialization, most manufacture had been the province of craftsmen and small firms. The Lowell System retained the traditional personal bonds between employer and employee even as the Lowell mills pioneered the industrial workplace. Before long, the new market realities of industrialization would make the Lowell management approach unsustainable.

An economic downturn in the 1830s led to the mills' first wage cuts. In the 1840s overexpansion in New England's textile industry brought further pressure on production and labor costs. Young female workers resisted the higher production quotas and lower wages. After 1848, the mills turned increasingly to Irish immigrants for cheap labor.

The Lowell System was abandoned by the 1850s. In its place came the employment practices that would predominate in 19th-century factories. Prospective workers, whether immigrant or native, would move to a firm's location. Many came with families, and it was common for all able family members to be put to work. The men and older children, both male and female, labored in the factory. Married women remained at home with younger children. Tenement housing was provided for the families within walking distance of the factory.

FACTORY TOWNS

The commercial success of the Lowell enterprise spurred the building of similar textile mills elsewhere on the Merrimack as well as along other Massachusetts and Connecticut rivers. These early mills were water-powered. Development of Pennsylvania's vast coal mines by the late 1820s made available a ready and inexpensive source of energy for steam engines. Water transport was soon bringing the coal to steam-powered mills in New Bedford, Fall River, Providence, and other New England coastal towns. The steam engine freed manufacturing from a dependence on water power, which meant factories could be located almost anywhere. With virtually no limit to the amount of power that could be supplied, factories could also be larger and larger.

The growth of the New England textile industry led to the manufacture of textile machinery. As the capabilities of mechanized production were exploited with successive innovations and inventions, factories turned out a rapidly expanding array of machines, tools, and other iron items. The discovery of massive iron ore deposits in the Great Lakes states after 1844 provided the raw material for the boom in factory production. Western Pennsylvania, with its enormous coal reserves and prox-imity to the Great Lakes region, emerged as the center of the American iron industry.

Between 1840 and 1860 American factories pioneered the fabrication and assembly of standardized parts in what was soon called the American system of manufacture. Factories produced growing quantities of newly devised threshing machines, harvesters, reapers, and other farm implements, beginning the mechanization of American agriculture. The Singer plant in New York City made the first sewing machines. Other factories churned out firearms, stoves, clocks, and various tools.

By 1860 America's initial manufacturing belt extended from north of Boston to New York City and then across New Jersey to Philadelphia. Industrialization brought a new landscape of mill and factory towns. Most of New England, much less most of America, remained overwhelmingly rural in 1860. But the die had been cast for an explosive growth in American industry in the decades after the Civil War. By 1890 the manufacturing belt would extend across New York to western Pennsylvania and northern Ohio. Major industrial areas were located around Cincinnati, Chicago, and St. Louis.

FROM FARMS TO CITIES

Cities were the dominant landmarks of the emerging industrial landscape. The United

Growth of Industry and Cities to 1900

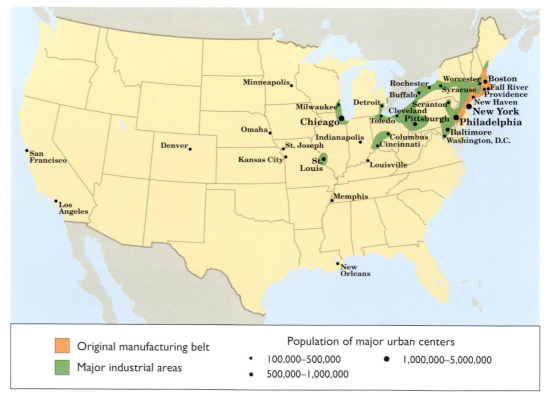

States, it has been observed, was born in the country and moved to the city. In 1790 only 5 percent of Americans lived in towns of at least 2,500 inhabitants—the threshold population long used to differentiate urban from rural areas. The largest city, Philadelphia, had some 42,000 residents, and only 5 cities in all had more than 10,000 inhabitants. All five were seaports, as the 18th century's urban economy was based on maritime commerce. Late 18th century cities clustered on the waterfront and were limited in size by the one to two miles residents could walk comfortably in their day-to-day lives.

As late as 1820 New York—by then the nation's leading port—had just 125,000 inhabitants, but American cities were on the verge of startling growth. In following decades, industrialization would turn cities into manufacturing centers. Advances in transportation and communication made cities the bustling hubs of America's burgeoning economy. New York's railroad links to the interior became as important to its stunning expansion as its seaborne links to other ports.

Manufacturing jobs drew rural migrants to cities as well as to the industrial towns

New York City, 1867   (Photo by Matthew Brady, *Broadway North from Spring Street*, Museum of the City of New York, gift of Edmund Dwight)

LEADING U.S. CITIES, 1790–1860

1790		1820		1860	
Philadelphia	42,444	New York	123,700	New York	1,080,330
New York	33,131	Philadelphia	112,800	Philadelphia	565,529
Boston	18,038	Baltimore	62,700	Baltimore	212,418
Charleston	16,359	Boston	43,300	Boston	177,840
Baltimore	13,503	New Orleans	27,200	New Orleans	168,675

Source: *Encyclopedia of American History*

dotting New England and the Middle Atlantic. Generations of America's surplus rural population flowed west. After 1840, increasing numbers of single men and women, as well as families, also migrated from the countryside to the city. Many of the young men and women married and assimilated into the new factory-dominated urban life. The bursting northeastern cities also became home to swelling ranks of immigrants.

By 1870 New York's population had climbed above one million. Another 14 cities had more than 100,000 residents and there were 168 places with populations over 10,000. Industrialization was creating dominant cities and outlying towns. It also was shifting the balance between rural and urban America. Urbanization, or increase in the number of urban residents in relation to rural residents, had resulted in 25 percent of Americans dwelling in urban areas in 1870. This urbanization was confined largely to the Northeast. The South, which had developed through slave agriculture, and the frontier West would not undergo industrialization until the 20th century.

American cities in the mid-1800s were densely packed warrens and grids of five-story buildings. Existing construction meth-ods, the lack of safe elevators, and difficulties in running water lines above five floors all restricted building heights. The limited daily reach of horse-drawn transport kept cities from extending much more than three or four miles. The jamming of ever larger numbers of people into the tight urban confines brought unprecedented crowding, with tenement housing forming the first industrial slums.

After 1870, advances in construction techniques enabled cities to soar upward, while elevated railroads and electric streetcars let them expand outward. This vertical and horizontal movement by the early 20th century had produced the modern city of skyscrapers, downtowns, and distinct commercial and residential neighborhoods.

THE IRON ROAD

In 1870 an immigrant arriving in New York could cross the entire continental expanse of America to San Francisco by rail. The transcontinental railroad, completed the year before, was a crowning achievement of the First Industrial Revolution. It also underscored the importance of steam age transportation, and rail travel in particular, to the industrialization, urbanization, and final settlement of the frontier that marked 19th-century America.

Steam power first revolutionized transportation with the development of the steamboat in 1807, followed by the first oceangoing steamship in 1819. Before long, steamships would bring successive waves of immigrants to America's shores. On water, steam power had supplanted the sail. On land, the challenge was to replace the horse that pulled a stagecoach or wagon with a steam engine, or "iron horse." By 1825, wheel-mounted steam engines, or locomotives, had been devised that could pull stagecoaches or wagons with flanged wheels along parallel iron rails. The rails made it easier to pull larger loads, because

From Farms to Cities, 1790–1870

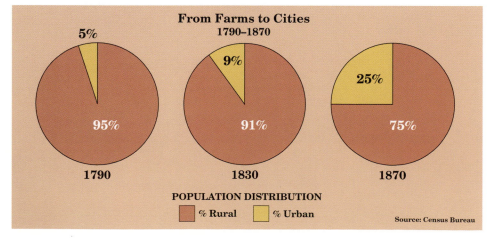

From Farms to Cities 1790–1870

5% / 95% — 1790
9% / 91% — 1830
25% / 75% — 1870

POPULATION DISTRIBUTION
■ % Rural   ■ % Urban

Source: Census Bureau

of reduced wheel friction, and gave the new transportation system its name.

The first American railroads were constructed in the late 1820s. In 1830 there were only 23 miles of track in operation, but the extraordinary potential of rail transport, especially for the movement of freight, was already manifestly evident. By 1840 the nation had almost 3,000 miles of railway, with local lines extending into every New England and Middle Atlantic state except Vermont. Over the next 20 years a railroad construction boom resulted in more than 30,000 miles of track which formed an iron network linking all the states east of the Mississippi River. The first railroad line crossed the Mississippi in 1856, and tracks reached as far west as St. Joseph, Missouri, on the eve of the Civil War.

More powerful steam engines were manufactured and passenger and freight cars were developed. The railroad became the workhorse of industrialization, carrying both raw materials and finished products. The railroads themselves became a giant industry, requiring growing numbers of workers and growing amounts of rolling stock and iron rails. The development of large-scale steel production techniques in the 1860s, prompted in part by the need for less brittle rails, signaled the end of iron's industrial reign. The astonishing expansion of the American steel industry after the Civil War was due in large part to the

Railroads and the West

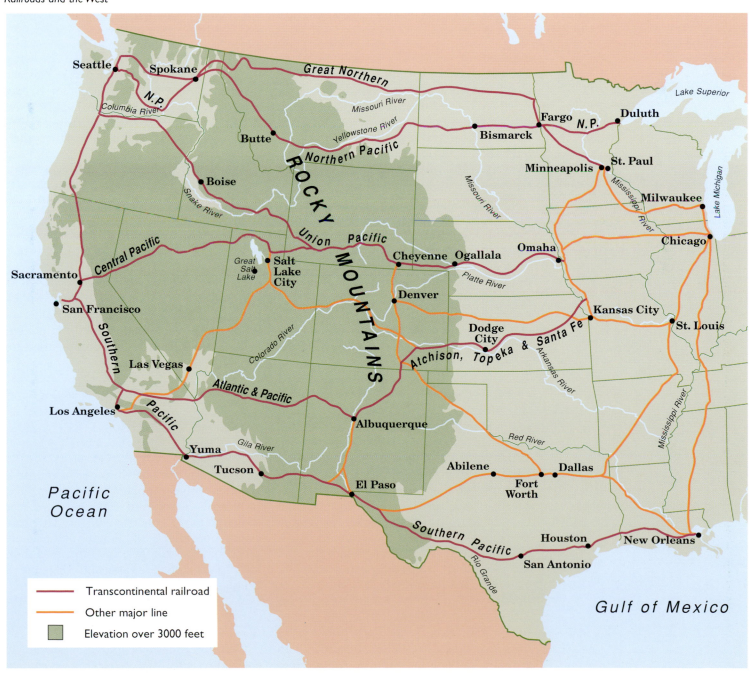

Building the Union Pacific Railroad   (Courtesy of the American Heritage Center, University of Wyoming)

demand for steel rails and bridge girders. The telegraph, in use after 1844 and run on electricity from steam-powered generators, provided the instantaneous communication needed to operate trains over extended distances. Telegraph lines paralleled railroad tracks across the nation.

Railroads were private ventures, but they needed public lands for their routes. In 1850 Congress made the first land grant to a railroad, giving the Illinois Central 2.5 million acres to build a line linking Chicago to Cairo in southern Illinois. As hoped, the railroad spurred development of the Illinois prairie, attracting thousands of settlers and spawning 37 new towns.

Between 1850 and 1871, when the federal land-grant policy ended, railroad companies received 155 million acres from the public domain, an area almost the size of Texas. Normally, companies were awarded alternating square-mile sections on either side of a projected track which they could sell to help finance construction costs. Railroads had a strong interest in the settlement of the West so as to ensure both buyers for their land and sufficient freight and passenger traffic on their lines.

The Mexican Cession in 1848 opened the way for railroads to link the Far West to the Mississippi valley. The landmark Pacific Railroad Act in 1862 provided the land for the first transcontinental railroad. Completed at Promontory, Utah, in 1869, the line followed the rough path of the Mormon and California trails from Omaha to San Francisco. By 1883 other land-grant lines crossed the West along northern, 35th parallel, and southern routes. All tied into

eastern tracks and all carried growing numbers of settlers to the West. Western railroads, most notably the Great Northern, which completed a line from St. Paul to Seattle in 1893, actively recruited immigrants for farm settlements along their routes.

By 1880 American railroads had 93,000 miles of track and employed 419,000 workers. The years 1860 to 1880 saw the full realization of the changes sparked by the First Industrial Revolution. Steel production was refined, industrial manufacture blossomed, and national transportation and communication networks (the railroad and telegraph) were completed. The groundwork had been laid for a Second Industrial Revolution after 1880 that, based on electric power, would again transform American life.

WORKERS AND SETTLERS WANTED

Constructing the transcontinental railroads required huge numbers of workers. The Industrial Revolution had hastened the dynamic natural increase in the American population after 1800. Better shelter, more plentiful food supplies, and improved diets all helped extend life expectancy. Despite its rapid growth, though, America's population could not keep up with either the demand for workers in industry or for settlers in the West.

Immigrants answered both needs. In the mid-1800s, the federal government continued to exercise no control over immigration. Under the Open Door policy, any and all were welcome across the nation's portals. Western states and territories took to recruiting immigrants as settlers. In 1845 Michigan appointed an agent to enlist settlers among immigrants on the docks of New York. Wisconsin soon followed suit. Minnesota sent advertisements to Europe in English, Welsh, Dutch, German, Norwegian, and Swedish and hired recruiting agents in Germany and Sweden. After 1850, 33 states and territorial governments eventually established offices in New York to attract newcomers. The competition spawned fierce rivalries. Pamphlets circulating in Europe extolled Iowa's Indian Summer, Minnesota's low mortality rate, or Wisconsin's location and railroads. Much of the advertising trumpeted the virtues of the American frontier.

Industry representatives also met the immigrant ships. New England factories, Pennsylvania steel mills, and Chicago stockyards all needed laborers. The railroads recruited both workers and settlers. Railroad companies operated special "immigrant trains" that carried settlers to areas they wanted colonized along their routes.

Federal land policy promoted settlement of the West and, indirectly, the immigration that supported it. After 1840 western political interests pushed for free public lands for homesteaders, small farmers willing to live on and work a plot in return for its eventual ownership. Southern legislators blocked federal homesteading measures in the 1850s, fearing the occupation of western lands by independent small farmers would limit the expansion and influence of slavery.

The withdrawal of Southern members during the Civil War cleared the way for Congress to pass the Homestead Act in 1862. The law provided 160 acres of surveyed public domain to any head of household age 21 or over who agreed to build a residence and live on the land for at least five years. The only cost was a small filing fee.

The act drew rural migrants from the East and Midwest who otherwise could not afford to resettle in the West. It also proved a lure to hundreds of thousands of immigrants from Europe. Even as the Civil War raged, 15,000 homestead claims were established. As the movement westward resumed in earnest in the decades after the war, 145 million acres were acquired by homesteaders.

OLD IMMIGRANTS

The word of free land spread quickly in Europe. Between 1868 and 1873 over 100,000 Swedes, hearing of the Homestead Act, set out across the Atlantic. The Swedes were part of a massive movement of some 10 million emigrants from northern Europe who journeyed to America between the end of the Civil War and 1890.

The Irish and German migrations that dominated the 1840s and 1850s resumed in force after the Civil War. Around 435,000 Irish arrived in America in the 1870s. Another 655,000 came in the 1880s. As before, Irish immigrants tended to locate in urban areas. Also reprising an earlier pattern, the second wave of German immigrants was drawn by the prospect of readily available farmlands. Whereas the Irish influx was heaviest in the 1850s, German migration, spurred by the Homestead Act, peaked in the 1880s at more than 1.4 million. Hundreds of thousands of German settlers made for the farm states and territories of the upper Midwest.

Word of the need for laborers echoed loudest in Great Britain, inducing an upsurge in immigration in the late 1800s. Most of the 1.3 million English newcomers between 1870 and 1890 were workers seeking better opportunities in the rapidly

Sources of U.S. Immigration, 1820–1890

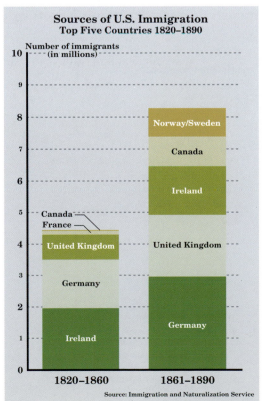

Sources of U.S. Immigration
Top Five Countries 1820–1890

Number of immigrants (in millions)

1820–1860 / 1861–1890

Source: Immigration and Naturalization Service

industrializing American economy. The ranks of largely unskilled laborers included numbers of experienced miners, craftsmen from building trades, and skilled industrial workers. The vast majority of the migrants were from urban areas. The relative handful of farmers amid this influx never amounted to much more than 10 percent of annual arrivals.

Roughly two-thirds of the workers were in what was considered the most productive age group of 15 to 39. Both men and women from England's surplus population sought employment in America, with females constituting as much as 40 percent of those taking passage. Men and women traveling alone or with friends outnumbered family groups by about eight to one.

Most of the English migrated to one of two regions. Many found work in the manufacturing belt extending across New England and the Middle Atlantic to the upper Ohio valley. Others went to the new mining, farming, and ranching areas west of the Mississippi River. English farmers favored settlement in Iowa and Kansas.

Interspersed among the English were small numbers of Welsh workers. Welsh industrialization dated to the early 1800s. Thus there was a ready supply of skilled laborers available for more lucrative employment in America. Wales had a population of less than two million in the 1800s, and the outflow of colliers, miners, quarrymen, and iron and steel workers never exceeded several thousand a decade. Well more than half of the English and Welsh workers eventually returned to Great

Britain. It is estimated that the permanent English and Welsh immigrant population in America increased by about 375,000 between 1870 and 1890.

Unlike many British, most Scandinavians came to stay. Scandinavian countries Norway, Denmark, Sweden, and Finland had shared interlocking histories for many centuries before the Napoleonic Wars once again rearranged the map of Europe in the early 1800s. By the close of this warfare in 1815, control of Norway had passed from Denmark to Sweden. Norway was recognized as a separate kingdom, but it remained under Swedish sovereignty until 1905, when it gained full independence. Reflecting the political ties, U.S. immigration records did not distinguish between Swedish and Norwegian entrants until 1871. Finland was made a part of Russia in 1809. The annexation separated Finland geopolitically from the rest of Scandinavia and precluded Finnish immigration to America until the early 20th century.

Emigration from Norway and Sweden to American occurred mostly in the late 1800s, but both Norwegians and Swedes had distant historical links to the New World. Norse ancestors of the Norwegians were the first Europeans to reach the Western Hemisphere, which they did in the early 11th century, briefly maintaining the settlement of Vinland in present-day Newfoundland. Sweden founded the small colony of New Sweden at the mouth of the Delaware River in 1638. Swedish involvement in the early settlement of America ended only 17 years later when New Swe-

Scandinavian Immigrants

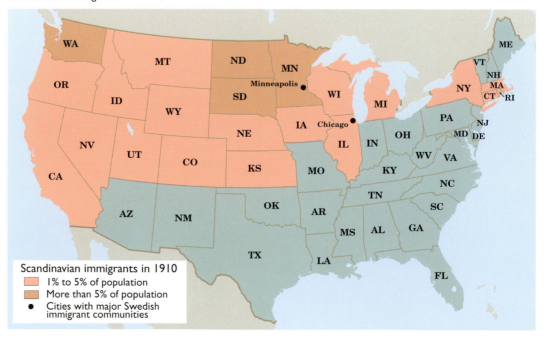

Scandinavian immigrants in 1910
■ 1% to 5% of population
■ More than 5% of population
● Cities with major Swedish immigrant communities

den was forcibly absorbed by the Dutch into New Netherland.

Over the next two centuries at most several hundred Norwegians and Swedes found their way to America. Sizable migration began after 1840, prompted by burgeoning rural populations in both countries. Arable land was scarce in both Norway and Sweden, and farm families were increasingly hard-pressed to divide their holdings among successive generations. Some 20,000 Norwegians and 15,000 Swedes arrived in America between 1840 and 1860. Both immigrant groups were dominated by family farmers in search of land. Norwegians and Swedes both put down roots mainly in Wisconsin and Minnesota, but Swedish farming communities were found in Illinois and Norwegian settlements in Iowa.

Crop failures and economic woes, as well as overpopulation, inspired the major migrations of Norwegians and Swedes after 1865. Norway, which experienced a dramatic population increase after 1820, saw nearly 98,000 of its rural folk immigrate to America in the 1860s. This outflow eased in the 1870s but surged again in the 1880s to more than 186,000. The Norwegians, many of whom were homesteaders, settled across the farm states of the upper Midwest.

Harvest failures caused a severe famine in Sweden in the late 1860s, precipitating the emigration of more than 100,000 Swedish homesteaders between 1868 and 1873. Conditions eased in Sweden until 1879, when new agricultural problems and downturns in the lumber and iron industries all conspired to produce a second and much larger exodus. In the 1880s almost 400,000 farmers and workers left for the American Midwest. The area between the Mississippi and St. Croix rivers in Minnesota became known as the Swedish Triangle. Swedish homesteaders migrating farther west played an important part in settling Nebraska and the Dakotas in the Great Plains. Many miners went to Michigan, while lumbermen from northern Sweden were attracted to the Pacific Northwest. Other workers, especially in the construction trades, flocked to Minneapolis and Chicago. A vibrant Swedish community formed in Chicago, as many single women also found work in the city as domestics. For a brief period in the early 20th century, Chicago had the largest Swedish population of any city other than Stockholm.

Only a very small number of Danes ventured to America from colonial times until the 1860s. What became an "America fever" in Denmark began in 1864, when the already-tiny country lost almost one-fourth of its territory in a war with Prussia and Austria. The defeat and dismemberment plunged Denmark into a long period of political and economic instability. Continued population growth outpaced the ability of its economy to absorb the swelling ranks of surplus farmers and laborers. The widespread unemployment that ensued made Denmark fertile ground for American immigrant recruiters.

Between 1870 and 1900, some 200,000 Danes immigrated to America. The outflow constituted almost one-tenth of Denmark's population. At first the migration was dominated by rural families. After 1890 young single workers, most of them male, predominated. The Danish immigrants dispersed across the American continent and assimilated quickly into a broad spectrum of occupations. Numbers settled in Iowa and Wisconsin. Danish farmers in the upper Midwest, reprising techniques pioneered in Denmark, became prominent in the development of the American dairy industry.

The forces driving emigration from northern Europe were largely spent by 1890. Overpopulation, in particular, had been ameliorated by the mass exodus. America, however, was not at a lack for newcomers. Even as immigration from northern Europe declined, a massive new influx from southern and eastern Europe was underway. Most of the southern and eastern European immigrant groups were coming to America for the first time and their millions of members became know as New Immigrants. Northern Europe's earlier emigrants were in turn referred to as Old Immigrants. In the years after 1890, the flow of New Immigrants would reach unprecedented levels.

GOLDEN MOUNTAIN

The call to America's shores reverberated not only in Europe but in Asia. The realization of Manifest Destiny extended U.S. sovereignty to the Pacific Ocean. It also opened America to emigration from beyond the Pacific. In the 1860s and 1870s tens of thousands of Chinese immigrants made San Francisco the gateway for Asia just as New York was for Europe.

The Chinese were the first to immigrate to the United States from Asia. Contact between China and America dated to the late 1700s and American participation in the China trade. By the early 1800s small numbers of Chinese crewmembers were serving

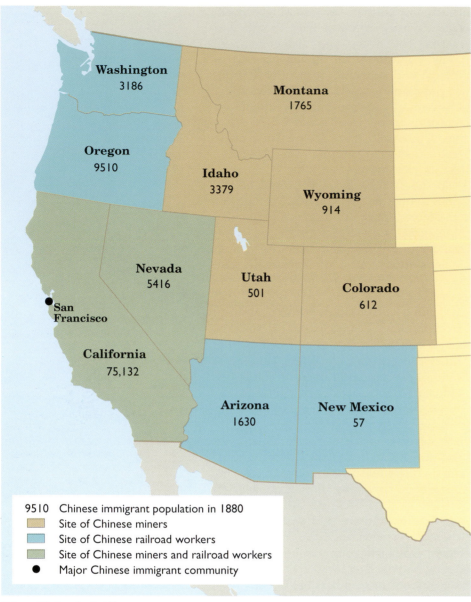

Chinese Workers in the West

1840 for work as manual laborers abroad. The exodus to Southeast Asia, Oceania, and both North and South America intensified during the unsuccessful Taiping Rebellion (1851–64) against the Manchu dynasty, which ravaged China and left 20 million dead.

After 1849 thousands of Chinese from the provinces of Fukien and Kwangtung adjoining the Western treaty ports sailed for California to work in the gold fields. Almost all went under the aegis of one of the "Six Companies," associations formed by Chinese merchants to gain a part of California's celebrated riches. The Chinese emigrants were obligated to repay the associations for transportation to California, and assistance once there, with one of two forms of contract labor. Some, especially during the early 1850s, agreed to work for an association for a specified time. Most arranged to pay off their debts through deductions from their wages. These contract laborers were willing migrants and not, as is often mistakenly assumed, part of the trade in "coolie" or involuntary labor, under which Chinese peasants were coerced into service and shipped abroad.

By 1852 21,000 Chinese were living in California. The Chinese district that formed in San Francisco was known as Chinatown, a moniker that became the standard name for Chinese enclaves in American cities. The Chinese called San Francisco, the main port of entry, the Golden Mountain, both for its shimmering image from the sea and for the riches beyond. Golden Mountain became Chinese slang for California and then all of America.

Some 40,000 Chinese arrived in America in the 1850s. Another 200,000 came to Golden Mountain from 1860 to 1882, when legislation was passed curtailing their further entry. Nearly all were males of working age and most were contract laborers. Many were married, but almost all left their families in China. At most several hundred eventually brought over their wives and children. The small ranks of female migrants included prostitutes, many of whom were taken to America by force and treated as virtual slaves. Some escaped and others finally earned their freedom. The importing of prostitutes, barred by U.S. law in 1875, was largely halted by the late 1870s. In 1880, there were 21 Chinese males in America for every Chinese female.

As California's gold fever subsided, many Chinese stayed to work in San Francisco's nascent cigar, shoe, and garment industries or in the Sacramento valley's rich agricultural areas. Many labored as farmhands much in the manner of the Mex-

on the American ships that brought furs and finished goods to southern China and returned home with silks and spices. A handful of Chinese seamen and merchants visited American ports in the first half of the 19th century.

In 1848 American ships brought word of the discovery of gold in California to the trading ports of southeastern China. At the time, the ancient Chinese empire was convulsed by upheaval and unrest. Defeated by Great Britain in the First Opium War (1839–42), China had been forced to abandon its stringent restrictions on foreign traders and open itself to the outside world and, consequently, to exploitation by European powers. The Chinese empire was in decline and its overwhelmingly peasant population chafed under the corrupt and oppressive rule of the Manchu dynasty.

Hundreds of thousands of impoverished peasants fled southern China after

ican migrant workers who later would toil in California's fields and orchards. Others farmed as sharecroppers or raised their own vegetables. Thousands of Chinese followed the Mining Frontier across the West. Chinese miners were part of the gold rushes in Nevada, Colorado, Idaho, Montana, and the Blacks Hills of South Dakota.

Chinese workers were engaged in building railroads in California as early as 1858. Most often, the Chinese were not employed individually but were contracted for in groups through a Chinese agent or foreman. In the 1860s Western railroads hired Chinese middlemen in Canton and other treaty ports to furnish contract laborers. The Central Pacific imported more than 10,000 Chinese to work on the San Francisco to Promontory Point link of the first transcontinental railroad. Chinese workers also helped build the western sections of the northern and southern transcontinental routes, as well as trunk and branch lines. As the tracks were finished, many of the workers settled in railroad towns in Washington and Oregon and from California across to Utah and Texas. In the Pacific Northwest thousands of Chinese subsequently found work in the salmon canneries.

Large numbers of the workers eventually returned to China. Most who stayed remained in the West. A small number of Chinese migrated to midwestern and eastern cities. Those who made it to New York would found the well-known Chinatown there in the mid-1870s. For a brief time after the Civil War, planters in Arkansas, Louisiana, and Mississippi tried using Chinese field hands to replace freed slaves, but this experiment soon gave way to black sharecropping. In 1880 there were slightly more than 100,000 Chinese immigrants in America, with the overwhelming majority dwelling in California.

CLOSING THE OPEN DOOR

In a sequence that exemplified the crazy-quilt peopling of the American West, Chinese workers from the Far East helped build the railroads that linked the former Mexican Southwest to the rest of the nation and aided the advance of native-born and European-immigrant settlers westward. The meeting of East and West beyond the Rockies did not go well. Chinese workers faced racism and hostility almost from the start. As early as 1852, Chinese miners in California's gold fields were harassed and attacked by white prospectors. Often, for their own safety, the Chinese were reduced to working the tailings of already-scoured areas. In San Francisco the Chinese were subjected to frequent intimidation and discrimination.

The racism became more virulent as the number of both Chinese and whites in the Far West increased. Most whites saw the Chinese as members of an inferior race. Chinese physical characteristics, such as Asian-shaped eyes, were denigrated and even imbued with nefarious meaning. The status of racial inferiority assigned to the Chinese was redolent of that associated with blacks and Native Americans. Like blacks, the Chinese were depicted as morally deficient, childlike, and lustful. Like Native Americans, they were considered heathens and barbarians.

Whites regarded Chinese culture, different as it was, as unassimilable. In stereo-

ANGEL ISLAND

Angel Island, the entry point for Asian newcomers in San Francisco Bay, became known as the Ellis Island of the West. Much like Ellis, it could be an "isle of tears." Angel was both a reception facility for immigrants and a detention center for those refused admission or otherwise awaiting deportation. It became a custom for detainees to write poems on the wooden barracks walls. In the following anonymous verse, the "Flowery Flag" is Cantonese slang for America, referring to its brightly hued banner.

I used to admire the land of the Flowery Flag as a country of abundance.
I immediately raised money and started my journey.
For over a month, I have experienced enough winds and waves.
Now on an extended sojourn in jail, I am subject to the ordeals of prison life.
I look up and see Oakland so close by.
I wish to go back to my motherland to carry the farmer's hoe.
Discontent fills my belly and it is difficult for me to sleep.
I just write these few lines to express what is on my mind.

IMMIGRANTS BY OCCUPATION GROUP, 1820–1890

	Total	No Occupation	Professional	Commercial	Skilled	Farmer	Servant	Labor	Miscellaneous
1820	8,385	4,910	105	933	1,090	874	139	334	—
1830	23,322	17,848	136	1,427	1,745	1,424	22	720	—
1840	84,066	39,164	481	5,311	10,811	18,476	183	9,640	—
1850	369,980	243,577	918	6,400	26,369	42,873	3,203	46,640	—
1860	153,640	67,874	792	11,207	19,342	21,742	1,415	31,268	—
1870	387,203	207,174	1,831	7,139	35,698	35,656	14,261	84,577	867
1880	457,257	217,446	1,773	7,916	49,929	47,204	18,580	105,012	9,397
1890	455,302	195,770	3,236	7,802	44,540	29,296	28,625	139,365	6,668

Sources: *Historical Statistics of the United States*, Immigration and Naturalization Service

typing typical of the time, they denounced Chinese neighborhoods as dens of gambling, prostitution, and opium smoking. The use of dogs and rats in Chinese cuisine was frequently cited as evidence of a racial depravity.

As long as America needed workers, the Chinese were tolerated, if not accepted. In 1868, as western railroad building boomed, the U.S. government concluded the Burlingame Treaty with China, formally establishing the right of Chinese to immigrate to American so as to guarantee a steady supply of cheap labor. Most of the Chinese working on the railroads lived in separate shantytowns that relocated along the tracks as lines were completed. Anti-Chinese sentiments flared into open hostility in the 1870s as the Chinese settled down and came into contact with the surging numbers of white settlers in the Far West.

Racial antagonisms were exacerbated by a downturn in the American economy. In the hard times that gripped the nation in the 1870s, many whites saw the Chinese as an economic as well as cultural threat. Chinese workers increasingly were perceived as endangering American livelihoods. Newspapers, politicians, and labor leaders across the country fanned fears of a "yellow peril" and called for an end to Chinese immigration. Some went so far as to advocate Chinese repatriation.

Anti-Chinese feelings turned violent. In 1871 rioters in Los Angeles killed 21 Chinese immigrants. Chinese across California were driven from their homes or otherwise terrorized by white vigilante groups and mobs. Similar attacks occurred in Washington, Oregon, and Colorado.

The anti-Chinese fervor drove the first closing of America's traditionally wide-open door to immigrants. It also helped bring about federal control of immigration. In 1875 Congress passed the first federal immigration law, prohibiting the entry of criminals, prostitutes, and unwilling contract laborers. The measure, aimed principally at Chinese migrants, marked the onset of federal regulation of immigration. It also presaged the end of the nation's Open Door immigration policy.

In 1879 President Rutherford B. Hayes, seizing the popular mood, warned against the "present Chinese invasion" (notwithstanding that the Chinese constituted .002 percent of the U.S. population) and endorsed "any suitable measures to discourage the Chinese from coming to our shores." In 1880 the Hayes administration negotiated a new treaty with China that permitted the United States to "regulate, limit, or suspend" the immigration of Chinese laborers. China, too weak to oppose the discriminating measure, was left with U.S. promises to protect Chinese workers already in America.

The treaty cleared the way for the Chinese Exclusion Act of 1882. The law suspended the entry of Chinese workers for 10 years. Officials, teachers, students, merchants, and those who "traveled for curiosity" were exempted. To preclude a Chinese presence in American, the act barred all foreign-born Chinese from acquiring U.S. citizenship. The legislation, the first ever to raise a restrictive barrier against a specific national group, represented the abandonment of the Open Door and its replacement by a Restrictive Door immigration policy. Between 1882 and 1921, when immigration was put on a quota system, Congress would impose progressively tighter restrictions on those welcome to America.

The effect of the Chinese Exclusion Act was immediate. Chinese immigration dropped from nearly 40,000 in 1882 to 8,000 in 1883 and to less than 100 by 1885. Despite U.S. assurances, violence against the Chinese continued to erupt in the 1880s and 1890s. In 1885 a mob murdered 28 Chinese in Rock Springs, Wyoming.

The Chinese Exclusion Act was extended in 1892 and made permanent in 1902. The Chinese population in America declined from its 1890 high of 107,000 to 62,000 in 1920, as many in the largely bachelor society died or returned to China. After 1890 Chinese in more rural areas migrated to the remaining Chinatowns. These tiny urban enclaves were sustained by a trickle of immigrants and family growth.

As Chinese immigration dwindled, European immigration soared. By the early 1880s more than 500,000 Europeans a year were disembarking at American ports. The regulation of immigration by the states was proving unworkable, with differing rules governing the entry of newcomers in major ports such as Boston, New York, and New Orleans. In 1882 Congress enacted the first comprehensive federal immigration legislation. The law established initial national standards for immigrants, but left the actual processing of newcomers to the states. The continuing influx of immigrants overwhelmed state facilities and soon compelled the federal government to assume full control over immigration. Under a sweeping immigration law passed in 1891, Congress created the Bureau of Immigration to oversee and administer a national immigration program, ushering in complete federal regulation of immigration.

THE GREAT PLAINS

Many of the European immigrants were destined for the Great Plains. All the major trends in 19th-century American migration came together in the settlement of the relatively flat, treeless area between the Mississippi valley and the Rockies. Indian removal, slavery, industrialization, immigration, and gold and land rushes all played a part in the peopling of the last open expanse of the American frontier.

In 1834 Congress set aside the Great Plains, then the westernmost frontier, as Indian Territory. U.S. territorial expansion after 1845 soon undermined pledges to protect the Indian lands from white encroachment. By the late 1840s American settlers headed for the Far West were streaming along the Santa Fe, Oregon, and Mormon trails that traversed Indian Territory in Kansas and Nebraska. The pioneers, drawn by California and the Pacific Northwest, saw the Plains as an area to cross rather than settle.

Industrialization provided the impetus to opening the central Plains to white development. The movement to build a transcontinental railroad along a central route led Congress to create the Kansas and Nebraska territories in 1854. In forming the territories, lawmakers shrank Indian Territory to the confines of Oklahoma. In following decades the Kaw in Kansas and the Omaha, Oto and Missouri, Pawnee, and Ponca in Nebraska were relocated to the truncated Indian reserve.

Kansas became a battleground in the deepening North-South conflict over slavery. The Kansas-Nebraska Act establishing the territory had set forth the novel doctrine of "popular sovereignty," under which residents in territories would decide for themselves whether to enter the Union as free or slave states. Both proslavery and antislavery groups rushed to settle Kansas so as to influence the territorial vote on slavery. In the North abolitionists formed the New England Emigrant Aid Company to recruit antislavery volunteers and help them relocate to Kansas. Southern proslavery forces mobilized in the slave state of Missouri, which shared a long border with Kansas.

In early 1854 the only American outposts in Kansas's 50 million acres of grassland were the army forts at Leavenworth and Riley. That July the Emigrant Aid Company settled Lawrence on the Kansas River in northeastern Kansas. At the same time

Sod house, c. 1890   (Western History Collections, University of Oklahoma Library)

slave-owning farmers moved into south-eastern Kansas from Missouri. By 1855 there were 8,500 settlers in the territory, with antislavery groups congregating around Lawrence and Topeka in the north and proslavery elements spreading out around Lecompton in the south.

Bitter conflict between the two sides kept the territory's politics in turmoil until the Civil War. A virtual guerrilla war between the groups gained the territory the name "Bleeding Kansas." Antislavery settlers in particular continued to flow into the territory and Kansas had slightly more than 100,000 inhabitants when it was admitted to the Union as a free state by a Northern-dominated Congress in 1861.

Nebraska, too far north to serve as a second testing ground for the extension of slavery, had only some 28,000 settlers in 1860. Most were family farmers who eked out an existence on small plots. Because there were no trees, they lived in earthen houses made of sod bricks, with scarce wooden boards used only for roofs.

Settlement of both Kansas and Nebraska, disrupted by the Civil War, was boosted in the late 1860s by a combination of railroads and cattle-raising. Omaha and Ogalla in Nebraska and Abilene, Ellsworth, Wichita, and Dodge City in Kansas developed as railroad towns. The railroad boom vaulted Nebraska to statehood in 1867. Destruction of the vast buffalo herds on the central Plains by railroad workers, settlers, and Indian-fighting soldiers allowed cattle ranching to thrive in the open ranges of western Kansas and Nebraska. Railroads and ranching were linked, as the cattle were driven to railheads in the towns that had sprung up along the tracks and shipped to Chicago. The 1870s and 1880s formed the era of the great cattle drives, as ranchers in Texas brought their herds north to the railroads. Abilene flourished as the terminus of the famed Chisholm Trail, while Dodge City became renowned as the raw frontier town at the end of the Western Trail.

In the 1870s German immigrants from Russia helped transform the central and northern Plains from a seemingly endless grassland into the granary of the world. The Germans, who had settled in southern Russia in the 1700s, had generations of experience farming that region's plains-like steppes. The Germans were enticed into colonizing the steppes in part by promises they could keep their traditional culture, but after 1862 they faced an increasingly intolerant czarist regime intent on their absorption into Russian society. Between 1870 and World War I, tens of thousands of these Germans fled to America, where many resettled in the Great Plains. As early as 1874 German settlers had introduced to Kansas the hard winter wheat known as Turkey Red, which they had grown in Russia.

Turkey Red and the hybrids developed from it made possible abundant wheat harvests. Homesteaders poured in to farm the open ranges. The onslaught sparked occasional "range wars," as farmers and ranchers fought over land. Farmers gained the upper hand for good when the brutal winter of 1886 decimated the open-range herds. The great cattle drives from the south ended, as Texas ranchers delivered their herds to new railheads in their own state.

Farm settlement pushed the populations of both Kansas and Nebraska over one million by 1890. Agricultural advances brought the cultivation of other grains,

Settlement of the Great Plains

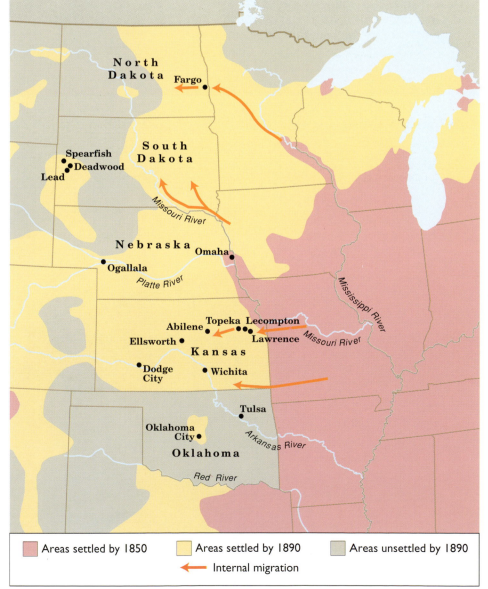

Areas settled by 1850   Areas settled by 1890   Areas unsettled by 1890
⟵ Internal migration

while mechanization permitted the harvesting of larger yields. The crops joined the burgeoning Great Plains agricultural output bound by rail to the East's expanding urban centers.

DAKOTA BOOMS

The northern Plains was organized as Dakota Territory in 1861. The area was opened to homesteading in 1863, but warfare with the Sioux impeded settlement. In 1868 the Sioux were forced to accept confinement to reservation lands in the Dakotas and Montana. The ensuing rush of settlers into the arable lands of eastern South Dakota became known as the First Dakota Boom. Homesteaders from Minnesota, Iowa, Wisconsin, and Illinois were joined by immigrants from Germany, Norway, and Sweden. The onrush raised the territory's population to more than 20,000 by 1873.

The following year gold was found in the Sioux-held Black Hills of western South Dakota, triggering a mining boom that brought thousands of prospectors into the rugged area. The Sioux fought the intrusion, but were compelled to cede the Black Hills in 1877. Mining towns with picturesque names such as Deadwood, Lead, and Spearfish anchored new farm settlements west of the Missouri River. By 1880 South Dakota had almost 100,000 inhabitants.

Construction of a transcontinental railroad route across North Dakota in the 1870s precipitated the Second Dakota Boom. Between 1878 and 1885 tens of millions of acres in North Dakota were claimed in homestead grants. North Dakota's population climbed from less than 40,000 in 1880 to almost 200,000 by the end of the decade. While cattle ranching was introduced in its western parts, wheat farming predominated in North Dakota, as it did in South Dakota. Almost all the Dakota Territory's eastern reaches were under cultivation when it was divided into the states of North and South Dakota in 1889.

OKLAHOMA LAND RUNS

Settlement of the northern Plains left Indian Territory in Oklahoma as the last undeveloped expanse in the West. Agitation by land-hungry whites to open the western half of Indian Territory to homesteading mounted in the 1880s. For prospective settlers, the lands of western Oklahoma seemed to be ripe for the taking, as only

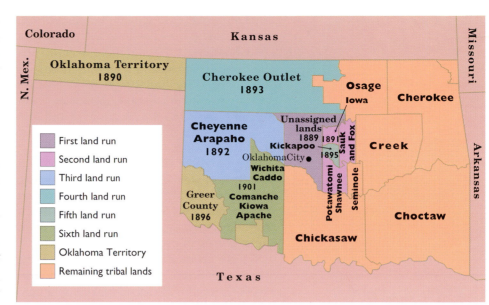

Oklahoma Land Runs

15,000 Indians at most lived on reservations in the untrammeled, Ohio-sized area.

Until the 1860s all of Indian Territory within present-day Oklahoma was the domain of the Five Civilized Tribes. The Five Tribes, which had adopted black slave-owning while in their original homelands in the South, brought thousands of slaves with them when they were removed to Indian Territory in the 1830s. During the Civil War, the Five Tribes sided with the Confederacy. Following the South's defeat, the tribes in 1866 were forced to free all their slaves and to cede all of western Oklahoma back to the U.S. government.

Most of the approximately 7,500 freed blacks remained in Oklahoma, starting their own farms or working as laborers for the Indians. The more than 50,000 members of the Five Tribes were confined to reservations in eastern Oklahoma. Western Oklahoma was used by the federal government for the relocation of tribes from former Indian Territory in Kansas and Nebraska as well as for reservations for southern Plains tribes subdued by the U.S. military. By 1889 all of Oklahoma, except for some 2 million acres of so-called Unassigned Lands in the center of Indian Territory, had been allocated to various tribes.

In the 1880s thousands of white squatters settled illegally in the sparsely populated western half of Indian Territory. Many were evicted by the U.S. Army, but broad political support for the settlement of Oklahoma led President Benjamin Harrison to announce on March 3, 1889, that the Unassigned Lands would be opened to homesteading at noon on April 22.

At the appointed hour, the sound of booming cannon sent 50,000 hopeful homesteaders racing by wagon, horse, and foot across the boundary lines of the central Oklahoma tract. By nightfall the entire area had been claimed and a literally hours-old Oklahoma City had 10,000 residents. The frenzied, astonishing spectacle soon became known as the Oklahoma Land Run.

More such runs were to follow. The settled part of Oklahoma was made a territory in 1890, with federal agents working diligently to extend its borders. As provided for under the 1887 General Allotment Act, Indian lands were converted from tribal to individual ownership, with the "left over" acreage set aside for white settlement. In 1891 the former reservations of the Iowa, Sauk and Fox, Potawatomi, and Shawnee were opened to the second Oklahoma Land Run. Cheyenne and Arapaho lands were occupied in 1892. The next year, in the fourth and largest land rush, more than 100,000 settlers poured into the area known as the Cherokee Outlet in northwestern Oklahoma.

The Oklahoma homesteaders gained the nickname Boomers. Those who snuck into an area before the starting gun were called Sooners. By 1901 the final two Boomer runs had incorporated all of the western half of Indian Territory into Oklahoma Territory. Discovery of oil around Tulsa brought white development of the Osage lands in northeastern Oklahoma by 1905. In 1906 all that remained of Indian Territory were the white-besieged holdings of the Five Tribes in eastern Oklahoma. In 1907 this last Indian enclave was joined with Oklahoma Territory in the new state of Oklahoma. A special census the same year found a population of more than 1.4 million, with settlers representing every state.

THE CLOSING OF THE FRONTIER

Oklahoma was the final piece to the puzzle assembled under Manifest Destiny. American settlement had spread first across and then throughout the continent. In 1890 the director of the U.S. Census observed that "there can hardly be said to be a frontier line." His words were widely understood as heralding the closing of the American frontier. Homesteading would continue in various forms until 1935, and millions more acres of public land would come under private development, but the West as the magic, open place that beckoned to millions was passing from view. In its place came the bustling metropolis. After 1890 the city was the new place of promise and the new locus of American migration.

At its dedication in 1886, the Statue of Liberty in New York Harbor towered over the city behind it. Only the spire of Trinity Church in lower Manhattan reached higher into the sky. Within 10 years, the 280-foot steeple itself would be dwarfed by the skyscrapers that sprouted around it. After 1890, New York and other American cities exploded upward and outward to create a new and completely different urban landscape.

Cities became a new urban frontier to which millions migrated in the hope of a better life. The years 1890 to 1940 are sometimes called the classic era of the modern American city, but this frontier was every bit as challenging as the wilderness frontier. Beneath New York's skyscrapers were the most densely packed slums in the world.

Many of those crowding into the tenements were immigrants. In the early 1900s, the Statue of Liberty welcomed to New York the largest and most concentrated burst of immigration in American history. Immigrants swelled the burgeoning cities of the North and Midwest. They were joined in the teeming urban centers by growing numbers of rural Americans displaced by the mechanization of agriculture. In the half-century after 1890, migration transformed America from a rural to an urban nation.

NEW IMMIGRANTS

In what became known as the Great Wave, more than 18 million newcomers crossed the nation's portals between 1891 and 1920. At its peak between 1905 and 1914, when World War I abruptly interrupted the massive influx, the volume often surpassed a previously unimaginable million immigrants a year.

The Great Wave was remarkable both for its size and for the new patterns of immigration it represented. The first decades of the 20th century saw more immigrants pour into America than during any comparable period in the nation's history. The overwhelming preponderance of the newcomers were from southern and eastern Europe. Because most were members of immigrant groups arriving for the first time in discernible numbers, they soon gained the appellation "New Immigrants."

The New Immigrants signified a dramatic shift in America's sources of immigration. Until the 1890s, almost all of the nation's many generations of immigrants had come from northern Europe. As the once-steady supply of so-called Old Immigrants waned for good in the late 1800s, America's native populace could not furnish enough workers for the nation's accelerating industrial expansion. Industry's seemingly insatiable demand for labor attracted a growing tide of newcomers from southern and eastern Europe. A turning point was reached in 1896, when for the first time the number of New Immigrants surpassed that of Old Immigrants. In 1910, over half of America's industrial workers were foreign-born. Most were New Immigrants.

NEW IMMIGRANTS BY GENDER AND AGE

| | Total | GENDER | | | | AGE | | | | | |
		Male	%	Female	%	Under 15	%	15–40	%	Over 40	%
1890	455,302	281,853	62	173,449	38	86,404	19	315,054	69	53,844	12
						Under 14		14–44		Over 44	
1900	448,572	304,148	68	144,424	32	54,624	12	370,382	83	23,566	5
1910	1,041,570	736,038	71	305,532	29	120,509	12	868,310	83	52,751	5
						Under 16		16–44			
1920	430,001	247,625	58	182,376	42	81,890	19	307,589	72	40,522	9

Source: *Historical Statistics of the United States*

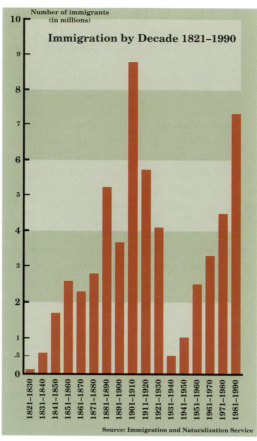

Number of immigrants
(in millions)

Immigration by Decade 1821–1990

Source: Immigration and Naturalization Service

Immigration by Decade, 1821–1990

The ready availability of employment, and the better life it promised, proved an overpowering lure to millions of impoverished peasants in southern and eastern Europe. Northern Europe had undergone significant industrialization by the late 19th century, but the southern and eastern tiers of the continent were just confronting a dislocating transition from agrarian to industrial economy. The Austro-Hungarian, Russian, and Turkish Ottoman empires, which for centuries had held sway over much of southern and eastern Europe, were in crisis. As they struggled to modernize, their still feudalistic societies were wracked by political unrest as well as social and economic upheaval. The chronic poverty endured by the average peasant was exacerbated by overpopulation and concomitant scarcity. Cholera and other epidemics claimed thousands. Many, especially Russian Jews, faced not only physical hardship but also religious or political persecution.

As the sometimes embellished word of America's golden opportunity spread, a growing human tide made its way to ports on both the Mediterranean and Baltic seas. There transatlantic steamship lines offered

Immigrants at Ellis Island, c. 1910   (By Courtesy of the Statue of Liberty National Monument)

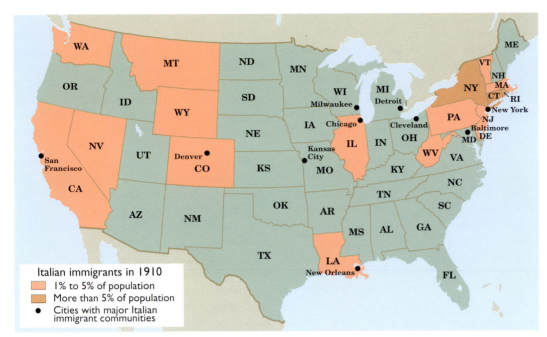

Italian Immigrants

relatively cheap passage to New York, the fabled gateway to America. Almost all the New Immigrants passed through the federal reception center opened in 1892 on Ellis Island, off the southern tip of Manhattan.

Until 1943, when it was converted to a detention center for deportees, the facility on Ellis was where more than three-quarters of the New Immigrants first set foot on American soil. Passage through the station for millions became the defining experience of arrival in America. After quarantine and customs procedures, the immigrants were subjected to medical exams, screened for potential indigency, and then interviewed by inspectors who recorded their entry. For most, Ellis was a symbol of hope and opportunity, but for those denied admission it became know as the Isle of Tears. Only a small percentage were rejected, but by 1910 this still amounted to more than 24,000 prospective newcomers a year. The mixture of expectation and dread was much the same on Angel Island in San Francisco Bay, where from 1910 to 1940 federal authorities operated a reception facility for Asian immigrants.

The swollen ranks of New Immigrants processing through Ellis Island reflected the extraordinary ethnic and religious diversity of southern and eastern Europe. The figures on their different numbers are at best approximations, as U.S. immigration inspectors often misidentified the various groups. One difficulty was the often confusing distinction between ethnicity and nationality. Many western and southern Slavs from the Austro-Hungarian Empire, for example, were not recorded as Czechs,

Slovaks, Slovenes, or Croats, but as Austrians or Hungarians. Poles were not listed as a separate category from 1899 to 1918, when Poland regained its independence after World War I. Adding to the diverse array, and the record-keeping confusion, were the first sizable numbers of immigrants from the Middle East.

The New Immigrants tended to be poorer, less educated, and less skilled than their Old Immigrant predecessors. Almost all settled in cities, where there was an incessant need for unskilled labor. The new immigrant groups filled the major industrial centers, creating an urban terrain of distinctive ethnic neighborhoods. By 1920 they comprised more than 40% of the residents of New York, Cleveland, and Chicago. Immigrants made up one-fourth of the populations of Boston, Buffalo, Philadelphia, Pittsburgh, and Detroit.

The new ethnic groups provoked a resurgent nativism that helped influence Congress in 1921 to enact legislation that virtually halted further immigration from southern and eastern Europe. The Great Wave was ended, but the thriving ethnic communities of New Immigrants and their children would remain the most dynamic demographic presence in American cities until after World War II.

SOUTHERN AND EASTERN EUROPE

Small numbers of immigrants from southern and eastern Europe had filtered into America since colonial times, but signifi-

DEPARTURE FOR AMERICA

Mary Antin grew up in Polotzk, in Russian-occupied Poland. In 1894, when she was 13, the word finally came to join her father in America, where he had gone ahead to make a new home for their family. In her book *The Promised Land* (1912), she remembered the poignant, chaotic departure from Polotzk.

On the day when our steamer ticket arrived, my mother did not go out ...

Before sunset the news was all over Polotzk that Hannah Hayye had received a steamer ticket for America. Then they began to come. Friends and foes, distant relatives and new acquaintances, young and old, wise and foolish, debtors and creditors, and mere neighbors—from every quarter of the city, from both sides of the Dvina, from over the Polota, from nowhere—a steady stream of them poured into our street, both day and night, till the hour of our departure....

What did they not ask, the eager, foolish, friendly people? They wanted to handle the ticket, and mother must read them what is written on it. How much did it cost? Was it all paid for? Were we going to have a foreign passport or did we intend to steal across the border? Were we not all going to have new dresses to travel in? Was it sure that we could get kosher food on the ship? And with the questions poured in suggestions, and solid chunks of advice were rammed in by nimble prophecies....And so on, and so on, till my poor mother was completely bewildered. And as the day set for our departure approached, the people came oftener and stayed longer, and rehearsed my mother in long messages for their friends in America ....The last night in Polotzk we slept at my uncle's house, having disposed of all our belongings, to the last three-legged stool, except such that we were taking with us.... I did not really sleep. Excitement kept me awake .... In the morning I was going away from Polotzk, forever and ever, I was going on a wonderful journey. I was going to America. How could I sleep?

cant migration from the region ensued only with the mass movements of the late 19th century. Most numerous of the New Immigrants were the roughly 4 million Italians who arrived between 1891 and 1920. Most were peasants from poverty-stricken southern Italy, where overpopulation and a devastating infestation of the crop disease phylloxera had pushed the centuries-old agricultural economy to virtual collapse.

At first the ranks of Italian immigrants were dominated by young men. Many came not so much as immigrants as sojourners, intending to work for a year or two and then return to Italy with sufficient money to improve life there. Eventually, large numbers of Italian immigrants did go back, but many of these in turn came back to settle in America. After 1900 Italian immigration became more stable as women and children increasingly joined the men bound overseas. Sometimes entire villages migrated together.

More than 75 percent of the Italians settled in the industrial cities of New York, New Jersey, Pennsylvania, and New England, but numbers went to every part of the country. There were Italian enclaves in Baltimore, Cleveland, Detroit, Chicago, Milwaukee, Kansas City, New Orleans, Denver, and San Francisco. Largest by far was the community in New York, where as elsewhere Italians became active in the fruit and vegetable business as well as finding employment in construction and heavy industry.

Also making the journey from southern Europe were Spaniards, Portuguese, and Greeks. In the only concerted burst of Spanish immigration to the United States, perhaps 100,000 Spaniards left their politically troubled homeland in the early 1900s. Most made their way to the former Spanish colonies of Florida, Louisiana, and California. More affluent and educated than most New Immigrants, they quickly assimilated into American society. In Portugal a long, successful effort by anticlerical republicans to overthrow the monarchy prompted about 185,000 Portuguese, mainly more conservative Catholic monarchists, to depart for America. Many came from seafaring islands and regions, and they migrated principally to the coastal towns of southern New England and California, where they assumed a major place in the local fishing industries.

Immigration from Greece was similar to that from Italy. A majority of the Greeks, who numbered some 350,000 by 1920, were young male sojourners from rural villages beset by overpopulation, recurrent crop failures, and grinding poverty. Many returned to Greece, while those who decided to stay in America often went back to their native land to choose a bride. The Greeks located mostly in New York, Detroit, Chicago, and San Francisco, but they also found their way to the industrial towns of New England, Atlanta, Milwaukee, and the mining regions of the Rocky Mountains. As family life took hold, the Greeks, much like the Japanese, became known for small business and store ownership.

From eastern Europe came as many as 4 million Slavs, although this figure is, at best, an uncertain estimate as the term "Slav" encompasses a number of ethnically related peoples. The Slavs are normally divided into three regional groups: the southern Slavs of the Balkan Peninsula, which include Bulgarians, Croatians, Macedonians, Montenegrins, Serbs, and Slovenes; the western Slavs, primarily Czechs, Poles, and Slovaks; and the eastern Slavs, including Russians and Ukrainians.

Despite their significant historical, cultural, religious, and linguistic differences, Slavic immigrants underwent a largely common experience in their relocation in America. Many came as sojourners, planning to return home, but many also came as families, intending to stay. Most migrated to the industrial centers, where they found work in the mines and factories. Some 80 percent of the Slavs settled in an area stretching from Boston and Baltimore across to Milwaukee and St. Louis. Major Slavic neighborhoods developed in New York, Philadelphia, Pittsburgh, Buffalo, Cleveland, Detroit, and Chicago. There was also a sizable Slavic presence in San Francisco and Los Angeles.

By far the most numerous of the Slavic immigrants were the Poles, with estimates of their numbers ranging as high as 2 million. The migration of other western Slavs totaled perhaps 500,000 Slovaks and 175,000 Czechs. From the Balkans emigrated maybe 400,000 Croatians, 300,000 Slovenes, 100,000 Serbs and Montenegrins, 50,000 Bulgarians, and 50,000 Macedonians. The Russian Empire saw about 250,000 Ukrainians depart and a somewhat smaller number of Russians.

There was a massive movement out of Russia, but it was of Russian Jews. About 2 million eastern European Jews were among the New Immigrants. While most came from areas that were part of the Russian Empire, there were also substantial migrations out of the Austro-Hungarian Empire and Romania.

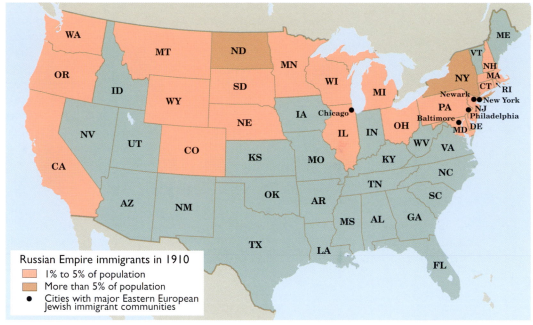

Russian Empire Immigrants

The very small Jewish presence in America that dated to early colonial times was first significantly augmented in the mid-1800s. Between 1830 and 1880 some 175,000 German Jews immigrated to America. Many left because of repressive laws in their native German principalities that limited where they could live or work. German Jews were also part of the larger German migration that resulted from industrialization's disruption of the peasant agricultural economy.

The influx from Germany pushed America's Jewish population from around 6,000 in 1830 to some 200,000 in 1880. Many of the German Jews were tradesmen or small merchants. In America they turned to peddling as a means of earning a livelihood. At the time there were few retail stores outside large cities, and peddling-based German Jewish communities were soon located in smaller cities across the country.

The eastern European Jews, most of whom arrived with few if any means, crowded into ghettos in the major cities of the Northeast and Midwest. Jewish neighborhoods grew rapidly in Baltimore, Newark, Philadelphia, Chicago, and especially New York. By 1910 there were 540,000 Jews living in the 1.5-square-mile area of the city's Lower East Side. In New York and elsewhere many of the newcomers found work in the garment districts, achieving, before long, a prominent place in the apparel trade.

The eastern European Jews migrated overwhelmingly as families. More than any other immigrant group, they came with no intention of ever returning home. Most were fleeing mounting persecution in eastern Europe, and America was not just a place of opportunity but also a refuge. In czarist Russia both dislocating internal social and economic changes and the rise of a nationalistic Slavism contributed to an increasingly virulent, government-countenanced anti-Semitism after 1880. Harsh, discriminatory measures against Jews were enacted, and pogroms were frequent. Conditions in Romania were equally repressive and were only slightly better in the Austro-Hungarian Empire. The growing hostility prompted fully one-third of eastern European Jewry to emigrate, with over 90% making for America. By 1920 America's Jewish population had climbed to about 4 million.

Also departing eastern Europe in significant numbers were perhaps 2 million Hungarians, 300,000 Lithuanians, and 85,000 Romanians. Although they differed ethnically and culturally, the three immigrant groups shared important characteristics. Most of their members were impoverished peasants drawn to America by the prospect of employment. Many were sojourners and as many as half returned to their homelands.

All three groups added once again to the new ethnic landscape of the manufacturing and mining belt that ran from New York to Chicago. Cleveland's Hungarian enclave grew so large it became known as the American Debrecen after the eastern Hungarian city. Chicago absorbed the largest concentration of Lithuanians, while Detroit was one of several cities with a small but vibrant Romanian presence.

…Half of Polotzk was at my uncle's gate in the morning, to conduct us to the railway station, and the other half was already there before we arrived.

The procession resembled both a funeral and a triumph. The women wept over us, reminding us eloquently of the perils of the sea, of the bewilderment of a foreign land, of the torments of homesickness that awaited us. They bewailed my mother's lot, who had to tear herself away from blood relations to go among strangers; who had to face gendarmes, ticket agents, and sailors, unprotected by a masculine escort; who had to care for four young children in the confusion of travel…

At the station the procession disbanded and became a mob. My uncle and my tall cousins did their best to protect us, but we wanderers were almost torn to pieces. They did get us into a car at last, but the riot on the station platform continued unquelled. When the warning bell rang out, it was drowned in a confounding babel of voices—fragments of oft-repeated messages, admonitions, lamentations, blessings, farewells—"Don't forget!"—"Take care of—" "Keep your tickets—" "Moshele—newspapers!" "Garlick is best!" "Happy journey!" "God help you!" "Good-bye! Good-bye!" "Remember—"

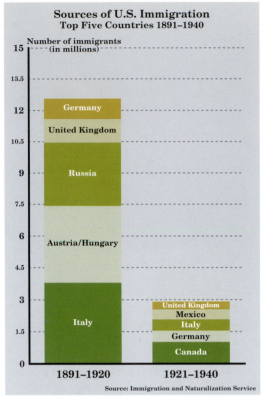

Sources of U.S. Immigration, 1891–1940

MIDDLE EAST

Persecution underlay the first real immigration from the Middle East. In the late 1800s Armenia, Lebanon, and Syria, all still part of the declining Ottoman Empire, were subjected to an increasingly brutal and intolerant rule by a beleaguered Turkish sultancy. The Ottoman regime, already beset by political turmoil, responded with unrestrained violence to Armenian efforts at greater freedom and autonomy. Several hundred thousand Armenians were massacred.

About 100,000 Armenians managed to escape to America. Most were peasants and many arrived virtually destitute. The Armenians settled primarily in Massachusetts and California, but numbers also found work as unskilled laborers in New York, Pennsylvania, Michigan, Illinois, and Wisconsin.

The Islamic Ottoman Empire, which long had tolerated the practice of other faiths, turned increasingly repressive in the 1890s. Christian Arabs, as well as the mostly Christian Armenians, faced religious persecution. Approximately 450,000 Middle Easterners fled the mounting Turkish oppression for America. Overwhelmingly Christian Arabs, they came mostly from Lebanon and Syria, as well as Iraq, Yemen, and Palestine. The exodus included some 125,000 Lebanese Maronites, 100,000 Greek

Orthodox, 50,000 Melkites, 10,000 Protestants, and 140,000 members of smaller Christian sects. Also migrating were around 25,000 Moslem Arabs. The Arab immigrants located in the major cities of New England, New York, Pennsylvania, Ohio, and Michigan. While retaining their various religious ties, many adopted American-sounding names and made every effort to blend into American society.

ADJUSTMENT AND ASSIMILATION

Virtually all the New Immigrants, including those fleeing persecution, came to America in some measure for economic reasons. Success in their adopted country depended in part on adjusting to American customs and on learning and using the English language. The new immigrant groups struggled with the issue of assimilation. Integration into American society often proved difficult. For many groups, there was also the desire to retain their traditional cultures and ways even as they adapted to life in America.

The New Immigrants took to forming mutual aid associations. Organizations such as the Society for Italian Immigrants, Polish National Alliance, and American Jewish Committee served both to help preserve Old World traditions and values and to assist members in making the often dislocating transition to a very different New World. Virtually every ethnic group had a benevolent society to aid the latest newcomers disembarking at New York's piers. Mutual aid associations were often key to immigrant survival in horrid conditions in the tenement neighborhoods of the early 1900s. They provided help with everything from access to work and shelter to emergency relief for the ill or destitute.

The plight of immigrants in the inner cities drew the attention of social reformers such as Jane Addams. In 1889 Addams established Hull House in Chicago, which became a model for similar settlement houses in other cities. The houses offered educational and recreational facilities to those living in the stifling urban neighborhoods.

The sudden, massive influx of new ethnic groups also drew the attention of civic and business leaders. Among Americans at the time there was little if any understanding of, much less support for, cultural pluralism, and it was widely assumed the New Immigrants should be assimilated into American society as quickly and completely as possible. Schools, civic groups, and employers undertook to "Americanize" the foreigners. Public secondary education emphasized an American history and culture reaching back to the English colonists of Jamestown and Plymouth. Voluntary agencies conducted thousands of English language and citizenship programs for adult immigrants. Major employers such as the Ford Motor Company instituted English classes for immigrant workers. In his acclaimed 1908 play *The Melting Pot*, Israel Zangwill celebrated America as a "great Melting Pot where all the races of Europe are melting and reforming."

The metaphor of the melting pot entered the national lexicon as an idealization of how immigrants were absorbed into America. In practice, however, the process was far from smooth or free of discord. Many of the immigrants not only resisted full Americanization, but also displayed little interest in mixing with other of the new ethnic groups. Ancient enmities were brought across the Atlantic. Conflict among various ethnic enclaves in the inner cities was common.

THE CLOSED DOOR

Despite the enthusiasm for Americanization, the New Immigrants were not always welcomed with open arms. The Great Wave precipitated an intense new nativism in America. Many Americans viewed the latest newcomers with suspicion if not outright hostility. Immigrants encountered widespread ethnic and religious prejudice and discrimination. Southern and eastern Europeans were characterized as inferior to prior northern European immigrant groups and subjected to venomous denigration. Eastern European Jews confronted anti-Semitism at every turn, manifested not only in discriminatory barriers to work and housing but also in physical harassment and even attack. Catholic immigrants, much as their Irish co-religionists decades before, were viewed as a threat to American Protestant values. The nativist American Protective Association, which flourished in the Midwest in the 1890s, was virulently anti-Catholic.

Most influential of the nativist organizations that appeared was the Immigration Restriction League, formed by a group of young patricians in Boston in 1894. League members argued that the New Immigrants, deemed less intelligent and energetic than the Old Immigrants who had founded and built the nation, were unsuited for assimilation or addition to the American melting pot. Sympathetic academics and intellectuals relied on the emerging fields of anthropology and genetics to fashion pseudo-scientific theories that supported the bigoted reasoning. The league was at the forefront of a budding movement in the early 1900s to limit immigration, campaigning for a literacy test for new arrivals. It was understood that while literacy in itself was not an ethnic screen, such a requirement would curtail the entry of less-educated southern and eastern Europeans. Nativist calls for a halt to immigration were echoed by labor organizations, worried that the flood of newcomers imperiled the jobs of native-born workers, and by temperance-favoring progressives who connected the immigrants to alcohol consumption and crime.

Since passage of the Chinese Exclusion Act in 1882, the federal government had pursued a Restrictive Door immigration policy, progressively excluding from entry aliens considered undesirable. Those denied admission included anarchists and saboteurs, potential charity cases, persons deemed morally unfit, and individuals afflicted with certain diseases. In 1911 the congressionally appointed Dillingham Commission on U.S. immigration policy, accepting the fallacious scientific evidence of southern and eastern European inferiori-

Asiatic Barred Zone and Asian-Pacific Triangle

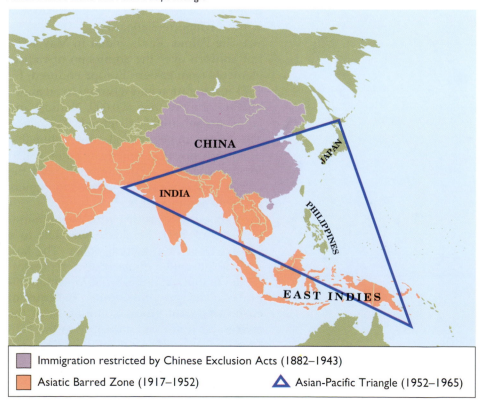

- ▪ Immigration restricted by Chinese Exclusion Acts (1882–1943)
- ▪ Asiatic Barred Zone (1917–1952)
- △ Asian-Pacific Triangle (1952–1965)

ty, recommended the imposition of an immigrant literacy test.

World War I drastically curtailed the influx from southern and eastern Europe, but not the mounting pressure to legislate its halt. In 1917 Congress passed a sweeping immigration law that instituted a literacy requirement for immigrants. The mood of the legislation was anti-Asian as well as anti-New Immigrant. The act added to the restrictions on Chinese and Japanese immigration from Asia. It established an Asiatic Barred Zone encompassing Afghanistan, Arabia, India, Indochina, and the East Indies, and blocked the entry of laborers from the area.

The 1917 legislation did not work as intended, as the literacy hurdle failed to prevent an upsurge in transatlantic immigration after World War I. Revolutionary upheaval in Russia heightened nativist fears that eastern European immigrants would bring with them a radical political ideology. Public concern over the entry of Bolsheviks, communists, and others considered subversive was accentuated by widespread labor unrest and a nationwide series of bombings and attempted bombings. During the so-called Red Scare of late 1919 and early 1920 (red being the color associated with radical political movements linked to the Russian Revolution), federal agents under Attorney General A. Mitchell Palmer arrested several thousand purported radicals. Those who were aliens were processed for deportation. In December 1919, for instance, the U.S. transport *Buford*, nicknamed "The Soviet Ark," set sail for Russia with 249 deportees aboard.

The Palmer Raids ended in May 1920, but concern over the admission of radical elements from eastern Europe endured. By 1921 immigration had returned to an annual level of more than 800,000. Nativist and labor organizations clamored for action. The American Legion and other nationalistic groups favoring Americanization called for a suspension of immigration until the large backlog of recently arrived foreigners could be assimilated.

Congress responded with the Immigration Act of 1921, heralding the shift to a Closed Door immigration policy. The law, which instituted a quota system, represented the first direct limits on European immigration. The legislation limited the entry of each immigrant group to 3 percent of the foreign-born of that nationality in the 1910 census. Use of the 1910 count ensured the quotas would cut most sharply into the ranks of New Immigrants. The act reduced overall immigration by almost two-thirds, while the numbers of immigrants from southern and eastern Europe fell abruptly to one-fourth of their pre-World War I levels.

The Closed Door was locked in place by the Immigration Act of 1924. The law created a national origins system as the basis for determining immigration quotas. As of July 1, 1927, the total number of immigrants allowed annually into the United States was set at 150,000. Each immigrant group was given a quota equal to the percentage of people of that ancestry or national origin in the 1920 census. In the interim, the quotas in the 1921 act were reduced to 2 percent of the 1890 census. In both cases, the total quotas for southern and eastern Europe amounted to only 20,000 a year.

The 1924 legislation included a measure that barred the admission of those ineligible for U.S. citizenship. The provision, which capitalized on a 1922 Supreme Court decision that U.S. naturalization law did not apply to Asians, succeeded in virtually ending further Japanese or other immigration from Asia. As with the 1921 law, the 1924 act placed no limit on emigration from Western Hemisphere countries. The preservation of good hemispheric relations was a factor, but the principal reason was to assure a continuing flow of Mexican agricultural workers.

By the late 1920s the once massive flood of newcomers from Europe had declined to a trickle. In the 1930s only 500,000 immigrants entered America as first the Great Depression and then the events leading up to World War II caused many northern European quotas to go unfilled. Although U.S. law did not yet distinguish between immigrants and refugees, many of the newcomers were in fact émigrés escaping the fascism then ascendant in Europe. The inflexibility of U.S. immigration law, as well as still widely prevalent nativist sentiments, prevented the admission of more than a small number of the Jewish refugees fleeing persecution in Nazi Germany. In 1939 the ship *St. Louis*, bearing more than 900 Jewish refugees, was turned away from America's shores. The refugees returned to Europe, where many subsequently perished in the Holocaust. The failure to save more Jewish refugees contributed to a post-World War II refashioning of U.S. refugee policy. Racial or ethnic restrictions on entry to America were eliminated in 1952, but the door to immigration was not reopened until 1965.

The New Immigrant communities ensconced in the nation's cities gradually absorbed into the American mainstream. Members of the second and third generations evinced little attachment to the Old

The Great Migration

World values so important to their parents and grandparents. In the course of two to three generations, most of the New Immigrant groups achieved a substantial measure of upward social mobility. Intermarriage, as much as adoption of the dominant culture's norms, made the succeeding generations indistinguishable from other Americans. The New Immigrants, reformed in the crucible of the melting pot, had blended into American society. In the process, they had expanded the definition of what it was to be American.

THE VANISHING FARMER

Even as the flow of New Immigrants dwindled, two other migrations converged in the nation's cities, sustaining the tilt to an urban demographic. First was the movement of hundreds of thousands of blacks from the rural South to the urban North. Paralleling this mass relocation was the continued shift of the farm populace to industrial employment.

GREAT MIGRATION

In the early 1900s racism in the North was less institutionalized than in the South, but just as pervasive. Before World War I most northern factories barred the employment of African Americans. The onset of hostilities in Europe in 1914 virtually halted the supply of immigrant labor on which American industry depended, even as a deepening involvement in the conflict stretched the nation's industrial capacity to its limits. Facing a severe labor shortage, firms took to hiring black workers. The limited black presence in the North soon had companies

INTERNAL MIGRATION, 1871–1940

The impact of the Great Migration of blacks northward is seen in this chart, which depicts internal migration from 1871 to 1940. The figures below, which represent the net population gain of the West and North, are obtained by subtracting the number of native-born persons departing these regions from the number of native-born persons moving there. The West is defined as the states west of the Mississippi River, while the North is defined as the states north of the Mason-Dixon Line.

	East to West Migration	South to North Migration
1871–1880	3,300,378	639,018
1881–1890	4,078,157	500,026
1891–1900	3,993,554	274,403
1901–1910	4,592,106	77,878
1911–1920	4,188,945	430,200
1921–1930	3,497,090	1,419,137
1931–1940	2,731,002	1,381,500

Source: *Historical Statistics of the United States*

sending recruiters to the South, where 90 percent of African Americans lived.

Some 400,000 black migrants were attracted northward by the prospect of wartime employment. Economic conditions in the South were bad in general, but especially so for the overwhelmingly rural black populace. A devastating boll weevil infestation ravaged cotton crops across the region, while widespread flooding in 1915 inundated thousands of farm acres in Alabama and Mississippi. Many black tenant farmers were reduced to abject poverty. Tens of thousands of farm families boarded trains bound for Chicago, Detroit, Cincinnati, Cleveland, Pittsburgh, Philadelphia, and New York. The rail links between southern rural black communities and northern cities carried not only male laborers headed to work in the automotive, steel, or other industries, but also young women hoping to find employment as domestics.

African Americans had more than economic reasons for leaving the South. White racism, always rampant, was especially acute in the early 20th century. Blacks suffered constant discrimination and intimidation. Jim Crow segregation was widely instituted, and a resurgent Ku Klux Klan subjected blacks to a virtual reign of terror. Lynchings and other mob violence against blacks were common. Many southern African Americans, deeply imbued with the biblical teachings of the mostly fundamentalist black churches, came to see the North as the Promised Land.

What became known as the Great Migration of blacks northward did not abate with the termination of World War I in 1918. An additional 100,000 African

Americans had made the trek by 1920. Another 750,000 followed in the next decade.

Harlem in New York was the most renowned of the black enclaves that emerged in northern cities. Over the course of the 1920s New York's black population increased from 150,000 to 330,000. By 1920 there were 235,000 black residents in Chicago, 220,000 in Philadelphia, and 120,000 in Detroit.

The North represented greater freedom and opportunity, but the promised land for most of the black migrants streaming into its cities turned out to be a ghetto. In New York and elsewhere African Americans were met by white hostility, scorn, and condemnation. Racial prejudice and discrimination posed intractable barriers to advancement or assimilation into the mainstream. Blacks were confined by segregation and limited employment possibilities into urban slum neighborhoods.

The shared struggle against adversity and inequality in the northern ghettos contributed to a new black racial consciousness and self-respect. Harlem, in particular, became the center of a newly self-confident black culture and life. Black organizations, most notably the National Urban League and the National Association for the Advancement of Colored People, concentrated on attaining better housing and jobs and full civil rights and equality.

The Great Migration was slowed to a virtual halt by the Great Depression. If anything, life in the rural South was more stable than in the urban North during the economic crisis. At most several hundred thousand blacks journeyed northward in the 1930s. Smaller numbers continued a separate but related migration to southern cities. Industrialization and urbanization came much later to the South than to the North or Midwest. Many New England textile mills had relocated to the South in the early 1900s, but the first real stirrings of industrial development in the region followed World War I. Thousands of southern blacks were lured by the prospect of employment to Atlanta, Birmingham, Memphis, and New Orleans.

By 1940 the Great Migration had shifted the locus of black America northward, but 77 percent of African Americans still resided in the South. Most still lived in rural areas. After 1940 southern industrialization and advances in agricultural technology would precipitate a second and even more massive exodus of blacks northward. The Great Migration, ultimately involving some 6 million African Americans between 1910 and 1970, would become by far the largest movement of a single group in American history.

MECHANIZATION OF THE LAND

The advent of labor-saving farm machinery meant that farms could become larger even as fewer workers were required. America's rural population declined by almost one million in the 1920s as the widespread

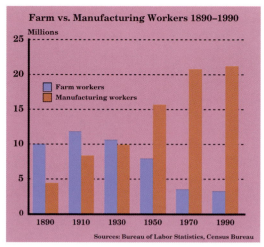

Farm vs. Manufacturing Workers, 1890–1990

introduction of gasoline tractors accelerated the migration from farms to cities. Mechanization was especially suited to the giant grain fields of the Great Plains. In the Midwest tens of thousands of farm families departed the land for nearby industrial centers.

The Great Depression stemmed the flow from rural areas, but the 1930s also witnessed an ongoing revolution in agricultural methods. Better crop strains, such as hybrid corn, were developed and improved livestock bred, while science brought to farming the use of chemical fertilizers, insecticides, and herbicides.

Harlem in the 1920s   (Frank Driggs/Archive Photos)

From Farms to Cities
1890–1990

1890
35%
65%

1940
56%   44%

1990
25%
75%

POPULATION DISTRIBUTION
■ % Rural   ■ % Urban

Source: Census Bureau

From Farms to Cities, 1890–1990

Dust Bowl

The combination of agricultural mechanization and high grain prices in the 1920s had enticed farmers in the southern Plains to plow up millions of acres of grassland to plant wheat. When a severe drought struck between 1934 and 1937, winds easily picked up the loose topsoil, no longer anchored by the grass, and swirled it into dense, rolling clouds dubbed "black blizzards." The area encompassing the Oklahoma and Texas panhandles and adjoining parts of Kansas, Colorado, and New Mexico was soon called the Dust Bowl. The ecological disaster drove upward of 60 percent of the population from the region. Thousands of families piled their possessions in trucks and made their way along Route 66 to the migrant labor camps of southern California. Their odyssey was chronicled by John Steinbeck in his novel *The Grapes of Wrath*.

Federal farm programs helped reverse the damage and by 1940 much of the Dust Bowl had been returned to grassland. After 1940, continued improvements in land management and farming techniques, supported by federal programs, would spur dramatic increases in agricultural productivity. The higher yields, tied increasingly to large-scale agricultural production, rendered the American farmer a vanishing figure.

In 1940 America's 6.1 million farms averaged 215 acres in size. Some 30 million Americans, or 23 percent of the population, lived on farms. By 1980 the number of farms had declined to 2.4 million, but the average size had grown to 431 acres. The number living on farms had fallen to 5.7 million, or less than 3 percent of the population.

Dust Bowl Migrants

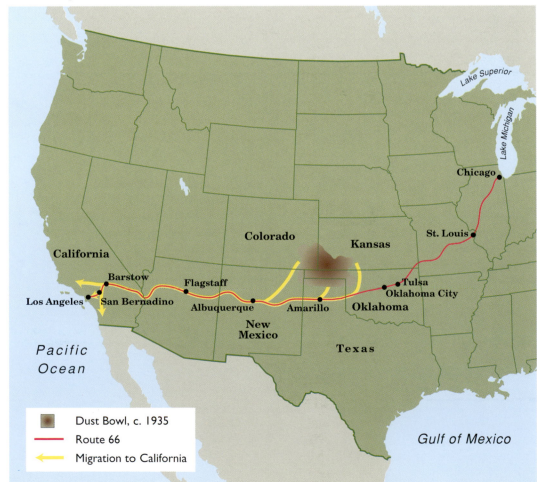

Dust Bowl, c. 1935
Route 66
Migration to California

"Okie" Madonna seeking refuge, 1939   (Oklahoma Historical Society)

The disappearing farmer was most evident in the South. Industrialization and the mechanization of southern agriculture uprooted some 20 million rural residents between 1940 and 1970. The development in 1944 of a mechanical cotton picker, which did the work of 50 people, forced black sharecroppers and field hands off the farms of the Cotton Belt. Most of the nearly one million black farmers who owned their own lands were no longer able to scratch out a living, as they were too poor to buy the new machines that were revolutionizing southern agriculture. Over 1.5 million African Americans left the South for northern cities in the 1940s. By the time the mass exodus finally subsided in the late 1960s, more than 2.5 million additional black Americans had departed. The volume was such that by 1970 50 percent of black Americans resided outside of the South.

Millions of white southerners also could not afford to keep their small farms.

In all, more than 15 million whites were dislocated by the changes sweeping the rural South. Many went north and west in search of employment. The defense industries of Southern California, in particular, became a powerful magnet. Numbers also moved to the rapidly expanding urban centers in the South.

MEXICAN FARMHANDS

The mechanization of agriculture did not alter the need for seasonal farmhands, especially in the cultivation and harvesting of fruit and vegetable crops. In the 1920s the need for agricultural workers drew hundreds of thousands of Mexican immigrants to the South and Southwest. Nearly 500,000 Mexicans entered the United States on permanent visas during the decade. Thousands more crossed the border informally. Most were migrant farmhands, but many took menial positions in industry and on the railroads.

The Great Depression not only halted the influx, but also actually reversed the direction of migration. Only 30,000 Mexicans came to the United States on permanent visas during the 1930s. At the same time 500,000 Mexicans already in America returned to Mexico. Many who lost or could not find jobs departed voluntarily. Many thousands of others were encouraged and even compelled to leave by federal, state, and local authorities. Mexican workers, eagerly welcomed in the 1920s, had suddenly become unwanted surplus laborers in the hard times that gripped the nation. The U.S. government, in cooperation with Mexican officials, sponsored a repatriation program that financed the transport of Mexicans south of the border. Many traveled on specially chartered trains.

The end of the Depression and the onset of World War II once again reversed the migratory flow. Wartime agricultural expansion and labor shortages caused American growers to look again to Mexican farm workers. In 1942 the U.S. and Mexican governments concluded an emergency wartime agreement that provided for the temporary admission of Mexican laborers to America. Mexican migrant workers soon played a vital role in the production of southwestern crops.

After the war both governments favored continuing the Bracero Program (which took its informal name from the Spanish word for "laborer"), and it was periodically extended. Over the years approximately 5 million *braceros* came to the United States, establishing a lasting pattern of Mexican migrant labor in the Southwest. The program was ended in 1964 amid concern in both the United States and Mexico over intolerable working conditions and other abuses of the migrant farmhands. Also at issue was illegal Mexican immigration, which would draw increased attention in subsequent decades.

NEW MANIFEST DESTINY

By 1890 the United States was an emerging industrial giant. Industrial prowess made possible the construction of modern cities and the development of large-scale agriculture. It also led a newly outward-looking nation to contemplate imperial ambitions, with far-reaching consequences for migration to America's shores.

Until 1890 America's attention had been directed inward, with settlement of the West the overarching focus of the nation's energies. Other than to further continental expansion, or promote overseas trade, the United States adhered to a foreign policy of isolationism, avoiding involvement in international affairs. As the long taming of the West drew to a close in the 1880s, America began to look beyond its borders for new commercial opportunities and even for new possessions. Proponents of an American imperialism argued that sustaining the nation's dynamic economic growth required new foreign markets and sources of raw materials. Overseas commerce, they noted, depended on a powerful navy, as would the assertion of possible colonial interests abroad. The arguments fell on receptive ears in Congress, which capitalized on the nation's new industrial might to launch a major naval construction program in 1890. To support its expanding sea power, America cast an increasingly covetous eye on potential overseas naval bases.

The basic thrust of U.S. foreign policy shifted in the 1890s from isolationism to imperialism. American expansionism abroad was justified under the banner of a New Manifest Destiny, which extended overseas the righteous credo of Manifest Destiny, with its belief in the preordained advance of American civilization. Manifest Destiny had carried U.S. sovereignty to the Pacific Ocean. New Manifest Destiny would plant the American flag in the Caribbean and Asia.

THE LAST FRONTIER

Even as the United States flirted with imperialism and the acquisition of overseas possessions, there remained one last unexplored frontier on American soil. The frontier declared closed in 1890 was that of the "lower" states. Far to the north along the Pacific Ocean was another, mostly frozen frontier. The coastal arc of present-day Alaska was first colonized by Russian fur traders in the late 1700s. In 1867 the United States purchased Alaska from a retrenching Russian Empire, partly because of its strategic location astride sea lanes and partly because of its fur and fish resources.

Alaska's frigid clime held little appeal to American settlers. In 1880 there were actually fewer American inhabitants than the roughly 700 Russian residents there in 1867. American exploitation of Alaska's resources began in 1878 with the establish-

Bering Sea

× Nome

Yukon River

Alaska

Circle

Fairbanks ×

Klondike Region

Valdez

Cordova

Gulf of Alaska

Juneau ×

Sitka

Pacific Ocean

CANADA

× Mining center
● Port
→ Gold rush migration

Seattle

Alaskan Gold Rush

ment of a fish cannery on Prince of Wales Island. Other canneries would be built among the numerous islands along the southeastern coast, but it was gold fever that provided the necessary warmth to draw Americans northward. The discovery of gold in 1880 near the town of Juneau, founded the same year, drew several thousand American prospectors to the Alaskan panhandle.

The 1890s ushered in the period of the great Alaskan gold rushes. In 1896 gold was found in the Klondike region of Canada, just 50 miles east of the central Alaskan border, triggering a manic invasion of the Yukon River basin. The ports of Cordova and Valdez were developed to support the onrush while such interior settlements as Fairbanks and Circle thrived as mining towns. A major strike at Nome on the western Alaskan coast in 1898 added another destination for the argonauts. In all more than 100,000 Americans set sail

for Alaska in the last three years of the 19th century.

While a majority of the gold seekers eventually left, enough stayed to establish a permanent American presence around mining, fish canning, and limited farming. A 1904 measure enabled homesteaders to purchase up to 160 acres at $2 an acre. Some 36,000 settlers had put down roots by 1910, leading to the introduction of territorial governance in 1912. Two years later Anchorage was founded as the hub of a budding Alaskan railroad. Alaska's isolation from the Lower 48, as well as the consolidation of mining into larger commercial operations, kept the territorial population fairly level until World War II. During the war, more than 200,000 military personnel were sent to Alaska to defend it against Japanese attack. Military construction boomed, with war pressures hastening completion of the Alaskan Highway linking the territory to the contiguous United States in 1942. After the war numbers of construction workers either remained in or returned to Alaska, as did discharged service members.

Between 1950 and 1960 the number of inhabitants jumped from 93,000 to 175,000. The construction of military early-warning stations and the discovery of vast "black gold" oil reserves spurred the development of northern Alaska. By the time Alaska became a state in 1959, the basic settlement pattern was set, with Fairbanks, Juneau, and especially Anchorage emerging as the anchors of an increasingly urban population.

Most of the interior of Alaska remains the province of native Eskimos, or Inuits. Contact with Americans, as with Russians before, exposed Eskimos to infectious diseases that decimated their ranks. The turn-of-the-century gold rushes altered Eskimo ways of life, with numbers of the migratory arctic dwellers eventually settling in mining towns. Later many found jobs as construction workers. Remoteness spared Alaska's native peoples from relocation to reservations. Moreover the introduction of effective medical care in the 1950s stemmed the decline in their population. In 1971 federal legislation preserved native areas for the Eskimo in the Alaskan interior as well as for the Tlingit in the Alaskan panhandle and for the Aleuts in the Aleutian Islands.

KINGDOM OF HAWAII

In the 1890s American naval planners were keenly aware of the Hawaiian Islands. Following discovery of the archipelago by British naval officer and explorer James Cook in 1778, the deepwater port of Pearl Harbor on the island of Oahu emerged as a major way station for American merchants plying the China trade. Soon ships were taking on sandalwood to exchange for silk, spices, and tea in Canton. Although the sandalwood trade declined from overcutting, Pearl Harbor became the major Pacific base for American whaling fleets in the first half of the 19th century. Smaller numbers of British and French vessels also stopped at the great natural harbor.

In 1810 Hawaiian warrior chief Kamehameha united the islands under his rule and founded the kingdom of Hawaii. The Western powers recognized the kingdom's independence, but the archipelago, 2,000 miles from the U.S. mainland, fell under increasing American sway.

American Protestant missionaries from New England first arrived in the islands in 1820. These missionaries proselytized not only Christianity but American civilization. They developed a Hawaiian alphabet, opened schools, and attempted to curtail

Mining camp during Alaskan gold rush   (P.E. Larrs Collection, PCA 41-35, Alaska State Library)

what they saw as licentious native customs, such as dancing. The missionaries were joined by American merchants and planters eager to trade with the whalers and to exploit the islands' rich agricultural promise. The first American sugar plantation was established in 1835.

The American presence undermined the ancient Hawaiian social system. Americans advised the monarchy on political organization and governance, steering the kingdom to close commercial ties with the United States. Even as their traditional world succumbed to outside pressure, the Hawaiians were ravaged by the diseases, notably smallpox and measles, that arrived with the American and European ships. From an estimated 300,000 islanders in 1778, the number of Hawaiians had fallen to about 85,000 in 1850.

As whaling declined in the mid-1800s, sugar emerged as the mainstay of the Hawaiian economy. American sugar growers faced a labor shortage, as the natives, apart from their diminishing numbers, balked at working on plantations. The answer was imported workers. Not unexpectedly, American planters targeted China, with its ready supply of cheap labor. Between 1852 and 1898 tens of thousands of Chinese contract laborers were brought to Hawaii. Until the 1880s the Chinese, who overwhelmingly were male, made up more than 90% of the islands' labor immigrants.

In the 1880s anti-Chinese sentiment similar to that on the U.S. mainland took hold among the American settlers on Hawaii. Such antipathy influenced planters to seek alternative sources of workers. Several thousand Portuguese immigrants from the Azores and Madeiras were recruited, but attention shifted primarily to Japan. Small numbers of Japanese contract laborers had been imported since 1868. More vigorous recruitment in the 1880s resulted in some 12,000 Japanese in Hawaii by 1890. After 1890, as restrictions on Chinese workers were tightened, Japanese immigration to the islands increased dramatically.

A Splendid Little War

By 1890 American settlers owned four-fifths of the land in Hawaii. For the Americans, the archipelago was a sugarcane paradise, where life revolved around the sugar industry. Ties with the United States were strengthened by the fact that almost all the sugar crop was shipped to U.S. markets. Trouble in paradise began in 1891 when Queen Liliuokalani ascended the Hawaiian throne determined to end the influence of white advisers over the kingdom. Her assertions of independence, in the settlers' eyes, jeopardized vital trade relations with the United States. In 1893 a group of American planters, aided by 150 Marines from a U.S. warship at anchor in Pearl Harbor, overthrew the monarchy in a bloodless coup. A republic was established with Sanford B. Dole, the scion of a leading missionary family, as president.

The republic promptly petitioned the United States for annexation. The petition drew a divided response in Washington. It was favored by the apostles of New Manifest Destiny but opposed by a coalition of nativists alarmed over Hawaii's considerable Asian population, domestic sugar interests fearful of tariff-free competition, and organized labor, which warned against the reintroduction of contract labor to the United States. Defeated in Congress in 1897, annexation would be driven the next year by the Spanish-American War.

The United States first flexed its military muscle on the world stage in 1898. The imperialist ambitions of New Manifest Destiny were translated into action when U.S. support for a Cuban revolt against Spanish colonial rule drew America into a brief conflict with Spain. In what Secretary of State John M. Hay called "a splendid little war," the United States forced Spain to cede control over Puerto Rico, Guam, and the Philippines as well as Cuba. During the conflict the navy used Pearl Harbor as a coaling station, underscoring Hawaii's strategic value and rekindling demands for its annexation. War fever swept aside all objections, and in July 1898 Congress voted to make the archipelago U.S. territory.

The Spanish-American War precipitated a national debate over imperialism. Anti-imperialists contended that retaining Spain's former colonies would contradict American ideals of self-rule and republican government. In its declaration of war against Spain, the United States had committed itself to Cuban independence. Despite postwar calls by American expansionists to annex the island, U.S. troops were withdrawn from the newly sovereign Cuba in 1902.

Guam, however, because of its key location in the western Pacific, proved irresistible as a navy base. In 1899 the small island, with its population of several thousand Chamorro-speaking Micronesians, was placed under the jurisdiction of the U.S. Navy. The same year the United States acquired the group of South Pacific islands since known as American Samoa. Because of the superb natural harbor at Pago Pago on Tutuila, the Polynesian-inhabited islands also fell under the navy's administration. The U.S. presence in the Pacific Islands, expanded during World War II, continues to this day. Guam and American Samoa were designated unincorporated U.S. territories in 1950 and 1951 respectively, permitting the migration of some 100,000 Pacific Islanders to the American mainland in the decades since.

The disposition of the Philippines occasioned a fierce political battle. Imperialists pressed for annexation, maintaining that the island chain would not only furnish important naval bases but also let the United States compete with European powers for commercial advantage in China. Responding to the anti-imperialists, annexationists argued that the Filipinos were unprepared for self-rule and needed enlightened American governance.

New Manifest Destiny's advocacy of American expansionism rested in part on a deep-seated racism. This racism, with its belief in the superiority of white American civilization, had previously been evident with Manifest Destiny. As the Native Americans and later the Chinese had learned, America's white settlers had regarded the West as a land reserved to them by Providence, with little or no room for those considered savages or heathens.

By the 1890s racist theorizing was more sophisticated. Many of New Manifest Destiny's adherents subscribed to the thinking of Social Darwinism, which applied British naturalist Charles Darwin's ideas of "natural selection" and "survival of the fittest" to human societies. Various races, Social Darwinists held, evolved or developed at different rates based on their inherent qualities. Social Darwinism provided a rationale for the widespread American belief in Anglo-Saxon superiority. The United States was said to owe its greatness to its Anglo-Saxon heritage. Imperialists maintained that with greatness came responsibilities. America, they asserted, bore an obligation to help assume the "white man's burden" of bringing progress to backward areas and civilizing allegedly inferior peoples, such as the Filipinos.

Anti-imperialists also were motivated by the white racism then in vogue. Where imperialists wanted to "Americanize" the Filipinos as part of a proposed colonialism, anti-imperialists opposed annexation of the Philippines in part because they did not want Filipinos, or other Asians, on American soil. The desire to keep supposedly inferior groups from diluting American society extended to more than Asians. Racist notions of Anglo-Saxon, and northern European, superiority animated efforts in the late 1890s and after to restrict the immigration of southern and eastern Europeans.

Ironically enough, given the condescending American attitudes, it was the Filipinos themselves who tipped the scales against annexation. A bloody four-year revolt against U.S. rule by independence-seeking Filipinos, finally crushed by American forces in 1902, ended any enthusiasm in the United States for colonialism. Henceforth American imperialist ambitions were channeled into the extension of U.S. influence abroad, rather than territorial aggrandizement.

The Philippines in 1902 was designated an unorganized U.S. territory in what was essentially a protectorate status. Under American governance Filipinos had the right to enter the United States freely, although they were barred by U.S. naturalization law from becoming American citizens. Because they were coming from a U.S. possession immigration statistics were not kept, but in an unanticipated consequence of New Manifest Destiny, more than 50,000 Filipinos journeyed to the American mainland between 1903 and 1934. Most settled in California where they toiled as seasonal agricultural workers, but small numbers found their way to Chicago, Detroit, Philadelphia, and New York.

By the early 1930s both nativists and labor interests were exerting pressure to curtail the Filipino migration. Their efforts reinforced a movement to fulfill the U.S. pledge made in 1916 eventually to grant the Philippines its independence. The Tydings-McDuffie Act in 1934 conferred commonwealth status on the archipelago in anticipation of full independence after a transitional period. The change in status closed the special Filipino door to America. Under the legislation Filipinos became aliens for immigration purposes. As such they fell under the stringent limits set by existing immigration law. Filipino entry to America was virtually halted until abolishment of the national-origins quota system in 1965. The Philippines gained full independence in 1946, but enduring U.S.-Philippine ties, including a continued American military presence in the islands, would provide the impetus for a major resurgence in Filipino immigration after 1965.

The unintended ripple effects of the Spanish-American War would ultimately include significant Puerto Rican migration to the United States. Puerto Rico became a U.S. protectorate in 1900. Immigration to the

NUYORICAN

New York since the 1920s has been the primary destination of Puerto Ricans coming to the American mainland. By the 1950s the city's burgeoning Puerto Rican community was well-established in Manhattan's Spanish Harlem. Other Puerto Rican neighborhoods formed in the South Bronx, Manhattan's Upper West Side (setting of the movie *West Side Story*), and the Williamsburg section of Brooklyn. New Yorican or Nuyorican became a slang term for Puerto Ricans making the city their home. Since the late 1940s there has been a continuous internal migration between San Juan and New York, as many Puerto Ricans have moved back and forth between island and mainland. Since 1970, growing numbers of Puerto Ricans, as well as successive generations born on the mainland, have settled across America.

PEOPLE OF PUERTO RICAN ORIGIN IN THE CONTINENTAL UNITED STATES

| | CONTINENTAL UNITED STATES | | NEW YORK CITY | | |
	Total	Total	Percent of U.S. Total	First Generation	Second Generation
1910	1,513	554	37	554	—
1930	52,774	—	—	—	—
1940	69,967	61,463	88	61,463	—
1950	301,375	245,880	82	187,420	58,460
1960	887,662	612,574	69	429,710	182,964
1970	1,391,463	817,712	55	473,300	344,412

Source: *Census Bureau*

United States grew rapidly after Puerto Ricans were granted U.S. citizenship in 1917, mainly in response to demands for greater political equality. Between 1900 and 1940 more than 60,000 Puerto Ricans sailed for the American mainland. Almost all went seeking employment and almost all settled in New York. The steady flow of economic migrants was virtually halted by World War II, which made the seaborne journey to New York too hazardous. After the war the advent of cheap air travel, coupled with a burgeoning population and continued high unemployment on the island, would produce a permanent, large-scale migration between Puerto Rico and the U.S. mainland.

ISSEI AND NISEI

Annexation brought Hawaii under the jurisdiction of the Chinese Exclusion Act, which halted altogether the importation of Chinese laborers. The influx of Japanese workers met the continued need for plantation labor. Migration had already given Hawaii a multiracial identity by 1900, when it was granted full territorial status. The archipelago's population of 154,000 comprised 29,000 whites and 125,000 native islanders and Asians, including 26,000 Chinese and 61,000 Japanese.

Hawaii was one of two destinations for Japanese immigrants to America. The other was California. Between 1890 and the implementation of a legal ban on Japanese immigration in 1924, well over 300,000 Japanese immigrated to the United States. The Japanese came mostly for economic reasons, but were free to do so only because of major changes in Japan.

In 1853 an American naval expedition under Commodore Matthew G. Perry succeeded in piercing Japan's long self-imposed isolation from the Western world. Perry's visit opened Japan to the West, which in turn brought a transformation of the island nation's feudal society. The hold of the shoguns, or warlords, on the imperial government was broken, and in 1868 the Meiji emperor was restored to full power. The Meiji Restoration ushered in a period of Westernization and modernization, including rapid industrialization. To accelerate Japan's development, the government encouraged greater contact with the West, going so far as to promote the recruitment of Japanese workers.

The demand for immigrant labor intensified in Hawaii in the early 1900s with the development of widespread pineapple cultivation. Thousands of farmers from Japan's rural prefectures were brought over on planter-contracted ships to work in the pineapple fields. Precise statistics on the

WARTIME INTERNMENT

For most Americans, World War II was a period of great national unity and purpose. On the home front literally everyone, it seemed, pulled together in supporting the war effort. For one group in particular, however, the war was brought home to America in a very different way.

Japan's surprise attack on Pearl Harbor in December 1941 aroused traditional anti-Asian sentiments on the American West Coast. The belief that the success of the attack was due in part to Japanese spies in Hawaii accentuated existing apprehensions over the loyalty of the Japanese-American community. Many in the U.S. government feared possible espionage or sabotage by Japanese immigrants still loyal to Japan.

In February 1942 President Franklin D. Roosevelt issued Executive Order 9066 authorizing the designation of restricted military areas from which specified residents could be excluded. Under the order, persons of Japanese ancestry were forcibly relocated from Washington, Oregon, California, and Arizona to internment camps in the American

Japanese-American migrant farmers, Sacramento, California, 1909   (By Courtesy of the National Japanese American Historical Society)

number of new arrivals were not kept, but the inflow boosted Hawaii's Japanese population to 110,000 in 1920.

Hawaiian planters, always alert to potential sources of labor, gained access to the ancient, hermetic kingdom of Korea through the efforts of Horace N. Allen, a Presbyterian missionary with long experience in the country who had been appointed American minister to the Korean government. Beginning in 1903, sugar

growers brought some 7,000 Koreans to Hawaii to work on their plantations. Japan abruptly halted the migration in 1905 when it gained control of Korea after its victory in the Russo-Japanese War. Japan first sealed Korea off from any contact with the outside world and then annexed it into the Japanese Empire in 1910. The very small number of Koreans entering the United States between 1910 and 1924 traveled on Japanese passports and were recorded as Japanese.

The first 27 Japanese immigrants landed in California in 1869. The failure of their small farm settlement discouraged any sizable immigration for several decades. Thus in 1890 there were maybe 3,000 Japanese on the American mainland.

In the 1890s Japanese were drawn to California by the need there for agricultural workers. Agriculture offered a clear avenue to advancement. A newcomer could progress from laborer to contract farming and then to outright purchase of a small truck farm. In the towns and cities Japanese at first were employed mainly in domestic service. Others worked in meatpacking, fishing, mining, logging, and on the railroads.

More than 100,000 Japanese arrived in California between 1901 and 1907 alone. As their numbers mounted, they found themselves less and less welcome. Rising anti-Japanese sentiments engendered both public and private discrimination. The Japanese and Korean Exclusion League, formed in San Francisco in 1905, reflected an increasingly ugly anti-Asian mood. The

Japanese girl awaiting transport to an assembly center, 1942   (National Archives)

league's stance against Japanese immigration echoed the arguments used in previous decades to justify the exclusion of Chinese workers. The Japanese were characterized as a racially inferior and alien people who did not fit into America's predominantly Anglo-Saxon society. In a charge that resonated powerfully with the league's heavily union membership, they were also blamed for taking jobs from native workers.

In 1906 nativists prevailed in a vote by the San Francisco school board to segregate Japanese and other Asian students, precipitating a diplomatic crisis with Japan, which protested the discriminatory action. President Theodore Roosevelt sought to defuse the international incident, persuading the school board to reverse its decision in early 1907. At the same time Roosevelt signed an executive order that barred foreign workers who had journeyed to an American possession from entering the United States. As California had wanted, this largely halted Japanese immigration from Hawaii to the mainland. In early 1908 the Roosevelt administration concluded a crisis-defusing diplomatic understanding with the Japanese government known as the Gentlemen's Agreement, under which Japan agreed to limit the immigration of its citizens to America. In return the United States pledged not to single out the Japanese as inferior or undesirable by prohibiting their immigration by law.

By 1914 the number of Japanese arriving on U.S. soil had been reduced by a third. With Japanese immigration curtailed,

Hawaiian sugar and pineapple growers after 1908 turned increasingly to Filipino workers. Between 1909 and 1934 about 113,000 Filipinos came to Hawaii. Most were single men and more then one-third eventually returned to their home islands. Another 18,000, tired of plantation life, moved on to the U.S. mainland in the expectation of greater opportunity.

Despite the growing hostility to their presence, the Japanese managed to establish the only large, successful Asian immigrant community in America before World War II. One reason was social. Between 1910 and 1924 many of the mostly male immigrants looked to marry and raise families. Many sent back to Japan for "picture brides," so called because the only contact these couple had in the arrangement of marriage was an exchange of photographs. The other key reason, tied to the development of families, was economic. The family-owned business, or farm, became the cornerstone of Japanese life. In more urban areas, Japanese families ran such small enterprises as laundries, barbershops, grocery stores, and rooming houses.

That the Japanese adapted so well to American life, paradoxically, only exacerbated fears on the West Coast about Japanese economic competition. The Japanese became targets of an institutional prejudice that was intended to discourage both their immigration and permanent residency in America. In 1913 the California legislature passed the Alien Land Act, which prohibited aliens "ineligible for citizenship," namely Japanese immigrants, from owning

interior. By November 1942 some 120,000 Japanese Americans had been removed from the West Coast and confined in one of 10 so-called relocation centers: Manzanar and Tule Lake in California; Gila River and Poston in Arizona; Topaz in Utah; Minidoka in Idaho; Heart Mountain in Wyoming; Granada in Colorado; and Jerome and Rohwer in Arkansas. In the process, many of the Japanese Americans lost their homes, possessions, and businesses.

Among those interred were many native-born citizens of Japanese descent, who deeply resented the questioning of their loyalty. In December 1944 the federal government announced that the relocation centers would be closed by the end of 1945.

Following their release, most of the Japanese Americans returned to the West Coast, where they began the painful process of rebuilding their lives and communities. A long drive for official redress finally culminated in creation of the Commission on Wartime Relocation and Internment of Civilians by Congress in 1980. In its 1982 report *Personal Justice Denied*, the commission found that the wartime internment of Japanese Americans had been a grave injustice and recommended a compensatory payment to its surviving victims. Federal legislation in 1988 proffered a formal apology to those incarcerated during the war and authorized a $20,000 payment to each.

World War II internment has long been associated in the public mind with Japanese Americans, but they were not alone in suffering this fate. About 12,000 German and Italian immigrants who were not citizens, as well as a small number of Bulgarians, Czechs, Hungarians, and Romanians, were also detained in a network of federally administered camps in the Midwest.

Japanese-American Internment

● Internment camps during World War II

agricultural lands. Antimiscegenation laws in a number of Western states forbade Japanese (and most other nonwhites) from marrying Caucasians. By the early 1920s the Japanese were casualties of a national mood that was not only anti-Asian but also anti-immigrant in general. The Japanese and Korean Exclusion League, renamed the Asiatic Exclusion League in 1908, saw its basic goal achieved in 1924, when Congress barred the further entry of Asians as part of sweeping new restrictions on immigration.

Because their initial immigration occurred almost entirely between 1890 and 1924, Japanese Americans had a deep sense of generational identity. Those in the immigrant or first generation were called *Issei*; those in the second, *Nisei*. (Later, *Sansei* was applied to those in the third generation and *Yonsei* to those in the fourth.)

The fact the *Nisei* were American citizens by birth enabled the Japanese-American communities in both California and Hawaii to navigate if not surmount many of the legal barriers to their advancement between 1924 and World War II. (Many families, for example, registered the deeds for their land under the names of their children.) In one of the saddest chapters in American ethnic history, most of the Japanese Americans in California were confined to internment camps as presumed potential internal security risks during World War II. During the 1950s most legal hurdles to *Issei* assimilation, such as the bars on naturalization and land ownership, were removed. Congress reopened the door to Japanese immigration in 1965.

Several factors spared the 150,000 Japanese on Hawaii from confinement during World War II. The imposition of martial law in the islands served to ease security concerns. Moreover it was logistically infeasible to intern one-third of the archipelago's population. Importantly, Hawaii's racially diverse society was less inclined to target a single group, such as the Japanese, for discrimination.

After World War II white immigration to Hawaii from the U.S. mainland increased, transforming the islands' demographic composition to roughly one-third Caucasian, one-third Japanese, and one-third Chinese, Filipino, and native Hawaiian. Intermarriage, which by 1950 had created an even greater diversity across these categories, continues to reshape Hawaii's mixed society. Over the past century intermarriage, as much as any factor, has reduced the number of native Hawaiians to fewer than 10,000 today.

Hawaii's diversity delayed its postwar bid for statehood. In the late 1940s and 1950s Southern senators blocked the admission of Hawaii to the Union, for fear the multiracial archipelago's representatives to Congress would vote for civil rights legislation. By 1959 the power of Southern segregationists had declined sufficiently to allow passage of legislation making Hawaii the 50th state. In the decades since it has retained its distinction as the only state with a majority Asian American population.

URBAN LANDSCAPES

America's diverse society has been recast again and again by immigration. In the first half of the 20th century, the mold, more often than not, was formed by the new urban centers that expanded across the American landscape. Westward migration continued in the decades after 1890, but the basic direction of America's population movement shifted to the new urban frontiers of the industrializing Northeast and Midwest. By 1920 54 million Americans were urban dwellers, comprising, for the first time, a majority of the population.

SECOND INDUSTRIAL REVOLUTION

Industrialization, with the jobs it created, remained the root cause of urbanization. The First Industrial Revolution had set America inexorably on the path to a manufacturing-based economy. Another burst of technological innovation between 1880 and 1920 would build on this foundation to make the United States the world's largest producer of industrial goods by 1930.

What launched this Second Industrial Revolution was the advent of electric power in the 1880s. Electricity quickly proved a much more flexible source of power than steam for industrial machinery. The electric welding machine was patented in 1886, attesting to the use of electricity in metallurgical and chemical processes. The application of science to industrial processes became a second catalyst for the surging growth of manufacturing, as firms turned out a mounting array of new and improved consumer items and office equipment. New industries formed around the production of petrochemicals, pharmaceuticals, and packaged foods.

New York City skyline, c. 1913 (Museum of the City of New York/Archive Photos)

The nationwide rail system permitted the high-volume flow of goods and materials necessary for the development of a modern industrial economy. Access to larger markets, as well as new production technologies, enabled firms to realize much greater economies of scale. Small businesses gave way to such giant industrial enterprises as John D. Rockefeller's Standard Oil Company. To oversee their massive, far-flung operations a new class of professional managers developed.

The Second Industrial Revolution transformed the American economy and, by extension, where people lived and worked. In 1890 agriculture remained by far the largest sector in the labor force. A half-century later, despite a much larger total acreage under cultivation, the number earning their livelihoods in farming had remained virtually unchanged at about 10 million. The equivalent of two generations of surplus rural population had left the land to work in the industrial economy. In 1940, those employed in manufacturing and related sectors of the economy totaled more than 20 million. Almost all made their homes in urban areas.

UPWARD AND OUTWARD

Major industrial enterprises needed large central offices for their management operations. So did the banks, investment firms, and insurance companies that arose in tandem with the industrial expansion. Cities, especially major transportation and communications hubs such as New York and Chicago, were the natural location for such offices.

The fact that space in urban areas was at a premium virtually mandated vertical development. Innovations in construction techniques and development of a safe passenger elevator permitted a sudden explosion of office buildings upward, transforming them into what marveling city dwellers, accustomed to five-story vistas, came to call "skyscrapers." (The term was coined in the 1890s, as was "skyline.") The 22-story Flatiron Building, the first steel-framed skyscraper, was completed in New York in 1904. By 1913 the city's 55-story Woolworth Building had ushered in a golden age of skyscraping office towers. Skyscrapers became the quintessential symbol of the dynamic new urban landscapes taking shape in the early 20th century. In ensuing decades multi-story structures would appear in every major American city.

Office buildings tended to cluster in the commercial districts that formed in the downtown, or central, areas of cities. They were joined by shops, especially the nascent department stores, and government facilities. Manufacturing was still found in these central business districts, but factories, which often needed extensive horizontal space, increasingly were situated farther out along transportation corridors.

Encircling the downtowns were residential neighborhoods. Most were defined by a combination of socioeconomic status and ethnicity or race. Immigrants in partic-

DUMBBELL TENEMENTS

In the November 1888 issue of *American Magazine*, journalist Allan Forman described the "dumbbell" tenements multiplying in New York City. The tenements took their informal name from the slight indentations on either side that permitted a minimal number of windows for ventilation. (The "view" from the window was of the adjacent building).

They are great prison-like structures of brick, with narrow doors and windows, cramped passages and steep rickety stairs. They are built through from one street to the other with a somewhat narrower building connecting them ...The narrow court-yard ... in the middle is a damp foul-smelling place, supposed to do duty as an air-shaft; had the foul fiend designed these great barracks they could not have been more villainously arranged to avoid any chance of ventilation.

The drainage is horrible, and even the Croton as it flows from a tap in the noisome courtyard, seemed to be contaminated by its surroundings and have a fetid smell.

Immigrant slum in New York City, c. 1890 (Jacob A. Riis Collection, *The Court at No. 24 Baxter Street ca. 1890*, Museum of the City of New York)

Development of the apartment building dated to the 1870s. Until then, merchants and other more-prosperous urban denizens had resided in single-family dwellings. As cities experienced the quickening pace of industrialization, the demand for space and the emergence of a burgeoning middle class gradually made separate residences unattainable to all but the wealthy.

Apartments, consciously designed as family homes with indoor plumbing, separate kitchens, and other then-modern amenities, became the housing of both choice and necessity for the growing ranks of managers and other white-collar professionals that flowed into cities with the organization of major corporate offices. By 1900 elevator-serviced apartment buildings were creating a new vertical urban habitat that could house previously unimagined numbers.

Vertical development alone could not absorb the surging migration into urban areas in the late 19th century. Cities pushed outward as well as upward. Expansion, though, was limited by the fact that residential neighborhoods had to be within daily reach of commercial districts or other workplaces, which was, at most, a couple of miles by horse-pulled omnibus or streetcar. With cities bursting at the seams, there was a pressing need for rapid transit that could not only traverse longer distances but also carry much larger numbers of passengers.

Development of the trolley in the 1880s inaugurated urban mass transit, as electric streetcars could cheaply transport thousands to work at upwards of 20 miles per hour. From the trolley it was only a short, albeit massive, step to the subway. Boston became the first American city to build a subway in 1897. New York opened its initial underground line in 1904. The subway, with its slightly surreal subterranean world, became as much an image of the new urban frontier as the skyscraper.

METROPOLIS AND SUBURB

The new rapid transit could extend the bounds of cities out to a radius of 10 miles or more. Suddenly possible was the giant city, or metropolis. In 1900 New York, Philadelphia, and Chicago had populations of more than one million. By 1940 they had been joined by Detroit and Los Angeles. Boston, Baltimore, Washington, Cleveland, and St. Louis all had more than 800,000 inhabitants.

While each of the cities differed in its particulars, the basic pattern of the metrop-

ular, both for mutual support and for cultural familiarity, congregated in ethnic neighborhoods.

Poor and working-class families, including most of the immigrants arriving after 1890, lived in tenements. The dreary four-to-six story walk-up buildings were stifling, cramped and lacked adequate plumbing. In many of the immigrant-swelled neighborhoods, each room, much less each apartment, likely contained an entire family.

Such conditions were not a disincentive to immigration, as housing for the urban poor was actually better in American cities that elsewhere in the world. Even still, the overcrowding, poor sanitation, and lack of ventilation made tenements breeding grounds for disease and other health problems. The death rate in slum areas was two to three times that in other urban districts.

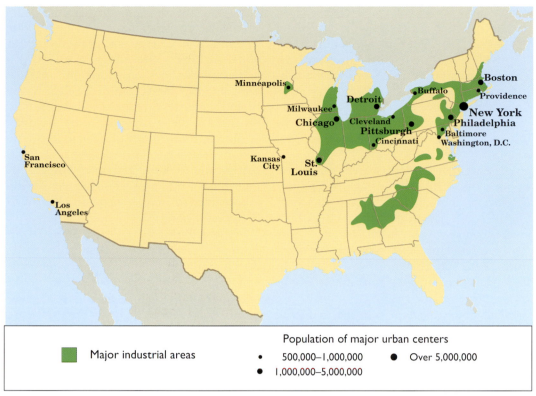

Major industrial areas

Population of major urban centers

• 500,000–1,000,000   ● Over 5,000,000

● 1,000,000–5,000,000

The Urban Frontier, 1920

olis was everywhere the same. Closest to the center, where the urban transit lines normally converged, were the tenement districts of those unable to afford better housing. Packed into these tight confines were the poor, unskilled workers, and recent immigrants. Farther out along the streetcar and subway lines were middle-class neighborhoods, with their blocks of apartment buildings and row houses. More affluent enclaves generally were found at the outer reaches of cities, where there was more space for larger, separate dwellings and where life was more bucolic and amenable.

The wealthy were not alone in wanting to escape the crowding, fetid conditions, noise, and crime of the central city. The desire to live near to but not in cities spurred the first suburbanization of the American landscape. Suburbs, in the sense

of smaller towns adjacent to major cities, had existed since colonial times. Examples included Charlestown across the Charles River from Boston, Greenwich Village some two miles north of New York on Manhattan Island, and the area around Society Hill outside Philadelphia. These and similar settlements had close social and economic ties with neighboring cities, but they were not suburbs in the more modern sense of places where residents commute to jobs in urban centers.

The term suburb, in common use in America by the mid-1800s, has long defied specific definition and even today remains somewhat vague and imprecise. Key to any characterization, at least since the advent of rail transport, has been the element of commuting. The American suburb for more than 100 years has been a residential community in the vicinity of a large city, to

LEADING U.S. CITIES 1900–1990

1900		1950		1990	
New York	3,437,202	New York	7,891,957	New York	7,322,564
Chicago	1,698,575	Chicago	3,620,962	Los Angeles	3,485,398
Philadelphia	1,293,697	Philadelphia	2,071,605	Chicago	2,783,726
St. Louis	575,238	Los Angeles	1,970,358	Houston	1,630,553
Boston	560,892	Detroit	1,849,568	Philadelphia	1,585,577

Sources: *Census Bureau, Encyclopedia of American History*

which many of its inhabitants journey daily to work. Though closely linked, suburbs are not part of cities, but separate political entities with their own local governments. There is no standard rule for how far a suburb can lie from a city, its minimum population density, or the percentage of its residents who must be commuters. Suburbs today can stretch out 50 or more miles from a city.

The term metropolitan area was coined to describe the larger agglomerations formed by cities and their suburbs. As used by the U.S. government, a metropolitan area encompasses a central city of at least 50,000 inhabitants and its suburban environs. These suburban areas are defined, in large measure, by a "significant level" of commuting into the city.

The first American suburbs to fit the more modern sense of the term appeared around 1815 with the onset of industrialization. Among the earliest was the village of Brooklyn, across the East River from downtown Manhattan. In 1814 Robert Fulton, who seven years earlier had invented the steamboat, won a concession to operate a steam ferry between Brooklyn and Manhattan, making it possible to commute daily to the Wall Street business district. Soon real estate developers were extolling Brooklyn's ready access to Manhattan, as well as its more salubrious clime. An 1819 advertisement celebrated Brooklyn Heights as an ideal location for "families who may desire" a permanent residence in "a select neighborhood" outside the inner city.

American cities in the early 19th century characteristically were sited on rivers, reflecting the era's dependence on waterborne transit. Frequently their confines were defined by water. The construction of ferry lines and bridges in the 1820s and 1830s opened neighboring areas to settlement. Suburbs expanded outside Boston, along the New Jersey shore across the Hudson River from Manhattan, across the Schuylkill River in Philadelphia, and on the other side of rivers at Buffalo, Pittsburgh, and Cleveland. The population in these places grew rapidly, often doubling or even tripling in a given decade. Most of the suburbs had their own local economies and few as yet had evolved into residential areas for large numbers of commuters. By 1860, however, Brooklyn, the archetypal 19th-century residential suburb, had more inhabitants than Boston.

Suburban life was already being cast as an American ideal by the mid-1800s. Writers as diverse as Catherine Beecher and Henry David Thoreau touted the value of yards and meadows as an antidote to the urban ills of crowding, noise, and grime. The suburban cottage was praised by influential architects Alexander Jackson Davis and Andrew Jackson Downing. In 1848 Downing, if a bit overenthusiastically, celebrated the deepening hold of suburban life on the American imagination. "Hundreds of thousands, formerly obliged to live in the crowded streets of cities, now find themselves able to enjoy a country cottage . . . and these suburban cottages enable the busy citizen to breathe freely, and keep alive his love for nature."

The widespread construction of commuter railroads in the 1880s facilitated the development of the first true dormitory, or "bedroom," suburbs. Suburban towns sprouted along the lines, normally at several mile intervals as this was the distance it took to start and stop steam engines. The towns often were not contiguous to each other or to the central city.

As cities expanded rapidly in the late 19th century, they generally absorbed adjoining suburbs into their boundaries. This had largely stopped by the early 1900s, as suburbs insisted on retaining their autonomy and distinct identity. The prototypical American suburb emerged as a place of spacious homes set back on broad, open, shrubbery-landscaped yards along wide, shady streets. The single-family, multi-storied house became in essence the American cottage. While most residents were commuters, small commercial districts, with their shopowners and merchants, appeared around the local train stops.

Anxious to take advantage of the burgeoning suburban movement, real estate developers between 1890 and 1920 recorded some 550,000 potential residential lots in the Chicago metropolitan area. By 1900 more than 100,000 commuters were streaming daily through Grand Central Terminal in Manhattan. The new railroad suburbs were white-collar enclaves, inhabited primarily by business and professional elites and their families. Most living in cities could not afford the new suburban lifestyle. High down payments and short-term mortgages put home ownership out of reach for much of the middle class, not to mention blue-collar workers.

Not all the suburbs suddenly dotting the American landscape were sylvan havens. The notable exceptions were the new factory towns that materialized after 1880 along the multiplying local freight lines in the industrializing Midwest. Many industries, favoring large, consolidated manufacturing operations, situated their massive plants outside of cities. The communities built to house the workers, unlike earlier factory towns, were more suburban than urban in design. The towns followed a common pattern. The factory or mill was located next to the railroad siding. Stretching out from it were uniform grid-like blocks of closely packed small frame or brick houses. The drab streets were broken only by the occasional church, school, or market. Often the community was designed, constructed, and controlled by the industrial firm, giving rise to the expression company town. Many if not most of the houses where the employees and their families lived were owned by the company. Examples of such industrial suburbs included Pullman, Illinois, founded by the railroad car firm in 1884; Granite City, Illinois, established outside St. Louis in 1893; and Gary, Indiana, created by the U.S. Steel Corporation in 1905.

After World War I the labor movement gradually broke the hold of industry on company towns. Conditions in the industrial suburbs improved, but the average worker still could not afford to purchase a home, much less move to more amenable surroundings. Until after World War II suburbia remained largely the province of the more affluent.

The frenzied economy of the Roaring 20s, symbolized by the manic speculation on Wall Street, drove a new burst of suburban development. During the 1920s suburbs around Buffalo, Cleveland, Detroit, Milwaukee, Atlanta, and Los Angeles doubled and redoubled in size. Shaker Heights outside Cleveland, with its winding roads, greenery, and French-, English-, and Colonial-style houses, came to embody the suburban ideal.

The suburban boom crashed with the stock market in 1929. New construction came to a virtual halt as the Great Depression tightened its grip on the nation. The dream of escape from the inner city, if anything, seemed even more remote to millions of urban residents squeezed into apartments and tenements. In 1940 only 20 million Americans, or 15 percent of a total population of 130 million, lived in suburban areas. New Deal federal housing programs, however, had already helped lay the groundwork for the massive suburban expansion that would follow World War II.

THE HORSELESS CARRIAGE

Also key to the growth of suburbia was the gasoline-powered automobile. Until the early 1900s, the state of the art in individual transport was still the horse-drawn carriage, limiting the distance suburbs could extend outward from their railroad stops.

The automobile and the suburb, 1930   (Cincinnati Museum)

FROM RAIL TO ROAD

	RAILROAD		AUTOMOBILE	
	Miles Track	Passenger- Train Cars in Service	Miles Surfaced Road	Automobiles in Use
1900	193,000	34,713	NA	8,000
1920	253,000	56,102	369,000	8,000,000
1940	234,000	38,308	1,367,000	27,000,000
1960	218,000	25,746	2,557,000	74,000,000
1980	178,000	4,347	3,206,000	105,000,000

Sources: *Historical Statistics of the United States; Statistical Abstract of the United States* (1996)

The refinement of steam engines in the mid-1800s had inspired efforts to build a self-propelled carriage, but early steam-powered vehicles proved too bulky, cumbersome, and difficult to operate. The critical breakthrough in the quest for a horseless carriage came with development of the internal combustion engine in 1876.

The first sale of an American-made automobile was in 1896. The car remained something of an expensive novelty until 1908, when introduction of the moderately priced Model T by the Ford Motor Company launched the automotive industry on a decades-long period of explosive growth. The number of cars on America's roads skyrocketed from 458,000 in 1910 to 23 million in 1930.

The motor vehicle, much as the railroad before it, revolutionized transportation and transformed American society. It became the driving force behind industrialization in the first half of the 20th century, accelerating in the process both urbanization and suburbanization. By 1920 the automobile industry was the primary impetus behind America's continued economic expansion. The location in the Midwest of the major automotive firms, most notably the Big Three of Ford, General Motors, and Chrysler, reinforced the region's emergence as the center of heavy industry. The smokestack became as much a marker of the industrialized Midwest as the skyscraper was of the metropolis.

The automobile's impact extended across the economy, from the booming petroleum industry to the sudden surge in the construction of streets and highways. America's meager, late-19th century network of dirt-and-gravel roads was manifestly inadequate to the burgeoning vehicular traffic. In the early 1900s New York, New Jersey and California were among the first states to begin building asphalt roadways designed expressly for motor vehicles. The enormous costs of construction, however, were virtually prohibitive for many localities. Mounting political pressure form rural states in particular soon induced Congress to reverse its long-standing opposition to federal involvement in road building. The landmark Federal Road Act of 1916 inaugurated what would become an enduring program of federal funding for highway construction. Almost prophetically, 1916 was also the year in which the nation's aggregate railroad track mileage peaked. The railroads would enjoy a golden age of intercity transit in the 1930s and 1940s, but it was the automobile that was ascendant.

America's 160,000 miles of surfaced road in 1905 increased steadily to more than 1.3 million miles in 1940 as the motor vehicle assumed a central role in the country's changing demographics. Motor transit connected the remotest rural area to the rest of the nation, forever altering the ease with which people could move or travel. Trucks delivered an increasingly critical part of the massive commerce necessary to sustain rapidly expanding cities and metropolitan areas. The automobile made the outer reaches of railroad suburbs more accessible, helping trigger the burst of suburban growth in the 1920s. Car ownership, and the personal mobility it provided, became part of the American dream. By 1930 there was one motor vehicle for every five persons in the country, by far the highest rate in the world. While car ownership remained beyond the means of most rural and urban Americans in the 1930s, the personal automobile became a fixture of the suburban middle class. The automobile's full impact on suburbia would follow World War II, when accelerating rates of car ownership would redefine commuting and reshape the suburban landscape.

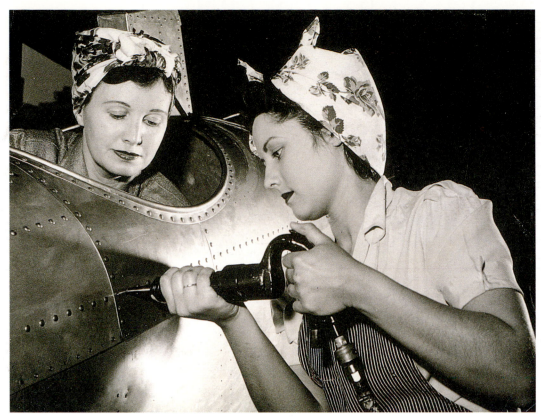

"Rosie the Riveter"   (Lambert/Archive Photos)

AMERICA GOES TO WAR

The massive involvement of the automotive industry was but one aspect of America's astonishing mobilization during World War II. More than 16 million men, and 300,000 women, served in uniform. A vast wartime expansion produced acute labor shortfalls. For the first time hundreds of thousands of women went to work in America's industrial plants and factories. The presence of women in the workplace was not entirely new, as after 1900 many of the clerical and sales jobs created in the new urban commercial and business districts had been filled by females. By 1930 2 million women were employed as secretaries, typists, and clerks and another 700,000 were in sales positions in stores. Many immigrant women labored in the infamous sweatshops of the garment industry. Most women held jobs only as temporary occupations until marriage, or to supplement family incomes.

The women in the wartime defense industries performed tasks traditionally associated with men. Rosie the Riveter, the nickname of a muscle-flexing woman in bandanna and overalls depicted in a wartime poster, became an enduring symbol of newly recognized female abilities. After the war most of the women returned to homemaking, but the gender barriers that had been broken would have a lasting impact on American society.

America emerged from World War II the dominant global military and economic power. American's new engagement in the world would greatly influence postwar immigration. Its newfound industrial might and pent-up consumer demand would fuel a postwar economic boom that enabled millions of returning servicemembers to fulfill the American dream of suburban life.

THE SUBURBAN FRONTIER
Migration Since 1945

After 1945 a new American frontier developed along the outer reaches of the nation's major cities and metropolitan areas. There millions of suburban pioneers created a novel and distinctively American landscape of mass-produced single-family homes in uniform subdivisions. In just 25 years America moved from an urban to a suburban nation. The migration to suburbia produced a new and very different locus to American society and life.

As America's suburbs flourished, its cities waned. Eighteen of the nation's 25 largest municipalities in 1950 experienced a net loss of population over the next three decades. During the same period, in contrast, suburbia gained more than 60 million inhabitants.

America reopened its door to immigration in 1965. Just as the death knell was being sounded for its inner cities in the early 1980s, a fresh surge of newcomers from Africa, Asia, the Caribbean, and Latin America helped revitalize Los Angeles, Miami, New York, and other urban areas. It also gave immigration to America a truly global character.

AMERICA RETURNS FROM WAR

The Great Depression had defined American life in the years before World War II. The herculean national effort during the war revitalized and transformed the economy, spurring new developments in technology as well as industrial production. The massive wartime mobilization reinforced a New Deal belief in federal action and fur-

ther expanded the role of the federal government. The conflict engaged the American people in an all-consuming common endeavor that very much helped restore a Depression-marred sense of national purpose and identity. U.S. victory in 1945 found the nation with a renewed self-confidence and optimism.

America emerged from the war with a much more mobile society. This mobility was both socioeconomic and geographic. The Servicemen's Readjustment Act of 1944 (better known as the GI Bill) provided financial assistance for up to four years of college for the 16 million World War II veterans. A combination of greater educational opportunities and a booming postwar economy made America history's first middle-class nation, with its wealth distributed broadly across society. Well-paying manufacturing jobs enabled millions of auto, steel, and other workers to join white-collar professionals in a huge middle class that could aspire to the American dream of a suburban lifestyle.

For the first time, most American families could afford their own car. From 26 million in 1945, the number of automobiles registered in the United States doubled to 53 million in 1955, and doubled again to 106 million by 1975. By 1980 fully half of all American households owned more than one motor vehicle. America went from the family car to the two-car family to virtually one car per adult by 1990. The seemingly ubiquitous auto provided the burgeoning middle class an unprecedented mobility, greatly extending where its growing numbers could live and work. In 1941 there were some 2,100 communities across the country with between 2,500 and 50,000 inhabitants that did not have any public transport and that

PASSENGER ARRIVALS AT U.S. PORTS

	By Sea	By Air
1940	379,000	43,000
1950	602,000	581,000
1960	754,000	2,358,000
1970	867,000	9,172,000

Source: *Historical Statistics of the United States*

Levittown (Levittown [Long Island] Public Library)

depended on private passenger vehicles for personal travel. Within another 30 years reliance on the personal automobile was the norm throughout a vast new suburbia.

There was also a much greater mobility in the air. World War II brought tremendous advances in aviation technology. After the war military transport was readily converted to commercial use. The airliner soon supplanted the railroad and the ocean liner as the primary means of long-distance travel. Introduction of the first passenger jets in 1958 gave air transport a decisive boost. The postwar aviation boom saw local and regional airlines connected to giant international carriers in a global aerial network. By the 1960s immigrants were no longer sailing but flying to America.

Aviation had a telling, but less direct, impact on internal migration. The automobile, and the moving van, remained the principal means of relocation, but air transport linked the nation closer together and made moving farther from friends and family more palatable to millions. It also aided commercial development, with its concomitant suburbia, in general, and the rise of the Sunbelt in particular.

SUBURBAN LANDSCAPES

Millions of Americans in 1945 were ready to move but had nowhere to go. Sixteen years

of Depression and war had left America with a severe housing shortage. After the war, the shortfall was exacerbated by marriage and birth rates that climbed dramatically. During the 1930s American families, hard-pressed financially, had fewer children and the population increased by less than a million a year. In 1946 a sudden surge in births pushed the population growth to 3 million. Newfound prosperity and the resumption of war-delayed personal lives by millions of returning servicemembers kept the birthrate at record levels through the mid-1960s. The 76 million Americans born between 1946 and 1964 quickly gained the moniker of the Baby Boom.

For new or growing families after the war, there were virtually no homes for sale or apartments for rent. By 1947 six million families were living with friends or relatives. Another 500,000 were temporarily in converted wartime housing. A bursting population, and its need for housing, constituted one of the two conditions underlying the postwar rush to suburbia. The other was the already deeply ingrained American preference for suburban life. Millions of urban apartment dwellers required little inducement to move to their own homes in greener surroundings.

The federal government, responding to the pressing need for housing, provided the nudge necessary to start the migration to suburbia rolling. An increase in federal mortgage insurance for developers, combined with special GI mortgages for veterans, made purchasing a suburban house actually cheaper than renting an urban apartment. Real estate developers, not surprisingly, were not long in taking advantage of the federal incentives.

SUBDIVISION BOOM

The opening of the postwar suburban frontier was at Hempstead, Long Island, a rural community 25 miles outside of New York City. In 1946 the family real estate development firm Levitt and Sons began acquiring 4,000 acres of potato farms in Hempstead, where they planned and built a private housing project that both revolutionized home construction and redefined suburbia. Under the gifted and prescient developer William J. Levitt, the firm pioneered the mass production of identical, inexpensive, modest suburban homes placed with repetitive precision on small individual lots. The construction process was divided into 27 distinct steps, with a separate crew for each task. Building materials and other components were prefabricated and preassembled to the extent possible. At peak production more than 30 houses were erected in a day.

On its completion in 1955 Levittown, as it was soon called, encompassed 17,450 single-family houses, as well as developer-built streets, parks, playgrounds, and pools. Allocation was made for schools, stores, and churches. There was no lack of GI mortgage-aided buyers. Some 1,400 homes were sold on a single day in March 1949. Some families waited in line four days. The largest development ever erected by a single builder, Levittown eventually housed 82,000 moderate-income residents.

Levittown was a subdivision, which became the norm for postwar suburbs. In a subdivision, a larger tract of land was divided by a developer into individual lots. Almost invariably, the developer also built the homes, and house and lot were sold together. In prewar suburbia, prospective homeowners typically purchased single lots and then oversaw the construction of their houses. Sited along the Wantagh Parkway, Levittown was also a forerunner of the postwar automobile suburb. Its inhabitants commuted to work by car, in marked contrast to residents of the railroad suburbs built before World War II.

The Suburban Frontier

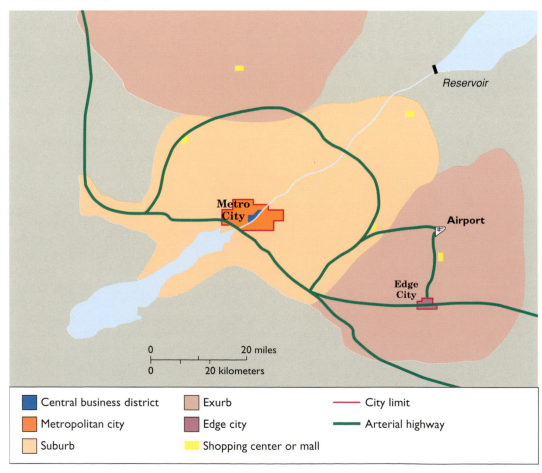

■ Central business district	■ Exurb	— City limit
■ Metropolitan city	■ Edge city	— Arterial highway
■ Suburb	■ Shopping center or mall	

Levittown was the prototype for the new suburban landscape that mushroomed across America. Similar subdivisions were built along the highways extending out from Boston, Baltimore, Washington, Cleveland, Chicago, Memphis, San Antonio, Houston, Denver, Phoenix, Los Angeles, San Francisco, and Portland. Many residents plied the highways to work in the urban centers, but the extraordinary flexibility provided by the car meant suburban denizens could also commute to jobs elsewhere in suburbia. In the 1950s the Levitts constructed a second Levittown on former broccoli and spinach farms in lower Bucks County, Pennsylvania. The development was a short drive from the new Fairless Works of the U.S. Steel Corporation, where a large percentage of the residents were employed.

In the 1960s a third Levittown went up in Willingboro, New Jersey, within distant commuting range of Philadelphia. By the 1960s suburban subdivisions were a fixture of every large metropolitan area. Between 1950 and 1970 the suburban population skyrocketed from 36 to 74 million, as a massive tide of prospective homeowners flowed from the cities into the new developments. In 1970, for the first time, more Americans lived in suburbs than in urban or rural areas.

The subdivision boom endured until 1973, when first an Arab oil embargo and then steep increases in oil prices disrupted America's record postwar economic growth. The high interest rates and double-digit inflation that ensued spelled the end of large-scale, tract-house subdivisions. Suburban development would continue, but the changing economy would alter both its nature and form.

The suburban landscape constructed across America between 1945 and 1973 exhibited a striking uniformity. The new subdivisions were located on the periphery of metropolitan areas, where larger tracts were available. They had relatively low population densities. Levittown on Long Island, with around 10,500 residents per square mile, was about average for a postwar development. Most noticeably, the subdivision tract houses, limited as they were to a few basic designs to aid mass production and hold down costs, spawned a stunning architectural monotony.

By the early 1960s social critics, most notably Lewis Mumford, were deriding the postwar suburbs as repetitive cultural wastelands. The subdivisions were condemned as places that promoted conformity, consumerism, and a stifling bourgeois lifestyle. What Mumford and other proponents of an allegedly richer, more communal urban life failed to grasp was that for millions of moderate-income Americans, the suburbs offered open space, the possibility of raising children in more favorable surroundings, and the first real chance at homeownership.

Postwar suburbia was built on inexpensive housing. Single-family suburban homes were never as affordable as between 1945 and 1973. There were several reasons why. Land, especially at the edges of metropolitan areas, was inexpensive. Often subdivisions were erected on former farmland, as the expansion of suburbia paralleled the consolidation of American agriculture into fewer, larger farms. Also inexpensive was the transport that brought suburban homes within manageable commuting range of workplaces. Low sticker prices and low gas costs, especially by international standards, made it almost irresistibly cheap to operate a car. Federal funds drove the construction of the new highways that crisscrossed suburbia, linking workplace and home. The Federal Highway Act of 1956 launched the building of a 41,000-mile interstate highway system that had the effect of connecting the suburbs into a national transportation network. Suburban shopping centers, for example, could be supplied directly by truck from anywhere across the country.

Another component of suburban affordability was the balloon-frame house. This American-invented method of construction uses two- by four-inch wooden studs to create a light but sturdy frame to which can be attached a clapboard, shingle, brick, or stucco exterior. The balloon frame both simplified home construction and lowered its cost. It also facilitated the mass production techniques employed by the Levitts and others.

Inexpensive land, transport, and construction methods were all important, but government played the central role in making suburban housing accessible to millions. The Federal Home Owners Loan Corporation (HOLC) was created by Congress in 1933 to stem home foreclosures during the Great Depression. During the 1920s the typical home mortgage was for 5 to 10 years. Often the loan was not paid off in full on the final payment, necessitating a renewal of the mortgage and leaving the homeowner at the mercy of interest rate changes. High down payments limited homeownership to the affluent, but when money was tight, as during the Depression, even the more well-to-do were hard-pressed to obtain a mortgage renewal. The HOLC introduced into standard practice long-term, amortized mortgages (meaning the entire loan and all interest due were divided into equal payments spread over the life of the debt). Such mortgages, which helped reverse home foreclosures, came into widespread use in postwar suburbia.

The HOLC was followed in 1934 by the Federal Housing Administration (FHA), formed to stimulate home construction by the private sector. Its primary means of doing so was by insuring long-term mortgages made by private institutions. Because there was very little risk to the lender, FHA-secured mortgages revolutionized the home finance industry. Minimum down payment requirements were reduced from at least 30 percent to as little as 10 percent, while interest rates on mortgages fell by 2 to 3 percentage points. The FHA also extended mortgages to 25 to 30 years, further lowering the monthly cost of a home purchase.

The full impact of FHA mortgage insurance was felt in the newly booming economy after World War II. In making housing widely affordable, the FHA was supplemented by the Veterans Administration (VA), which secured the low-interest mortgages provided to World War II veterans by the GI Bill. The FHA and VA programs reflected the heavy governmental subsidization of suburbia. The financing of highways, roads, sewers, and other infrastructure was also a manifestation of public policies that favored the suburb over the city.

The single most important public subsidy to individual home ownership has been the federal income tax code. Since enactment of the present federal income tax in 1913, both mortgage insurance and local property taxes have been deductible items. This had little impact on the average American until after World War II, when higher tax rates made residential tax benefits a key component of home ownership for millions.

The impact of the FHA and VA mortgage programs was greatest in the heyday of the subdivision from 1945 to 1973. After 1973, sharp increases in house prices made the single-family home much less affordable to middle-income Americans, but federal subsidies continued to influence the purchase of suburban dwellings. Since its establishment in 1965, the Department of Housing and Urban Development has overseen ongoing federal mortgage insurance programs. Similarly, VA-secured mortgages have been provided to successive genera-

tions of veterans. If anything, escalating real estate values in recent decades have increased the tax advantage to millions of the mortgage interest and property tax deductions. In something of an irony, a growing percentage of these tax subsidies, widely understood to benefit the broad middle class, is going to more affluent suburbanites, whose large mortgages involve substantial deductible interest payments.

Government also had a part in the racial homogeneity of postwar suburbia. Racial prejudice was the other catalyst, along with affordable housing, for the exodus from the cities to the suburbs after World War II. Many urban middle-class whites did not want to live near the poorer minorities that were appearing in growing numbers in the inner cities. The massive movement of African Americans from the rural South to the urban North gained a new momentum in the 1940s. Also making their way to the larger industrial cities were Puerto Ricans, especially to New York, and Mexicans, most notably on the West Coast but also in the Midwest.

As blacks in particular poured into the older ghetto neighborhoods of northern and midwestern cities, many urban whites found a new motivation to depart for the suburbs. The movement away from the presence of blacks became known as "white flight." Many who fled were fearful of crime and declining neighborhoods and schools; almost all wanted to avoid integration with blacks.

The suburbs were constructed as white enclaves. Few African Americans at the time could afford even modest suburban homes, but those who could were effectively excluded from suburbia by pervasive discrimination. Segregation in the North was as marked as in the South. Real estate agents, mortgage companies, and banks all refused to transact or finance black home-ownership. The prejudice against African Americans was overt and systematic. Often it was officially proclaimed. The Levitt development firm, for example, for two decades had a publicly stated policy of not selling to blacks. In 1960 not one African American was living in the Long Island Levittown.

The discrimination was fully allowable under existing law. The federal government from the close of World War II until the mid-1960s only haltingly grappled with the second-class citizenship of African Americans. State and municipal governments in the North did not codify segregation in the law, as in the South, but they readily tolerated it in practice. Local suburban govern-

Urban blight, New York City   (Archive Photos)

ments often relied on zoning codes, which regulated land use, not only to control commercial development in residential areas but also to keep out unwanted persons, including blacks. Minimum lot and setback requirements, for instance, restricted the construction of lower income housing that might accommodate minorities or those of limited means.

Things began to change with the landmark federal Civil Rights Act of 1964. Subsequent civil rights legislation progressively outlawed discriminatory housing practices, but the opening of suburbs to African Americans was a slow and tortuous process. Institutional racism was banned, but a subtle private racism endured. In recent decades many suburbs have gained black residents, but even today African Americans are far from welcome in numerous white suburban enclaves.

After World War II African Americans moved in overwhelming numbers from farms to cities. Continuation of the prewar Great Migration out of the rural South brought more than 4 million African Americans into northern cities between 1940 and 1970. By 1970 50 percent of all African Americans resided in the North. Many of the blacks who remained in the South also moved from rural areas to the region's burgeoning urban centers.

In little more than a generation black Americans underwent a profound shift from a largely rural to a largely urban existence. By 1970, 75 percent of African Ameri-

cans lived in urban areas. Blacks became widely associated with an urban identity. This was due in part to the more visible presence of blacks in cities, especially as whites were leaving, and in part to the development of a black underclass in the urban ghettos. The stereotype of the poor urban black, however, obscured the development of a substantial black middle class after World War II.

Black social mobility was dramatically altered by the civil rights movement of the 1960s. After 1964, new educational and employment opportunities, as well as full political and legal rights, enabled millions of African Americans for the first time to attain the American dream of a better life. As blacks entered the middle class they chose, much as other Americans, to move to suburbia. Black advancement coincided with the halting integration of suburbs. By 1990 roughly one-third of the nation's 30 million African Americans were part of a new black suburban middle class. Another third, mostly urban, lived on lower middle class or working class incomes. A final third, whether urban or rural, remained trapped in poverty, with about 10 percent of African Americans caught in the ghetto underclass.

MEGALOPOLIS

The relentless postwar spread of suburbia gave rise to the term urban sprawl. Metropolitan areas extended outward in a hodge-podge of subdivisions, highways, and shopping centers. The suburban shopping center as a separate, planned conglomeration of stores for vehicle-bound customers dated to the 1930s. In 1946 there were only eight such parking-surrounded retail centers across America, but their numbers quickly multiplied as growing legions of automobile-owning families moved to the suburbs. The first enclosed, climate-controlled mall was introduced near Minneapolis in 1956. The indoor mall soon became a fixture on the suburban landscape. In the 1970s great super or mega-malls were developed that incorporated eateries, cinemas, skating rinks, and other amusements, as well as fountains and tree-lined walks. The mall became not only a shopping center but also a locus of suburban life.

Metropolitan areas grew so large they began to overlap one another. By the 1960s the area between Boston and New York was a vast megalopolis, a continuous urban and suburban expanse incorporating several or more cities. This megalopolis eventually extended to Philadelphia, and then Washington. Chicago and Milwaukee were similarly connected, as were Los Angeles and San Diego.

The migration to suburbia had a powerful impact on cities. As the middle class departed, cities saw a decline in long-established neighborhoods, as well as in the commercial activity that sustained their downtowns. Few suburbanites, beguiled by the convenience and attractiveness of malls, returned to shop in urban department stores. Middle-class residents were also taxpayers and with their loss came a drop in tax revenues. Municipal governments found themselves with fewer funds just as the percentage of their lower-income inhabitants, many of whom needed public assistance, was rising.

Former industrial centers were hit hard by a decline in manufacturing and the disappearance of solid-paying jobs. By the mid-1970s many cities, especially in the industrialized Northeast and Midwest, were caught in a downward cycle. To cope with such problems as low-income housing shortages, worsening schools, and drug-related crime, they often raised taxes. The escalating taxation caused remaining businesses to flee, further shrinking the tax base. Deteriorating conditions in turn caused more firms, as well as more of the dwindling middle-class residents, to leave.

Two developments in the 1980s reversed this downward spiral. First was an infusion of immigration that provided a new lifeblood for cities. Second was a dramatic shift in the American economy from manufacturing to service industries. Long-standing commercial centers such as Boston, New York, Philadelphia, and Chicago all revived as hubs of a new information economy. These cities, which had suffered a decades-long population loss, have all seen the number of their residents hold steady or even slightly increase since 1980. As part of this urban revival, contemporary metropolises have added convention and cultural centers amid their postmodern office towers. Still, even the most vibrant cities are no longer a lure to an American populace wedded to suburbia. Immigration sustains the more dynamic urban centers, while other cities, mainly in the midwestern manufacturing belt, continue to struggle to adapt to a changing economy.

POST-INDUSTRIAL AMERICA

The automotive industry, anchored in the Midwest, was at the forefront of American technology through World War II. The automobile, in ever newer models, figured everywhere in the postwar growth of suburbia, but after 1945 it was the aerospace industry that drove technological advancement. Air and space flight requirements spurred breakthroughs in composite materials, electronics, robotics, and optics. American industry by the 1960s had entered a new high-technology era. This era would reshape the suburban landscape, creating a new terrain of exurbs and edge cities.

The linchpin of this new world was the computer. Much as electricity was the catalyst for the Second Industrial Revolution (1880–1920), which sparked America's rapid industrialization in the early 20th century, the computer was central to the technological revolution that transformed the nation's economy between 1950 and 1990. Some call this period a Third Industrial Revolution because of the profound changes it wrought in industrial production, especially in manufacturing.

Computers altered both the industrial workplace and its work force. They created extraordinary new capabilities in areas as diverse as industrial design and inventory control, but their greatest impact was in automation. Automated assembly lines and other production processes not only increased output and improved quality control, but also reduced the need for manufacturing workers.

Automation was one of two reasons manufacturing jobs constituted a shrinking percentage of the total labor force after 1960. The other was the globalization of the economy. Overseas competition from countries with much lower labor costs, and often with more efficient plants and production methods, caused a major shakeout of America's heavy industries in the 1970s. The steel industry rebounded from a precipitate drop in production by streamlining and modernizing operations, but the number of steelworkers dropped from 457,000 in 1975 to 164,000 by 1990. The automotive industry was similarly impacted. By 1980 Japan was the world's leading auto producer. American-made car sales fell from a record 12.8 million in 1978 to only 6.9 million in 1982. Chastened American automakers retooled, cutting capacity and personnel, and regained their competitiveness, but production remained at much lower levels.

In the 1980s light manufacturing also shifted overseas. In some instances foreign firms produced goods at much lower cost, knocking out American businesses. In others, American firms switched their manufacturing operations abroad to take advantage of much cheaper labor pools. In either case, the importance of manufacturing to the American economy declined.

At the same time service industries, due in no small part to the computer, experienced explosive growth. Constant advances in data processing, for instance, opened up entirely new avenues in banking, medicine, and electronic media. Also flourishing were high technology enterprises that concentrated on information-based products, such as software, pharmaceuticals, and telecommunications equipment. Since its commercial advent in 1951, the computer itself has progressed from mainframe to minicomputer to microcomputer, spawning a whole range of new industries. These industries have become part of a new Information Age, in which computers are playing an increasingly central role not only in commerce, but also in virtually every aspect of life.

By 1990 America had entered what has been termed a post-industrial economy, in which its traditional manufacturing base had been supplanted by high technology and service industries. The transition to a post-industrial America has had a lasting impact on the nation's demographics.

FROM FROSTBELT TO SUNBELT

The retrenchment of America's smokestack industries left in its wake a landscape of obsolete, rundown, and abandoned factories and plants. The older manufacturing areas of the Northeast and Midwest became known as the Rustbelt. Skilled blue-collar workers who had lost well-paying jobs struggled to hold on to their suburban middle class lives. Employment at a comparable income was virtually unavailable, as much of the Rustbelt suffered from a general economic downturn.

By the mid-1970s many Rustbelt workers and their families were joining the massive migration then underway to the Sunbelt, the southern tier of the country extending below the 37th parallel from Virginia across to California. The workers were lured by the region's dynamic economy and greater opportunity, as well as its lower cost of living and attractive climate.

Since World War II millions of middle-class professionals and retirees, as well as displaced industrial workers, have departed the Northeast and Midwest for the South and Southwest. This migration has made the Sunbelt the fastest growing part of the nation for more than four decades. The broader Northeast and Midwest area was tagged with the moniker the Frostbelt, conveying its diminished appeal, especially to retirees craving a warmer clime. With the emergence of its Rustbelt in the 1970s, the Frostbelt was seen as a region in decline, as opposed to the up-and-coming Sunbelt.

	Manufacturing Workers (in millions)	Service Workers (in millions)
1950	15.6	7.2
1960	17.1	10
1970	20.7	20.4
1980	21.9	28.8
1990	21.3	39.3

Source: *Statistical Abstract of the United States (1996)*

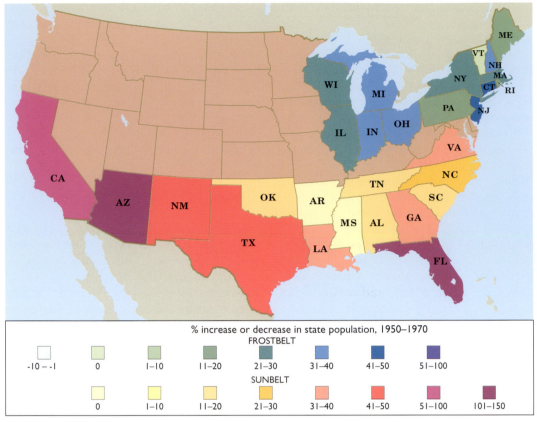

From Frostbelt to Sunbelt, 1950–1970

Between 1950 and 1990 the U.S. population rose by almost 100 million, from just over 150 million to just under 250 million. Almost two-thirds of this increase was absorbed by the Sunbelt. The region's number of inhabitants jumped 127 percent, climbing from 52 million to 118 million. In contrast the Frostbelt, encompassing the

From Frostbelt to Sunbelt, 1970–1990

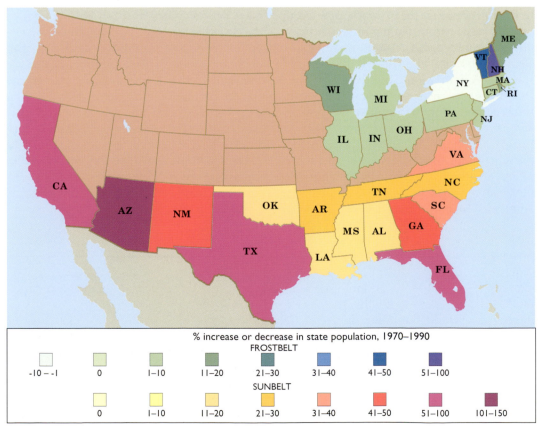

area north of the Ohio River from New Jersey to the Mississippi River, went from 70 million residents in 1950 to 89 million in 1970, and then barely increased to 93 million in 1990.

The Sunbelt's stunning population growth was closely connected to an equally spectacular postwar economic expansion. The pump for this surging economy was primed with federal dollars. Much of the nation's rapid military build-up during World War II had been located in the South or Southwest. Continued defense spending in the Sunbelt after the war both stimulated economic activity and drew skilled workers to the region. Burgeoning aerospace and other defense industries in southern California in particular helped catapult that state's population from 11 million in 1950 to 16 million by the end of the decade.

Equally important was the still relatively new federal Social Security program, which for the first time provided most Americans with a stable retirement. Increases in life expectancy contributed to the growing ranks of retirees by the 1960s. Between 1950 and 1970 the number of Americans age 65 and over climbed from 12 to 20 million. Arizona and Florida, with their low taxes, inexpensive housing, and year-round leisure activities, became powerful draws to northern retirees. Social Security-backed retirement incomes enabled millions to move. A constant influx of retirees helped quadruple Florida's 1950 population of roughly 3 million to almost 13 million by 1990.

Much of the development of southern Florida, interestingly, hinged on the widespread introduction of air conditioning. So did growth in the desert Southwest. The air conditioner, in a sense, was to a lower Sunbelt home what the furnace was to a Frostbelt home.

Oil and gas exploration made Texas and Oklahoma boom states in the 1950s and 1960s. Abundant natural energy was part of the Sunbelt's favorable business climate, which also included low taxation, inexpensive labor, and an appealing quality of life that enticed skilled professionals to its environs. By the 1970s the Sunbelt had emerged as a center of high-technology chemical, aerospace, and electronics industries. Its high-technology base, and the fact that it had never relied on manufacturing, enabled the region to embrace the shift by then underway to a post-industrial economy.

Recreation and tourism industries capitalized on the beaches and endless summer weather of Florida and southern California. By the 1960s life in the suburban expanses of southern California had become the dream of millions. California became almost an emblem of the Sunbelt's ascendancy, as its seemingly inexhaustible supply of newcomers by 1970 had pushed it past New York as the most populous state. By 1990 California, with 30 million residents, was home to one in every eight Americans.

The movement from the Frostbelt to the Sunbelt has become the largest interregional population shift in American history. It reversed an almost century-long migration into the industrializing Northeast and Midwest and resumed the westward march, largely stopped after 1910, of the nation's geographical center of population. The flow into the Sunbelt has continued unabated in the 1990s, although it has somewhat shifted course. With the end of the Cold War, reductions in defense spending slowed southern California's decades-long boom, while service industries spurred new growth in Texas and the upper South. North Carolina's emergence as a high technology research center has brought a mounting influx of businesses and new residents. Of arguably greatest significance, the continued aging of the American populace has produced an ever larger number of retirees. While most still flock to Florida and Arizona, many are now also settling in retirement communities across the Sunbelt.

EXURBS AND EDGE CITIES

Most of the growth in the Sunbelt has occurred in metropolitan areas. Both urban centers and outlying suburbs expanded rapidly. In 1950 only one of the nation's 10 largest cities, Los Angeles, was located in the Sunbelt. By 1990 it had been joined by Dallas, Houston, San Antonio, Phoenix, and San Diego. The population of Phoenix increased by an astounding 800 percent; that of San Diego and Houston by a still-amazing 300 percent.

The suburban frontier moved southward in the 1970s. In the North escalating home prices, higher financing costs, and declining real incomes all conspired to slow the rush to suburbia, but in the South and Southwest the combination of economic and population growth had the opposite effect. During this decade America's suburbs gained some 22 million new residents, with much of the increase coming in the Sunbelt. Subdivisions were still built, but individual home construction became the norm. Suburban expansion was especially strong around Atlanta, Dallas, and Houston. In 1980, 80 percent of the Atlanta metropolitan area's 2 million inhabitants could be found in its rapidly multiplying suburbs.

Recovery from the oil shocks and stagflation of the 1970s brought a resurgence of suburban construction in the Northeast after 1980, even as suburban development continued to sweep the South. Migration within suburbia became an important phenomenon, as many suburban-raised Baby Boomers established families and purchased their own homes. The Baby Boomlet, the nickname affixed to the upswing in births as the huge Baby Boom generation itself began to have children, helped add another 24 million residents to suburbia in the 1980s. By 1990 120 million Americans, virtually 50 percent of the population, lived in suburban areas extending over tens of thousands of square miles.

As metropolitan areas expanded, suburbs were built farther and farther from cities. But the growing distance between the two different spheres was not just geographic. By the 1970s suburbs were falling out of the orbit of cities, as fewer and fewer of their residents were commuting to work in urban centers. This was especially true on the outer reaches of metropolitan areas, where a new and different kind of suburb was taking hold.

The term exurbia had been coined in the 1950s to describe the outer fringes of suburbia. By the 1970s its cousin "exurb" was being applied to the communities, suburban-like but, autonomous of the central city, appear on the edges of metropolitan areas. The exurb was a residential place of single-family homes, but unlike traditional suburbs, it had no cultural or social, much less commuting, links to an urban center.

Many exurban residents worked in office parks. A high-technology revolution in communications, married to advances in data processing, enabled businesses in the 1970s to decentralize their operations. Increasingly, it was no longer necessary to keep different departments under a single roof or even to be centrally located in a city. Many firms, especially in the service industries, chose to move all or part of their operations to greener surroundings. Often the corporate headquarters relocated. By 1985, for example, more than 16 million feet of office space had been built in an exurban stretch of Morris and Somerset counties in New Jersey to absorb business activities moving from New York City. A similar amount of office space went up in exurban areas in Westchester County, New York, and Fairfield County, Connecticut.

In the 1980s exurbia proved a natural locale for the emerging post-industrial economy. New high-technology firms sprouted along Route 128 outside Boston, in Silicon Valley around San Jose, California, and amid the environs of Seattle. A new exurban landscape developed of office and light industrial parks, corporate and convention centers, and research facilities. Interspersed were the malls and local office areas that accompanied the growing number of exurbs.

The rise of suburbia and then exurbia has produced a new kind of centerless city. Instead of developing as a traditional downtown surrounded by residential districts, these cities have emerged as an

Major Metropolitan Areas, 1990

agglomeration or clustering of office and retail buildings large enough to constitute a distinct, more urban entity. Examples include Irvine and Costa Mesa in Orange County, California, Schaumburg west of Chicago, and Chesterfield outside of St. Louis. These urbanized areas have been called edge cities, to convey both their location and mold-breaking identity. Similar to the nation's older cities today, they are more workplace than bedroom, and their populations are swelled each workday morning by commuters. They often contain such urban fixtures as hotels and entertainment centers, but their landmark feature is the single-family home.

Edge cities are connected to the outside world more by satellite than highway. They fit, much as exurbia does, the new Information Age that is linking together an increasingly global commerce. The exurban fringe in the 1990s has paced the continued growth of metropolitan areas, sustaining America's progression to a predominantly suburban nation.

FROM EVERY SHORE

The Information Age was new, but not the connections it provided Americans to the rest of the globe. America has been deeply involved in the world since World War II. This engagement has caused the nation to open its door to refugees and to reopen its door to immigrants. Ultimately, it has given America a truly global immigration. American society has become a microcosm of the world, with its latest members coming from literally every foreign region and shore. Its newly diverse populace has changed the face of America and prompted a new pondering of the nation's identity.

After World War I the United States returned to its historic policy of isolationism. Foreigners, or at least most foreigners, were also out of favor. After decades of a massive flow of newcomers, strict immigration quotas were enacted in the early 1920s. A ban on immigration from the Middle East and Asia, reflecting the prejudices of the time, limited what little continuing influx there was to Europe. An ethnic bias against southern and eastern Europe, enshrined in the 1924 immigration law, ensured that the quotas for that continent favored its northern and western parts. In the 1930s America kept its distance from both Europe and Asia, even as the rise of fascism in Germany and Italy and an expansionist militarism in Japan swept the world toward crisis.

World War II thrust the nation into leadership of the Allied fight against the Axis powers, with unanticipated consequences for U.S. immigration policy. In 1943, Congress repealed the various Chinese exclusion acts, acknowledging that the discriminatory measures contradicted the spirit of the U.S.-Chinese wartime alliance. Congress also wanted to dispel Japanese propaganda in Asia, which asserted that Americans did not see the Chinese, or other Asians, as equals. Chinese immigrants received only a token annual quota of 105, but it was the symbolism that mattered, as racist assumptions of Asian inferiority built into U.S. immigration law were starting to crumble.

Love as well as war helped undermine U.S. barriers to immigration. The War Brides Act in 1945 was the first in a series of federal measures that permitted the admission of the alien spouses and children of American veterans who had married during the war. The same open immigration status was subsequently extended to the spouses, children, and fiance(e)s of members of the armed forces serving overseas after the war. Admissions under these provisions, which were outside existing quota limits, soon included some 5,000 Chinese and 800 Japanese brides, further chipping away at the bigoted logic of the still-substantial restrictions on Asian immigration.

REFUGEES AND COLD WAR

The American servicemembers stationed overseas after World War II at first were on occupation duty in Germany and Japan. At the conflict's end the United States found itself the dominant power in a world devastated by six years of fighting. Much of Europe and Asia lay in ruins. It was evident that America would have to remain engaged overseas and assume a leadership role if the world were to recover from war. Americans also widely believed that U.S. isolationism in the 1930s had contributed to the outbreak of hostilities. There was broad national support for a new internationalist foreign policy intended to prevent another global conflict.

Among the most pressing immediate postwar problems were the millions of refugees or displaced persons in Germany, Austria, and Italy. Many had been imported by the Nazis to work in forced labor camps; others had fled westward before the advancing Soviet army. Large numbers eventually returned home. Most of the displaced persons from Eastern Europe, which

ESCAPEES FROM COMMUNISM

"The countries of Eastern Europe have fallen under the Communist yolk—they are silenced, fenced off by barbed wire and minefields—no one passes their borders but at the risk of his life. We do not need to be protected against immigrants from these countries—on the contrary we want to stretch out a helping hand, to save those who have managed to flee into Western Europe, to succor those who are brave enough to escape from barbarism, to welcome and restore them against the day when their countries will, as we hope, be free again ..."

President Harry S Truman, in a message to Congress (1952)

REFUGEES AND ASYLEES, 1946–1990

Since 1980 U.S. law has defined a refugee as any person outside of his or her country of nationality who is unable or unwilling to return home because of persecution or a well-founded fear of persecution. This persecution can be based on race, religion, nationality, membership in a particular social group, or political opinion. America since 1945 has accepted millions of refugees from around the world. Almost all have become permanent residents and most have become U.S. citizens. Included in the figures of refugees granted permanent residence below are also much smaller numbers of asylees. An asylee conforms to the same definition as a refugee, with the only difference being the location of the person upon application for sanctuary in America. The asylee is already in the United States or at a port of entry, whereas the refugee is granted sanctuary while still outside the country and then admitted by special visa.

	1946–50	1951–60	1961–70	1971–80	1981–90	Total
Europe	211,983	456,146	55,235	71,858	155,512	950,734
Africa	20	1,768	5,486	2,991	22,149	32,414
Asia	1,106	33,422	19,895	210,683	712,092	977,198
Oceania	7	75	21	37	22	162
North America	163	831	132,068	252,633	121,840	507,535
South America	32	74	123	1,244	1,976	3,449
Total	213,311	492,316	212,828	539,446	1,013,591	2,471,492

Source: *Immigration and Naturalization Service*

had fallen under the control of the Soviet Union, resisted repatriation, however, out of fear of political or religious persecution. Allied refugee camps also housed thousands of Jewish survivors of the Holocaust.

In December 1945 President Harry S Truman, citing a humanitarian crisis, issued a presidential directive authorizing the emergency admission of 40,000 displaced persons a year from Europe. The Directive on Displaced Persons was the first U.S. measure specifically addressing refugees. Significantly, refugees entering America were to count against Europe's immigration quotas.

Because of complications in reallocating these quotas, only 40,000 refugees had been admitted by 1948. With more than a million displaced persons still in Europe, Congress that year enacted the Displaced Persons Act. The first U.S. refugee legislation, it ultimately permitted the entry of 400,000 displaced persons over a four-year period. To speed the flow of refugees, while preserving the quota system, the act applied their admission against future allocations.

In part, Congress was motivated to pass the refugee legislation by the burgeoning Cold War with the Soviet Union. Refugee issues assumed an increasingly important place in America's anticommunist foreign policy. As leader of the Free World, America saw it as both a strategic and moral imperative to offer haven to those fleeing communism in Eastern Europe. Such "escapees"

deserved support, while their existence was presented as living proof of the bankruptcy of the Soviet system.

The Cold War as much as any factor drove a major overhaul of U.S. immigration law. In 1952 American and communist Chinese forces were locked in bitter stalemate in the Korean War. There was a general consensus among U.S. policymakers that the nation's racist bars to immigration were undercutting its position not only in Asia but also around the world. The Immigration and Nationality Act of 1952 removed all racial restrictions on immigration and naturalization. The statute retained the national origins system of quotas, but revised it to accommodate those now eligible for entry. The bulk of the roughly 150,000 quotas each year, however, still went to Europe. The Asiatic Barred Zone created in 1917 was replaced by an Asian-Pacific Triangle. Most countries in the triangle, bounded by Pakistan, Japan, and the Pacific Islands north of New Zealand, received the minimum annual immigration quota of 100. Asians were still discriminated against, but the door to immigration was being nudged open.

The importance attached to refugee admissions in the West's struggle against communism was manifested in 1953 in the Refugee Relief Act. The legislation represented a major departure from basic immigration policy, authorizing 214,000 special refugee visas outside quota limits. Most entering under the provision were refugees and "escapees" from Eastern Europe, but their ranks also included small numbers of Asians. In 1957 the Refugee-Escapee Act provided for the acceptance of those fleeing Hungary in the aftermath of the failed 1956 revolt against Soviet rule. The act reflected America's sense of responsibility for the Hungarian freedom fighters who had risked their lives partly in the mistaken expectation of direct U.S. support for their rebellion. Some 38,000 Hungarian refugees eventually made their way to America.

Cold War refugee issues shifted much closer to home following Fidel Castro's successful revolution in Cuba in 1959. As Castro moved to align Cuba with the Soviet Union and communism, more than 150,000 Cubans fled to America. The outflow was halted in 1962 by deepening U.S.-Cuban confrontation in the aftermath of the Cuban Missile Crisis. In 1965 Castro publicly invited his domestic critics to leave Cuba. After President Lyndon Johnson announced that the United States would accept any Cubans able to depart the communist nation, American and Cuban authorities negotiated an agreement establishing daily refugee flights from Havana to Miami. Dubbed the Freedom Flight Program, the airlift brought more than 250,000 Cubans to the United States before it was unilaterally terminated by Cuba in 1973. The first limits on immigration from the Western Hemisphere had been imposed in 1965, but the Cubans were admitted under a blanket refugee status. Most settled in Miami, with a sizable Cuban exile community also taking hold in northeastern New Jersey's Hudson County.

In 1960 Congress approved the Fair Share Refugee Act as part of U.S. participation in the United Nations-sponsored World Refugee Year. A major goal of the designated year, running from July 1, 1959, to June 30, 1960, was the final resettlement of the remaining post-World War II refugees in Europe. As its "fair share," America agreed to shoulder up to a quarter of the year's additional refugee admissions. The Migration and Refugee Assistance Act in 1962 helped implement this pledge, while also furnishing additional monies for refugee assistance programs.

THE REOPENED DOOR

The funding to assist refugees in America was part of a liberalizing national attitude toward immigration. The civil rights movement had cast in stark relief the contradiction between America's ideals and the racism and prejudice that marred its institutions and laws. By 1965 the bigotry embedded in the national origins quota system was no longer publicly acceptable or politically tenable. At a time when East-West Cold War competition was shifting to the Third World, the immigration code's discrimination against Africans and Asians was seen as impeding the development of good relations with the new postcolonial nations of Africa and Asia.

At President Johnson's urging, Congress enacted the Immigration Act of 1965. The landmark legislation gave America a new, Reopened Door immigration policy. The act terminated the national origins system, abolishing all quotas based on race or ethnicity. It eliminated the 1952 designation of an Asian-Pacific Triangle and mandated equal immigration access regardless of nationality.

The annual cap on immigration visas was raised to 290,000. Of this total, 170,000 were set aside for the Eastern Hemisphere. No more than 20,000 immigrants could come from the same country in any given year. The preference given since 1952 to immigrants with needed professional skills was changed to an emphasis on family reunification and the granting of visas to the family members of citizens and resident aliens. In a provision that would actually increase annual immigration well above 290,000, the spouses, children, and parents of citizens were not subject to numerical restrictions.

In a departure from the tradition of providing open access to other Western Hemisphere nations, the remaining 120,000 annual visas were allocated to these countries. The per-country limit and family preference system did not apply to the region

Percentage of Population Foreign Born, 1850–1990

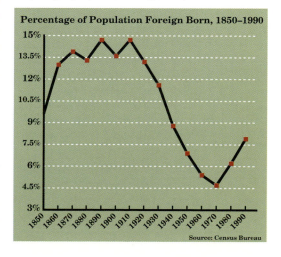

Percentage of Population Foreign Born, 1850–1990

15%
13.5%
12%
10.5%
9%
7.5%
6%
4.5%
3%

1850 1860 1870 1880 1890 1900 1910 1920 1930 1940 1950 1960 1970 1980 1990

Source: Census Bureau

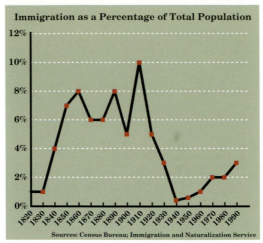

Immigration as a Percentage of Total Population

until passage of the Western Hemisphere Act in 1976 standardized U.S. immigration policy worldwide.

In another precedent-setting step, refugee admissions for the first time in 1965 were incorporated into immigration law. Up to 6 percent, or 10,200, of each year's immigration visas were set aside for refugees.

THE NEWEST IMMIGRANTS

The 1965 legislation had a profound impact on the patterns of migration to America. The law meant little change in visa allocations to Europe, but it opened the door to immigration from Africa and especially Asia. Between 1961 and 1970, America accepted 1.2 million newcomers from Europe, more than twice the 425,000 immigrants from Asia. Within another decade, however, the proportions had virtually reversed. Between 1971 and 1980, the number of European immigrants declined to 800,000, while the volume of Asian newcomers jumped to 1.6 million.

With western Europe enjoying unprecedented peace and prosperity, there was little incentive for emigration. In the 1980s European immigration to the United States plateaued at some 760,000 even as the numbers arriving from Asia climbed again to 2.7 million. These trends continued into the 1990s. The collapse of the Berlin Wall in 1989 allowed an upsurge in emigration from Eastern Europe in the early 1990s, but Asians remained the dominant presence among those coming to America.

Joining the newest immigrants to America were mounting numbers of Latin Americans and, to a lesser degree, Africans. The number of immigrants from Central and South America increased from 800,000 between 1961 and 1970 to 2.6 million between 1981 and 1990. During the same two decades emigration from Africa to the United States rose from 29,000 to 177,000. By 1995 almost 80 percent of the newcomers crossing America's portals each year were from regions that had become significant sources of immigration only after 1965.

Sources of U.S. Immigration, 1941–1990

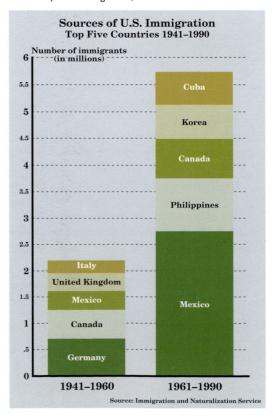

Major Immigrant Destinations, 1995

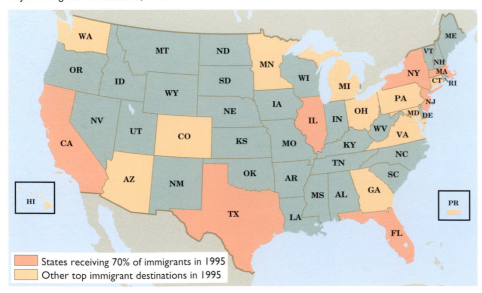

MAJOR IMMIGRANT STATES, 1995

Rank	State or Territory	Number of Immigrants
1	California	166,482
2	New York	128,406
3	Florida	62,023
4	Texas	49,963
5	New Jersey	39,729
6	Illinois	33,898
7	Massachusetts	20,523
8	Virginia	16,319
9	Washington	15,862
10	Pennsylvania	15,065
11	Maryland	15,055
12	Michigan	14,135
13	Georgia	12,381
14	Connecticut	9,240
15	Ohio	8,585
16	Minnesota	8,111
17	Colorado	7,713
18	Arizona	7,700
19	Hawaii	7,537
20	Puerto Rico	7,160
	Other	74,574
	Total all states and territories	720,461

Source: Immigration and Naturalization Service

TOP 15 IMMIGRANT COUNTRIES OF BIRTH, 1995

Rank	Country of Birth	Number of Immigrants
1	Mexico	89,932
2	Phillipines	50,984
3	Vietnam	41,752
4	Dominican Republic	38,512
5	China, People's Republic	35,463
6	India	34,748
7	Cuba	17,937
8	Ukraine	17,432
9	Jamaica	16,398
10	Korea	16,047
11	Russia	14,560
12	Haiti	14,021
13	Poland	13,824
14	Canada	12,932
15	United Kingdom	12,427
	Other	293,492
	Total	720,461

Source: Immigration and Naturalization Service

AFRICA

Immigration from Africa prior to 1965 had been limited both by U.S. law and Europe's colonial grip on the continent. The collapse of the British, French, Belgian, and Portuguese colonial regimes in the 1960s and 1970s produced small but discernible numbers of white Africans migrating to America. Their emigration reflected a desire to no longer reside in former colonies that had gained independence under black African governance. The white Africans, mostly from former British colonies, blended almost imperceptibly into American society. Since the dramatic changes ensuing in the late 1980s that brought black majority rule to South Africa, a small but steady flow of white South Africans has immigrated to America.

Decolonization also opened the way to growing numbers of black African immigrants. By 1970 there were some 13,000 black Africans in America. Almost all were from Ghana, Nigeria, Kenya, and Ethiopia. Most of the newcomers initially settled in or near African-American communities. More recently, as their numbers have increased, black African immigrants, similar to previous generations of newcomers, have tended to locate in ethnic enclaves. Most reside in major cities, most notably New York and Washington, D.C.

Postcolonial political unrest in Africa has both limited the countries furnishing immigrants to America and the total volume of migration. Annual immigration, which reached the mid-30,000s in 1990, has remained at roughly this level through the mid-1990s. The remote living conditions of many black Africans, as well as the very low average annual incomes in sub-Saharan Africa, have also mitigated against a larger migration. Ghanaians and Nigerians continue to predominate among black African immigrants, but small numbers are found from virtually every country and ethnic group.

ASIA

Post–1965 emigration from Asia, in contrast, has been facilitated by close postwar American ties to the region. American engagement in the Korean War resulted in a permanent U.S. military presence in South Korea. The Korean spouses of American servicemembers established an early pattern of migration to America that after 1965 developed into a major influx. Key to the

Korean festival in Los Angeles   (Herald-Examiner Collection/ Los Angeles Public Library)

Korean migration were the family preferences built into the 1965 immigration law. Prior to 1965 immigrant families could be separated for years as members overseas waited for scarce immigration quotas. The 1965 provisions, meant to support family reunification across international borders, enabled tens of thousands of Koreans to come to America outside the new visa limits imposed on each country and hemisphere. In a process sometimes referred to as chain migration, Koreans in America would sponsor the automatic or expedited admission of close relatives still in Korea. These entrants in turn would sponsor other family members.

Post-1965 Immigrants

O Significant African immigrant community
O Significant Asian immigrant community
O Significant Hispanic immigrant community

Between 1965 and 1990, approximately 675,000 Koreans immigrated to America. At first women constituted a pronounced majority, but the gender ratio moved toward balance as more families migrated. Korean immigrants from the start tended to be well educated. Many came in the hope of better opportunity, but a fair number left Korea out of disenchantment with the country's military-dominated government.

Koreans settled overwhelmingly in and around New York and Los Angeles. Many opened their own small family businesses shortly after arrival. In the 1980s it was estimated that 75% of the fruit-and-vegetable stores in New York City were Korean-owned. The emphasis on family, education, and entrepreneurship helped make Korean immigrants a "success story" often cited by proponents of immigration. Koreans adapted quickly to American life and attained a rapid upward social mobility. Both a booming economy and the institution of democratic rule in South Korea brought a slight drop in Korean immigration in the early 1990s.

Chain migration also contributed to an upsurge in immigration among two groups with prior histories of migration to America. The imposition of communist rule on the mainland precluded emigration from the People's Republic of China, but nearly 500,000 Chinese immigrated to America from Hong Kong and Taiwan between 1970 and 1990. Most located initially in the existing Chinese-American communities in San Francisco and New York. Because they have migrated under much different circumstances than Chinese laborers in the 1800s, and arrived in a much less hostile place, the latest waves of Chinese immigrants have fared much better in America. The easing of restrictions on emigration by communist China has helped the Chinese influx to continue unabated in the 1990s, consistently placing the Chinese among the most numerous immigrant groups each year.

U.S. colonial rule in the Philippines before World War II and an enduring U.S. military presence there after the war provided the basis for a resumption in earnest of Filipino immigration after 1965. The Filipino-American community in California was the destination of most of the first newcomers to pass through the suddenly reopened door to America. Family reunification helped sustain an influx that reached 900,000 Filipinos between 1970 and 1990. Almost two-thirds of recent Filipino immigrants have been professionals. Large numbers have been physicians and nurses. Since the 1970s American hospitals, especially in urban areas, have depended on Filipino nurses to fill critical shortages, and there is now an established pattern of Filipino nursing school graduates migrating to waiting employment in America. California remains the home to most Filipino immigrants, but since the 1980s Filipinos have settled increasingly across the nation.

At most no more than a few thousand Asian Indians immigrated to America before World War II. Almost all the more than 600,000 Indians in America in 1990 were post-1965 immigrants and their offspring. The vast majority of recent Indian immigrants, much like the Filipinos, have been well-trained and educated professionals. Many have come to work in information technology industries. Many others, also seeking greater opportunity, have become entrepreneurs. Often those running small retail businesses in need of employees have sponsored the arrival of additional family members as chain migrants. Indian nuclear families, while smaller on average than for other Asian immigrant groups, tend to be highly cohesive and have aided a swift assimilation across America.

Boat People

The circumstances surrounding the entry of more than one million Vietnamese, Cambodians, and Laotians since 1975 are very different than those for other recent, large Asian immigrant groups. The Southeast Asians have come as refugees, not as traditional immigrants, and few have arrived with the qualifications or means to take full advantage of their new freedom in America. The long U.S. involvement in the Vietnam War created new ties to a part of the world previously unknown to most Americans. The United States disengaged from the fighting in Indochina in 1973, but retained a close advisory role with South Vietnamese government. When South Vietnam succumbed to North Vietnamese invasion in 1975, America accepted some 140,000 Vietnamese refugees fleeing the new communist regime. Their admission was animated by a sense of obligation to the nation's former wartime allies. America's door was similarly opened to a much smaller number of refugees from Cambodia, which had been overrun by the communist Khmer Rouge.

Because existing refugee quotas could not possibly accommodate the sudden flood tide, Congress passed the Indochina Migration and Refugee Assistance Act in 1975. The temporary measure both authorized the special admission of Indochinese

Vietnamese boat people   (DOD Visual Information Center)

refugees and established a program of domestic resettlement assistance.

Most of the initial group of Indochinese refugees escaped by air in the waning days of the war. Internal crisis in Vietnam in 1978, as well as a Vietnamese invasion of Cambodia the same year, provoked a second and much larger flight of Vietnamese and Cambodian refugees. As turmoil enveloped the region, refugees from communist Laos joined the exodus. Hundreds of thousands crossed by land to Thailand or set out to sea in small boats.

The huge numbers of seaborne refugees, most crammed into rickety crafts with few provisions, gave rise to the expression "boat people." Thousands of the boat people perished at sea or were preyed on by pirates. Those that survived ended up in refugee camps across Southeast Asia. The United States reaffirmed its policy of offering a home to refugees of the Vietnam War and its aftermath, accepting an additional half-million Vietnamese, Cambodians, and Laotians by 1985. As the refugee camps were finally emptied, Indochinese refugee admissions declined in the late 1980s. The end of the Cold War, however, has brought a rapprochement between the United States and Vietnam that has helped sustain a sizable Vietnamese immigration in the 1990s.

Most Indochinese refugees have struggled in America. Many were not equipped for life in a modern urban society. An often painful adjustment period has enabled growing numbers to make some progress up the socioeconomic ladder, but many live in poverty or conditions near to it. Despite a concerted effort by the U.S. government to settle Indochinese refugees across the country, the Vietnamese have ended up residing primarily in southern California and along the Gulf Coast of Texas and the Deep South. The smaller numbers of Cambodians and Laotians are more dispersed.

LATIN AMERICA

Boat people soon proved to be more than an Asian phenomenon. In 1980 Fidel Castro again declared that anyone desiring to leave Cuba could do so. He opened the Cuban port of Mariel and encouraged Florida's Cuban exile community to retrieve any relatives still on the island nation.

Within days Miami's staunchly anti-Castro Cuban-American community had launched a "freedom flotilla" of hundreds of small boats and was transporting thousands of Cuban émigrés from Mariel back to Florida. The sudden, unexpected refugee flow was countenanced by President Jimmy Carter, who announced America would welcome those fleeing Cuba with "an open heart and open arms." Over four months the boatlift brought more than 130,000 Cubans to America's shores before Castro just as abruptly closed Mariel's port. As before, most of the latest Cuban newcomers located in Miami and in Hudson County, New Jersey, where they quickly assimilated into the successful Cuban-American communities.

The readily apparent insufficiency of the refugee quotas in the 1965 immigration act led to enactment of the Refugee Act of 1980. The legislation separated refugee and immigrant admissions into two separate categories. There was no longer a hard ceiling on the number of refugee visas to be issued annually. Instead, the president would determine each year's allocation in consultation with Congress. Since 1990 annual refugee admissions have averaged about 125,000.

In 1994 another flotilla of Cuban boat people suddenly appeared off southern Florida's shore. Unlike the Mariel boatlift, this exodus, while tolerated by Cuban authorities, was spontaneous and uncoordinated. With the Cold War over, the United States was no longer willing to grant automatic asylum to Cuban émigrés or to see its orderly refugee program disrupted. U.S. and Cuban authorities negotiated an agreement that ended the seaborne flight and routinized Cuban immigration to America.

The more than 800,000 Cubans who have entered the United States since 1960 rank, along with Mexicans, as one of the two large Latin American immigrant groups. Most of the Caribbean, Central America, and South America historically has had little tradition of immigration to America. For South America this has not substantively changed in recent decades, as only relatively small numbers have migrated to the United States, most notably Argentines, Colombians, and Ecuadorians.

Caribbean Migration Since 1945

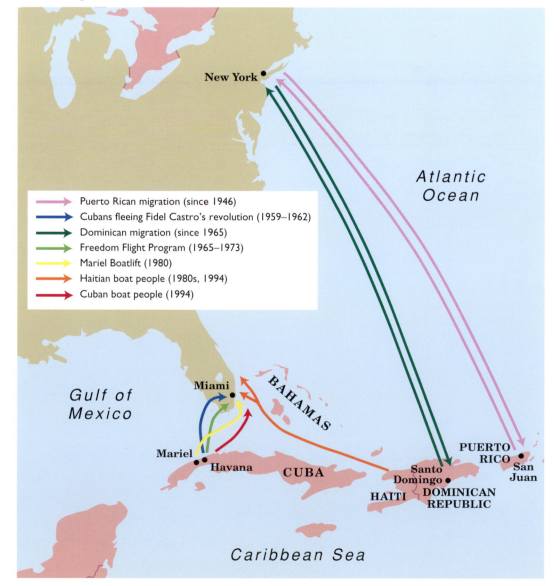

Since the 1960s the case has been much different with the Caribbean and Central America. The island of Hispaniola, just a few miles from Cuba, has produced two significant, but very distinct and separate, recent migrations to America. Hispaniola is divided between the Spanish-speaking Dominican Republic and French Creole-speaking Haiti. Dominican immigration, which started to build in the 1960s, has been very similar to Puerto Rican migration to America. The Dominicans have also settled overwhelmingly in New York City. Many are also sojourners, traveling back and forth between New York and their homeland. This makes it difficult to determine their actual numbers in America, but estimates are in the hundreds of thousands. Unlike Puerto Ricans, however, Dominicans do not have the benefit of automatic entry. To circumvent immigrant quotas, many are in America as undocumented or illegal entrants.

Beginning in the 1970s Haitians in growing numbers made their way to America to escape the grinding poverty and political repression of their nation. By 1980 estimates of the Haitians in America ranged from 100,000 to 300,000, as many had entered illicitly outside immigration channels. In the early 1980s a mounting flow of Haitian boat people started landing along Florida's east coast. The U.S. government resisted granting the Haitians refugee status, claiming they were economic migrants, and most were interned before finally gaining legal entry to America. Political conditions improved in Haiti in the mid-1980s, stemming the flow, only to worsen again in the early 1990s. A much larger surge of Haitian boat people in 1994 ultimately helped induce the United States to intervene militarily in Haiti to restore democratic governance to the troubled nation and stop the exodus. Haitian migration has been much reduced, but a thriving Haitian-American community in New York remains a locus for those who continue to come.

Feet People

Regional crisis prompted the first serious migration from Central America in the 1980s. Guatemala, El Salvador, and

Migrant Farmworkers   (Archives of Labor and Urban Affairs, Wayne State University)

Nicaragua were all wracked by civil war. Cold War concerns over potential Soviet-sponsored communist states in the area caused the United States to become involved indirectly in the conflicts in El Salvador and Nicaragua. America in turn became a haven for persons fearing possible persecution or worse at the hands of those on the other side of the struggles. The term "feet people" was coined to describe the refugees from these bitter conflicts who made their way northward to America, many of whom just wanted to escape the seeming madness and wanton violence of the wars.

More than 200,000 El Salvadorans, over 100,000 Guatemalans, and a somewhat smaller number of Nicaraguans found their way to America in the 1980s. Some had immigrant visas; a smaller percentage were granted asylum. Most, however, entered or remained illegally. Those without documentation survived in the underground economy, most often in or near the sizable Central American enclaves that developed in the Southwest and Florida. The resolution of all three civil wars in the 1990s removed the impetus for further refugees, but left a considerable Central American presence in America and established a continuing pattern of chain and other migration.

AROUND THE DOOR

Not only Guatemalans or Haitians but also millions of other aspiring immigrants around the world since 1965 have been unable to squeeze through America's reopened door. The door was thrust back open, but it was still only so wide. Denied admission, growing numbers resorted to illegal entry. By the 1980s illegal immigration had become a major concern. Nowhere was the issue more pronounced than with Mexican migration.

Mexico since World War II has been the single largest source of migration to America. Between 1946 and 1964 the long-established flow of Mexicans into America was governed by the Bracero Program, which permitted the recurring entry of migrant workers while limiting other immigration. During these same years, however, more than 5 million Mexicans crossed into America illegally, most in search of seasonal agricultural work in the Southwest. The entry of so many additional farmhands contributed to the exodus then underway of rural Mexican Americans into Los Angeles,

El Paso, San Antonio, and other southwestern cities.

Most of the illegal Mexican entrants returned home each year, but sizable numbers eventually settled in the burgeoning urban Mexican enclaves. Termination of the Bracero Program, and the employment it provided to excess Mexican workers, if anything increased the flow of illegal immigrants to America. The Mexican presence in America was also heightened by renewed legal immigration, as chain migration after 1965 helped spur the ongoing movement of Mexican Americans into the cities of the upper Midwest. Over one million Mexican immigrants entered legally through America's open door in the 1960s and 1970s.

As many if not more came around the door. By 1980 there were upward of 4 million persons of Mexican birth in America. As many as half were in the country illegally. The problem of illegal immigration, identified widely in the public mind with Mexicans, precipitated an intense national debate. On the one side were those who favored tighter border controls and greater enforcement of deportation laws. On the other were those who argued against such strict measures, claiming they would both contradict American ideals and prove ineffective. The only way to stop illegal immigration, this latter group has contended, is to remove its underlying causes.

In 1986 Congress responded by approving the Immigration Reform and Control Act. The measure reflected a compromise strategy for dealing with illegal immigration. On the one hand, it provided for granting amnesty to illegal aliens in America since before 1982. On the other, it strength-

Undocumented Immigrants, 1995

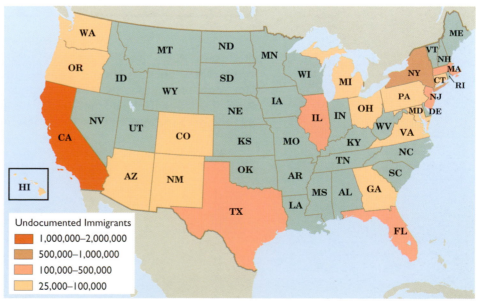

Undocumented Immigrants
- 1,000,000–2,000,000
- 500,000–1,000,000
- 100,000–500,000
- 25,000–100,000

UNDOCUMENTED IMMIGRANTS, BY NATIONALITY

There is considerable disagreement over the actual scope of illegal immigration in the 1990s—partly because there is no way to figure the exact number of undocumented aliens in America (many of whom are seeking to avoid detection and deportation) and partly because those on either side of the issue tend either to minimize or overstate the problem. Below are estimates prepared by the Immigration and Naturalization Service in 1992 of the number of illegal immigrants in America at any given time.

Country	Estimated # Undocumented Immigrants
Mexico	1,321,000
El Salvador	327,000
Guatemala	129,000
Canada	97,000
Poland	91,000
Philippines	90,000
Haiti	88,000
Bahamas	71,000
Nicaragua	68,000
Italy	67,000
Honduras	61,000
Colombia	59,000
Ecuador	45,000
Jamaica	42,000
Dominican Republic	40,000
Trinidad & Tobago	39,000
Ireland	36,000
Portugal	31,000
Pakistan	30,000
India	28,000

Source: Immigration and Naturalization Service

the provisions of the law, including 2.2 million Mexicans. Neither the stricter enforcement nor the employer sanctions, however, succeeded in stemming a virtually unabated illegal immigration, and the nation continued to wrestle with the issue in the 1990s. In 1995 there were an estimated 4 million illegal aliens in America.

By the late 1980s, legal immigration had reached the highest rates since the early 1900s. Congress moved to constrain a further upward swing in annual immigration levels, while preserving the family-reunification orientation of the U.S. immigration law. The Immigration Act of 1990 kept the existing non-quota entry provisions for immediate family members, but otherwise tightened family-sponsored immigration quotas under a new, flexible cap on immigrant visas of 675,000 a year. The act served to help stabilize legal immigration at about one million entrants annually in the 1990s.

MULTICULTURAL AMERICA

Immigration since 1965, with its predominantly Asian and Latin-American cast, has become part of a larger debate over an increasingly more diverse American identity. In recent decades cultural pluralism has gained much credence as an alternative to the traditional vision of a single America people. This multicultural perspective sees America as a mosaic of different groups rather than a melting pot blending them into one. Multiculturalism's proponents celebrate the new hues of America's most recent immigrants. Those favoring the notion of Americans as one people point out that most of the most recent immigrant groups have assimilated into American society at a remarkable rate.

Immigration, providing either ore for a melting pot or pieces for a mosaic, will continue to affect, and be affected by, the debate over national identity. At the least, if existing immigration laws remain unchanged, current immigration trends will make America even more diverse in the 21st century.

ened procedures for the enforcement of immigration laws. It also imposed legal sanctions on employers hiring undocumented aliens in the belief that employment was the primary incentive for illegal immigration.

More than 3 million illegal aliens applied for adjustment to legal status under

SELECTED BIBLIOGRAPHY

Asante, Molefi K. and Mark T. Mattson. *Historical and Cultural Atlas of African Americans*. New York: Macmillan, 1992.

Bailyn, Bernard. *The Peopling of British North America*. New York: Vintage Books, 1988.

Brinton, Daniel G. *The Lenape and Their Legends*. New York: AMS Press, 1969.

Brown, Dee. *Bury My Heart at Wounded Knee*. New York: Holt, Rinehart and Winston, 1970.

Burton, Rosemary, Richard Cavendish, and Bernard Stonehouse. *Journeys of the Great Explorers*. New York: Facts On File, 1992.

Chudacoff, Howard P. *The Evolution of American Urban Society*. Englewood Cliffs, N.J.: Prentice-Hall, 1975.

Clark, Judith Freeman. *America's Gilded Age: An Eyewitness History*. New York: Facts On File, 1992.

Coe, Michael, Dean Snow, and Elizabeth Benson. *Atlas of Ancient America*. New York: Facts On File, 1989.

Cooke, Jacob Ernest, ed. *Encyclopedia of the North American Colonies*. New York: Scribner's, 1993.

Daniels, Roger. *Asian America: Chinese and Japanese in the United States Since 1850*. Seattle: University of Washington Press, 1988.

_____.*Coming to America: A History of Immigration and Ethnicity in American Life*. New York: Harper Perennial, 1991.

Dinnerstein, Leonard, Roger L. Nichols, and David M. Reimers. *Natives and Strangers: Blacks, Indians, and Immigrants in America*. New York: Oxford University Press, 1990.

Edmonds, Margot and Ella E. Clark. *Voices of the Wind*. New York: Facts On File, 1989.

Farb, Peter. *Man's Rise to Civilization as Shown by the Indians of North America From Primeval Times to the Coming of the Industrial State*. New York: Dutton, 1968.

Fernandez-Shaw, Carlos M. *The Hispanic Presence in North America: From 1492 to Today*. New York: Facts On File, 1987.

Foner, Eric. *A Short History of Reconstruction, 1863–1877*. New York: Harper and Row, 1990.

Frank, Irene M. and David M. Brownstone. *The American Way West*. New York: Facts On File, 1991.

Garreau, Joel. *Edge City: Life on the New Frontier*. New York: Doubleday, 1991.

Garrett, Wilbur E., ed. *Historical Atlas of the United States*. Washington, D.C.: National Geographic Society, 1988.

Gates, Henry Louis Jr., ed. *The Classic Slave Narratives*. New York: Mentor, 1987.

Heyerdahl, Thor. *Kon-Tiki*. New York: Pocket Books, 1962.

Hutchinson, E.P. *Legislative History of American Immigration Policy 1798–1965*. Philadelphia: University of Pennsylvania Press, 1981.

Jackson, Helen. *A Century of Dishonor*. New York: Barnes and Noble, 1993.

Jackson, Kenneth T. *Crabgrass Frontier: The Suburbanization of the United States*. New York: Oxford University Press, 1985.

Johnson, Adrian. *America Explored: A Cartographical History of the Exploration of North America*. New York: Viking, 1974.

Kolchin, Peter. *American Slavery, 1619–1877.* New York: Hill and Wang, 1993.

Kouwenhoven, John A. *The Columbia Historical Portrait of New York.* New York: Doubleday, 1953.

Kranz, Rachel. *The Biographical Dictionary of Black Americans.* New York: Facts On File, 1992.

Kupperman, Karen Ordahl. *Roanoke: The Abandoned Colony.* New York: Barnes and Noble, 1993.

Lemann, Nicholas. *The Promised Land: The Great Black Migration and How It Changed America.* New York: Vintage Books, 1992.

LeMay, Michael C. *From Open Door to Dutch Door: An Analysis of U.S. Immigration Policy Since 1820.* New York: Praeger, 1987.

Lewis, Richard S. *From Vinland to Mars.* New York: Quadrangle Books, 1976.

Liesner, Thelma. *One Hundred Years of Economic Statistics.* New York: Facts On File, 1989.

Limerick, Patricia Nelson. *The Legacy of Conquest: The Unbroken Past of the American West.* New York: Norton, 1987.

Lister, Robert H. and Florence C. Lister. *Those Who Came Before.* Tucson: University of Arizona Press, 1983.

Marlita, Reddy A., ed. *Statistical Record of Native North Americans.* Detroit: Gale Research, 1993.

Martin, Albro. *Railroads Triumphant: The Growth, Rejection, and Rebirth of a Vital American Force.* New York: Oxford University Press, 1992.

McEvedy, Colin and Richard Jones. *Atlas of World Population History.* New York: Penguin, 1980.

Mittelberger, Gottlieb. *Journey to Pennsylvania.* ed. and tr. Oscar Handlin and John Clive. Cambridge: Harvard University Press, 1960.

Morgan, Ted. *A Shovel of Stars: The Making of the American West 1800 to the Present.* New York: Simon and Schuster, 1995.

_____.*Wilderness at Dawn: The Settling of the North American Continent.* New York: Simon and Schuster, 1993.

Morris, Jeffrey B. and Richard B. Morris, eds. *Encyclopedia of American History,* (7th ed.). New York: HarperCollins, 1996.

Morrison, Samuel Eliot. *The European Discovery of America: The Northern Voyages.* New York: Oxford University Press, 1971.

Niiya, Brian, ed. *Japanese American History: An A-to-Z Reference from 1868 to the Present.* New York: Facts On File, 1993.

Obregon, Mauricio. *Argonauts to Astronauts.* New York: Harper and Row, 1980.

Prucha, Francis Paul. *American Indian Policy in the Formative Years.* Cambridge: Harvard University Press, 1962.

Prucha, Francis Paul, ed. *Documents of United States Indian Policy.* Lincoln: University of Nebraska Press, 1975.

Rae, Noel, ed. *Witnessing America.* New York: Penguin Reference, 1996.

Ravitch, Diane. *The American Reader: Words That Moved a Nation.* New York: HarperCollins, 1991.

Ridge, Martin and Ray Allen Billington. *America's Frontier Story: A Documentary History of Westward Expansion.* New York: Holt, Rinehart and Winston, 1969.

Salmoral, Manuel Lucena. *America 1492: Portrait of a Continent Five Hundred Years Ago.* New York: Facts On File, 1990.

Satz, Ronald N. *American Indian Policy in the Jacksonian Era.* Lincoln: University of Nebraska Press, 1975.

Scott, John Anthony. *Settlers on the Eastern Shore.* New York: Facts On File, 1991.

Smithsonian Institution. *Handbook of North American Indians.* Washington, D.C.: U.S. Government Printing Office, 1988.

Spangenburg, Ray and Diane K. Moser. *The Story of America's Roads.* New York: Facts On File, 1992.

Stone, Norman, ed. *The Times Atlas of World History*. Maplewood, N.J.: Hammond, 1991.

Takaki, Ronald. *A Different Mirror: A History of Multicultural America*. Boston: Little, Brown, 1993.

Taylor, Theodore W. *The Bureau of Indian Affairs*. Boulder, Colorado: Westview Press, 1984.

Thernstrom, Stephan, ed. *Harvard Encyclopedia of American Ethnic Groups*. Cambridge: Harvard University Press, 1980.

Thornton, Russell. *American Indian Holocaust and Survival: A Population History Since 1492*. Norman: University of Oklahoma Press, 1987.

Tunnard, Christopher and Henry Hope Reed. *American Skyline: The Growth and Form of Our Cities and Towns*. New York: Mentor Books, 1956.

Turner, Frederick Jackson. *The Frontier in American History*. New York: Holt, 1920.

Tyler, Lyman S. *A History of Indian Policy*. Washington, D.C.: Government Printing Office, 1973.

United States History Atlas. Maplewood, N.J.: Hammond, 1984.

U.S. Bureau of the Census. *Historical Statistics of the United States, Colonial Times to 1970*. Washington, D.C.: U.S. Government Printing Office, 1975.

_____.*Statistical Abstract of the United States: 1996*. Washington, D.C.: U.S. Government Printing Office, 1996.

U.S. Immigration and Naturalization Service. *Statistical Yearbook of the Immigration and Naturalization Service, 1996*. Washington, D.C.: U.S. Government Printing Office, 1997.

_____.*Statistical Yearbook of the Immigration and Naturalization Service, 1990*. Washington, D.C.: U.S. Government Printing Office, 1991.

The Vinland Sagas: the Norse Discovery of America. tr. Magnus Magnusson and Hermann Palsson. New York: New York University Press, 1966.

Waldman, Carl. *Atlas of the North American Indian*. New York: Facts On File, 1988.

_____.*Encyclopedia of Native American Tribes*. New York: Facts On File, 1988.

Waldman, Carl and Alan Wexler. *Who Was Who in World Exploration*. New York: Facts On File, 1992.

Weber, David J. *The Spanish Frontier in North America*. New Haven, Conn.: Yale University Press, 1992.

Wexler, Sanford. *Westward Expansion: An Eyewitness History*. New York: Facts On File, 1991.

Williams, Trevor I. *The History of Invention: From Stone Axes to Silicon Chips*. New York: Facts On File, 1987.